Contemporary's

GED

Short Course

Contemporary's

GED

Short Course

Coordinating Editor, Patricia Mulcrone, Ed.D.
Professor/Chair, Adult Educational Development
William Rainey Harper College
Palatine, Illinois

CB

CONTEMPORARY BOOKS

a division of NTC/CONTEMPORARY PUBLISHING GROUP
Lincolnwood, Illinois USA

Library of Congress Cataloging-in-Publication Data

Contemporary's GED short course / coordinating editor, Patricia Mulcrone.
       p.   cm.
     Includes index.
     ISBN 0-8092-3034-8
     1. General educational develpment tests—Study guides.   I. Mulcrone,
Patricia.   II. Contemporary Books.
LB3060.33.G45C6697   1997
373.126′2—dc21   96-40529
                                                CIP

Contributing Writers

Reading Skills
Noreen Giles
Patricia Mulcrone

Test 1: Writing Skills
Karen A. Fox
Judith Gallagher

Test 2: Social Studies
Dan M. Fox
Karen Gibbons
Virginia Lowe

Test 3: Science
Bruce R. Brown
Robert P. Mitchell

Test 4: Literature and the Arts
Karen A. Fox
Noreen Giles
Anne V. McGravie

Test 5: Mathematics
Jerry Howett
Janice Phillips

Patricia Mulcrone gratefully acknowledges the expertise of:

Janice S. Phillips, Assitant Professor of Adult Educational Development at
William Rainey Harper College, who served as a consultant for the mathematics
sections of *Contemporary's GED Short Course*

Patricia A. Best, Associate Professor of Adult Educational Development at
William Rainey Harper College, who served as a consultant for the social studies
and science sections of *Contemporary's GED Short Course*

Pages xi–xiii constitute an extension of this copyright page.

Published originally as *Contemporary's Essential GED*

CONTENTS

ACKNOWLEDGMENTS

Cartoon on page 8 by Jim Morin. Copyright 1992 by the *Miami Herald*. Reprinted by permission.

Map on page 12 from *World Geography* by Preston E. James and Nelda Davis, © 1985. Reprinted by permission of the Glencoe division of the Macmillan/McGraw-Hill School Publishing Company.

Excerpt on page 21 from *Song of Solomon* by Toni Morrison. Permission granted by International Creative Management, Inc. Copyright 1977 by Toni Morrison.

Poem on page 21, "Tom Merritt," in *Spoon River Anthology* by Edgar Lee Masters. Originally published by the Macmillan Company. Permission by Ellen C. Masters.

Excerpt on page 22 from *Pygmalion* in *Four Modern Plays* by Bernard Shaw. Reprinted by permission of The Society of Authors Ltd.

Excerpt on page 206 from "The Short Happy Life of Francis Macomber." Reprinted by permission of Charles Scribner's Sons, an imprint of Macmillan Publishing Company, from *The Short Stories of Ernest Hemingway*. Copyright 1936 by Ernest Hemingway; renewal © 1964 by Mary Hemingway.

Excerpt on pages 206–207 from "The Possibility of Evil" by Shirley Jackson. Copyright 1965 by Stanley Edgar Hyman. Reprinted with the permission of Laurence Hyman, Barry Hyman, Jai Holly and Sarah Stewart.

Excerpt on page 208 from "Everything That Rises Must Converge" in *The Complete Stories* by Flannery O'Connor. Copyright 1961, 1965 by the Estate of Mary Flannery O'Connor. Reprinted by permission of Farrar, Straus & Giroux, Inc.

Excerpt on pages 209–210 from *The Bell Jar* by Sylvia Plath. Copyright 1971 by Harper & Row Publishers, Inc. Reprinted by permission of HarperCollins Publishers, Inc.

Review on page 211 by Anne Whitehouse. Copyright 1993 by the New York Times Company. Reprinted by permission.

Poem on page 213, "Oh, When I Was in Love with You," from *The Collected Poems of A. E. Housman* by A. E. Housman. Copyright 1939, 1940, © 1965 by Henry Holt and Company, Inc. Copyright 1967, 1968 by Robert E. Symons. Reprinted by permission of Henry Holt and Company, Inc.

Poem on page 214, "On Being a Woman," in *The Portable Dorothy Parker* by Dorothy Parker. Introduction by Brendan Gill. Copyright 1928, renewed © 1956 by Dorothy Parker. Used by permission of Viking Penguin, a division of Penguin Books USA Inc.

Poem on pages 215–216, "History." Copyright 1977 by Gary Soto. Used by permission of Gary Soto.

Poem on page 216, "maggie and milly and molly and may," is reprinted from *Complete Poems, 1904–1962* by E. E. Cummings. Edited by George J. Firmage, by permission of Liveright Publishing Corporation. Copyright 1923, 1925, 1926, 1931, 1935, 1938–1940, 1944–1962 by E. E. Cummings. Copyright 1961, 1963, 1966–1968 by Marion Morehouse Cummings. Copyright 1972–1991 by the Trustees for the E. E. Cummings Trust.

Poem on page 217, "Jazz Fantasia," in *Smoke and Steel* by Carl Sandburg, © 1920 by Harcourt Brace & Company and renewed 1948 by Carl Sandburg, reprinted by permission of the publisher.

Poem on page 218, "My Papa's Waltz," © 1942 by Hearst Magazines, Inc., from *The Collected Poems of Theodore Roethke* by Theodore Roethke. Used by permission of Doubleday, a division of Bantam Doubleday Dell Publishing Group, Inc.

Poem on pages 219–220, "Memory," by Trevor Nunn in *Cats: The Book of the Musical*, incorporating lines from "Rhapsody on a Windy Night" in *Collected Poems 1909–1962* by T. S. Eliot, © 1936 by Harcourt Brace & Company, © 1964, 1963 by T. S. Eliot, reprinted by permission of the publisher.

Poem on pages 219–220, "Memory," from *Cats: The Book of the Musical*. Words by Trevor Nunn after T. S. Eliot. Reprinted by permission of Faber and Faber Ltd. © 1981 by Trevor Nunn/Set Copyrights Ltd.

Excerpt on page 220 from "Chicago" in *Chicago Poems* by Carl Sandburg, reprinted by permission of Harcourt Brace & Company.

Poem on page 221 from *The Poetry of Robert Frost* edited by Edward Connery Latham. Copyright 1923, © 1969 by Henry Holt and Company, Inc. Copyright 1942, 1951 by Robert Frost. Copyright 1970 by Lesley Frost Ballantine. Reprinted by permission of Henry Holt and Company, Inc.

Excerpt on page 221 from "An Indian Summer Day on the Prairie" in *Collected Poems of Vachel Lindsay* (New York: Macmillan, 1925).

Poem on page 222, "Because I Could Not Stop for Death," by Emily Dickinson. Reprinted by permission of the publishers and the Trustees of Amherst College from *The Poems of Emily Dickinson*, Thomas H. Johnson, ed., Cambridge, Mass.: The Belknap Press of Harvard University Press, © 1951, 1955, 1979, 1983 by the President and Fellows of Harvard College.

Review on page 223 by Stephen C. Levi, October 1992. Reprinted by permission of *Small Press Review*.

Excerpt on pages 277–228 from *'night, Mother* by Marsha Norman. Copyright 1983 by Marsha Norman. Reprinted by permission of Hill and Wang, a division of Farrar, Straus & Giroux, Inc.

Excerpt on pages 229–230, *I Never Sang for My Father*, by Robert Anderson. Reprinted by permission of International Creative Management.

Excerpt on page 235 from *Hard Times* by Studs Terkel. Copyright 1970 by Studs Terkel. Reprinted by permission of Pantheon Books, a division of Random House, Inc.

Excerpt on page 236 from *Nigger: An Autobiography* by Dick Gregory. Copyright 1964 by Dick Gregory Enterprises, Inc. Used by permission of the publisher, Dutton, an imprint of New American Library, a division of Penguin Books USA Inc.

Essay on pages 239–240, "The Computer Is Down." Reprinted by permission of The Putnam Publishing Group from *You Can Fool All of the People All of the Time* by Art Buchwald. Copyright 1985 by Art Buchwald.

Excerpt on page 240 from "The Dark Side of the Boom" by Mary S. Glucksman. Reprinted by permission of *Omni*, © 1991, Omni Publications International, Ltd.

Review on page 243 reprinted by permission of *People Weekly* © 1993 Time Inc.

Review on page 245 reprinted by permission from *TV Guide® Magazine*. Copyright 1993 by News America Publications, Inc.

Cartoon on page 358 by Tom Toles, © 1991, the *Buffalo News*. Reprinted by permission of Universal Press Syndicate. All rights reserved.

Excerpt on page 361 from *Newsweek*, May 14, © 1993, Newsweek, Inc. All rights reserved. Reprinted by permission.

Map and key on page 362 from *U.S. News & World Report*, © January 28, 1991. Reprinted by permission of *U.S. News & World Report*.

Excerpt on page 377 from "Girls of Summer" by Marie Brenner. Copyright 1993 by The New York Times Company. Reprinted by permission.

Excerpt on page 378 from *There Will Come Soft Rains* by Ray Bradbury. Reprinted by permission of Don Congdon Associates, Inc. Copyright 1950, renewed 1977 by Ray Bradbury.

Excerpt on pages 379–380 from "He" in *Flowering Judas and Other Stories*, © 1930 and renewed 1958 by Katherine Anne Porter, reprinted by permission of Harcourt Brace & Company.

Poem on page 381, "25th High School Reunion," by Linda Pastan in *The Five Stages of Grief*. Reprinted by permission of W. W. Norton & Company, Inc.

Excerpt on page 382 from *The House of Ramon Iglesia*. Copyright 1983 by Jose Rivera.

Review on page 383, " 'White Rose' Celebrates Anti-Nazi Heroes," by Lawrence Bommer, theater critic for the *Chicago Tribune*. Reprinted by permission of the author.

Review on pages 384–385 909 of the book *In My Place*. Reprinted by permission of PhoebeLou Adams, *The Atlantic Monthly*.

The editor has made every effort to trace the ownership of all copyrighted material, and necessary permissions have been secured in most cases. Should there prove to be any question regarding the use of any material, regret is here expressed for such error. Upon notification of any such oversight, proper acknowledgment will be made in future editions.

TO THE STUDENT

IS THIS BOOK FOR YOU?

There are many ways to go about preparing for the GED Tests.

Do you like an all-in-one approach in one comprehensive volume? If so, *Contemporary's GED: How to Prepare for the High School Equivalency Examination* is for you.

Do you like a separate book for each of the five content areas? If so, Contemporary's GED Satellite Series is for you:

Test 1: Writing Skills
Test 2: Social Studies
Test 3: Science
Test 4: Literature and the Arts
Test 5: Mathematics

Do you need less of a review? *Essential GED* is for you if most of these statements generally describe you:

I attended two or more years of high school.
I did not leave high school because the classes were too hard.
I usually understand most of what I read including a newspaper
    like *U.S.A. Today*.
I am good at finding other sources when I need to find out more
    information. (These sources include people, newspapers, magazines,
    books, radio, television, computer software, etc.)
I like to be in charge of my own learning and work well on my own.

WHY TAKE THE GED TESTS?

If you're studying to pass the GED Test battery, you're in good company. In 1994, the most recent year for which figures are available, over 750,000 people took the tests. Of this number, nearly 450,000 actually received their certificates. Why do so many people choose to take the GED Tests? Some do so to get a job or to get a better one than they already have. Others take the tests so that they can go on to college or vocational school. Still others pursue their GED diplomas to feel better about themselves or to set good examples for their children. Americans and Canadians from all walks of life have passed their GED Tests and obtained diplomas. Some well-known graduates have included people in the fields of entertainment, government, business, and other areas.

HOW WILL THIS BOOK HELP?

This book has a number of features designed to help make the task of preparing for the actual GED Test easier as well as effective and enjoyable.

- A preliminary reading skills section explains the six levels of thinking skills—knowledge, comprehension, application, analysis, synthesis, and evaluation.

- A special essay section helps to prepare you for the Writing Skills portion of the GED Test.
- A variety of exercise types and questions maintain interest—matching, fill-in-the blank, true-false, multiple-choice, and short essay questions.
- Half-length Post-Tests that are simulated GED Tests present questions in the format, level of difficulty, and percentages you will find on the actual tests.
- An answer key (coded by skill level) for each section explains the correct answers for the exercises.
- Evaluation charts for the Pre-Tests and Post-Tests help pinpoint weaknesses and refer you to the specific pages for review.

WHAT DOES *GED* STAND FOR?

GED stands for General Educational Development. The GED Test battery is a national examination developed by the GED Testing Service of the American Council on Education. The credential received for passing the test is widely recognized by colleges, training schools, and employers as equivalent to a high school diploma. While the GED Test measures skills and knowledge normally acquired in four years of high school, much that you have learned informally or through other types of training can help you pass the test. The GED Test is available in English, French, and Spanish and on audio-cassette, in Braille, and in large print.

WHAT SHOULD I KNOW TO PASS THE TEST?

The GED Test consists of five examinations in the areas of writing skills, social studies, science, literature and the arts, and mathematics. The chart below outlines the main content areas, the breakdown of questions, and the time allowed per test.

THE GED TESTS			
Test	Minutes	Questions	Percentage
1: Writing Skills Part 1: Conventions of English	75	55	Sentence Structure 35% Usage 35% Mechanics 30%
Part 2: The Essay	45	1 topic	
2: Social Studies	85	64	History 25% Economics 20% Political Science 20% Geography 15%* Behavioral Sciences 20%
3: Science	95	66	Life Sciences 50% Physical Sciences 50%
4: Literature and the Arts	65	45	Popular Literature 50% Classical Literature 25% Commentary 25%
5: Mathematics	90	56	Arithmetic 50% Algebra 30% Geometry 20%

*In Canada, 20% of the test is based on Geography and 15% on Behavioral Sciences.

On all five tests, you are expected to demonstrate the ability to think about many issues. You are also tested on knowledge and skills you have acquired from life experiences, television, radio, books and newspapers, consumer products, and advertising.

WHO MAY TAKE THE TESTS?

In the United States, Canada, and many U.S. territories, people who have not graduated from high school and who meet specific eligibility requirements (age, residency, etc.) may take the tests. Since eligibility requirements vary, it would be useful to contact your local GED testing center or the director of adult education in your state, province, or territory for specific information.

WHAT IS A PASSING SCORE ON THE GED?

Again this varies from area to area. To find out what you need to pass the test, contact your local GED testing center. However, you must keep two scores in mind. One score represents the minimum score you must get on each test. For example, if your state requires minimum scores of 40, you must get at least 40 points on every test. Additionally, you must meet the requirements of a minimum average score on all five tests. For example, if your state requires a minimum average score of 45, you must get a total of 225 points to pass. The two scores together, the minimum score and the minimum average score, determine whether you pass or fail the GED Test.

MAY I RETAKE THE TEST?

You are allowed to retake some or all of the test. Again the regulations governing the number of times that you may retake the tests and the time you must wait before retaking them are set by your state, province, or territory. Some states require you to take a review class or to study on your own for a certain amount of time before taking the test again.

HOW CAN I BEST PREPARE FOR THE TEST?

Many community colleges, public schools, adult education centers, libraries, churches, and other institutions offer GED preparation classes. Some television stations broadcast classes to prepare people for the test. If you cannot find a GED preparation class locally, contact the director of adult education in your state, province, or territory or call the GED Hotline (800-62-MY-GED). This hotline will give you telephone numbers and addresses of adult education and testing centers in your area. The hotline is staffed 24 hours a day, seven days a week.

IF I STUDY ON MY OWN, HOW MUCH TIME SHOULD I ALLOW TO PREPARE?

It depends on your readiness in each of the five subject areas; however, you should probably allow three to six months to do the following:

1. Read the introductory section of the book.

2. Take and score the five Pre-Tests. Decide which areas you need to focus on the most.

3. Read and complete the exercises in those areas that you decided to focus on.

4. Take the Post-Tests to determine how much improvement you've made.

5. Review the test-taking tips below.

6. Contact the GED administrator or the director of adult education in your state, province, or territory and arrange to take the GED.

TEST-TAKING TIPS FOR SUCCESS

1. **Prepare physically.** Get plenty of rest and eat a well-balanced meal before the test. Avoid last-minute cramming.

2. **Arrive early.** Be at the testing center at least 15 to 20 minutes before the starting time.

3. **Think positively.** Tell yourself you will do well.

4. **Relax during the test.** Take half a minute several times during the test to stretch and breathe deeply, especially if you are feeling anxious or confused.

5. **Read the test directions carefully.** Ask any questions about the test or about filling in the answer form before the test begins.

6. **Know the time limit for each test.** If you have time left after answering all the questions, go back and check your answers.

7. **Have a strategy for answering questions.** Read through the reading passages or look over the materials once, and then answer the questions that follow. Read each question two or three times to make sure you understand it. It is best to refer back to the passage or illustration in order to confirm your answer choice. Some people like to guide their reading by skimming the questions before reading a passage.

8. **Don't spend a lot of time on difficult questions.** If you're not sure of an answer, go on to the next question. Answer easier questions first and then go back to the harder questions. However, when you skip a question, be sure that you have skipped the same number on your answer sheet. Be sure not to throw off your whole answer key.

9. **Answer every question on the test.** If you're not sure of an answer, take an educated guess. When you leave a question unanswered, you will always lose points, but you can possibly gain points if you make a correct guess. If you must guess, try to eliminate one or more of the answers that you are sure are not correct. Then choose from the remaining answers.

10. **Clearly fill in the circle for each answer choice.** If you erase something, erase it completely. Be sure that you give only one answer per question; otherwise, no answer will count.

11. **Practice test-taking.** Use the exercises, reviews, and especially the Post-Tests in this book to better understand your test-taking habits and weaknesses. Use them to practice different strategies such as skimming questions first or skipping hard questions until the end.

HOW TO USE THIS BOOK

1. This book has been designed to help you succeed on the test. You may not have to work through all of the five sections in this book. In some areas you are likely to have stronger skills than in others. However, before you begin this book you should take the Pre-Tests. These will give you a preview of what the five tests include and help you to identify which areas you need to concentrate on most. Use the Evaluation Charts at the end of the Pre-Test Answer Keys to pinpoint the types of questions you answered incorrectly and to determine what skills you need extra work in.

2. Review the reading skills section to understand the six levels of thinking and how these levels are reflected on the GED Test.

3. In order to best prepare for the test, we recommend that you work through the entire book. An alternative method is to work through the subject areas that needed strengthening as indicated by the Pre-Test scores.

4. Take the Post-Tests at the end of the book. These tests will help you determine whether you are ready for the actual GED Test and, if not, what areas of the book you need to review. The Evaluation Charts are especially helpful in making this decision.

5. Seek further instruction through other books, if necessary. Contemporary Books publishes a wide range of materials to help you prepare for the tests. Additional titles that Contemporary offers are listed on page xv. These books are designed for home study or classroom use. Our GED preparation books are available through schools and bookstores and directly from the publisher. For the visually impaired, a large-print version is available. For further information, call Library Reproduction Service (LRS) at (800) 255-5002.

Finally, we'd like to hear from you. If our materials have helped you to pass the test or if you feel that we can do a better job preparing you, write to us at the address on the back of the book to let us know. We hope you enjoy studying for the GED Test with our materials and wish you the greatest success.

PRE-TESTS

GENERAL DIRECTIONS: The Pre-Tests will help you determine what you need to study in this book. They are one-quarter-length tests in the format and level of difficulty of the real GED Test. The results of these tests will help you map out a plan of study. We recommend the following approach to the Pre-Tests.

1. Take only one Pre-Test at a time. Don't attempt to do all of the tests at one sitting. Read the directions before you start a test. Use the answer grid at the beginning of each test to mark your choices.

2. After you finish each Pre-Test, check the answers in the answer key and fill in the Evaluation Chart for that test. Answer keys and Evaluation Charts are on pages 397–407. For all of the questions that you miss, read explanations of the correct answers.

3. Based on the information in the Evaluation Charts, you may choose to do one of two things:

   • If you miss half or more of the questions in a Pre-Test, you should work through the entire subject area.

   • If you miss fewer than half of the questions, focus on particular areas of the test that gave you difficulty.

4. Although these are Pre-Tests, you should give them your best effort. If an item seems difficult, mark it and come back later. Always answer every question—even if you have to make an "educated guess." Sometimes you may know more than you give yourself credit for. Also, on the real GED Tests a blank counts as a wrong answer. It's always wise to answer every question as best you can.

5. Answer each question as carefully as possible, choosing the best of five answer choices and blackening in the grid. The Math Pre-Test requires that you work each problem and write your answer on the blank line. If you find a question too difficult, do not waste time on it. Work ahead and come back to it later when you can think it through carefully.

6. When you have completed the test, check your work with the answers and explanations at the end of the section.

7. Use the Evaluation Charts on the pages indicated to determine which areas you need to review most:
   • Pre-Test 1, page 397
   • Pre-Test 2, page 400
   • Pre-Test 3, page 402
   • Pre-Test 4, page 404
   • Pre-Test 5, page 407

Time Allowed for Each Pre-Test

Writing Skills	Part 1	19 minutes
	Part 2	45 minutes
Social Studies		21 minutes
Science		24 minutes
Literature and the Arts		17 minutes
Mathematics		23 minutes

PRE-TEST 1: WRITING SKILLS
Part 1: Conventions of English

Directions: Part 1 of the Writing Skills Pre-Test consists of 15 multiple-choice questions. The questions are based on paragraphs that contain numbered sentences. Most sentences contain errors, but a few may be correct as written. Read the paragraphs and then answer the questions based on them. For each item, choose the answer that would result in a needed correction to the sentence, the best rewriting of the sentence or sentences, or the most effective combination of sentences. The best answer must be consistent with the meaning and tone of the rest of the paragraph. If you think the original is the best version, choose option (1).

PRE-TEST 1: WRITING SKILLS ANSWER GRID

1 ① ② ③ ④ ⑤   5 ① ② ③ ④ ⑤   9 ① ② ③ ④ ⑤   13 ① ② ③ ④ ⑤

2 ① ② ③ ④ ⑤   6 ① ② ③ ④ ⑤   10 ① ② ③ ④ ⑤   14 ① ② ③ ④ ⑤

3 ① ② ③ ④ ⑤   7 ① ② ③ ④ ⑤   11 ① ② ③ ④ ⑤   15 ① ② ③ ④ ⑤

4 ① ② ③ ④ ⑤   8 ① ② ③ ④ ⑤   12 ① ② ③ ④ ⑤

Questions 1–9 refer to the following passage.

(1) Most fire-related death's result from household fires, yet many people do not have fire extinguishers in their homes. (2) There is smoke detectors in many homes to warn residents of a fire, but fire extinguishers can actually help people fight fires. (3) In most cases, everyone should evacuate a home when a fire has started or the smoke alarm sounds. (4) Someone outside the home should call the fire department. (5) However, if a fire extinguisher is handy, a quick-thinking person often can use them to put out a small fire. (6) There are several types of fire extinguishers on the market, and each are suitable for particular types of fire. (7) Most extinguishers coming with instructions, and they are very easy to operate. (8) Fire departments may be contacted for training in operating extinguishers. (9) A person should keep in mind some basic safety rules when you are deciding whether or not to use a fire extinguisher. (10) Buying a fire extinguisher knowing how to use it, and placing it in a location familiar to all family members can help protect families against fire.

1. Sentence 1: **Most fire-related death's result from household fires, yet many people do not have fire extinguishers in their homes.**
   (1) replace *death's* with *deaths*
   (2) change *result* to *results*
   (3) remove the comma after *fires*
   (4) change *have* to *has*
   (5) replace *their* with *there*

2. Sentence 2: **There is smoke detectors in many homes to warn residents of a fire, but fire extinguishers can actually help people fight fires.**
   (1) There is
   (2) Their is
   (3) They're is
   (4) There are
   (5) Their are

3. Sentences 3 and 4: **In most cases, everyone should evacuate a home when a fire has started or the smoke alarm sounds. Someone outside the home should call the fire department.**
   (1) sounds, and someone
   (2) sounds and call
   (3) sounds, or someone
   (4) sounds unless someone
   (5) sounds and should call

4. Sentence 5: **However, if a fire extinguisher is handy, a quick-thinking person often can use them to put out a small fire.**
   (1) them
   (2) him
   (3) it
   (4) they
   (5) theirs

5. Sentence 6: **There are several types of fire extinguishers on the market, and each are suitable for particular types of fire.**
   (1) replace *There are* with *There is*
   (2) remove the comma after *market*
   (3) replace *and* with *or*
   (4) replace *each are* with *each is*
   (5) change the spelling of *particular* to *particuler*

6. Sentence 7: **Most <u>extinguishers coming with</u> instructions, and they are very easy to operate.**
    (1) coming with instructions
    (2) change *coming* to *come*
    (3) extinguishers comes
    (4) extinguishers, coming
    (5) coming, with

7. Sentence 8: **Fire departments may be contacted for training in operating extinguishers.**
    (1) replace *departments* with *Departments*
    (2) replace *may be* with *were*
    (3) change the spelling of *operating* to *opperating*
    (4) replace *departments* with *department's*
    (5) no correction is necessary

8. Sentence 9: **A person should keep in mind some basic safety <u>rules when you are deciding</u> whether or not to use a fire extinguisher.**
    (1) rules when you are deciding
    (2) rules when deciding
    (3) rules you decide
    (4) rules when you decided
    (5) rules. You are deciding

9. Sentence 10: **Buying a fire extinguisher knowing how to use it, and placing it in a location familiar to all family members can help protect families against fire.**
    (1) insert a comma after *extinguisher*
    (2) change *placing* to *place*
    (3) replace *members* with *member's*
    (4) insert a comma after *help*
    (5) change the spelling of *families* to *familys*

Questions 10–15 refer to the following passage.

(1) A european concept in overnight lodging known as "bed and breakfast" is becoming popular in the United States. (2) Private citizens act as hosts and rent out spare bedrooms in there homes. (3) Saying that they feel safer and like being treated as guests, the bed and breakfast hosts make them feel at home. (4) Travelers can learn much about the history and people of the local area; for example, visitors currently stayed on Wisconsin dairy farms and in restored log cabins in Kentucky. (5) The hosts also benefit from running such a business because they can stay home, make money, and meeting a variety of people. (6) Most state tourism departments and some travel agencies with bed and breakfast listings.

10. Sentence 1: **A european concept in overnight lodging known as "bed and breakfast" is becoming popular in the United States.**
    (1) change *european* to *European*
    (2) replace *known* with *is known*
    (3) replace *is* with *are*
    (4) replace *States* with *states*
    (5) no correction is necessary

11. Sentence 2: **Private citizens act as hosts and rent out spare bedrooms in there homes.**
    (1) replace *citizens* with *citizen's*
    (2) change *act* to *acted*
    (3) change *rent* to *renting*
    (4) add a comma after *hosts*
    (5) replace *there* with *their*

12. Sentence 3: **Saying that they feel safer and like being treated as guests, <u>the bed and breakfast hosts make them feel at home.</u>**
    (1) the bed and breakfast hosts make them feel at home.
    (2) feeling at home with the bed and breakfast hosts.
    (3) the bed and breakfast hosts feel at home with travelers.
    (4) are the bed and breakfast hosts feeling at home.
    (5) the travelers feel at home with the bed and breakfast hosts.

13. Sentence 4: **Travelers can learn much about the history and people of the local area; for example, visitors currently stayed on Wisconsin dairy farms and in restored log cabins in Kentucky.**
(1) replace *can* with *did*
(2) remove the comma after *example*
(3) replace *stayed* with *can stay*
(4) add a comma after *farms*
(5) no correction is necessary

14. Sentence 5: **The hosts also benefit from running such a business because they can stay at home, make money, and meeting a variety of people.**
(1) and meeting
(2) and meet
(3) to meet
(4) and be meeting
(5) get to meet

15. Sentence 6: **Most state tourism departments and some travel agencies with bed and breakfast listings.**
(1) change *with* to *have*
(2) change *tourism* to *Tourism*
(3) insert a comma after *departments*
(4) insert a comma after *agencies*
(5) change *with* to *has*

Answers begin on page 397.

Part 2: The Essay

Directions: This part of the test is designed to find out how well you write. The test has one question that asks you to present an opinion on an issue or to explain something. In preparing your answer to this question you should take the following steps:

1. Read all of the information accompanying the question.

2. Plan your answer carefully before you write.

3. Use scratch paper to mark any notes.

4. Write your answer on a separate sheet of paper.

5. Read carefully what you have written and make any changes that will improve your writing.

6. Check your paragraphing, sentence structure, spelling, punctuation, capitalization, and usage and make any necessary corrections.

Take 45 minutes to plan and write on the following topic. Write legibly and use a ball-point pen.

Topic

People decide to obtain a GED certificate for a wide variety of reasons. Some are interested in changing jobs; others simply want to finish something they started a long time ago. Why have you decided to study for the GED? Explain your decision and what you hope to gain by it. Be sure to give examples and to be specific.

Information on evaluating your essay is on page 398.

PRE-TEST 2: SOCIAL STUDIES

Directions: The Social Studies Pre-Test consists of 15 multiple-choice questions. Some of the questions are based on a map, chart, graph, cartoon, or reading passage. Read the passage or study the illustration carefully before you choose an answer.

PRE-TEST 2: SOCIAL STUDIES ANSWER GRID

1 ① ② ③ ④ ⑤   5 ① ② ③ ④ ⑤   9 ① ② ③ ④ ⑤   13 ① ② ③ ④ ⑤

2 ① ② ③ ④ ⑤   6 ① ② ③ ④ ⑤   10 ① ② ③ ④ ⑤   14 ① ② ③ ④ ⑤

3 ① ② ③ ④ ⑤   7 ① ② ③ ④ ⑤   11 ① ② ③ ④ ⑤   15 ① ② ③ ④ ⑤

4 ① ② ③ ④ ⑤   8 ① ② ③ ④ ⑤   12 ① ② ③ ④ ⑤

1. American consumers are not spending their money as freely as they have in the past. As a result, sales of personal computers have been affected. According to the dynamics of supply and demand, what will happen to the price of computers? The price will
   (1) increase to make up for the loss in profits
   (2) remain the same because the cost to manufacture computers stays the same
   (3) decrease to encourage consumers to buy them
   (4) increase in order for manufacturers to improve the quality of computers
   (5) remain the same because fewer computers will be available for sale

Question 2 is based on the cartoon below.

2. The cartoonist is suggesting that
   (1) terrorists have bigger and better weapons than ever before
   (2) terrorists deliberately use the media to publicize and promote their causes
   (3) terrorists cover their faces because they are afraid to be identified by the media
   (4) to terrorists, the media is the real enemy
   (5) terrorists want to dominate the world

Questions 3 and 4 are based on the bar graph below.

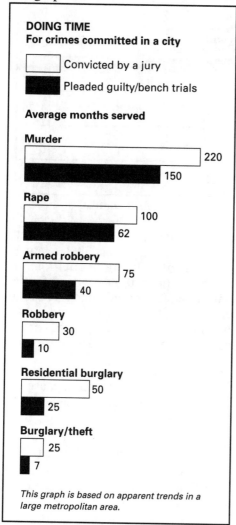

DOING TIME
For crimes committed in a city

☐ Convicted by a jury

■ Pleaded guilty/bench trials

Average months served

Murder
220
150

Rape
100
62

Armed robbery
75
40

Robbery
30
10

Residential burglary
50
25

Burglary/theft
25
7

This graph is based on apparent trends in a large metropolitan area.

3. Which of the following statements is best supported by the information in the graph?
  (1) Accused criminals are better off insisting on their right to a jury trial.
  (2) In this city, accused criminals are better off pleading guilty and accepting a bench trial presided over by a judge.
  (3) Juries do not understand the impact of their decisions.
  (4) Criminal courts in this city are harsher on criminals than in most cities.
  (5) Criminal courts in this city are more lenient with convictions than in most cities.

4. What values are being given priority by juries in criminal cases in this city?
  (1) the punishment of the criminal over the safety of the community
  (2) the needs of the criminal over the advice of the judge
  (3) the life of the criminal over the needs of the community
  (4) the safety of the community over sympathy for the criminal
  (5) the rights of the criminal over a strict interpretation of the law

Question 5 is based on the paragraph below.

The Monroe Doctrine demanded that Europe stay out of the affairs of the Americas. President Theodore Roosevelt used the doctrine to support a position on imperialism that came to be called the "Roosevelt Corollary." It stated that the United States had a right to take action in troubled areas of the Americas needing our "civilizing power."

5. In which incident would Roosevelt have used the corollary to defend his actions?
   (1) his approval of England's colonization of India and Egypt
   (2) the United Nations' participation in a conference to end French-German rivalry in Morocco
   (3) his support for the Open Door policy for trade with China
   (4) his negotiating an informal understanding between the United States and Japan to end unwanted immigration
   (5) the aiding of Panamanian rebels against the Colombian government

6. Before the Civil War, Virginia was united; however, in 1863, West Virginia chose to become independent. Which is the most reasonable cause of West Virginia's secession from the rest of the state?
   (1) The state was too large for only one legislature.
   (2) West Virginia was defeated by the North early in the war.
   (3) Richmond, Virginia, became the capital of the Confederacy.
   (4) There were no slave owners in West Virginia.
   (5) Political differences existed between western Virginia and the eastern part of the state.

Questions 7 and 8 are based on the following graph and passage.

Percentage of married women who hold full-time jobs and have children under 18 and husbands who work		
	18.4%	1950
	27.8%	1960
38.7%		1970
54.1%		1980
66.3%		1990

Source: *Scholastic Update Magazine*

The way a male or female acts or is expected to act in society is called a *role*. The traditional role for the husband in the American family has been breadwinner, while the wife's role has been homemaker. According to the bar graph above, however, family roles are changing.

7. Which of the following is *least likely* to be considered a cause of the changing role of married women in the family?
   (1) increased expenses requiring a second income in many families
   (2) more women wanting careers in addition to raising a family
   (3) the lack of respect accorded the traditional role of homemaker
   (4) increased availability of day-care centers and professional babysitters
   (5) more job opportunities for women than ever before

8. According to the bar graph, during which time period was there the greatest increase in the percentage of married women in the work force?
   (1) Before 1950
   (2) 1950–1960
   (3) 1960–1970
   (4) 1970–1980
   (5) 1980–1990

9. Between 1937 and 1957, the birthrate rose from 18.7 to 25.3 per 1,000 people. The most likely cause of this "baby boom" was
   (1) the return of young American soldiers from war
   (2) the growth of the urban/suburban areas after World War II
   (3) the increased mobility of the American family of the 1950s
   (4) the continuing expansion of the middle class and its new wealth
   (5) the relaxing of moral sanctions against artificial birth control methods

10. Increased personal income lets people purchase more goods and services. For example, spending for houses and cars increases as people feel comfortable in making long-term investments. In such a climate, business would likely
    (1) increase production to provide greater quantities of goods
    (2) lower the sales tax on the products
    (3) spend less money on new equipment and machinery
    (4) sell the products to foreign nations
    (5) distribute the products equally throughout the country

Question 11 is based on the following graph.

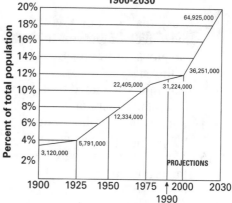

U.S. POPULATION, AGE 65 AND OLDER
1900-2030

11. The number of people in the United States over the age of 65 is increasing dramatically. Which one of the following governmental programs would be most directly affected by this growth?
    (1) veterans' benefits
    (2) national defense
    (3) job training and employment programs
    (4) food stamps
    (5) social security

Questions 12 and 13 are based on the following passage.

In 1992, Australia's Prime Minister, Paul Keating, urged that the country cut its remaining political ties with Britain and become a republic instead of a commonwealth. Britain is no longer a major factor in Australia's economic security. Today, almost half of Australia's exports go to Asia, and Asian immigration to Australia is on the rise. With a declining economy, Australians must decide where their best interests lie.

12. Based on the information in the passage, you can conclude that

   (1) Paul Keating is in favor of continued commonwealth status.

   (2) Australia's economy will most likely improve if it develops further relations with Asia.

   (3) Australia is isolated to maintain its economy.

   (4) Politics has nothing to do with geographic location.

   (5) Many Australians agree with the prime minister.

13. The decision facing the Commonwealth of Australia is most similar to

   (1) the decision to transfer Hong Kong from British rule to Chinese rule

   (2) the decision of the Commonwealth of Kentucky to join the United States

   (3) the decision to adopt Guam as a territory of the United States

   (4) the decision of Puerto Rico about whether to request statehood or remain a commonwealth

   (5) the decision of the thirteen original American colonies to form a new nation

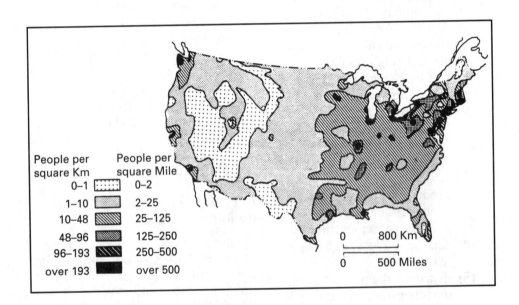

People per square Km		People per square Mile
0–1		0–2
1–10		2–25
10–48		25–125
48–96		125–250
96–193		250–500
over 193		over 500

0   800 Km

0   500 Miles

Question 14 is based on the map on page 12.

14. Based on the map, the region of the country with the greatest population density is the
(1) Midwest
(2) Southwest
(3) Northwest
(4) Southeast
(5) Northeast

Question 15 is based on the following passage.

Vice President Andrew Johnson succeeded Lincoln as president after Lincoln's assassination. Johnson was from Tennessee and was the only southern senator not to join the Confederacy when the war broke out. Lincoln had trusted him totally, but many in Congress did not. In spite of Johnson's refusal to join the Confederacy, his every action appeared to be suspiciously pro-South to them.

15. Which of the following actions of Johnson's does *not* support these congressmen's opinion of him?
(1) his issuing a proclamation forgiving most Confederates
(2) his demand that Confederate states ratify the Thirteenth Amendment abolishing slavery
(3) his veto of the civil rights bill that guaranteed rights to freed slaves
(4) his veto of the Freedman's Bureau bill that had been approved without the input of the southern states
(5) his opposition to the Fourteenth Amendment, which toughened Congress's stand against former Confederate loyalists

Answers begin on page 399.

PRE-TEST 3: SCIENCE

Directions: The Science Pre-Test consists of 15 multiple-choice questions. Some of the questions are based on a chart, graph, diagram, or reading passage.

Our blood consists of a liquid, the straw-colored *plasma*, in which are suspended red blood cells, white blood cells, and *platelets*. Red blood cells are used to transport oxygen throughout the body. The different types of white blood cells are used to fight infections. Platelets are important in blood clotting.

1. Based on the passage above, which of the following blood components would be used to repair an open wound?
   (1) plasma and white blood cells
   (2) red blood cells
   (3) white blood cells
   (4) platelets
   (5) white blood cells and platelets

The leaf is a flat organ composed of two layers of photosynthetic cells sandwiched between the epidermal, or outer, layers. The epidermal layers are coated with a waxy covering called the *cuticle*, which prevents the loss of gas and water. Tiny holes, called *stomata*, provide openings for the entry of carbon dioxide and the exit of oxygen.

2. Based on the information above, the leaf "breathes" through its
   (1) photosynthetic cells
   (2) veins
   (3) cuticle
   (4) epidermal layers
   (5) stomata

Question 3 is based on the following table.

Energy Expenditure	
Activity	**Calories per Hour**
sitting at rest	15
walking	130–200
running	500–900
bicycling	240
swimming	200–700
writing	20

3. According to the table, for a person concerned with weight loss which would be the most efficient weight-loss exercise for the time spent?
   (1) bicycling
   (2) swimming
   (3) walking
   (4) writing
   (5) running

S	N	N	S

4. As the two bar magnets above are brought closer together, what do you predict will happen?
   (1) They will attract each other.
   (2) They will repel each other.
   (3) They will cancel out each other's magnetic field.
   (4) They will create an alternating current.
   (5) Nothing will happen.

Questions 5 and 6 are based on the following passage.

Charles Darwin proposed the theory of natural selection in 1859. The theory holds that those species that are best adapted to the conditions under which they live will survive, and those that are not adapted will perish.

An example of this theory is illustrated by the experience of the peppered moth that was once common near Manchester, England, an industrial city.

Before the industrial revolution, the light-colored form of this moth was common and the dark-colored form was rare. As Manchester's environment became increasingly polluted, however, the tree trunks on which the peppered moth lived became blackened by soot. The light-colored form of the moth stood out against the dark tree trunks and was eaten by birds, which destroyed 99 percent of the light-colored moths.

In the absence of the light-colored moths, the rare dark moths became more common and filled the vacancy left by the light-colored moths. In the 1950s, however, Manchester's industries were cleaned up, and the light-colored moth became the more common type again.

5. Based on the passage, the cause of the light-colored moth's disappearance was
   (1) an inability to tolerate a polluted environment
   (2) the birds' preference for its taste
   (3) an insecticide that killed it
   (4) the reduced number of eggs laid by female moths
   (5) its inability to blend in with its environment

6. Based on the information in the passage, you can infer that
   (1) forms of life in a community are influenced by nature's laws
   (2) human activity can have significant ecological impact on an environment
   (3) Darwin's theory works only under ideal circumstances
   (4) all forms of life must fend for themselves
   (5) moths can thrive under the worst conditions

7. Acetylsalicylic acid (aspirin) is known to retard the blood-clotting process. This can have both positive and negative effects. One positive application of this knowledge is the use of aspirin to
   (1) relieve pain
   (2) reduce inflammation
   (3) reduce the possibility of stroke
   (4) act as a stimulant
   (5) stop bleeding

Questions 8 and 9 are based on the following passage.

There is, perhaps, no part of the world where the early geological periods can be studied with so much ease and precision as in the United States. Along the northern border between Canada and the United States, there runs a low line of hills known as the Laurentian Hills. Insignificant in height, nowhere rising more than two thousand feet above the level of the sea, these are nevertheless the first mountains that broke the uniform level of Earth's surface and lifted themselves above the waters. Their low stature, as compared with that of other, loftier mountain ranges, is in accordance with an invariable rule by which the relative age of mountains may be estimated. The oldest mountains are the lowest, while the younger and more recent ones tower above their elders and are usually more jagged and dislocated.

8. In the United States, early geological periods
   (1) can be studied only along the country's northern border
   (2) can be studied only in the Rocky Mountains
   (3) can be studied easily and precisely
   (4) are not as visible as in the rest of the world
   (5) can be studied only in the Appalachian Mountains

9. The relationship between low mountain ranges and high mountain ranges can be described *best* in terms of
   (1) old age and youth
   (2) the Laurentian Hills
   (3) the Swiss Alps and the Himalayas
   (4) dislocation and thickness
   (5) their location in either Canada or the United States

Question 10 is based on the information and table below.

Heat is able to pass from one molecule to another. This is called *heat conduction*. In the table that follows, the numbers (called coefficients) indicate the relative rates of heat transfer in the materials listed.

Heat Conduction Coefficients	
Material	**Coefficient**
silver	100
copper	92
aluminum	50
iron	11
glass	0.20
water	0.12
wood	0.03
air	0.006
perfect vacuum	0

10. The table identifies the best conductors as
(1) gases
(2) natural materials
(3) metals
(4) liquids
(5) compounds

Question 11 is based on the following passage.

Loess is a deposit of windblown dust that slowly blankets large areas and often covers existing land forms. A distinctive sedimentary deposit, loess was laid down long ago. It may cover as much as one-tenth of Earth's surface and is particularly widespread in semiarid regions along the margins of great deserts. The equatorial tropics and the areas covered by continental glaciers are free of loess.

11. A nation in which loess would likely be found today is
(1) Republic of the Congo
(2) Iceland
(3) Japan
(4) United States
(5) Ecuador

Question 12 is based on the following information.

The Fathometer is a device used for determining ocean depths. It operates by sending sound waves under water. A sudden pulse of sound is transmitted by a ship and then picked up again after it has been reflected, or echoed, from the sea bottom, and the elapsed time is recorded. Knowing the time and the speed of sound waves through water, the depth of the sea at any point may be computed, often to the nearest foot.

12. From the information in the passage, you can conclude that
(1) the depth of the ocean is already known
(2) the speed at which underwater sound waves travel from the ocean's surface to the bottom remains constant
(3) Fathometers show only approximate depths and are, therefore, unreliable
(4) Fathometers work best in shallow waters
(5) Fathometers operate on scientific and not mathematical principles

Questions 13 and 14 are based on the following information.

The most common organic acids are formic acid and acetic acid. Formic acid occurs naturally in red ants and in pine needles. In concentrated form it can burn the skin; however, diluted formic acid is used for its germicidal properties. Acetic acid is responsible for the sour taste of pickles and sharp odors that can burn the nostrils. Cider vinegar contains 3 to 6 percent acetic acid and is made by the natural oxidation of apple cider.

13. The main idea of the passage above is that
   (1) organic acids can be both harmful and beneficial
   (2) formic acid is a part of vinegar
   (3) pine needles contain acetic acid
   (4) undiluted formic acid is used as a germicide
   (5) apple cider turns into formic acid

14. The passage supports the statement that
   (1) all acids are harmful to humans
   (2) only organic acids are useful to humans
   (3) organic acids in diluted form are useful to humans
   (4) inorganic acids in diluted form are useful to humans
   (5) only diluted inorganic acids are beneficial to humans

Question 15 is based on the chart below.

Transfusion Relationship		
Blood Type	Can Receive Blood from	Acts as Donor to
O	O	O, A, B, AB
A	A, O	A, AB
B	B, O	B, AB
AB	O, A, B, AB	AB

15. Which of the following blood types can be regarded as a universal donor?
   (1) O
   (2) A
   (3) B
   (4) AB
   (5) all blood types

Answers begin on page 401.

PRE-TEST 4:
LITERATURE AND THE ARTS

Directions: The Literature and the Arts Pre-Test consists of 12 multiple-choice questions. These questions are based on passages of fiction and nonfiction prose, poetry, drama, and commentaries on literature and the arts.

PRE-TEST 4: LITERATURE AND THE ARTS ANSWER GRID

1 ① ② ③ ④ ⑤   4 ① ② ③ ④ ⑤   7 ① ② ③ ④ ⑤   10 ① ② ③ ④ ⑤

2 ① ② ③ ④ ⑤   5 ① ② ③ ④ ⑤   8 ① ② ③ ④ ⑤   11 ① ② ③ ④ ⑤

3 ① ② ③ ④ ⑤   6 ① ② ③ ④ ⑤   9 ① ② ③ ④ ⑤   12 ① ② ③ ④ ⑤

Read each excerpt and choose the best answer to each question.

Questions 1–3 refer to the following biographical sketch.

HOW DID ELVIS PRESLEY ACHIEVE RECOGNITION?

Success often comes to those with humble beginnings. Elvis Aaron Presley was born on January 8, 1935, in Tupelo,
5 Mississippi. He first sang in a church choir and taught himself to play the guitar, but he never learned to read music. By 1953, he had moved to Memphis,
10 Tennessee, graduated from high school, and enrolled in night school to become an electrician. That year, while recording some test pressings
15 at Sun Records, Presley was heard by the company president. As a result of the president's recognition, Presley's first record, "That's All Right,
20 Mama," was cut in 1954.

He toured the South, and in 1955 five of his records were released simultaneously. His first national television
25 appearance was that year on Jackie Gleason's "The Stage Show," but Presley became known for his appearance on "The Ed Sullivan Show," where
30 the young singer gyrated as he sang "rock 'n' roll" music. In later TV performances Presley was photographed only from the waist up because his
35 motions were considered obscene.

"Elvis the Pelvis" began his film career in 1956 with *Love Me Tender* and signed a long-term
40 film contract. The movie critics were not always kind, but teenagers flocked to Presley's films. Within a few short years, Presley had established a career
45 that would span twenty-five years of ups and downs and make him one of the most popular entertainers in history. Long after his untimely death at
50 age 42, Presley would be remembered as "The King of Rock 'n' Roll."

1. The last sentence reveals that the author's attitude toward Presley is one of
   (1) indifference
   (2) admiration
   (3) disgust
   (4) disbelief
   (5) sarcasm

2. The main idea of the sketch is that
   (1) there has always been obscenity on television
   (2) singers are more successful if they appear in films
   (3) celebrities are usually more famous after their death
   (4) success always comes to those who work hard
   (5) opportunity and luck are often as important as hard work

3. The statement that "success often comes to those with humble beginnings" would apply best to which of the following historical figures?
   (1) multimillionaire Pierre DuPont
   (2) John F. Kennedy
   (3) Franklin D. Roosevelt
   (4) Abraham Lincoln
   (5) oil billionaire J. Paul Getty

Questions 4 and 5 refer to the following excerpt from a novel.

HOW DOES THE PERSON FEEL?

Once again he did his Christmas shopping in a Rexall drugstore. It was late, the day before Christmas Eve, and he
5 hadn't had the spirit or energy or presence of mind to do it earlier or thoughtfully. Boredom, which had begun as a mild infection, now took him over completely.
10 No activity seemed worth the doing, no conversation worth having. The fluttery preparations at home seemed fake and dingy. His mother was going on
15 as she did every year about the incredible price of trees and butter. As though their tree would be anything other than it had always been: the huge shadowy
20 thing in the corner burdened with decorations she had had since she was a girl. As if her fruitcakes were edible, or her turkey done all the way
25 to the bone. His father gave them all envelopes of varying amounts of money, never thinking that just once they might like something he actually went into
30 a department store and selected.

—Toni Morrison, excerpted from *Song of Solomon*, 1977

4. The son waits until the last minute to do his Christmas shopping because he
 (1) is following the example set by his father
 (2) couldn't go shopping until he received his paycheck
 (3) hasn't any idea what to buy for his parents
 (4) doesn't really care what gifts he buys
 (5) spent all his money on a Christmas tree

5. Which of the following methods does the author rely on most heavily in creating character in this excerpt?
 (1) showing the character's actual speech patterns
 (2) showing what other characters say about the character
 (3) revealing the character's private thoughts
 (4) describing the character's physical features
 (5) showing the character in action

Questions 6 and 7 refer to the following poem.

WHAT HAPPENED TO TOM MERRITT?
Tom Merritt

At first I suspected something—
She acted so calm and absent-minded.
5 And one day I heard the back door shut,
As I entered the front, and I saw him slink
Back of the smokehouse
10 into the lot,
And across the field.
And I meant to kill him on sight.
But that day, walking
15 near Fourth Bridge,
Without a stick or a stone at hand,
All of the sudden I saw him standing,
20 Scared to death, holding his rabbits,
And all I could say was, "Don't, Don't, Don't,"
As he aimed and fired at my
25 heart.

—Edgar Lee Masters, 1915

6. Who is the speaker in this poem?
   (1) Merritt's wife
   (2) a murderer
   (3) Tom Merritt
   (4) God
   (5) the sheriff

7. The poem mainly uses which of the following techniques?
   (1) rhyme—the repetition of two or more vowel sounds
   (2) verse—a division of a poem into distinct parts
   (3) rhythm—an emphasis on certain words or syllables (beat)
   (4) free verse—the absence of rhyme and a regular rhythmic pattern
   (5) personification—the attributing to an animal or thing some human activity or quality

Questions 8 and 9 refer to the following excerpt from a play.

WHAT DOES HIGGINS THINK OF WOMEN?

PICKERING: Excuse the straight question, Higgins. Are you a man of good character where women are concerned?

HIGGINS: [*Moodily.*] Have you ever met a man of good character where women are concerned?

PICKERING: Yes: very frequently.

HIGGINS: [*Dogmatically, lifting himself on his hands to the level of the piano, and sitting on it with a bounce.*] Well, I haven't. I find that the moment I let a woman make friends with me, she becomes jealous, exacting, suspicious, and a damned nuisance. I find that the moment I let myself make friends with a woman, I become selfish and tyrannical. Women upset everything. When you let them into your life, you find that the woman is driving at one thing and you're driving at another.

PICKERING: At what, for example?

HIGGINS: [*Coming off the piano restlessly.*] Oh, Lord knows! I suppose the woman wants to live her own life; and the man wants to live his; and each tries to drag the other on to the wrong track. One wants to go north and the other south; and the result is that both have to go east, though they both hate the east wind. [*He sits down on the bench at the keyboard.*] So here I am, a confirmed old bachelor, and likely to remain so.

PICKERING: [*Rising and standing over him gravely.*] Come, Higgins! You know what I mean. If I'm to be in this business I shall feel responsible for that girl. I hope it's understood that no advantage is to be taken of her position.

HIGGINS: What! That thing! Sacred, I assure you. [*Rising to explain.*] You see, she'll be a pupil; and teaching would be impossible unless pupils were sacred. I've taught scores of American millionairesses how to speak English: the best looking women in the world. I'm seasoned. They might as well be blocks of wood. I might as well be a block of wood.

—George Bernard Shaw, excerpted from *Pygmalion*, 1913

8. Higgins's negative attitude toward women is based on his
  (1) recent divorce
  (2) lack of contact with women
  (3) desire to meet beautiful women
  (4) previous experience with women
  (5) upcoming marriage

9. "One wants to go north and the other south; and the result is that both have to go east, though they both hate the east wind."

The playwright includes this reference to show that
  (1) relationships are stronger if both parties sacrifice
  (2) couples often come from different regions of the country
  (3) compromise can have negative effects upon a relationship
  (4) trust is the most important element of a relationship
  (5) women have equal rights in all relationships

Questions 10–12 refer to the following excerpt from a commentary.

DOES TV STEREOTYPE?

Hispanics may be the fastest-growing minority group in the USA, but they are sorely under-represented on prime-time tele-
5   vision.
While 9 percent of the U.S. population is Hispanic, only 2 percent of prime-time characters were during a week surveyed by
10   *USA Today.*
Asians and Native Americans also were underrepresented, with Asians 1 percent of TV's players vs. 3 percent of the U.S.
15   population and Native Americans

1 percent of TV's characters vs. 4 percent in real life.
The problem lies in percep-tions, says Ray Blanco of the
20   National Hispanic Academy of Media Arts & Sciences.
"People tend to think that all Hispanics don't speak English, only watch Spanish-language TV
25   and don't have a disposable income, which is not the case," Blanco says.
Hispanic roles that do exist, Blanco adds, often reinforce
30   derogatory stereotypes.
Actor Marco Sanchez agrees. "I can't tell you how frustrating it was to go on auditions and know I'd be considered for one of four
35   roles: the drug dealer, the gang member, the lover, or the street-wise youth with a heart of gold."
Sanchez, the son of Cuban immigrants, says his mother
40   suggested he change his name, "but I refused to compromise a part of myself to get a job."

—Donna Gable, excerpted
from "TV's Limited Visions
of Hispanics,"
August 30, 1993,
USA Today

10. According to the excerpt, the fastest-growing minority group in the United States is
  (1) Hispanics
  (2) Asians
  (3) Native Americans
  (4) Cubans
  (5) African Americans

11. The mother of actor Marco Sanchez suggested that he change his name because
- **(1)** casting agents found it hard to remember
- **(2)** people kept misspelling and mispronouncing the name
- **(3)** it was not an appropriate name for a stage and screen star
- **(4)** people kept mistaking him for someone with a similar name
- **(5)** it limited the kinds of characters he was allowed to play

12. If Marco Sanchez were offered the following roles, which would he most likely pick?
- **(1)** a drug dealer in a made-for-TV movie
- **(2)** the lead in a Shakespearean comedy
- **(3)** a gang leader on a weekly drama series
- **(4)** a streetwise youth in a feature film
- **(5)** the love interest of a married woman in a soap opera

Answers begin on page 403.

Pre-Test 5: Mathematics

Directions: The Mathematics Pre-Test consists of 30 items. It offers you the opportunity to test both your computational and problem-solving skills. These are not multiple-choice items, so you will have to work as accurately and carefully as possible. Be sure to use any diagrams or charts that are provided with the problems.

PRE-TEST 5: MATHEMATICS ANSWERS

1 _____	9 _____	17 _____	25 _____
2 _____	10 _____	18 _____	26 _____
3 _____	11 _____	19 _____	27 _____
4 _____	12 _____	20 _____	28 _____
5 _____	13 _____	21 _____	29 _____
6 _____	14 _____	22 _____	30 _____
7 _____	15 _____	23 _____	
8 _____	16 _____	24 _____	

You may find these formulas useful in solving some of the following problems.

FORMULAS

Description	Formula
AREA (A) of a	
square	$A = s^2$ where s = side
rectangle	$A = lw$ where l = length, w = width
triangle	$A = \frac{1}{2} bh$ where b = base, h = height
circle	$A = \pi r^2$ where $\pi \cong 3.14$, r = radius
PERIMETER (P) of a	
square	$P = 4s$ where s = side
rectangle	$P = 2l + 2w$ where l = length, w = width
circle—circumference (C)	$C = \pi d$ where $\pi \cong 3.14$, d = diameter
VOLUME (V) of a	
cube	$V = s^3$ where s = side
rectangular container	$V = lwh$ where l = length, w = width, h = height
Pythagorean theorem	$c^2 = a^2 + b^2$ where c = hypotenuse, a and b are legs of a right triangle
distance (d) between two points in a plane	$d = \sqrt{(x_2 - x_1)^2 + (y_2 - y_1)^2}$ where (x_1, y_1) and (x_2, y_2) are two points in a plane
slope of a line (m)	$m = \dfrac{y_2 - y_1}{x_2 - x_1}$ where (x_1, y_1) and (x_2, y_2) are two points in a plane

Solve each problem.

1. Divide 5310 by 9.

2. What is .38 divided by .4?

3. Corey needs $120 to buy a new coat. She has saved the money she received from four dividend checks of $16.75 each. How much more money must she add to those savings to play for the coat?

4. $1\frac{1}{4} - \frac{3}{4} =$

5. $4\frac{1}{5} \times \frac{1}{2} =$

Question 6 is based on the chart below, which compares the growth of four local companies.

	Sales	
	1991	**1995**
Magic Marketing	$ 323,000	$ 904,400
Futures Marketing	$ 630,000	$ 925,000
Townley Agency	$ 264,000	$1,497,000
Billings Printing	$2,000,000	$6,000,000

6. If Magic Marketing continues to have approximately the same rate of growth for the 4 years to 1999, what will be the projected sales in 1999 (to the nearest million dollars)?

7. On the first day of their vacation, the Morales family drove 312 miles in 6 hours. At that rate, how far will they travel the next day if they drive for 8 hours?

8. Find 72% of $350.

9. Find the length of the diagonal brace used to reinforce the barn door.

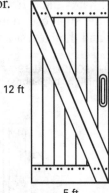

12 ft

5 ft

10. Nick's time card shows his hours for one week. If he works 8 hours per day before earning overtime, find Nick's total pay before deductions.

PHILLIPS CORPORATION time card		
Name: Nick Acino **SS#:** 002-00-0021		
Date	**From**	**To**
7/8	8:30 A.M.	4:30 P.M.
7/9	8:30 A.M.	5:15 P.M.
7/10	8:00 A.M.	4:30 P.M.
7/11	8:30 A.M.	6:00 P.M.
7/12	8:30 A.M.	4:45 P.M.

Total Regular Hours _____ at $8.40
Overtime Hours _____ at $12.60
(over 40 hours)

11. In the formula for the circumference of a circle, the *d* stands for the diameter, which is twice the radius, *r*. If $\pi \cong 3.14$ and $r = 3$, choose the expression below that could be used to find the circumference of the circle.

(1) (3.14) (3)

(2) (3.14) (6)

(3) (3.14) (1.5)

(4) (3.14) (3^2)

(5) not enough information is given

12. Write 273,000 in scientific notation.

13. There were many increases in gasohol sales over a nine-year period. What is the difference between the smallest annual increase and the largest annual increase?

GASOHOL SALES
(in millions of gallons)

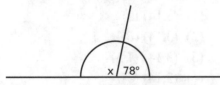

14. Find the number of square *yards* of sod needed to cover the circular putting green shown below
(*Hint:* 9 sq ft = 1 sq yd)

15 ft

15. Find the measure of angle *x* in the illustration below.

x / 78°

16. Main Street and Union Avenue are parallel roads as shown below.

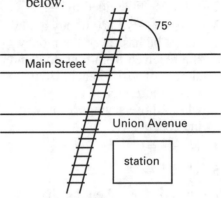

75°

Main Street

Union Avenue

station

The railroad tracks cut across both streets. What is the angle measure of the land on which the station rests, based on the formation given in the diagram above?

17. Solve for *x*: $14 = \frac{x}{5}$

18. Solve for *x*: $4x - 9 = 7$

19. Solve for *x*: $3(x - 2) - 3 = x + 5$

20. Evaluate: $-4 + (-3) - (-2)$

21. If $x = -2$ and $y = 5$, find the value of the expression $5y - 3x^2$.

22. Miguel has fourteen coins in this pocket. He has one more dime than quarters and three more nickels that dimes. How many of each coin does he have?

23. Using the diagram below, find the measure of angle *A*.

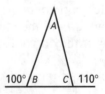

100° / *B*   *C* \ 110°

24. If one kilogram = 2.2 pounds, does a 3-kilogram roast beef weigh more or less than a 6-pound roast?

25. To find the height of the evergreen in his backyard, Doug sketched the information shown here.

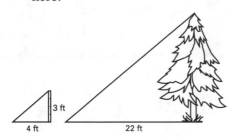

He placed a yardstick parallel to the tree and compared its shadow on the ground with the length of the shadow of the tree. How tall is the tree?

Questions 26 and 27 are based on this drawing.

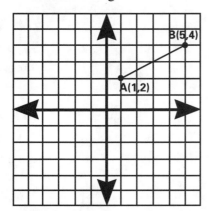

26. Find the length of the line segment from point *A* to point *B*.

27. Find the slope of the line *AB*.

28. Look at the triangle below. What is the measure of ∠ *b*?

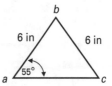

29. In a standard deck of 52 playing cards, what is the probability of drawing an ace on one draw?

30. Evaluate:

$$\sqrt{25} + (4 \times 3)^2 - (5 \times 2)$$

READING SKILLS FOR THE GED

Developing strong reading and reasoning skills is key to your success on the GED Tests. This section focuses on skills that are used on all of the tests and particularly in the content areas of science, social studies, and literature and the arts. These skills are called comprehension, application, analysis, synthesis, and evaluation.

The questions on the GED will test your ability to comprehend, apply, analyze, and evaluate what you read. The reading skills can be understood as layers of a pyramid. Each higher-level skill rests on the skill that precedes it. Each skill is a stepping-stone to a higher one.

PYRAMID OF THINKING SKILLS

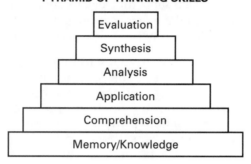

Evaluation
Synthesis
Analysis
Application
Comprehension
Memory/Knowledge

Memory (knowledge), sometimes referred to as *recall*, is the foundation of the pyramid. At the memory level, you recall facts and answer the questions *who, what, when, where,* and *how.* Other tests that you took in school may have focused heavily on memory-based questions in which you had to recall facts. On the GED Tests, however, you will have to manipulate, or work with, the information that you read and that you hold in your memory.

When you *comprehend* something, you understand what you read. You show your understanding by being able to *paraphrase,* that is, interpret or explain in your own words what something means. This skill involves putting one meaning into other words, identifying the main idea or key thought, and making inferences (sometimes referred to as reading between the lines).

Another way to show that you comprehend language is by *understanding idiomatic expressions.* Read and show that you comprehend (understand) the following paragraph by paraphrasing the numbered words or phrases. Write the intended meaning for each.

Carmen really needed to <u>brush up on</u> her Spanish. If she didn't <u>get cold feet</u> and wasn't <u>broke</u> by the end of the month, she was going to Mexico. <u>Her heart was set</u> on a trip, but she was <u>up to her ears in</u> work at the real estate office.

1. _____   4. _____

2. _____   5. _____

3. _____

[Possible answers: review, become cautious, out of money, She really wanted to go, overwhelmed by the amount of]

Another way you might show your comprehension of material is to *summarize*, or restate, the main idea. The main idea sums up what the writer is trying to get across. For example, if you answer the phone at work for an absent coworker, and the caller gives you a long story about the reason for the call, you generally won't write down every word the caller says. You will summarize the message or simply write down the key thought or purpose of the call. You also might jot down key words or summarize main ideas when you take class notes.

Comprehension also involves recognizing the main idea regardless of its location in the paragraph. The main idea is often stated first. Details that support the main idea are included in the sentences that follow. Occasionally, writers put the main idea in the middle or at the end of a paragraph. Then the author must ensure that enough supporting details are included before or after to "add up" to the main point the writer is trying to make. Read the following passage to identify the main idea. Where is it stated in the passage?

> Weather is one of many variables that affect the nation's agricultural economy, and it is the most unpredictable. Northern farmers who hope for record harvests have frequently seen crops wiped out by droughts, seeds washed away by torrential rains, and early spring planting plans thwarted by frozen ground. You might think that a farmer's problems are solved by lots of sunshine, plentiful rain, and year-round warm temperatures. Well, think again! In recent years, orange growers in Florida have had their hopes dashed by unexpected subfreezing temperatures. These cold temperatures have resulted in reduced harvests.

[Answer: the first sentence]

Reading between the lines is also a component of comprehension. In those instances, the author expects you to draw appropriate *inferences*, or conclusions. Read the following passage to draw an inference regarding the unstated main idea of the passage. Then pick out one stated detail that does *not* help you arrive at the main idea.

The Priceless Gift

> A young boy's dramatic adventure unfolds several years before the Soviet Union breaks up into the Commonwealth of Independent States. Picture a little Ukrainian boy coming to the United States with his parents. His parents decide to return to the Soviet Union, but he refuses to accompany them. Six years later, the boy, now twelve years old, receives a gift. The gift is something that native-born American children take for granted. It's a gift for a young boy who rode his bicycle to a relative's house and hid there for five days to avoid leaving the United States against his will. But this gift is wrapped in yards of legal red tape.
>
> Before the boy earned the gift, he had to ignore the wishes of his parents and his native country. He had to learn to accept a whole new way of life without his parents

and brother. He had to learn the English language and learn the ways of elementary school students in Chicago. He had to get used to grocery stores with plenty of food, unrestricted movement on the streets, and the option of celebrating religious holidays. He had to attempt to lead a normal life in spite of all the media attention. He knew the gift could not be bought with money; it was priceless.

[Answers: The unstated main idea of the passage is that the boy earned the right to become a U.S. citizen. Some details which help you arrive at the unstated main idea are the following: The gift was *wrapped with yards of legal red tape. The gift is something that native-born American children take for granted. The gift could not be bought with money. He had to learn to accept a whole new way of life.* . . . The fact that the boy was a twelve-year-old student in Chicago does not help you determine the main idea because there are thousands of twelve-year-old boys in any city.]

Application is applying what you read. On the GED Tests, you will have to use information given to you and apply it in a problem-solving situation. The information that you will be given may be in the form of a definition, scientific theory, or principle. You will encounter application questions primarily in the areas of science and social studies; however, the Literature and the Arts Test will contain some as well. To practice your skill in applying definitions, read the following passage about forms of drama and answer the questions that follow.

> The major forms of drama are *comedy* and *tragedy*. Comedies generally are light and amusing. They usually begin in humorously difficult situations and always end happily. Not all comedies are funny and lighthearted, although the majority are. Types of comedy include *slapstick*, a form of physical comedy that includes pratfalls and pie-in-the-face acts. *Farce* is a type of comedy that features exaggerated circumstances, improbable plots, and foolish action and dialogue.
>
> Tragedies often begin happily and always end in disaster. The main character is usually good, but loses to an opponent in a conflict and is either ruined or killed. The major reason for the main character's failure is the tragic flaw—the human weakness that has made the tragic hero or heroine vulnerable.
>
> Somewhere between comedy and tragedy lies *melodrama*, a type of drama that relies on sentimentality, exaggerates emotion, and provides thrilling action.

1. The boisterous humor featured by comedians such as the Three Stooges, Jerry Lewis, and Charlie Chaplin would be classified best as
   (1) comedy
   (2) tragedy
   (3) slapstick
   (4) farce
   (5) melodrama

2. One of the most popular television programs of the last decade was "Cheers." This classic look at the human condition from the points of view of the lively characters in a Boston barroom would be described best as

(1) comedy
(2) tragedy
(3) slapstick
(4) farce
(5) melodrama

[Answers: **1. (3)**; **2. (1)**]

Application in social studies and science will challenge your ability to apply given ideas in different situations. You need to be able to distinguish *propaganda,* which is information provided in such a way as to influence or slant the opinion or feelings of the audience that receives the message. You need to be able to recognize five techniques used by propagandists: *name-calling* (unfavorable names), *glittering generalities* (high-sounding, vague terms), *bandwagoning* (doing what everyone is doing), *transferring* (associating respect or power), and *card-stacking* (choosing favorable points only) .

Analysis is analyzing what you read. When you analyze something, you take it apart. You examine the elements to understand better what makes up its whole. In literature and the arts, the skill of analysis is used to determine the *author's style*, or choice of words; style helps to create *tone*, or attitude toward the subject and reader.

Another skill of analysis is distinguishing facts from opinions and hypotheses. *Facts* can be proved to be true by using one or more of the five senses. Newspapers and magazine articles are based largely on facts. *Opinions* are beliefs that may or may not be supported by facts. Opinions express feelings or ideas and are influenced greatly by one's background, values, and outlook on life. For example, editorials and columns in newspapers generally present a writer's opinions along with the facts. *Hypotheses* are educated guesses that are made to explain a phenomenon or an event. Hypotheses may be proved or disproved by the passage of time or the acquiring of additional information.

Formulating a hypothesis is an important step in the *scientific method.* The scientific method is a system of investigation on which all scientific inquiry is based. Most science courses offer at least a bare summary of the procedure. It can be reduced to six steps:

1. Identify and state the problem.
2. Collect information.
3. Make a hypothesis.
4. Make a prediction on the basis of the hypothesis.
5. Make observations and perform experiments to test the hypothesis.
6. Draw a conclusion.

When the results of an experiment or observation can be explained by a hypothesis, a *theory* is formed. When a theory has few exceptions, it is called a *law*. Let's apply these six steps to solve a problem.

We went to fish at our favorite lake, but the fishing was terrible. The water was very clear, and we didn't see any plants growing at the bottom of the lake at all. We were told a few weeks earlier that there had been a heavy die-off of fish. We called the Environmental Protection Agency. Agency officials said that they think the lake is a victim of acid rain. Water tests and an examination of frozen fish samples confirmed the belief that the high level of acidity in the lake had killed all life.

1. *Problem:* The fishing at our favorite lake was terrible.
2. *Information (observable facts):* The water was clear, there were no plants, and there was a recent die-off of fish.
3. *Hypothesis:* The lake may be a victim of acid rain.
4. *Prediction:* If the lake is acidic, a pattern will show up in water and fish samples.
5. *Experiment:* All tests prove positive for the characteristics of acid rain; our results agree with our prediction.
6. *Conclusion:* The lake has been affected by acid rain.

The scientific method is based on logical reasoning. When you draw conclusions that support evidence gathered in an investigation, you are following logic. Two methods of reasoning that are involved in logic are *inductive reasoning* and *deductive reasoning.*

Inductive reasoning involves drawing a conclusion by going from the specific to the general. In following induction, you observe the behavior or characteristics of members of a class or group and then apply this information to the unobserved members of the group. In other words, you generalize about the other members of the group. To see how a scientist follows inductive reasoning, read the following passage:

Scientific evidence from field studies of golden eagles indicates that the pesticide DDT is threatening the existence of our birds of prey. Raptors such as hawks and eagles provide a service by controlling rodents that damage our food crops. Although DDT does not poison the birds directly, it can interfere with their metabolism, causing them to produce eggs with thinner shells that break easily. Also, the birds' ability to store toxic materials in the fatty tissues weakens the offspring, increasing mortality.

[Answer: A specific statement that can be made from this study is that DDT is threatening golden eagles (birds of prey). Based on this observation, scientists can generalize that other birds of prey living in the same region as golden eagles are similarly threatened by DDT.]

Deductive reasoning involves drawing a conclusion by applying a generalization to a specific example or case. In the case above, scientists who have found that our birds of prey are threatened by DDT may infer that bald eagles, red-tailed hawks, falcons, great horned owls, and other raptors in the area are also being threatened. For a valid conclusion to be drawn, the generalization must be known, accepted, and true. If the generalization is faulty, it cannot be applied to a specific example.

Writers and speakers may not always follow logic in expressing their views. Sometimes, they make statements or write essays that are based on information that is not true. They often do this to influence the opinions of their audience. Read the statement below and consider the assumption being made.

> All who receive welfare benefits under the AFDC (Aid to Families with Dependent Children) program should be forced to do community work if they want to keep their benefits.

An assumption that the speaker has made is that everyone who receives welfare benefits under AFDC is able to work. This is not necessarily the case for all recipients. In fact, according to statistics, most of the recipients are actually children, who, of course, cannot go to work.

Directions: Read the statements below to detect the assumption made by the writer. Then complete the statements that follow by filling in the blank with the appropriate word or words.

1. All unwed mothers should be forced to complete high school before receiving any welfare benefits. The speaker assumes that all who receive benefits are _____.

[Possible answers: high school dropouts or adults (rather than children)]

2. In professional and collegiate sports, all athletes should undergo mandatory drug testing. The speaker assumes that professional and collegiate athletes are guilty of _____.

[Possible answer: drug abuse]

Another skill of analysis is *recognizing organizational patterns.* Textbooks and reading passages in social studies and science are organized according to certain patterns. Also, literary works such as novels, short stories, plays, and forms of nonfiction are based on organizational patterns. Three common patterns used in writing are *cause and effect, comparison and contrast,* and *sequence,* or time order. Organizational patterns can be the framework for entire books as well as single paragraphs. Often, there is a mixing of these three patterns within both single paragraphs and longer selections. However, generally you can see a predominant pattern within paragraphs of longer selections.

The cause and effect pattern shows a relationship between events. We connect causes with effects every day. For example, members of the baby-boom generation, who had delayed starting their families, are now parents of school-age children. This change in the American family unit has caused an increase in school enrollment and has slowed the school closings that were characteristic of the 1970s and 1980s. Several results came from the single cause: increase in family size.

The cause-and-effect relationship is frequently signaled by key words such as *because, since, therefore, as a result, consequently, accordingly, if . . . then, led to, brought about, the outcome was, the end result was,* and *was responsible for.*

A writer uses the comparison/contrast pattern to explain or show the similarities and differences among ideas, people, or things. A writer who points out how two or more things are alike is making a comparison; one who points out how they are different is using contrast.

Words and phrases that signal comparisons include *like, likewise, also, similarly, on the one hand, in the same way or fashion,* and *compared to.* Words and phrases that signal contrasts include *however, but, on the other hand, differently, on the contrary, while, although, yet, conversely, on the other side of the coin, versus, in contrast to,* and *either . . . or.*

Often, writers organize their works on the basis of sequence, sometimes known as time order. With this pattern of organization, events follow a series. Sequence is especially common in social studies when a writer describes historical events. It is also used widely in science writing to outline the steps in an experiment. Sequence is used as a pattern of organization in literature as well. In novels, short stories, and plays, plot events must follow a sequence. Often, this sequence has a cause-and-effect pattern. Some words and phrases that signal sequence include *on (a certain date—e.g., January 1), not long after, now, before, next, then, when, first, second,* and *third.*

Directions: An *allegory* is a story in which the characters are symbolic; that is, they stand for abstract qualities. The plot events in an allegory reveal a truth or generalization about life. Read the following summary of the famous short story "The Devil and Daniel Webster" by Stephen Vincent Benét. Then write *1* for the event that occurs first, *2* for the event that occurs second and so on.

The tale begins in New Hampshire during the time of Daniel Webster, a great lawyer and orator who aspired to be president of the United States. A local farmer, Jabez Stone, gets tired of poor crops and lack of prosperity. Enter the stranger, a lawyer, Mr. Scratch (the devil), who offers to make Stone prosperous in return for his soul. Mr. Scratch then draws up a contract. Jabez Stone pricks his finger and signs with his blood. Afterward, every year for six years, the stranger visits Stone to remind him of the contract.

On the seventh year, the stranger comes to collect Stone's soul. Jabez pleads for and receives a three-year extension. After the years pass, it is time for him to surrender the deed. Jabez Stone then goes to Daniel Webster to ask him to plead his case. When Daniel Webster visits Stone, the stranger appears.

The two argue strongly, but the stranger demands his due. Daniel Webster then asks for a trial including a courtroom, judge, and jury. Twelve men enter who have come from afar and who have the "fires of hell still upon them."

After Daniel Webster pleads the case all night, the defense rests. The jury finds for the defendant, Jabez Stone, and the judge and jury leave. Finally, the stranger signs a document promising never to bother Jabez Stone and is never seen in New Hampshire again.

_____ **a.** The stranger visits Jabez Stone to remind him of his contract.

_____ **b.** Jabez Stone tires of his lack of prosperity.

_____ **c.** Daniel Webster argues with Mr. Scratch at Stone's house.

_____ **d.** Mr. Scratch finally comes to collect from Jabez Stone.

_____ **e.** The jury rules in favor of Jabez Stone.

[Answers: **a.** 2, **b.** 1, **c.** 4, **d.** 3, and **e.** 5]

You will encounter the *synthesis* level of critical thinking skills in the Writing Skills section of this book. Synthesis involves putting elements together to create a whole, as in a piece of writing. By writing paragraphs about science, social studies, or literature and the arts, you will be strengthening your skills in synthesis.

When you *evaluate* something, you make a judgment. You decide how well or poorly an idea or object meets certain standards. For example, when you evaluate a movie, you judge it according to the quality of its acting, directing, cinematography, sound track, and other standards. Standards by which a judgment is made are called *criteria*. Criteria may be either subjective or objective.

Objective criteria are standards that are not affected by an individual's personal tastes, beliefs, or opinions about what is being judged. *Subjective* criteria are standards that are affected by an individual's personal tastes, beliefs, or opinions. The following situation illustrates the difference between objective and subjective criteria. Read the paragraph and answer the questions that follow.

A young couple is purchasing their first home. They have two small school-age children. They must consider several factors in the decision to buy a home. In the space provided, write *O* if the standard is objective and *S* if it is subjective.

_____ **1.** the closeness, in walking distance, to the nearest school

_____ **2.** the attractiveness of the other homes on the block

_____ **3.** the community's tax rate compared to other communities

[Answers: **1.** O, **2.** S, **3.** O]

Before you reach a decision or draw a conclusion, you need to consider the *adequacy of facts*. You need to evaluate the information that is available. Is there enough information to make this decision? Is this decision supported adequately by the facts?

When you don't have all the facts, you can't make an informed decision. Suppose you were interested in an issue in your community, such as "Should a low-rent apartment building be torn down to make room for a new high-rise building?" To be able to judge how you feel about the issue, you need to know all the facts. You need to know how many people will be affected by tearing down the building and what kinds of rents will be charged in the new building. You also need to know whether the construction company will hire community residents to work on the project. All of these facts (and others) will help you decide where you stand on the issue.

Similarly, when you answer questions on the GED Tests, you may need to determine whether there is enough information to support the writer's conclusion or point of view.

When people make decisions, they are, in part, influenced by facts. But we all have deeply held *values* and personal *beliefs* that influence our decision making. Many of the literature selections that you read on the GED Tests will consist of *commentaries*—writers' opinions of various types of literary and artistic works. These commentaries are based on the writers' own values. In social studies and science-related issues, personal values have a big impact on decision making.

Directions: In each situation described below, there is a conflict between two competing sets of values. On the lines following each paragraph, write the two values that are in conflict.

1. Myrna wants to marry Sam, settle down, and have a family. However, she knows that while her family likes Sam personally, family members object to the marriage because Sam's religious background is different from their own.

   Myrna has to choose between _____

   and _____.

[Answer: her desire to marry Sam and loyalty to her family]

2. One of the most controversial areas of scientific research is genetic engineering. Advocates of genetic engineering maintain that they will be able to prevent many genetically based birth defects such as Down's syndrome and sickle-cell anemia. Opponents of genetic engineering warn that this research tampers with nature and will lead to attempts to create a genetically "pure" master race.

   A scientist who is approached to do genetic research must choose

   between _____ and

   _____.

[Answer: the possibility of preventing birth defects and the possible danger of contributing to the creation of a "genetically superior" master race]

SAMPLE QUESTIONS FOR CRITICAL THINKING

To summarize the levels of critical thinking, there are definite clues which tell you the intended levels of reasoning. Here are some sample questions and statements:

KNOWLEDGE

What is the second step in solving for . . . ?

Where is that species of . . . often found . . . ?

Recall the main points of . . . .

Identify the common features of . . . .

Define the meaning of . . . .

COMPREHENSION

Summarize the *main functions of* . . . .

What was the author's *main purpose* in . . . ?

What are the *supporting details* of . . . ?

Why do you *believe* that . . . assumed that . . . ?

Translate . . . into . . . .

APPLICATION

If . . . lived today, what *would* . . . ?

What kinds of activities *would occupy* . . . ?

How can we *demonstrate the need* for . . . ?

Can you *apply the theory* of . . . to . . . ?

Follow the . . . *rule* to . . . .

ANALYSIS

Give an *example* of . . . .

Can you *illustrate* the concept of . . . ?

Trace the *events* that led to . . . .

What are the *effects* of . . . ?

Compare and contrast the two . . . .

SYNTHESIS

Write an *essay* about the following topic.

Arrange . . . into an introduction, a body, and a conclusion.

Indicate all your relevant knowledge about . . . .

Express your *reaction* or *mental image* to . . . .

Synthesize your overall impression of . . . .

EVALUATION

What *arguments* would you use to consider . . . ?

How *knowledgeable* were the *sources* for . . . ?

Did you notice any *fallacies* or mistakes of logic in . . . ?

The sports team offered many *testimonials* about . . . .

What *role* did *values* play in . . . ?

TEST 1: WRITING SKILLS

The GED Writing Skills Test consists of two parts. Each part is discussed separately below.

Part 1: Conventions of English

What's on the test?

Part 1 is a multiple-choice test of 55 questions. You will have 75 minutes to answer these questions. In this part, several passages will be followed by questions about the sentences within the passage. Some questions will ask you to locate errors in the passage, while other questions may ask you to restate an idea in different words. The questions will test your knowledge of sentence structure, grammar and usage, punctuation, spelling, and capitalization.

Part 1 of the test can be broken down into the following content areas:

Sentence Structure 35%
Usage 35%
Mechanics 30%

What kinds of questions are on the test?

Three types of questions will appear on the GED Writing Skills Test. In the *sentence correction* type, you'll see a sentence followed by the question, "What correction should be made to this sentence?" The five answer choices will focus on different parts of the sentence and deal with different grammar and usage issues.

Example: Sentence 1: **Time flies, when you're having fun.**

What correction should be made to this sentence?
(1) replace *flies* with *flys*
(2) remove the comma after *flies*
(3) replace *you're* with *your*
(4) insert a comma after *having*
(5) no correction is necessary

Note that this question tests your understanding of spelling, comma rules, possessives, and contractions. The correct answer is (2) remove the comma after *flies*.

In another question type, *sentence revision*, a sentence from the passage will be given with a part underlined. You will need to choose the best way to rewrite that underlined portion. The first answer choice in this question type is always the original version of the sentence, and this version is sometimes the correct answer!

Example: Sentence 2: **Frustration is an emotion we all have to deal <u>with, the</u> question is how to handle it well.**

Which of the following is the best way to rewrite the underlined portion of this sentence? If you think the original is the best way to write the sentence, choose option (1).
(1) with, the
(2) with the
(3) with and the
(4) with. The
(5) with however the

This question tests your understanding of sentence structure and combining. Choice (4) is the best way to write these two sentences. The other choices create incorrect sentence structures.

The last question type, *construction shift*, asks you to choose the best way to rewrite a sentence or combine two sentences. In this type of question, *the original sentences contain no error*. Your job is to understand how the ideas are related in a sentence and which of the answer choices has the same meaning as the original sentence.

Example: Sentence 3: **Although the female candidate ran a good race, she didn't receive enough votes.**

If you rewrote sentence 3 beginning with *The female candidate ran a good race*, the next word should be

(1) and   **(2)** which   **(3)** but   **(4)** so   **(5)** to

As you can see, the original sentence has no error. To answer this question, you must see the contrasting relationship between the two ideas of the sentence and choose (3). The word *but* correctly shows contrast.

Part 2: The Essay
You will be given 45 minutes to complete Part 2 of the Writing Skills Test. In this part, you will be given a topic and told to write a composition of about 200 words. You will not be given a choice of topics, but you will not need any special information or knowledge in order to write the essay. The topic will draw on your general knowledge and ask you to explain something about a common issue or problem. In this part of the Writing Skills Test, you should be able to plan and organize your thinking on an issue, and you should be able to communicate these thoughts clearly on paper.

1
<u>BASIC ENGLISH USAGE</u>
What Is Standard English?

The Writing Skills Test examines your knowledge of standard written English, language that is acceptable at all times and places. It is the language of all kinds of communication, such as in books, newspapers, and magazines, as well as in school and business. In general, when you read something in print, you are reading standard English. When someone gives a prepared presentation or speech, the speaker usually uses standard English.

Nonstandard English does not follow the rules of grammar and usage. In casual conversation, we may use nonstandard English. In fact, incorrect expressions we use in our daily speech may sound "right" to our ears because we are used to hearing them. In this chapter, you'll learn how to correct many common usage errors we make in both speech and writing— problems with pronouns and verb tenses, for example. Of course, whether or not you follow all the rules of standard English in conversation, you will need to know these rules for the Writing Skills Test.

Writing in Complete Sentences

One major difference between spoken and written English is that we do not always speak in complete sentences. For example, in a telephone conversation you might mix complete sentences with *fragments*, groups of words that are not complete sentences.

CHARACTERISTICS OF A COMPLETE SENTENCE

1. A complete sentence contains a *complete thought*. It does not leave unanswered questions.
2. A complete sentence must have a *subject* that tells whom or what the sentence is about.
3. A complete sentence must have a *predicate* that tells what the subject is or does.

In the following sentences the subjects and predicates are labeled. Compare these sentences with the characteristics listed in the box.

| Subject | Predicate |

Ripoff's Appliance Co. / is located on Airport Road next to the Wal-Mart.
We / sell air conditioners sometimes.
The warehouse / might have some.

While we often speak without including both a subject and a predicate in our sentences, we must always write in complete sentences—sentences containing both a subject and a predicate. Complete sentences are a feature of standard written English that will be important on the Writing Skills Test, both Part 1 and Part 2.

Parts of Speech

Subjects and predicates are built from the parts of speech. You will not have to define or explain these terms on the Writing Skills Test, but a knowledge of these major parts of speech and their functions will help you understand how standard English is put together.

BASIC PARTS OF SPEECH

Part of Speech	Function	Examples
noun	names person, place, thing, or idea	**John** drove to **Milwaukee** to give a **speech** about **democracy.**
pronoun	replaces a noun	**Somebody** showed **him** and **me** a picture of **it.**
verb	shows action or state of being (is, are, was, were, being, be, been)	Jim **is** tall. He **plays** basketball. Lew **looked** for a job.
conjunction	joins words and groups of words	Meg was here, **but** she left. Misha **and** I got home at noon.
adjective	modifies a noun; denotes a quality	We enjoyed the **colorful** trees in the **nature** preserve.
adverb	modifies a verb or other elements; expresses degree	The rain came **quickly** and **relentlessly**.

What Is a Noun?

People, places, and things are usually easy to recognize as nouns. Sometimes ideas are a little harder. Some examples of this category of nouns are *democracy, capitalism, courage, love, time,* and *anger.*

Noun as a Subject

A noun can be the **subject** of a sentence. Think of the subject as the main noun or the *actor* in the sentence. Ask yourself, "Who or what is doing something or being described in this sentence?"

The following sentence contains several nouns in **bold** type, but only one is the subject. Which one?

The **movers** packed the **truck** with **furniture** such as **beds, chairs,** and **tables.**

[Answer: movers]

Singular and Plural Nouns

Singular means "one" (single). ***Plural*** means "more than one." Rules for forming plurals often depend on combinations of ***vowels*** and ***consonants*** at the ends of words. You may know that all the letters of the alphabet are divided into these two groups. The vowels are *a, e, i o,* and *u* (and sometimes *y*). All the other letters are consonants.

Rules for Forming Plural Nouns

1. Add *s* to most nouns.
cup ⟶ cups   desk ⟶ desks

2. Add *es* to words ending with *s, sh, ch, x,* and *z*.
boss ⟶ bosses   fox ⟶ foxes

3. Add *s* to nouns ending in *y* if a vowel comes before the *y*.
driveway ⟶ driveways   valley ⟶ valleys

4. Change the *y* to *i* and add *es* to a word ending in *y* if a consonant comes before the *y*.
candy ⟶ candies   company ⟶ companies

5. Change the *f* to *v* and add *es* to some words ending in *f* or *fe*.
loaf ⟶ loaves   wife ⟶ wives

For most words ending in *f* or *ff* simply add an *s*.
chief ⟶ chiefs   roof ⟶ roofs

6. A few nouns do not change form when they are made plural.
deer ⟶ deer   sheep ⟶ sheep

7. A few nouns are made plural by changing their spelling. You can find the plurals in any dictionary.
goose ⟶ geese   child ⟶ children

> **ANSWERS TO EXERCISES IN THIS CHAPTER BEGIN ON PAGE 409.**

EXERCISE 1: PLURAL NOUNS

Directions: Write the correct plural form of each of the following words. Put in parentheses ( ) the number of the rule that applies.

Singular	Plural	Singular	Plural
1. country	_____	**6.** factory	_____
2. home	_____	**7.** race	_____
3. business	_____	**8.** life	_____
4. alloy	_____	**9.** woman	_____
5. car	_____	**10.** dish	_____

Possessive Nouns

Many people confuse possessive nouns and plural nouns. Look at *neighbors* and *neighbor's* in the following sentences. Which shows ownership, or possession?

My neighbors have loud parties on the weekends. My neighbor's car had to be dragged out of the ditch.

In the second sentence, *neighbor's* shows possession—the neighbor owns a car. Notice the possessive ending: *'s*.

Rules for Forming Possessive Nouns

Study the following rules for forming possessive nouns.

1. Add *'s* to form most singular possessive nouns.
   desk of the secretary ⟶ the secretary's desk

2. Add *'* to plural nouns to form most plural possessive nouns.
   decision of the managers ⟶ the managers' decision

3. Add *'s* to plural nouns that do not end in *s*.
   department for children ⟶ children's department

BE CAREFUL NOT TO USE *'s* TO FORM PLURALS.
   INCORRECT: I saw three bus's at the station.
   CORRECT: I saw three buses at the station.

EXERCISE 2: POSSESSIVE NOUNS
Directions: Insert apostrophes wherever they belong in the following sentences. Remember, not all nouns ending in *s* are possessive.

   Example: The girls' meeting ended when their votes had been counted.

1. Over the past two years, the Wagners house has become worn around the doors and windows.

2. Childrens pants and toddlers playsuits are marked down at Emilys favorite shop.

What Is a Verb?

In any sentence, the ***verb*** is the key word that names what the subject is or does. The two types of verbs are ***action verbs*** and ***linking verbs***. Some verbs show mental action *(think, believe, wish)*, and others show physical action *(run, leave, swim)*.

While an action verb tells what the subject is doing, linking verbs do not express action. Instead, they link the subject to words that describe the subject. No action is shown in the following sentences; but the subjects, *Joel* and *We*, are connected to words that describe them, *tall* and *angry*.

Examples: Joel **is** tall.   We **are** angry.

Is and *are* are forms of the most common linking verb, the verb *to be*. Forms of *to be* as well as some other common linking verbs are shown in the box below.

COMMON LINKING VERBS
is, am, are, was, were, be, being, been, appear, seem, become

---

For practice, fill in the blanks in the sentences below with forms of the linking verbs in the box.

She _____ calm during the GED Test.

David _____ very nervous about his job interview.

Tenses of Regular Verbs

PAST: Yesterday Brandon **wanted** to play outside.
PRESENT: Today Brandon **wants** to play outside.
FUTURE: Tomorrow Brandon **will want** to play outside.

One of the ways writers let you know when events take place is through verb tense. Some verb tenses are formed using a single word, such as *wants.* Other tenses require a verb phrase, such as *will want.* In the verb phrase *will want, want* is the *base verb* and *will* is a *helping verb.* To form all verb tenses, you need the base verb. For some, you also need to use helping verbs, as you will see as you review the verb tenses.

Knowing how to form different verb tenses correctly is very important for the Writing Skills Test. *Regular verbs* are verbs that form the simple past tense and the *past participle* (used to form the perfect tenses) by adding *ed* to the base verb. Naturally, the tenses of regular verbs are the easiest to master.

The Simple Tenses

The *simple present* tense is used for something that is happening now, something that happens regularly, or something that is always true. The simple present is the base form of the verb unless the subject is *he, she, it,* or a singular noun. For these subjects, add *s* (or *es* if the verb ends in a hissing sound such as *s, sh, ch, x,* and *z*).

Examples: I **look** terrible today.
Gary **washes** his car every morning.
The sun **rises** in the east.

The *simple past* tense shows action that occurred in the past. To form the simple past of any regular verb, add *ed* to the base verb.

Example: Wilson **dunked** his cat in the bathtub last night.

The *simple future* tense shows action that will happen in the future. Form the simple future for any subject by using *will* with the base verb.

Example: Tomorrow Becky Brown **will learn** to juggle.

EXERCISE 3: THE SIMPLE TENSES
Directions: Fill in the correct simple tense form of the verb indicated in the parentheses. Time clues such as *yesterday, today,* and *tomorrow* in the sentences will help you decide whether to use past, present, or future.

1. (walk) Next week Fred _____ to work while his car is being fixed.
2. (appear) Right now the store manager _____ very distressed.
3. (plant) In March of 1994 Rayleen _____ those daffodils.

The Continuing Tenses

The *continuing tenses* show action continuing in the past, present, or future, as in the following examples. As you can see, the continuing tenses are formed by combining helping verbs with the base form of the verb plus *ing*.

> PAST: The crew **was working** on the roof all last week.
> PRESENT: Right now the children **are watching** a dreadful TV show.
> FUTURE: I **will be knitting** this sweater for months.

CONTINUING TENSES			
Present continuing	I he, she, it* we, you, they**	am is are	I am looking. He is looking. You are looking.
Past continuing	I, he, she, it* we, you, they**	was were	I was looking. We were looking.
Future continuing	all subjects	will be	They will be looking.
* or any singular noun **or any plural noun			

EXERCISE 4: THE CONTINUING TENSES
Directions: Fill in the correct continuing tense form of the verb indicated in parentheses. Time clues such as *yesterday, today,* and *tomorrow* in the sentences will help you decide.

1. (bark) Now that blasted dog _____ again!
2. (cook) By next month I _____ in the kitchen of my own restaurant.
3. (sleep) On yesterday's show, Tad _____ during the fight between Hillary and Roy.

The Perfect Tenses

The *perfect tenses* show action completed before or continuing to a specific time. These tenses are used to show more specific time relationships than the simple or continuing tenses.

The *present perfect* tense shows that an action started in the past and either continues into the present or has just been completed.

Examples: Al **has fished** in this river since 1920.
The Barhams **have repaired** their back porch.

The *past perfect* tense shows that an action was completed before a specific time in the past.

Example: By midnight last Tuesday, the boys **had washed** forty-six cars.

The *future perfect* tense shows that an action will be completed by a specific time in the future.

Example: By 4:00 tomorrow, I **will have mowed** every blade of this grass.

PERFECT TENSES			
Present perfect	he, she it* I, you, we, they**	has have	She has looked You have looked.
Past perfect	all subjects	had	We had looked.
Future perfect	all subjects	will have	They will have looked.
*or any singular noun **or any plural noun			

EXERCISE 5: THE PERFECT TENSES

Directions: Fill in the correct perfect tense form of the verb indicated in parentheses. Pay careful attention to the meaning of each sentence before you decide whether to use the past, present, or future perfect.

Example: (paint) Merle Watson recently <u>painted</u> his house lavender with purple trim.

1. (attend) Lucy is enrolled in a Lamaze class. She _____ every session so far.

2. (work) Before going into the army, Warren _____ in a fish canning factory.

3. (mail) By next October, Ms. Eggebraaten _____ Christmas gifts to her relatives in Europe.

Spelling Regular Verb Forms

Not all verbs change form by adding *ed* or *ing* to the base verb. Following are five rules for adding *ed* and *ing* that cover all regular verbs. Study each rule.

1. **When *ed* and *ing* are added to most regular verbs, the spelling of the base verb does not change.**
   watch ⟶ watched, watching   walk ⟶ walked, walking

2. **If the base verb ends in *y* preceded by a consonant, change the *y* to *i* when adding *ed*, but keep the *y* when adding *ing*.**
   rely ⟶ relied, relying   cry ⟶ cried, crying

3. **If the base verb ends with a silent *e*, drop the *e* before adding *ed* or *ing*.**
   like ⟶ liked, liking   memorize ⟶ memorized, memorizing

4. **If the base verb ends in *e*, drop the silent *e* when adding *ed*, but change the *ie* to *y* when adding *ing*.**
   tie ⟶ tied, tying

5. **If the base verb ends in a single vowel and a single consonant other than *h*, *w*, or *x*, and if the accent falls on the last (or only) syllable of the verb, double the final consonant of the base verb when adding *ed* or *ing*. Otherwise, keep the normal spelling.**
   refer ⟶ referred, referring   relax ⟶ relaxed, relaxing

Irregular Verbs

English would be a much easier language if all verbs shifted in tense according to the regular patterns. However, many English verbs are irregular. When you study irregular verbs, you need to learn the simple present, the simple past, and the past participle, which is used to form the perfect tenses.

Have, Do, and *Be*

Make sure you know the three most common irregular verbs: *have, do,* and *be*. If you are not sure of the forms of these verbs, practice them.

	Present	Past	Past Participle
I, you, we, they** he, she, it*	have has	had	had
I, you, we, they** he, she, it*	do does	did	done
I he, she, it* you, we, they**	am is are	was/were	been
*or any singular noun	**or any plural noun		

The most common mistake people make with irregular verbs is confusing the past participle with the simple past tense. Remember, the past participle is used to form the perfect tenses, so a helping verb (*has, have,* or *had*) must always be used with a past participle.

INCORRECT: I done my chores.
CORRECT: I did my chores.
CORRECT: I have done my chores.

Other Common Irregular Verbs

For a list of the simple present, simple past, and past participle forms of common irregular verbs, consult Contemporary's other books listed on page xv.

EXERCISE 6: VERBS
Directions: Read the following passage and answer the questions. Be sure that all verb tenses are correct and that verb forms are spelled correctly.

(1) Videocassette recorders (VCRs) give TV watchers more choice in television programs. (2) Many viewers taped shows to watch later. (3) For example, people who work during the day had recorded daytime news programs, talk shows, movies, and soap operas. (4) Sometimes a family has went out for the evening and has turned on the VCR.

In each sentence, which is the best way to write the underlined portion? If you think the original is the best way to write the sentence, choose option (1).

1. Sentence 2: **Many viewers <u>taped</u> shows to watch later.**
   (1) taped
   (2) tapped
   (3) tape
   (4) had tapped
   (5) had taped

2. Sentence 3: **For example, people who work during the day <u>had recorded</u> daytime news programs, talk shows, movies, and soap operas.**
   (1) had recorded
   (2) record
   (3) will be recording
   (4) will have recorded
   (5) recorded

3. Sentence 4: **Sometimes a family <u>has went</u> out for the evening and has turned on the VCR.**
   (1) has went
   (2) has gone
   (3) will have gone
   (4) went
   (5) goes

Subject-Verb Agreement

Agreement makes the English language easier to understand. *Subject-verb agreement* means that you have chosen the correct verb form to match the number and person of the subject.

The Basic Pattern

If the subject of a present-tense verb is *he, she, it* (but not *I* or *you*), or any singular noun, the verb must end in *s* or *es*. Verbs ending in a hissing sound (*s, sh, ch, x, z*) take an *es* ending. Note that the forms of irregular verbs for *he, she,* and *it* always end in *s*.

The elderly women **walk** in the mall every day.
The elderly woman **walks** in the mall every day.

Subject-Verb Agreement Problems

You have to worry about subject-verb agreement only in the present tense, with one exception. The irregular verb *be* changes form for different subjects in the past tense as well (see page 52). Keep subject-verb agreement in mind when you see contractions. If you have trouble figuring out the correct form, take the contraction apart. For example, *doesn't* means *does not*, and *don't* means *do not*.

INCORRECT: She don't (do not) care.
CORRECT: She doesn't (does not) care.

1. Compound Subjects

The following rules apply to compound subjects and verbs.

If the parts of a compound subject are connected by *and*, the subject is always plural and the verb does not end in *s*.

Example: Mr. Tidwell and his daughter **row** the boat together.

If the parts of a compound subject are connected by *or* or *nor*, the verb agrees with the part of the subject closer to it.

Examples: Mr. Tidwell or his **daughters row** the boat.
His daughters or **Mr. Tidwell rows** the boat.

2. Inverted Order

In some sentences, especially questions, the verb comes before the subject. If you have trouble finding the subject of these sentences, mentally rearrange the word order:

(Is, Are) the twins hiding in the garage?
[Rearranged: The **twins are** hiding in the garage.]

Here (goes, go) the Bensons on their way to the races.
[Rearranged: The **Bensons go** here on their way to the races.]

3. Interrupting Phrases

The subject and verb of a sentence are often separated by two types of phrases: prepositional phrases and phrases that add information to the subject. Neither type of phrase affects agreement between subject and verb.

Some of the most common prepositions are *of, in, for, to, from, with, on,* and *by.* The prepositional phrases in the following example sentences are in *italics.* They are not part of the subject. The subject and verb are in **bold** type.

> *Examples:* The **papers** *on the desk* **are** very important.
> The **bushel** *of peaches* **has been sold.**

Other interrupting phrases may seem to make the subject plural, but they do not. They often start with words such as *as well as, in addition to,* and *like.* These phrases are set off by commas.

> *Examples:* **Clay**, along with his parents, **is** headed for the game.
> **Marcia,** like her coworkers, **is** going on strike.

4. Indefinite Pronouns

There are three groups of indefinite pronouns. Some are always singular, some are always plural, and some can be either singular or plural, depending on their antecedents (see chart below). Singular indefinite pronouns almost always end in *one* or *body.*

INDEFINITE PRONOUNS			
Singular		**Plural**	**Singular or Plural** *(depending upon their use)*
everyone	everybody	both	some
someone	somebody	few	any
no one	nobody	many	none
anyone	anybody	several	most
one	each (one)		all
either (one)	neither (one)		

EXERCISE 7: SUBJECT-VERB AGREEMENT

Directions: Underline the subject; then underline the correct verb in parentheses.

1. Down the street (runs, run) the racers in the Boston Marathon.

2. Neither her sons nor Letitia (visits, visit) the dentist often.

3. A sandwich and a glass of juice (is, are) plenty of lunch for me.

4. The crowd of his enthusiastic supporters (were, was) cheering.

5. Clara, like her parents and grandparents, (is, are) committed to the goal of a high school diploma.

What Is a Pronoun?

A *pronoun* is a word that replaces and refers to a noun. Usually, you use pronouns to avoid repeating the same nouns over and over. There are three important groups of pronouns. Each group has different functions in a sentence.

Subject Pronouns *act as the subject of a verb*		Object Pronouns *never act as the subject of a verb*		Possessive Pronouns *show ownership*	
singular	*plural*	*singular*	*plural*	*appear with another noun*	*stand alone*
I	we	me	us	my	mine
you	you	you	you	your	yours
he		him		his	his
she	they	her	them	her	hers
it		it		its	
who	who	whom	whom	our	ours
				their	theirs
				whose	whose

Subject and Object Pronouns

The following hints will help you decide when to use subject and object pronouns. Correct pronouns are in **bold** type.

Hint 1: Ask yourself whether the pronoun is the subject of a verb.

Example: Rebecca brought the flowers to (they, **them**).

Hint 2: Cross out any nouns connected to the pronoun with *and*. Then look at the pronoun alone to see if it is the subject of a verb.

Example: Bill and (**they**, them) went to a movie.

Possessives and Contractions

A possessive noun such as *Gerald's* shows ownership. So does the possessive pronoun *his*, which you could use to substitute for *Gerald's*. However, unlike the possessive noun, the possessive pronoun does not contain an apostrophe (').

Possessive Pronoun	Contraction
its	it's (it is)
theirs	there's (there is)
their	they're (they are)
your	you're (you are)
whose	who's (who is)

If you can't decide whether to use a contraction in a sentence, try substituting the two words that the contraction stands for. The correct choices are in **bold** type.

>*Examples:* I can't believe (your, **you're**) going to do that!
>(**Whose**, Who's) house do you think this is, young lady?

EXERCISE 8: POSSESSIVE PRONOUNS AND CONTRACTIONS
Directions: Underline the correct word to complete each sentence.

1. (Your, You're) not ready to move out of the house at age twelve.

2. (Theirs, There's) no one here by that name, Officer.

3. (Whose, Who's) coat is lying in the back corner of the bar?

Identifying Antecedents

The noun that a pronoun replaces and refers to is called its ***antecedent.*** The relationship between a pronoun and its antecedent must be clear and correct. There are several specific pronoun problems that you are likely to find on the Writing Skills Test.

>*Example:* Jenny told Bob how much **she** loves roses. [The pronoun *she* replaces and refers to the noun *Jenny*.]

Pronouns often refer to antecedents in other sentences.

>*Example:* Jim has the children for the weekend. I'll be getting **them** back from **him** Sunday night.

EXERCISE 9: IDENTIFYING ANTECEDENTS
Directions: Read the following paragraph. Fill in the correct antecedent for each pronoun.

Murray and Dee went to church yesterday with their new baby Marissa for the first time. Upon getting her out of the car, they were surrounded by eager friends who wanted to see Marissa.

Pronoun	Antecedent		Pronoun	Antecedent
1. their	_____		**3.** they	_____
2. her	_____		**4.** who	_____

Pronoun-Antecedent Agreement: Relative Pronouns

Relative pronouns (*who, which,* and *that*) are often used to link two ideas in a sentence. These relative pronouns must agree with their antecedents according to the following rules.

1. *Who (whom, whose)* can refer only to humans.
2. The relative pronoun *which* can refer only to nonhumans.
3. *That* can refer to either humans or nonhumans.

EXERCISE 10: RELATIVE PRONOUNS
Directions: Underline the antecedent for the relative pronoun in each sentence. Then underline the correct relative pronoun in parentheses.

1. The woman (who, which) is sitting on the floor is the photographer.

2. The door (who, that) is slightly ajar leads to the chamber of horrors.

3. Time, (who, which) waits for no man, waits for no woman either.

Agreement in Number

As you check for pronoun agreement errors on the Writing Skills Test, keep in mind that the antecedent of a pronoun is not always in the same sentence as the pronoun. Find the pronoun in the following passage that does not agree in number with the rest of the passage and correct it.

Word processors are miracles of technology. Because of **them**, correction fluid no longer stains the clothing and fingers of typists. **They** have eliminated typing and retyping drafts of the same material. **Its** quiet clicking has replaced the noisy thudding of typewriters. Many of **them** even check grammar and spelling.

[Answer: replace *Its* with *Their*]

Compound Antecedents

The antecedent of a pronoun is not always a single noun. Sometimes the antecedent is made up of two nouns connected by *and, or,* or *nor.* In this example, the two nouns in the antecedent are connected by *and.* The pronoun is plural.

Example: **Mark and Tim** showed up for **their** swim team practice.

And makes a *compound antecedent* (an antecedent of more than one noun) plural. Use a plural pronoun to refer to a compound antecedent joined by *and.* When a compound antecedent is joined by *or* or *nor,* the rule is different. *Or* and *nor* separate the nouns in a compound antecedent. The pronoun must agree with the closest antecedent.

Examples: Either **Mark or his brothers** will show up for **their** swim practice.
Either **his brothers or Mark** will show up for **his** swim practice.

EXERCISE 11: AGREEMENT IN NUMBER

Directions: Cross out incorrect pronouns in this passage and write in correct ones, making sure pronouns agree in number.

Over the last twenty years, Knoxville's population center, once clustered around their small downtown area, has shifted westward. However, their downtown area may become more important again in future years. Many of the city's older buildings are being restored, and its newer downtown buildings are lovely, too.

No Antecedent

Some pronouns are used without any antecedent at all. The pronouns *it, this,* and *they* commonly appear without an antecedent. Here's an example:

VAGUE: When I went to the public library, they told me I needed two pieces of identification to get a library card.

CLEAR: When I went to the public library, a **librarian** told me I needed two pieces of identification to get a library card.

EXERCISE 12: CLARIFYING ANTECEDENTS

Directions: Look for confusing pronoun reference. Cross out any vague references and make your correction above the sentence. If a sentence is written clearly, write *C* in the blank.

Example: When I went to the hospital, the doctor gave me eighteen stitches.

_____ **1.** I wrote to Ken and his sisters, but they did not respond.

_____ **2.** Dion asked Tony if he thought he would win the contest.

_____ **3.** When the quarterback made the touchdown in the final seconds of the game, it went wild in the stands.

_____ **4.** Sam thought he left his checkbook at home but later couldn't find it.

Keeping Track of Person

Read this paragraph and try to keep track of the pronouns.

A person should register to vote as soon as you turn eighteen. He should realize that it is your right to vote in a democracy. To register, he must be a U.S. citizen and a resident of the area in which you vote. Two convenient places he can register to vote are his local library and your post office.

The pronouns shift in **person** (from *you* to *he* and back again). Within a passage, the pronouns should not shift from one person to another. Use the second person *you/your* or the third person *he/his* throughout. Also, "a person" agrees with *he*; but "a person" should be changed to *you* if the other pronouns used are in the second person.

> First person: I, me, my, mine, we, us, our, ours
> Second person: you, your, yours
> Third person: he, she, it, him, her, his, hers, its, they, them, they, theirs

EXERCISE 13: AGREEMENT IN PERSON

Directions: Find which of the pronouns in **bold** type need to be corrected in the following passage.

Most of us think that having running water and electricity is normal. As a result, **you** might be surprised at the simple mud huts many Africans live in. Even when **you** are out of work here, **we** can get help from government agencies, including welfare or unemployment income. **We** may not all have lives of luxury, but **you** easily forget that people in many other countries feel lucky to earn only pennies per day.

2
SENTENCE STRUCTURE
Three Characteristics of a Sentence

Two characteristics of a complete sentence are a **subject** and a **predicate**. Together the subject and predicate must express a **complete thought**. A group of words that does not meet these requirements is a fragment. Can you identify the fragments in the following conversation?

(1) DAD: Where's John?
(2) SIS: Went to a job interview.
(3) DAD: Who drove him?
(4) SIS: His friend Jean.

[Answer: The fragments are **(2)** and **(4)**. **(1)** and **(3)** have meaning on their own and are complete sentences.]

Sentence fragments are often difficult to detect because they make sense when read with the sentences around them. When proofreading for sentence fragments, make sure each group of words has meaning when standing alone. Read backwards, sentence by sentence, in order to see each sentence in isolation.

ANSWERS TO EXERCISES IN THIS CHAPTER BEGIN ON PAGE 410.

EXERCISE 1: REWRITING FRAGMENTS
Directions: Rewrite the following paragraph, correcting all of the sentence fragments. Add a missing subject or predicate or join two fragments together.

> When President John F. Kennedy was inaugurated in 1960, he stated, "Ask not what your country can do for you; ask what you can do for your country." His philosophy did much for U.S. citizens and underdeveloped areas of the world. For example, the Peace Corps. This program sent volunteers. Into underdeveloped areas of the world. These volunteers educated the citizens of those countries in basic survival skills. The main goal was for the countries to become more self-sufficient. And also relations between the U.S. and these countries to be improved.

Sentence Combining

Sometimes you will want to make one sentence out of two simple sentences.

Example: Those nails are for the paneling. The others can be used for hanging pictures.

[Answer: Those nails are for the paneling, and the others can be used for hanging pictures.]

The combined sentence you have just seen is made up of two independent clauses joined by a comma plus *and*. A *clause* is a group of words that contains a subject and a verb. An *independent clause* can stand on its own as a complete sentence. The following joining words, or *coordinating conjunctions*, are used with a comma to combine independent clauses: *and, but, or, nor, for, so, yet.* Notice that the joining words have different meanings.

Coordinating Conjunction	Meaning
and	adds information
but, yet	shows an opposite
or	shows a choice
nor	rejects both choices
for	links effect to cause
so	links cause to effect

EXERCISE 2: CONJUNCTIONS

Directions: Choose a logical conjunction from the chart above to connect each pair of sentences. Then, on a separate sheet of paper, rewrite them as one sentence. Be sure to punctuate each new sentence correctly.

Example: I don't want to work. I need a job.

[Answer: I don't want to work, but I need a job.]

1. We are planning a Fourth of July picnic. We hope all of you can attend.
2. He did not study for his driver's test. He passed it.
3. Al has always wanted his own business. He opened a restaurant.

Clues About Commas

If a coordinating conjunction does not connect two complete thoughts, do not use a comma.

NO COMMA NEEDED: Sue and Bruce are married. All of us went but Maureen.

COMMA NEEDED: (two complete thoughts): Sue is married, but Tina is not.
Most of the girls went, but Maureen stayed home.

EXERCISE 3: USING COMMAS CORRECTLY

Directions: Place commas where they are needed. Some of the sentences are correct as written.

1. She took off her coat and hung it in the closet.
2. She took off her coat and she hung it in the closet.
3. Our son has a learning disability but is doing well in school.
4. Our son has a learning disability but he is doing well in school.

Run-ons and Comma Splices

INCORRECT: You should see Brooke, my fifteen-year-old daughter her hair is pink and seventeen different lengths it is hideous she has the wildest haircut I've ever seen.

There are actually four complete thoughts, ending in *daughter, lengths, hideous,* and *seen.* The sentence is one long **run-on**. When two or more sentences are joined without correct punctuation or conjunctions, the result is a run-on. You can correct run-ons by dividing them into separate sentences or combining the ideas with proper punctuation and conjunctions.

CORRECT: You should see Brooke, my fifteen-year-old daughter. Her hair is pink and seventeen different lengths, and it is hideous. She has the wildest haircut I've ever seen.

Another type of error, a **comma splice**, results when two complete sentences are joined by a comma without a conjunction. A comma splice can be separated into two sentences, or a logical conjunction can be placed after the comma:

INCORRECT: She did this right before our big family reunion, all of my relatives are going to think she is a creature from outer space.

CORRECT: She did this right before our big family reunion. All of my relatives are going to think she is a creature from outer space.

CORRECT: She did this right before our big family reunion, so all of my relatives are going to think she is a creature from outer space.

EXERCISE 4: RUN-ONS AND COMMA SPLICES

Directions: Divide run-on sentences (and those with comma splices) into separate sentences, or combine them correctly using a comma with *and, but, for, or, nor, so,* or *yet.* If a sentence is correct as written, write *C* in the space.

_____ **1.** Kyle broke his leg he was taken to the emergency room.

_____ **2.** Is a storm "watch" less serious than a storm "warning"?

_____ **3.** I'd rather have hay fever than food allergies, at least I can eat!

EXERCISE 5: SENTENCE STRUCTURE PRACTICE

Directions: The following paragraph may contain any type of error studied so far. Make corrections, as needed, at critical points (underlined).

(1) Recently psychologists have been researching birth <u>order, their</u> research suggests that personality and intelligence are based partly on where a child ranks in the family. (2) One of their theories is that the first child receives more of the parents' attention than later <u>children so</u> firstborns tend to be more intellectual. (3) Later children must share their parents with the oldest <u>child they</u> pattern their behavior after the older siblings and peers.

Using Conjunctive Adverbs

Choose the conjunctive adverb that has the correct meaning. The chart below can help you learn what words to use and when to use them.

Conjunctive Adverb	Meaning
moreover furthermore in addition	adds related information (like *and*)
however nevertheless on the other hand	shows a contrast (like *but*)

therefore
consequently
	links cause to effect
	    (like *so*) or
	explains relationship
	    between two ideas

otherwise	shows an alternative (like *or*)
for instance for example	gives specifics to illustrate a general idea
then	shows time order

Use the correct punctuation. A semicolon comes before all conjunctive adverbs. A comma comes after all conjunctive adverbs except *then*.

Examples: Barbara is from Iowa; however, she now lives in Illinois.
Barbara moved to Illinois; then she moved to New York.

EXERCISE 6: CONJUNCTIVE ADVERBS

Directions: Write the letter of the correct conjunctive adverb to complete each sentence. Be sure the meaning of the conjunctive adverb relates the clauses logically.

1. He was qualified for the job; _____ he got it.

   (a) therefore   **(b)** however   **(c)** instead

2. The steak is very good; _____, you might prefer the chicken.

   (a) consequently   **(b)** on the other hand   **(c)** for example

3. The company is in financial trouble; _____, workers may be laid off.

   (a) nevertheless   **(b)** however   **(c)** as a result

EXERCISE 7: COMBINING SENTENCES

Directions: Combine each pair of sentences in <u>two</u> different ways, using any correct sentence structure. Be sure you punctuate your new sentences correctly and use logical conjunctions. Use the charts on pages 62–64 to help you.

1. The salesperson was very polite. She listened to my complaints.

2. My friends give me advice. I do not always listen to them.

3. I could drive you to work in the morning. You could take the subway.

Joining Dependent and Independent Clauses

A *dependent clause* cannot stand alone as a complete sentence. It "depends" on another clause—an *independent clause*, which has a subject and a verb and can stand alone as a sentence. Such clauses are joined by a *subordinating conjunction*. When the dependent clause comes first, a comma separates the two clauses. When the independent clause comes first, no comma is needed.

Examples: Dirk ran on the ice. He fell.
[Independent clause. Independent clause.]

Because Dirk ran on the ice, he fell.
[Dependent clause, independent clause.]

Dirk fell **because** he ran on the ice.
[Independent clause, dependent clause.]

Following is a list of some common subordinating conjunctions, grouped according to meaning.

Subordinating Conjunction			Meaning
before	after	while	shows time relationship
when	whenever	until	
because	since	so that	shows cause or effect
if	unless		shows the condition under which something will happen
though	although	even though	shows a contrast
as though	as if		shows similarity
where	wherever		shows place

EXERCISE 8: DEPENDENT CLAUSES
PART A
Directions: Use the previous list of subordinating conjunctions to fill in the blank. There are several possible answers in each case.

1. _____ Ray was afraid of water, he took swimming lessons.

2. I'm not going to the class reunion _____ my closest friends won't be there.

3. Celia stayed with her mother _____ the nurse returned.

PART B
Directions: Combine each pair of sentences by changing one of them into a dependent clause, using one of the subordinating conjunctions listed on the previous page. Be sure to place a comma after introductory dependent clauses.

> ***Examples:*** Russell attempted to bribe a police officer. Russell was arrested.
>
> **When** he attempted to bribe a police officer, **Russell was arrested**.

1. We arrived at the church late. We missed their wedding ceremony.

2. Rose was angry with her babysitter. She said she would not hire the young girl again.

3. We drove into the parking lot. We noticed that the store was closed.

EXERCISE 9: STRUCTURE AND USAGE
Directions: Read the following paragraph and look for errors in sentence structure and usage. Some sentences need corrections. In other sentences, you need to rewrite the underlined portion. If you think the original is the best way, choose option (1).

(1) Ownership in a corporation is represented by the number of shares of stock a person owns, however, by buying stock, a person becomes an owner of the business. (2) When a corporation is successful, its stockholders reap the benefits. (3) They are paid a share of the increased profits in addition, the value of their stock increases. (4) If the business is not a success stockholders may see the value of their stock decrease. (5) If the value decreases enough, he may lose their entire investment.

1. Sentence 1: **Ownership in a corporation is represented by the number of shares of stock a person <u>owns, however,</u> by buying stock, a person becomes an owner of the business.**
   (1) owns, however, by
   (2) owns; however, by
   (3) owns, however by
   (4) owns; therefore, by
   (5) owns, therefore, by

2. Sentence 2: **When a corporation is successful, its stockholders reap the benefits.**
   (1) no correction is necessary
   (2) change *is* to *are*
   (3) remove the comma after *successful*
   (4) replace *its* with *it's*
   (5) replace *When* with *Then*

3. Sentence 3: **They are paid a share of the increased <u>profits in addition, the</u> value of their stock increases.**
   (1) profits in addition, the
   (2) profits, in addition the
   (3) profits; in addition, the
   (4) profits for example, the
   (5) profits; for example, the

4. Sentence 4: **If the business is not a success stockholders may see the value of their stock decrease.**
   (1) replace *if* with *though*
   (2) insert a comma after *success*
   (3) change *stockholders* to *stockholders'*
   (4) change *may see* to *are seeing*
   (5) replace *their* with *his*

5. Sentence 5: **If the value decreases enough, he may lose their entire investment.**
   (1) no correction is necessary
   (2) replace *he* with *they*
   (3) change *lose* to *lost*
   (4) replace *their* with *his*
   (5) remove the comma after *enough*

Sequence of Tenses

The following sentence is made up of two independent clauses, so it has two subjects and two verbs in it. Look at the verbs carefully.

INCORRECT: The student **reads** the chapter, but he **was** unable to answer the test questions. [present tense, simple past tense]

CORRECT: The student **read** the chapter, but he **is** unable to answer the test questions. [simple past tense, present tense]

CORRECT: The student **had read** the chapter, but he **was** unable to answer the test questions. [past perfect tense, simple past tense]

Special Helping Verbs

- If one clause is in the present tense, use one of the present or future helping verbs (*can, shall, will, may,* or *must*) in the other clause.
- If one clause is in the past tense, use one of the past helping verbs (*could, should, would, might,* or *had to*) in the other clause.

EXERCISE 10: CORRECT VERB SEQUENCE
Directions: In the following sentences, underline the correct verb in parentheses.

1. When Connie applied for the job, she (should take, should have taken) her references along with her.

2. If Mary is smart, she (will call, called) her boss about the problem.

3. Eileen was really sorry that she (had slept, is sleeping) through the movie.

4. If we had sold the house, we (could have moved, can move) earlier.

Dangling and Misplaced Modifiers

Another way to combine sentences is to use **modifying phrases**, phrases that describe or add information. A correct sentence will always (1) make clear exactly what a modifying phrase modifies and (2) place the modifying phrase as close as possible to the word it modifies.

INCORRECT: Growling loudly, we heard the guard dog.
CORRECT: We heard the guard dog growling loudly.

INCORRECT: The deer crossed in front of the driver with huge antlers.
CORRECT: The deer with huge antlers crossed in front of the driver.

In addition to being misplaced, modifiers also may "dangle." A sentence with a **dangling modifier** contains no word for the modifier to modify.

INCORRECT: Stepping on the brakes too fast, the car slid.
CORRECT: When I stepped on the brakes too fast, the car slid.

INCORRECT: An accident was reported while watching the news.
CORRECT: While watching the news, I heard an accident reported.

EXERCISE 11: DANGLING AND MISPLACED MODIFIERS
Directions: Underline the modifying phrase in each of the following sentences. Rewrite each sentence that contains a dangling or misplaced modifier.

INCORRECT: Wearing gloves, the parrot perched on the hand of the trainer.
CORRECT: The parrot perched on the hand of the trainer wearing gloves.

1. Nailed to the wall, Rich saw the "No Smoking" sign.

2. While taking a shower, the telephone rang.

3. When traveling through Colorado, my luggage was lost on the train.

4. We heard the dog under the table whining for food.

Parallel Structure

In sentences, two or more elements that have the same function must be written in the same form to be considered "parallel."

NOT PARALLEL: She prefers dancing, singing, and to act.
PARALLEL: She prefers dancing, singing, and acting.

NOT PARALLEL: The model is tall, slim, and has attractive looks.
PARALLEL: The model is tall, slim, and attractive.

EXERCISE 12: PARALLELISM

Directions: In the blank, write the letter of the correct sentence from each pair.

_____ 1. **(a)** Thomas Edison invented the electric light bulb, and he started motion pictures, and the phonograph.
(b) Thomas Edison invented the electric light bulb, the motion picture, and the phonograph.

_____ 2. **(a)** To have a good job, live alone, and enjoy herself are Vicki's goals.
(b) To have a good job, be living alone, and enjoy herself are Vicki's goals.

_____ 3. **(a)** I promise to be loving, cherish, and honor you.
(b) I promise to love, cherish, and honor you.

EXERCISE 13: STRUCTURE AND USAGE

Directions: Read the following paragraph, checking for errors in sequence of tenses, misplaced and dangling modifiers, parallel structure, and sentence structure and usage. Then make needed corrections to sentences, or rewrite underlined portions. If the original is the best way, choose option (1).

(1) As the rest of our family played trivia games, our youngest children felt left out of the fun, ages five and six. (2) Feeling sorry for them, new questions are being written by us that young children can answer. (3) We try to think of questions that they would find interesting and challenging but not to frustrate them. (4) We ask them about subjects they have learned about in school. (5) Other questions draw on information in the books we read to them.

1. Sentence 1: **As the rest of our family played trivia games, <u>our youngest children felt left out of the fun, ages five and six.</u>**
   (1) our youngest children felt left out of the fun, ages five and six
   (2) their youngest children felt left out of the fun, ages five and six
   (3) our youngest children, ages five and six, felt left out of the fun
   (4) their youngest children, ages five and six, felt left out of the fun
   (5) our youngest, ages five and six, children felt left out of the fun

2. Sentence 2: **Feeling sorry for them, <u>new questions are being written by us</u> that young children can answer.**
   (1) new questions are being written by us
   (2) new questions written by us
   (3) new questions have been written by us
   (4) we are writing new questions
   (5) they are writing new questions

3. Sentence 3: **We try to think of questions that they would find interesting and challenging but not <u>to frustrate them</u>.**
   (1) to frustrate them
   (2) frustrating them
   (3) to frustrating them
   (4) frustrated
   (5) frustrating

4. Sentences 4 and 5: **We ask them about <u>subjects they have learned about in school. Other questions draw on information</u> in the books we read to them.**
   (1) subjects they have learned about in school and information
   (2) subjects they have learned about in school but draw on
   (3) subjects they have learned about in school; instead, we
   (4) subjects they have learned about in school. As well as information
   (5) subjects they have learned about in school, not information

3
MECHANICS

When we read, we rely on the signals of capitalization and punctuation to help us understand the writing. We also must be able to recognize the words by accurate spelling. We have all read, or tried to read, writing that contains so many mistakes that it fails to communicate. The material in this chapter focuses on those issues that may appear on the Writing Skills Test.

Capitalization

Always capitalize **_proper nouns_**, or names. In each blank, write a proper noun and be sure to capitalize it.

Common Nouns (General)	Proper Nouns (Specific)
woman	_Bette Midler_
street	_____
nation	_____
holiday	_____
doctor	_____

Other Capitalization Rules

1. **Capitalize a word used as a person's title, but not those used as general labels.**

   Examples: Representing the state of Illinois is Senator Carol Moseley Braun.

   I went to see the doctor about a lingering cough.

2. **Capitalize the specific names of places. Also capitalize words derived from the specific names of places. Don't capitalize general geographical terms.**

   Examples: My Russian boyfriend likes French dressing on his salad.

   Washington Square in New York City is the setting of a famous novel.

   We drove east until we came to a four-lane highway.

3. **Capitalize names of special days and words used as part of a date. Don't capitalize the names of seasons unless they are part of an event.**

   Examples: My sister was born on Independence Day.

   The celebration was held on Monday, January 22.

   A fund-raiser for the group home will be held in the spring.

   The Spring Fling was a fund-raiser for the group home.

EXERCISE 1: CAPITALIZATION RULES
Directions: Rewrite the following sentences, putting in capital letters where they belong and taking out those that are incorrect. The number of errors each sentence has is in parentheses.

1. The mayor of chestertown requested assistance from governor kelly. (3 errors)

2. We will meet on wednesday, august 9, at lincoln center in memphis, tennessee. (6 errors)

3. Drive North to baker avenue, then turn left at Kennedy highway. (4 errors)

4. The ohio river is a beautiful river. (2 errors)

Punctuation

As you know, every sentence ends with a period (.), a question mark (?), or an exclamation point (!). Watch out for end punctuation that is missing or incorrect. Because a group of words ends with a period or a question mark does not mean it is a complete sentence.

INCORRECT: Cleaned the garage.
CORRECT: Peter cleaned the garage.

INCORRECT: The man running the roulette wheel?
CORRECT: Who is the man running the roulette wheel?

The Comma

Commas are used for specific reasons. Unnecessary commas are just as incorrect as missing ones! Following are some helpful rules.

1. **Use a comma with a coordinating conjunction to join two independent clauses.**

   INCORRECT: Jill finished her exams, and went home for Christmas.
   CORRECT: Jill finished her exams, **and** she went home for Christmas.

2. **Put a comma after introductory dependent clauses.**

   INCORRECT: I would take a class, if I had time.
   CORRECT: **If I had the time**, I would take a class.

3. **Use commas to set off three types of phrases.**

   (1) Introductory or interrupting phrases: The phrases in **bold** type introduce or interrupt the main flow of the sentence. Notice that these phrases never contain the subject or verb of a sentence. They simply add an additional thought to the sentence.

   CORRECT: **As usual**, no one wants to take out the garbage.
   The goal, **of course**, is to score the most touchdowns.

(2) Modifying phrases: Phrases, set off by commas, describe or modify another word in the sentence.

CORRECT: **Chattering happily,** the children rode off to the picnic.
Alan Morse, **the manager of our plant**, is ill.

(3) Adverb phrases: Adverb phrases do not join two complete sentences; they simply add new meaning.

CORRECT: We could, **on the other hand**, eat at McDonald's.
Mrs. Mugford, **in addition**, is a member of the lunch committee.

4. **Use commas to separate items in a series (a list of three or more items, actions, or descriptions).**

CORRECT: Children love to eat **pizza, hot dogs, and peanut butter.**
Sid **jogs, lifts weights, and plays handball.**

EXERCISE 2: USING COMMAS

Directions: Insert eight commas needed in the body of the following letter.

Dear Mom,

Because I do not have enough money I will not be coming home for spring vacation. Unfortunately I need to stay here in Des Moines and work. I did not of course waste my money; but I did not allow enough in my budget for an airline ticket. You will understand that I can't come I know. I'd really love to be home in March but I can't afford a ticket until June. Please call Sue Pam and Linda for me and relay the message.

Love always,

Dawn

Semicolon

Use a semicolon to join two or more independent clauses that are related in thought.

Example: Jeff and Jennifer are planning a June wedding; many relatives will travel here from a distance to attend.

Use a semicolon to separate two independent clauses joined by a conjunctive adverb (*however, consequently, moreover, therefore,* etc.). Use a comma following the conjunctive adverb.

Example: I will check your files; however, your account seems to be in order.

Apostrophe

1. Use an apostrophe to show possession.

Add *'s* to all singular nouns. Add *'s* to plural nouns not ending in *s*. Add *'* to plural nouns ending in *s*.

Examples: I ran into a **child's** bicycle in the driveway.
The **children's** bicycles are in the basement.
My three **brothers'** rooms are always neat and clean.

2. Use an apostrophe to replace missing letters in contractions.

Example: **They're** going to lunch at the Ritz-Carlton.

EXERCISE 3: PUNCTUATION REVIEW

Directions: Each sentence below contains *one* error in punctuation. Find and correct each error.

1. To strip the paint from the woodwork, you will need, a gallon of stripper, old rags, a scraper, a paintbrush, steel wool, and a mask to protect you from the fumes.

2. She hasn't returned the dresses to the store, because she lost the receipt.

3. I love to stay up late and watch old movies, as a result, I have difficulty getting up in the morning.

4. I'd like to attend your party; however I will be out of town that weekend.

5. It isnt a good idea to arrive late for a business appointment.

Spelling

Those students who are concerned with their ability to spell words correctly are referred to *Contemporary's GED: How to Prepare for the High School Equivalency Examination* (1994) or to *GED Test 1: Writing Skills* (1994). In those references, you will find general spelling tips, frequently misspelled words, and sound-alike words.

4
PREPARING FOR THE GED WRITING SAMPLE

A written composition may present accurate usage, contain no errors in mechanics, have well-structured, complete sentences, but say nothing. Good writing must say something—convey an explanation, present an opinion with logical and accurate support, or describe someone or something. The writing process can be compared to an exercise workout: you go through a series of steps to reach the desired result. A writing "workout" is an exercise program for our minds, helping us clarify our thoughts and get them on paper.

The Writing Process

The writing process can be broken down into the following five stages.

1. **Prewriting.** Brainstorm for a topic by using mapping, clustering, or organizing strategies.
2. **Drafting.** Write a first draft based on prewriting activities.
3. **Revising.** Write a second draft. Do a self-check based on what you like or dislike about the writing.
4. **Editing.** Check mechanics, spelling, punctuation, and grammar.
5. **Publishing.** Write for a purpose—for example, family stories, the GED Essay Test.

Warming Up to Writing

Think of the kinds of writing you already do. You probably write many things in your daily life—lists (grocery lists, shopping lists, items, gift lists, things to do); notes (to family members, friends, teachers; on greeting cards or post cards); letters (business, personal, job application, to newspapers or magazines); and diary or journal writing. Are there other kinds of writing you do that are not listed?

Building Material for Writing

Keeping informed and writing about your daily experiences, thoughts, and conversations will help you build your resources for writing. Some suggestions are

1. Keep a journal (daily events, experiences, ideas).
2. Think about discussions with others (methods of persuasion).
3. Read with a writer's point of view (development of ideas, paragraph organization, and context clues).
4. Try writing something you haven't written before (surprise letters, family stories, etc.).

EXERCISE 1: WARMING UP

1. Write a note to someone or a journal entry of four or five sentences.

2. Think of a memorable day in your life and write a few lines describing the day or event.

Topic, Audience, and Purpose

The *topic* is the subject of your writing—what you are writing about. If you write a letter to a landlord, the topic may be "high rent," "longer lease," or "broken appliance."

Once you have a topic, you need to determine your *purpose*. What point do you want to make? Why are you writing? to tell a story? to describe? to inform? to persuade? If you are writing a letter of complaint to the credit department of a store, then your purpose is to state the problem, explain your opinion, and offer a solution.

Your purpose also depends on who is reading your writing—the *audience*. While diaries and journals are personal, most other types of writing are meant to be read. For example, you might write a letter of application to a personnel director. An essay is usually meant for "general readership" so that anyone reading it can understand it.

EXERCISE 2: TOPIC, AUDIENCE, AND PURPOSE
Directions: Read the following ending paragraph from a short letter and identify **1.** the writer, **2.** the topic, **3.** the purpose, and **4.** the reader (audience).

> For these reasons, I am asking that Erik be excused from your class next Friday. I hope that this absence will not hurt his progress in your history class. Please send homework with him.

> Thank you.

Prewriting Paragraphs

Have you ever helped people move from one home to another? If they are packed and organized, the hard part is done before you come. Writing is the same way. If you plan and organize your ideas before you write, the writing itself is much easier and the end product is better.

Brainstorming for Paragraphs

You have taken a major step in the writing process. You have considered your topic, purpose, and audience. Once you have determined what point you want to make, you need to come up with ideas to put into your paragraph. This process is often called *brainstorming*.

To brainstorm, simply list rapidly all the ideas you can think of about your topic. Don't stop to edit or evaluate your ideas; don't worry about spelling or try to write complete sentences. A "whirlwind" of ideas should come to you as you think about the ways in which you can support your topic.

Here's an example of brainstorming:

Topic: garage sales
Topic sentence: It takes a lot of organization to get ready for a garage sale.

Brainstorm list:
sort and price items
clean out the closets and the basement
keep the neighbor's kids out of my yard
borrow tables
take out an ad in the newspaper
make and post signs

Structure of a Paragraph

A *paragraph* is a group of sentences written about one topic or main idea. A paragraph has two very important components: *a topic sentence* and *supporting sentences*. The topic sentence states the main idea of the paragraph and often appears at the beginning. The supporting sentences back up and explain the main idea—giving evidence, examples, and reasons. A paragraph may also have a concluding sentence, which sums up or restates the main idea.

In the following example, notice that the first sentence is the topic sentence. It "sets the stage" for the paragraph. The supporting sentences explain the main idea, and the concluding sentence summarizes without repeating.

> Karate lessons have really improved Jay's self-esteem. He is a small boy and not very athletically inclined, but after watching and loving the Karate Kid movies, he became interested in karate. He has taken lessons now for six months and feels very good about himself. As he advances in the classes, he gains confidence and seems to relate better to his friends. Jay is now more self-assured as he works toward his goal—a black belt!

Writing the Topic Sentence

The topic sentence is the most important sentence of a paragraph. It is often the first sentence of the paragraph, and it states the purpose of your piece of writing. Think of the topic sentence as an "umbrella" sentence. The supporting sentences should all belong under the main idea stated in the topic sentence: *Karate lessons have really improved Jay's self-esteem.*

EXERCISE 3: WRITING TOPIC SENTENCES
Directions: Each of these paragraphs needs a good topic sentence. Read the supporting and concluding sentences; then write a topic sentence.

> On sunny days, I have a lot of energy and feel good about myself. I'm usually easy to get along with when the sun shines. When it rains, I feel blue and do not want to work. I look forward to sledding with my children, so I'm happy when it snows. As you can see, if I never looked outside, I would be a more contented person.

> Buying tickets at the gate reminds me of the excitement I experienced at the yearly event. Sitting on the horse on the merry-go-round brings back many memories, and the music has not changed. The aromas of the fudge, popcorn, and cotton candy remind me of how I'd spend a month's allowance on food at the amusement park. Even now, when I get up my nerve and ride the roller coaster, I get sick. Some things never change!

Selecting and Organizing Ideas

You need to select the ideas you will use. Can you use all of the ideas on your brainstorm list, or should you cross out some? You want to eliminate irrelevant ideas, ideas that do not support your topic sentence.

But what order will you write them in? Every topic and every paragraph is different, so there's no one way to put ideas in order. You can put things in time order, least-to-most-important order, or another order that works for your subject.

Here is the brainstorm list from page 77 with the irrelevant ideas eliminated. The remaining ideas are numbered in the order in which the writer will perform the tasks—time order.

2. sort and price items
1. clean out the closets and the basement
4. borrow tables
3. take out an ad in the newspaper
5. make and post signs

Writing a Rough Draft

Now you're ready to create a paragraph—a first draft. As you write, use your numbered brainstorm list as a guide. You don't have to follow it exactly, of course. But if you have done a good job of prewriting, you have already done most of the work—all that's left is turning the items on your list into supporting sentences and adding a concluding sentence.

Remember that you are writing a rough draft. Your paragraph does not have to be perfect on the first try. Just work on getting the ideas on paper. You can polish the writing and make corrections later. Use wide margins and leave space between lines. Keep in mind the following features of a paragraph.

1. The first word is indented.

2. A paragraph has a topic sentence that tells a main idea.

3. A paragraph has several sentences that support the main idea.

EXERCISE 4: WRITING A ROUGH DRAFT
Directions: Make a brainstorm list. Write a rough draft of a paragraph. Be sure to save your work.

EXERCISE 5: PRACTICING THE WRITING PROCESS
Directions: Choose two of the following topics.

1. your favorite type of car
2. your least favorite musician or rock group
3. a friend or relative whom you admire

For each topic, do the following.

- Write a topic sentence that tells the main idea of your paragraph.
- Brainstorm ideas to support your topic sentence.
- Select and order the ideas you want to use in a paragraph.
- Write a rough draft of each paragraph.

Revising Your Rough Draft

Once you have drafted a paragraph, it's a good idea to take a break from it for a while. Then think about what you wanted to say. Read your paragraph as if you were the audience. Did you fully develop your main idea? Is your topic sentence clear and supported? Is there a closing sentence? Ask yourself these questions:

- What's good about my paragraph?
- What don't I like about it?
- What can I do to improve it?

This step in the writing process is called *revising*. The revision process is a "second chance." It is an opportunity to move words and sentences, add ideas, remove or rewrite irrelevant sentences, and clarify confusingly worded sentences. Rather than copying your paragraph over, make your changes in the spaces between the lines and the margins on each side. Don't worry about mechanical errors yet. You will have a chance to edit later.

Look at the following sample rough draft. It needs some work. What would you do to strengthen it?

> Thanksgiving is a day to relax. The rest of our family usually sleeps late. Mom or Dad gets up at 6:00 A.M. to prepare the turkey, then the dutiful parent goes back to bed. Because our aunts, uncles, and cousins bring food, there are only last-minute preparations, so there is plenty of time to sit and talk or play cards. Little children run all over, making it difficult to have a quiet conversation. After a big meal at 1:00 and a long afternoon of visiting, we are all thankful for our time spent together.

Two changes that would strengthen the paragraph would be (1) reverse the second and third sentences and (2) eliminate or revise the sentence "Little children run all over, making it difficult to have a quiet conversation." This sentence does not support the topic sentence; it is an irrelevant idea.

EXERCISE 6: REVISING A ROUGH DRAFT

Directions: Choose two of the paragraphs you wrote earlier. Revise each one, making sure that your main idea is stated clearly and well supported. Be sure to save your work.

Editing

Now you will want to refine your paragraph by making corrections in usage, sentence structure, and mechanics. You have done a lot of editing in previous chapters, so you have some experience in looking for errors. In the example below, see how the writer has used markings to indicate corrections neatly and carefully.

> About a week before the sale date, I call the *n*ewspaper, and list the items in an ~~advertizement~~ *advertisement*. The ~~hole~~ *whole* family helps me clean the garage for the sale. The day before the sale, I borrow tables and arrange all of the items.

Four Types of Writing

Type of Writing	Purpose
Narrative	to narrate, or tell a story
Descriptive	to describe something
Informative	to inform or explain with facts
Persuasive	to persuade the reader to agree

Narrative Writing

The purpose of narrative writing is to tell a story, usually in time order. If a story is not told in the correct sequence, the listener or reader will not understand the story. Read the following paragraph and notice that the narrator, a police officer, relates in time order the events of a typical domestic call.

One of the most difficult aspects of my job is answering the domestic dispute call. Many of these disputes involve violence, often a man beating a woman or children. When my partner and I arrive, we first check for weapons. Next we quickly decide which person is the aggressive one. We may then try to avoid arrest by counseling all members of the household. If necessary, my partner or I take one of the people outside to calm down. Because victims are often too afraid to sign a complaint against their abusers, we may leave the home not knowing if the people living there are safe. For these reasons, the domestic call is one of the most frustrating for police officers.

Words that help you follow the sequence of ideas in a paragraph are called *transitions*. The following words are helpful in narrative writing because they indicate time order.

after	before	then
during	finally	when
first	second	later
meanwhile	next	now

Scan the example paragraph about domestic dispute calls, underlining transition words that show time order.

[Answer: *When, first, Next, then*]

EXERCISE 7: PRACTICING NARRATIVE WRITING
Directions: Write a narrative paragraph. Be sure your paragraph has a topic sentence and presents events in correct time order. Use transition words to help your reader follow the flow of your ideas. Tell a story about an occasion you remember clearly from your childhood.

Descriptive Writing

Writing that draws a mental picture for the reader is descriptive writing. A writer may use all five senses, describing how something looks, smells, feels, tastes, and sounds. It's very important to include specific details in descriptive writing to ensure that the reader can "picture" what is described. However, when you write, avoid vague, overused words such as *very, nice, pretty, good, great, bad,* etc. Instead, use more specific words that tell the reader exactly what you mean. Try to avoid flowery and repetitive language.

Here is a sample of descriptive writing. What is the problem with it?

> Rich and Heather have a new baby. She was born on November 10, and they named her Meghan. She is a pretty baby and is really large. They sent some pictures of her at a few days old. She sure is cute.

This paragraph is vague. We know that Meghan is pretty and large, but we have no idea what she actually looks like. Notice how the following improved paragraph gives us many more specific details.

> Meghan Brady Marmor appeared on November 10 as a nine-pound, round-faced, dark-eyed, gorgeous little girl. Her parents, Rich and Heather, proudly sent us pictures of their first daughter. Her wispy, wheat-colored hair peeked out from a green, hooded sleeper. Like most newborns, she has no neck, and her cheeks look as if they were formed from the soft material of a doll. Because she is so big, she does not look like a fragile infant. Instead, she looks like a miniature toddler, very alert and ready to take on the world.

EXERCISE 8: USING DESCRIPTIVE WRITING

Directions: Rewrite the following vague, dull sentences. Load them with interesting, specific details. Use your imagination!

1. I got a great job.　**2.** It's a funny movie.　**3.** He's a neat guy.

Example:　We bought a nice car.

We finally bought a luxurious, full-sized family car, which is metallic gray with a dark blue interior and loaded with extras like cruise control, stereo and cassette player, and power locks and windows.

EXERCISE 9: WRITING A DESCRIPTIVE PARAGRAPH

Directions: You're supposed to meet an old family friend at the airport. She has not seen you since you were five. Write a descriptive paragraph about yourself and what you'll be wearing so she will know you at the airport. Be sure to use specific details to draw a picture for the reader.

Informative Writing

Informative writing presents facts. The writer's opinion is not included. A very common example of informative writing is the news story, which explains something to the reader. Other common examples of informative writing are recipes and instructions for assembling toys and furniture.

Many writers present information to (1) explain the causes of an effect or (2) explain the effects of a cause. Read the paragraph in Exercise 10 carefully to see how it is organized according to cause and effect. The paragraph gives a cause in the topic sentence. The supporting sentences list the effects.

EXERCISE 10 : CAUSE AND EFFECT

Directions: Identify the six effects of the Wilsons' divorce.

The Wilsons recently filed for divorce. As a result, the family home will be sold, and a property settlement must be decided. Mrs. Wilson, who has worked part-time for several years, may seek full-time employment. Since the separation, Mr. Wilson has moved into an apartment while Mrs. Wilson and the children are living with her sister. The Wilsons' lives have certainly changed in the last two months.

Transition Words in a Cause-Effect Paragraph		
as a result	because	consequently
for	for this reason	if . . . then
then	therefore	thus

EXERCISE 11: INFORMATIVE WRITING—CAUSE AND EFFECT

Directions: Choose one of the following topics and write a paragraph showing the causes or effects.

1. Write a paragraph explaining why you decided to prepare for the GED Test. (Your paragraph should discuss the *causes*.)

2. Write a paragraph explaining how studying for the GED Test has affected your life. (Your paragraph should discuss the *effects*.)

Persuasive Writing

Persuasive writing expresses an opinion. The writer's purpose is to "sell" a particular point of view or line of reasoning to the reader. A persuasive writer must be able to state an opinion and then focus on clear and logical reasons.

Stating an Opinion

Which of the following opening paragraphs do you think is the more persuasive?

A tax increase to pay for expansion of the community college might be a good idea, but there are good reasons to vote against it, too. It's a very tough issue to decide.

A tax increase to pay for expansion of the community college now will help our town meet the demands of the future. Though it will be costly, an improved community college is an excellent idea.

The second one is much stronger because it states a clear point of view. The writer of the first paragraph would have a tough time convincing anyone to vote either for or against the tax increase! The writer of the second paragraph takes a firm position on the issue.

Giving Supporting Reasons

Once a writer has a good topic sentence for a persuasive paragraph, he or she needs some supporting reasons. Why would expansion of the community college benefit the community in the future?

> **Topic sentence:** A tax increase to pay for expansion of the community college now will help our community meet the demands of the future.

Brainstorm list:

1. people won't have to go out of town for so many educational programs
2. most people won't vote for a tax increase
3. new industries coming into area will require new training programs
4. classes already overcrowded; enrollment rising

You should have crossed out 2, which argues against the writer's opinion instead of supporting it.

EXERCISE 12: WRITING PERSUASIVE PARAGRAPHS

Directions: Write a persuasive paragraph on the following topic.

> When a man or woman runs for public office, his or her personal life often becomes front-page news. Sometimes a candidate's private life even affects his or her chances of winning an election. Does the public have a right to know about the private lives of political figures?

Comparison/Contrast Development

A useful technique for organizing ideas in many persuasive paragraphs is *comparison/contrast*.

> **Topic sentence:** A cat makes a better pet than a dog does for people who live in the city.

Cats	Dogs
use litter pan indoors	have to be walked outdoors
are good company without being demanding	have to be played with frequently
don't need a lot of space	need large area to run

This chart lists the writer's ideas in a useful form. The following paragraph is based on the ideas in the chart. Underline words that signal comparison/contrast relationships between ideas.

> A cat makes a better pet than a dog does for people who live in the city. While a cat can use a convenient indoor litter pan, a dog has to be walked outdoors several times every day. Cats are good company, but they are not demanding. Dogs, on the other hand, need to be played with frequently, or they will be unhappy. Cats

don't need a lot of space to run and play, but dogs need a large area to run in and take up a lot of space in a city apartment. A cat is the right choice for a city person who wants a pet's companionship.

You might have underlined *better, while*, *but*, and *on the other hand.*

EXERCISE 13: USING COMPARISON/CONTRAST TO PERSUADE
Directions: Use comparison/contrast development to write a persuasive paragraph: Choose two states or towns you are familiar with. Decide which of the two states or towns is a nicer place to live in and write a paragraph persuading others that you have made the right choice.

Examples of the Four Types of Writing

Narrative Writing: Tell a story about
(1) the best day of your life (or worst day)
(2) your biggest mistake (or best work)

Descriptive Writing: Use vivid description and specific language to describe
(1) a room in your home
(2) the physical appearance of a person you know well

Informative Writing: Explain carefully to your readers
(1) the importance of proper nutrition
(2) some tips for reducing utility costs in the home

Persuasive Writing: State your opinion and give strong supporting reasons for or against
(1) smoking in public places
(2) prayer in the public schools

Writing an Essay

If you can write a good paragraph, you can apply that ability to longer pieces of writing. There are many similarities between paragraphs and essays. The goals of writing a paragraph and an essay are the same: to discuss one main idea, to provide plenty of support for the idea, and to stay on topic throughout the piece. The structure of an essay is also similar to that of a paragraph:

Paragraph	Essay
Topic sentence	Introductory paragraph
Supporting sentences	Body paragraphs
Concluding sentence	Concluding paragraph

As you read the following descriptions of the parts of an essay, think of a paragraph s-t-r-e-t-c-h-e-d.

- The *introductory paragraph* contains the *thesis statement*, which tells the reader the main idea, or purpose, of your essay. The introduction should also preview the major points you will be making to support your thesis statement.

- The main part of your essay is the *body*. As the supporting sentences of a paragraph support your topic sentence, the body paragraphs of an essay support your thesis statement. Each major supporting idea is developed in a paragraph. In your body paragraphs, you may want to use cause-effect, comparison/contrast, or sequence of events to organize your ideas.

- The *concluding paragraph* of an essay should contain a reworded version of the thesis statement to remind the reader of your main point. You can expand on your conclusion by ending with a suggestion or recommendation.

Prewriting for an Essay

Read the following outline. The writer has grouped details and examples under main headings that tell how each paragraph will develop a single idea supporting the thesis statement.

Paragraph 1: Introduction
Thesis statement: Our elementary school needs more crossing guards.

Paragraph 2: two dangerous intersections a few blocks from school
A. one at Lincoln St. and Davis Ave.
B. another at Plum St. and Morton St.

Paragraph 3: many children leave and return to school at the noon hour
A. morning kindergartners leave at 11:30
B. some students go home for lunch at 12:00 and return
C. the afternoon kindergartners arrive at 12:15

Paragraph 4: increase in traffic this year because of the new shopping mall
A. on Oak St., four blocks from school
B. more traffic everywhere because of mall

Paragraph 5: Conclusion: For these reasons, I recommend that the principal request at least four more guards.
A. parents or senior citizens might be free at noon
B. school must make sure children are safe

Drafting an Essay

With your paragraphs planned and outlined, you can draft your essay. All of the prewriting steps lead to the rough draft. Leave wide margins and space between lines to make changes later. When writing a *rough draft*, keep your outline plan next to you. Use words and phrases from the plan as the basis for your sentences.

Begin to develop your own personal writing process as you practice writing these longer pieces. Many experienced writers complete the introduction and conclusion after they have written the body paragraphs. You are not breaking any rules of writing if you start with the body paragraphs, write a strong conclusion, then go back and add a general introduction to your thesis statement.

Next, you will read the rough draft of the essay on the crossing guard topic. The thesis statement is in **bold** type. As you read the rough draft, notice that the writer did not stick strictly to the outline; instead, he used it as a guide, changing wording in several places. You might notice places where the writer's thoughts are hard to follow. Underline these sections and try to think of changes that would improve them.

OUTLINE
Paragraph 1: Introduction
Thesis: Our elementary school needs more crossing guards.

Many parents of children attending Jefferson School are concerned about the safety of their children walking to and from school. Although older students act as crossing guards before and after school, they can't do the whole job. Unguarded intersections near the school, noon hour comings and goings, and the general increase in traffic from the new mall all make walking dangerous, especially for young children. **Our elementary school needs more crossing guards.**

Paragraph 2: two dangerous intersections
A. Lincoln and Davis
B. Plum and Morton

We should hire guards to cover two very dangerous intersections located a few blocks from school. One is the intersection of Lincoln Street and Davis Avenue, where there is a "Yield" sign that drivers often miss. The other is at Plum Street and Morton Street, where there have been several accidents recently. An alert adult crossing guard is needed at each of the intersections whenever children are crossing.

Paragraph 3: children leave and return at noon
A. morning kindergartners leave at 11:30
B. students go home for lunch and return
C. afternoon kindergartners arrive at 12:15

Many children leave and return to school around the noon hour. When morning kindergartners are dismissed at 11:30, many five-year-olds walk home. There are no crossing guards on duty anywhere. At 12:00, many students go home for lunch and return around 12:45. The afternoon kindergartners arrive between noon and 12:15, so there are many children crossing unguarded intersections. Many parents drive their kids to school.

Paragraph 4: increase in traffic
A. new mall on Oak
B. more traffic

There has been an increase in traffic this year because of the new Oak Street Mall, four blocks from school. The traffic count is up in all areas of our neighborhood.

Paragraph 5:
Conclusion: For these reasons, I recommend that the principal request at least four more guards.
A. parents or senior citizens
B. school must ensure safety

For these reasons, the principal should request that the school board hire at least four more crossing guards. Some parents are willing to volunteer temporarily, but we feel that the school district should provide the funds for ensuring the safety of the students over the long term.

Revising the Essay

Before you revise, take a break from the writing process. Leave the essay alone for a while. Look at your own writing as objectively as you can. When you revise, read first as a reader. What does it say to you? Then read as the writer. What can be rewritten or rearranged so that the ideas are clear and the purpose is supported? You can change the order of sentences or paragraphs, add or delete material, rewrite sentences, insert transition words, and so on.

Checklist for Revising an Essay

- ❏ Does the introduction preview my body paragraphs?
- ❏ Does my thesis statement give my essay a clear purpose?
- ❏ Are my ideas arranged logically in body paragraphs that support my thesis statement?
- ❏ Will my reader be able to understand how my ideas fit together and support my thesis statement?
- ❏ Are there any irrelevant ideas?
- ❏ What's good about my essay?
- ❏ What don't I like about my essay?
- ❏ What can I do to improve my essay?

Editing Your Essay

Editing means checking for surface errors in your writing—misspelled words, comma splices, incorrectly capitalized words, etc. If the appearance of your paper detracts from your purpose, your reader will not be able to appreciate fully what you have written. Even minor errors can cause confusion for the reader and make your ideas hard to understand. Many writers read their papers backwards, word by word, to look for spelling errors. It's also helpful to read backwards sentence by sentence while checking for fragments.

EXERCISE 14: EDITING YOUR ESSAY

Directions: Edit an essay you have been working on, checking for surface errors. Check that all sentences express complete thoughts. Check for correctness or consistency of the following: verb tenses, references of pronouns to antecedents, combination of ideas and conjunctions, punctuation (especially commas and apostrophes), and spelling.

The GED Essay

Common Questions About the GED Essay

- **How much time will I have? How long should the essay be?**
  You will have up to 45 minutes for writing an essay of about 200 words. Two hundred words is only a guideline; you will not be penalized if you write more words or fewer words—as long as you express your ideas well. You will need to use a ballpoint pen. You'll be given scratch paper, but your notes will not be scored.

- **Why is there an essay on the GED Test?**
  Many educators and employers feel that writing is an important skill needed by every adult. For the GED Tests to truly represent a high school education, GED examinees need to show that they can write.

- **What is the essay topic like?**
  You will be asked to present an opinion or explanation of an issue with which all adults are familiar. You will be expected to support your explanation with appropriate and specific reasons, details, and examples. The topic will be broad enough that many approaches to the essay will be possible.

- **How will the essays be scored?**
  Readers trained in standards developed by the GED Testing Service will read and score your essay on a scale of 1–6. The readers evaluate the essay for its overall effectiveness; in fact, your paper can contain some errors and still receive a high score. To score well, you should be able to plan an essay that effectively supports a central idea. You should also be able to use correct grammar and spelling most of the time.

- **What are the standards for the scores?**
  Here are descriptions of papers at each level of the scoring guide.

  6 Papers show a clear organizational plan. Writers are able to support well-reasoned views with thorough, specific, and relevant detail. The papers are interestingly written and contain few errors.

  5 Papers are well organized, and ideas are supported convincingly, but they are not as smoothly written as 6 papers. These essays are generally correct but contain some errors.

  4 Papers show that writers organized their ideas and provided some support for their views. They contain more errors, but the errors do not prevent readers from understanding the essays.

  3 Papers are somewhat organized or developed, but in a limited and unconvincing way. Use of standard English is weak, and essays fail to accomplish their writers' purposes.

  2 Papers lack a clear purpose. They are disorganized, and little or no support is given for the writers' ideas. Errors in standard English are frequent and may prevent readers' understanding of these essays.

1 Papers show no purpose or organization. Writers are unable to express themselves in correct English.

NOTE: Papers that are blank, illegible, or written on a topic other than the one assigned cannot be scored, and a Writing Skills Test composite score cannot be reported.

- **What should I study in order to prepare for the essay?**
  Spend your study time learning the writing process and how to put it to work in a test situation. Practice writing timed essays and plan how you will use your time when you take the test.

Making the Most of Your Time

You should learn to adapt the writing process to the testing situation. You need to have a strategy for using your time well when you take the test. Study the following description of how you might approach the essay. Think about how you could adapt this strategy to suit your writing style.

Prewrite (5–10 minutes): Study the topic, think about the choices you have and the different directions you might take; then jot down a thesis statement for your essay. Quickly brainstorm ideas to support your thesis statement. Organize your brainstorm list by numbering ideas, drawing arrows between ideas that belong together, or jot down a rough outline.

Draft (25–30 minutes): Neatly write a rough copy in ink, keeping in mind that you won't have time to recopy the essay. Leave wide margins so that you can go back and add ideas and make corrections. As you write, be sure to keep the overall organizational plan of your essay in mind.

Revise and edit (5–10 minutes): Read over your essay. Look for changes you can make that will make your ideas clearer to the reader, such as adding paragraph breaks or transition words. Make sure you have included a clear thesis statement in your introduction and that your supporting paragraphs are relevant and well organized. Then correct spelling, punctuation, and other mechanical errors.

Sample Topics

Here are some essay topics that are similar to the ones that may be used as Part 2 of the Writing Skills Test. Use the skills you have been learning and manage your time carefully. You should spend about forty-five minutes on your essay.

1. How have the roles of men and/or women changed in the last twenty years? How have these affected the members of a family?
2. Personal qualities such as generosity, good humor, and selfishness are among the things that make us like or dislike a person. Identify a quality that you either admire or dislike in a person and explain why and how it affects you.

3. What are the effects of joint custody on children of divorced parents? You may describe the positive effects, the negative effects, or both.
4. Many people find that holidays are difficult times as well as joyous ones. Sad and lonely experiences may be as common for some people as parties and family gatherings are for others. Why do people often feel unhappy emotions during holidays?
5. As citizens in a democracy, we have the right to vote, yet many do not go to the polls. Explain why many citizens do not vote.
6. Frustration and anger are emotions that all people feel at one time or another. However, some people are able to recognize and control their feelings, while others resort to unkind actions and even violence when they are angry. Why are some people able to control themselves and their actions better than other people?

TEST 2: SOCIAL STUDIES

The GED Social Studies Test consists of multiple-choice questions. These questions require you to know some of the basic social studies concepts that will be covered in this book. However, the test emphasizes your ability to think about these concepts. You will not have to recall an isolated fact or date as on some other tests. Rather, you will read a passage or look at an illustration and answer questions based on it.

To answer successfully, you will need to have an understanding of basic social studies concepts and be able to interpret illustrations and reading passages. You will also need to show that you can understand what you read, apply information to a new situation, analyze relationships among ideas, and make judgments about the material presented.

How many questions are on the test?

There are 64 multiple-choice questions, and you will be given 85 minutes to complete the test. Approximately two-thirds of the questions will be based on reading passages of up to 250 words each, and one-third will be based on visuals—maps, charts, graphs, or political cartoons. Look at the Post-Test at the end of this book. This Post-Test is based on the real GED Test.

What's on the test?

The GED Social Studies Test can be broken down into the content areas it covers and the skills it tests. The content of the tests is as follows: Behavioral Science—20%; U.S. History—25%; Political Science—20%; Economics—20%; and Geography—15%. (In Canada, 15% is behavioral science, 25% is Canadian history, 20% is political science, 20% is economics, and 20% is geography.)

These essential social studies concepts are covered in Chapters 1–5 of this section. However, keep in mind that a given question may draw from a number of these subjects. It's difficult to discuss society or people without touching on a number of topics. For example, a question on the U.S. Constitution may draw from material covered in both political science and history.

Also, remember that you are being tested on your ability to think through certain ideas and concepts. You will be asked to do more than just find an answer that was given in a passage. Thinking skills that you will be tested on include the following: Understanding Ideas—20%; Applying Ideas—30%; Analyzing Ideas—30%; and Evaluating Ideas—20%.

1
THE BEHAVIORAL SCIENCES

Behavioral science is the area in social studies that concerns how human beings behave as individuals and within groups and cultures. The Social Studies Test will include questions on three subjects in behavioral science: anthropology, sociology, and psychology.

Although each subject overlaps the others to some extent, this section examines each one individually. Each of the behavioral sciences focuses on a specific aspect of humankind. Anthropology addresses the question *Who are humans?* Sociology answers the question *To what groups do people belong?* Psychology deals with the complex question *How do people think and behave?*

Anthropology: Who Are Humans?

Have you ever wondered about the human race in general—about who we are, where we came from, how we are alike, and how we are different? *Anthropology* is the science that tries to answer these and many other questions about human origins and civilizations.

The word anthropology comes from two Greek words: *anthropos* meaning "man" and *logos* meaning "study of." Of course, the study of "man" includes all of humankind—men and women. Anthropology has two branches: physical anthropology and cultural anthropology. *Physical anthropologists* study human ancestry to understand how humans have biologically adapted to a variety of environments found throughout the world. *Cultural anthropologists* study how people live in groups and how they have developed the tools of culture, such as language, religion, and technology, in order to survive. *Culture* is the shared, learned behavior that people develop from group experiences.

Research in the field of anthropology has led to many surprising discoveries about humans and their adaptation to their environment. For example, in India in 1913, the "wolf children" were found. They were two ten-year-old boys who lived with three wolves. The boys would eat only raw food. They never smiled or talked. They avoided humans, but allowed a dog to eat with them. Even after they were captured by hunters, the children could not be taught any human behaviors and died a short time later.

A physical anthropologist might ask these questions about this phenomenon: How did humans survive among wolves? How did the boys' bodies adapt to the wolves' way of life? How were they accepted and raised by these animals? A cultural anthropologist might ask: How could two boys learn to live with wolves? How did the human beings communicate with these animals?

Although each observes human behavior from different perspectives, both the physical and cultural anthropologist raise and answer questions that contribute to our overall knowledge about human beings in their varying environments.

EXERCISE 1: PHYSICAL AND CULTURAL ANTHROPOLOGY
Directions: Write *P* in front of the topic that a physical anthropologist would study and *C* in front of the topic a cultural anthropologist would study.

_____ **1.** fossils of bones of prehistoric people

_____ **2.** hieroglyphics found on the walls of an Egyptian cave

_____ **3.** a people's preference for raw meat

Culture

Culture consists of the knowledge, beliefs, and learned human behavior shared by a group of people. It includes the way we think, feel, and behave as we adapt to our environment. Humans can adapt to many environments that lower animals cannot. This is because we have the intelligence and creativity to develop culture.

In fact, humans *must* create culture in order to adapt and survive. For a culture to continue to exist, it must satisfy certain basic needs of its members. These needs, common to all cultures, are called ***cultural universals***. Among them are food, shelter, language, family, belief system, economic system, and political system.

Customs

We study various cultures so that we may increase our understanding of other people throughout the world. We study their ***customs***, the patterns of behavior shared by the members of a specific culture. The customs are based upon the values that each culture believes to be important. For example, eating with a knife and fork is an established custom in our society. In the United States, family, school, and church are the major institutions that transmit culture to young people.

Values, Ethnocentrism, and Cultural Relativity

Values are beliefs that direct and influence behavior. For example, a fundamental value in American life is the belief that all people are created equal. Values can include freedom, equality, fairness, and individualism. While observing other cultures, anthropologists are careful not to judge the culture they study according to their own values. Judging another culture according to one's own values is called ***ethnocentrism***. For example, an American who condemns child-rearing practices in Asia because they are different from ours is practicing ethnocentrism. Anthropologists attempt to study each culture realizing that each is different yet satisfying to its members.

The opposite of ethnocentrism is ***cultural relativity***, judging each culture by using that particular culture's values. Recognizing differences among cultures increases our understanding of the varieties of ways in which people can adapt to the environment.

Sociology: To What Groups Do People Belong?

People belong to many different groups. You may be a parent, a spouse, a brother, a sister, or a friend. You obviously are a student, for you are studying for the GED Test. All of these roles that you play indicate your membership in different groups.

Sociology studies how humans interact with other humans. We develop relationships and learn to behave in accordance with the beliefs and values of the society in which we live. Sociologists define a *group* as two or more persons who communicate with each other. Merely being together, however, does not constitute a group relationship. All of the people on a bus or in a room are not considered a group unless they interact—unless they communicate with one another.

Types of Groups

Sociologists divide groups into two categories based upon the group's influence on the individual. *Primary groups* are most important and immediate to a person. Your family is the most primary of all groups. Most people have close, personal relationships with family members. From this group, you form your habits, beliefs, and attitudes. Though not quite as close as your family, personal friends with whom you share intimacies also are members of a primary group to which you belong.

Group relationships that are less personal and exert less influence on an individual are called *secondary groups*. The people you work with or the other students in your class are examples of secondary groups to which you belong. Your communication with co-workers and fellow students tends to be specific and brief. These relationships are usually temporary and impersonal. However, when you work as a team with the same people over a period of time, relationships with co-workers can begin to resemble those with close friends or family.

EXERCISE 2: PRIMARY AND SECONDARY GROUPS
Directions: Write *P* if the situation describes a primary group and *S* if it describes a secondary group.

_____ **1.** students in math class _____ **2.** family _____ **3.** people in a town of 120

Social Institutions

An *institution* is a system organized by society to provide for its members' basic needs. The major function of most institutions is to transmit to citizens their culture's customs and values. In advanced societies, institutions are of five major types: family, religious, economic, political, and educational. The most important of these is the family.

Socialization and the Family

The family is the first group to which we belong. The most important function of a family is reproduction of the species. For a society to survive, new members must be continually added. After a child is born, the family is responsible for protecting and caring for the child and teaching him or her the appropriate customs and behaviors. This teaching process is called *socialization*.

Humans must learn to be human. The wolf children described in the anthropology section were biologically human. However, they had never been socialized as humans and, as a result, never adjusted to human society. On occasion, newspapers and magazines report cases of people being raised without contact with other humans.

Nuclear and Extended Families

The structure that the family takes depends upon the customs and values of the society. Traditionally, the family structure in the United States has been nuclear. A *nuclear* family is centered around a father, mother, and children. Other societies are based upon an extended family structure. In the *extended* family, the nuclear family has been extended to include grandparents, great-grandparents, and sometimes other relatives. In the extended family structure, all adults are responsible for the care and upbringing of all of the children.

EXERCISE 3: NUCLEAR AND EXTENDED FAMILIES
Directions: Write *N* in the space if the situation below describes a nuclear family and *E* if it describes an extended family.

_____ **1.** In Japan, India, Iran, Turkey, and many countries of Africa, the family unit consists of three generations living together.

_____ **2.** The dominant culture of the United States dictates that in most cases only two generations—parents and their children—live together as a family unit.

_____ **3.** The Hopi, Navajo, and Iroquois Indians require that a newly married couple establish residence with the wife's family.

Social Structure

Many societies are divided into categories called social classes. Members of a *social class* possess similar levels of prestige. *Stratification* refers to the way that society is divided into classes. Placement of people into social classes is based upon society's values and behaviors.

In the United States, the social classes are based upon economic values—how much one earns. The upper, middle, and lower classes are distinguished by the wealth and power of the individuals. The upper class is far more wealthy and powerful than the lower class.

Social class is an example of **ascribed** (automatically attained) **status,** since one is born into it, but it is not permanent. As one moves upward from one level to a higher one, the new social class is considered an **achieved** (earned) **status**. Some societies prohibit this **social mobility** (change in status).

In India, for example, the traditional social structure was a *caste system*. People were born into one of the five levels (classes) of the caste system. They were prohibited from changing levels. Thus, the ascribed status remained for the rest of a person's life, regardless of any attempt to rise above it.

EXERCISE 4: SOCIAL STRATIFICATION
Directions: Read the statements below. Write *CL* in the space if it describes a class system and *CA* if it describes a caste system.

_____ **1.** promotes ambition and self-improvement

_____ **2.** has strict social structure

_____ **3.** makes available many job choices

Psychology: How Do People Think and Behave?

Psychology, the study of human behavior, attempts to answer the questions that concern why human beings think and behave as they do. Three of the components psychologists study and analyze are thinking and learning processes, personality, and social environment.

The Thinking and Learning Process

Because people must learn to be human, learning is the basis for human behavior. According to the behaviorist school of psychology, *learning* is a permanent change in behavior that results from past experience.

Psychologists have identified many ways by which humans learn. Each of the ways represents an increasing level of sophistication by the learner. On the most basic level, people learn to respond to a stimulus (an event that causes a response or reaction). This is called *conditioning*. More sophisticated forms of learning involve reasoning and working out solutions to problems.

EXERCISE 5: TYPES OF LEARNING
Directions: Read the definitions and apply them to the questions that follow.

classical conditioning—After a stimulus has been introduced several times, a person learns to respond in a certain way. Some reinforcement (either a reward or a punishment) is part of the conditioning process.

operant conditioning—Learning results from interacting with the environment. In operant conditioning there is no direct stimulus. People do things because they want to gain something or to avoid some outcome.

trial-and-error learning—A person solves a problem after trying several possibilities and finally arrives at the right answer or achieves the goal.

cognitive perception—Learning is the result of a logical thought process. The mind takes in information, reorganizes it, and adapts the information to fit a new situation.

maze learning—Learning requires a series of responses in order for the goal to be reached. The responses are often made by trial and error, but maze learning also requires that an individual follow a logical thought process in solving a problem.

1. An infant cries when she wakes up in a dark room. At the sound of the baby's voice, the father goes to the room, picks her up, and turns on the light. The baby stops crying. The father continues this for several weeks. One night, he turns on the light before he picks up the baby. To his surprise, the baby stops crying. Thus, turning on the light has caused the same response as picking up the baby. This is an example of
   (1) classical conditioning
   (2) operant conditioning
   (3) trial-and-error learning
   (4) cognitive perception
   (5) maze learning

2. A child is told that birds fly. While playing outside, the child sees an airplane fly overhead. Based on his stored knowledge, the child tells his mother that he has seen a bird. His mother tells him, "No, dear, that's an airplane," and explains the differences between the two. The next time he sees an object flying, he will be able to know whether it is an airplane or a bird. This is an example of
   (1) classical conditioning
   (2) operant conditioning
   (3) trial-and-error learning
   (4) cognitive perception
   (5) maze learning

Personality

To a great degree, our personality influences the way in which we behave. *Personality* can be summed up as the traits a person exhibits in the way he or she behaves, adjusts, and relates to others and the environment. Because no two people are exactly alike, it follows that no two personalities can be duplicates. There are, however, similarities in behaviors among people, and it is these similarities that psychologists study to better understand human behavior.

The study of personality is so complex that even psychologists do not all agree about how this facet of human behavior can be explained. Briefly described in this section are four theories that psychologists rely on to understand personality: psychoanalytic theory, superiority and compensation theory, anxiety theory, and self-actualization theory.

Psychoanalytic Theory   According to Sigmund Freud, much of personality comes from unconscious, hidden instincts and desires. The three parts that make up the personality are the *id* (pleasure-seeking drive to satisfy the needs of food, sex, and self-protection), the *ego* (a check on the id's search for pleasure), and the *superego* (the conscience). Personalities develop from childhood experiences according to this theory.

Superiority and Compensation Theory   Alfred Adler believed that personality is shaped by a striving for superiority. The failure of people to be strong or powerful can result in a feeling of inferiority; the awareness of one's weakness makes a person strive especially hard to overcome it. Some adult problems are attributed to feelings of inadequacy in childhood.

Anxiety Theory   Karen Horney thought that people become anxious when they worry about not becoming who they want to be. To lessen their anxiety, they adopt behaviors or needs to help them adjust. The anxiety theory explains how adults develop neurotic needs—learned needs—to reduce anxiety. For example, an excessive washing of hands may result from an overwhelming emphasis on childhood cleanliness by a parent.

Self-Actualization Theory   Abraham Maslow believed that human personality is motivated to satisfy certain needs in life. These needs are expressed in the form of a hierarchy (a ranking in order of importance). Maslow's pyramid of needs includes the *physiological* (survival—food, shelter, and clothing), *safety and security* (desire for order and predictability), *belongingness* (social attachments), *esteem* (recognition and respect from others), and *self-actualization* (the highest human need—to fulfill one's potential). Maslow believed that appeals to the higher-order needs are the most motivational for human beings, and the failure to satisfy such needs are a cause of frustration and unhappiness.

Defense Mechanisms

Compensation was described as a part of Adler's theory of personality. A person compensates for a shortcoming by striving hard to overcome it. *Defense mechanisms* are devices adopted to reduce frustration in achieving one's goals. Some of them include

repression—keeping thoughts buried, that, if admitted, might arouse anxiety

   Example: Mary doesn't like dentists' drills, so she conveniently "forgets" her dental appointment.

projection—hiding the source of the conflict by blaming others

   Example: Jim needs an A on the math test to pass the course. He'd like to cheat, but his conscience won't let him. Instead, he accuses innocent students who do well on the test of cheating.

displacement—substituting one object or goal with another

   Example: Ralph gets angry with his boss but is afraid to tell him off. Instead, he comes home and picks a fight with his wife.

rationalization—assigning the reason for failure to something else.

   Example: Hector wasn't good enough to make the basketball team's first string, so he blames the coach for being prejudiced against him.

reaction formation—completely disguising a motive by showing
   opposite behavior

   Example: Deep down, June hates her father, but she appears to be
      overly concerned about his comfort and health.

EXERCISE 6: DEFENSE MECHANISMS

Directions: Reread the definitions on pages 99–100 and choose the best
answer for each of the following situations.

1. According to the "sour grapes" fable, a fox wanted a cluster of grapes
   that was out of his reach. Because he couldn't get the grapes, he turned
   away from them saying that they were sour and not worth having
   anyway. The defense mechanism described is
   (1) repression
   (2) projection
   (3) displacement
   (4) rationalization
   (5) reaction formation

2. Michael, angry because his team lost the football game, kicks his dog
   when it runs up to him. The defense mechanism described is
   (1) repression
   (2) projection
   (3) displacement
   (4) rationalization
   (5) reaction formation

Social Environment

People behave differently when they are alone from when they are in a
group. Social environment greatly influences how humans behave. *Social
psychologists* study the effects of groups on individuals. Social psychologists
are concerned with two areas: social attitudes and group behavior.

Social attitudes involve the actions, beliefs, and feelings of people toward
groups and classes of people. By studying attitudes, social psychologists are
able to understand how people are attracted to and repelled by one another.

Group behavior involves the different ways individuals behave in groups.
An example of the influence of the group on individual behavior is the
adolescent peer group. After a child reaches a certain age, his or her peer
group becomes more important to him or her than the family.

Social psychologists have found that when people become members of
certain types of groups, they become anonymous—they lose their individual
identity and become part of the crowd. This "loss of identity" enables them to
do things that they would not ordinarily do as individuals. Two examples of
these groups are mobs and vigilante groups. A positive example is a group of
rescuers working together to help victims of an earthquake.

2
<u>U.S. HISTORY</u>

Why study the past? We study the past because each of us is a result of those who came before. By understanding their triumphs and failures, we can better understand events that take place in our society today and better prepare ourselves for the future. History is largely a recording of cause-and-effect relationships. Historians study these connections between events. This chapter will include *highlights* of the most important events in U.S. history. For a more extensive overview of U.S. history in narrative form, consult *Contemporary's GED: How to Prepare for the High School Equivalency Examination* (1994).

A New Nation in a New World

Exploration and Colonization The news of Columbus' voyage to America in 1492 led to more voyages of exploration by Spain, Portugal, France, and England during the 1500s and 1600s. All these countries, and a few other European nations, laid claim to parts of the Americas, and most of them had colonial settlements there by the early 1700s. The rights of the Native Americans (Indians) were ignored, and huge numbers of them died of European diseases brought to America or were killed in wars with the Europeans.

France developed a large colony in Canada. England had thirteen colonies spread along the Atlantic coast from Maine to the edge of Spanish Florida. Conflicts over other claims on land in North America and elsewhere led to a 1754–1763 war between England and France (called the *French and Indian War* in America because each side had Indian allies). An English victory resulted in England's taking over most of France's North American claims.

The Colonial Period Each English colony was governed by a council or governor acting for the English monarch. The colonists, mostly English, but also including many Dutch and German settlers and smaller numbers of other Europeans, had differing customs and religious and political ideas. Economic opportunities abounded, and North America's abundant natural resources led to the development of industries in shipbuilding, mining, fur trading, and fishing.

To help pay its expenses for the French and Indian War, England tried to gain revenue from America. The colonists resisted, claiming that since they were not represented in Parliament (the British legislature), Parliament had no right to tax them. The British government tried one scheme after another: taxes on imports such as sugar and tea, a stamp tax, and finally a group of laws the colonists called the *Intolerable Acts*—acts of Parliament meant to force the colonists to obey all British laws—including tax laws. The colonists resisted.

Revolution and Independence Colonial protests led to violent resistance and then to war between the colonists and British soldiers. Representatives from the colonies, meeting in a Continental Congress in Philadelphia, approved a *Declaration of Independence* in 1776. The *Revolutionary War* lasted until 1781, when American forces led by George Washington, aided by a powerful force from France, captured a large British army at Yorktown, Virginia. In a peace treaty signed in Paris two years later, the British acknowledged the independence of the United States.

ANSWERS TO EXERCISES IN THIS CHAPTER BEGIN ON PAGE 413.

EXERCISE 1: A NEW NATION
Directions: Match the *cause* in the left column with its *effect* in the right column.

_____ **1.** England and France both claim lands in North America

_____ **2.** the Declaration of Independence

_____ **3.** colonists refuse to pay British taxes

(a) Revolutionary War

(b) the Intolerable Acts

(c) French and Indian War

The Early Republic

During the Revolutionary War, the Americans set up a government under the *Articles of Confederation*. After years of rule by English kings, the Americans did not trust a powerful central government, so they left most power with the individual states. This, however, led to disputes over issues such as the issuing of money, trade, and defense. Under the Articles, each state had the right to print its own money, trade between states was often taxed like foreign imports, and, during the war, troops were ill-equipped and often unpaid by the states that sent them. To solve these and other problems, the Continental Congress called for a Constitutional Convention to revise the Articles of Confederation. The Convention, which met in Philadelphia in 1787, went much further.

The U. S. Constitution The delegates sent by the states to Philadelphia wrote a totally new constitution. The convention was filled with disagreements—over what kind of legislature should be established, how the populations of the states should be counted for purposes of taxation and representation, slavery, and a host of other issues, big and small.

Through a series of compromises, a constitution was finally drafted. There would be a bicameral (two houses) legislature. Each state would be represented in the House of Representatives according to its population. Large states would have more representatives than small states, but in the Senate, each state would have equal representation—two senators. Another compromise, over the slavery issue, determined that slaves would be counted as three-fifths of a person for purposes of taxation and representation, but they would not be allowed to vote. The slave trade itself would be abolished in 1808, but no action was taken to end slavery.

The Campaign for Ratification Once the U.S. Constitution was drafted and approved by the delegates, a lively campaign over ratification (approval) by the states began. The country split into two basic camps, the *Federalists,* who favored the strong central government the Constitution would establish, and the *Anti-Federalists,* who wanted to maintain the sovereignty (supreme power) of the states. Ratification was approved, and in March 1779 George Washington was sworn in as the new nation's first president.

EXERCISE 2: THE BEGINNING OF AMERICAN GOVERNMENT
Directions: Read the following statements. Write *T* before each true statement and *F* before each false statement.

_____ **1.** After the Revolution, most powers of the government were held by the states.

_____ **2.** The Articles of Confederation were inadequate in addressing issues that were common to the thirteen states.

_____ **3.** The Articles of Confederation and the Constitution are two names for the same document.

EXERCISE 3: DISPUTES AND COMPROMISES
Directions: Choose the best answer for each of the following questions.

1. Counting slaves as only three-fifths of the population was favorable to the northern states because it
   (1) limited the number of senators representing the South
   (2) limited the South's number of seats in the House of Representatives
   (3) was based on the amount of property for taxing purposes
   (4) kept slavery from spreading
   (5) equalized the number of representatives from the North and South

2. Today, many conservatives—Democrats and Republicans alike—are strong supporters of states' rights. These Americans would likely have been supporters of
   (1) anti-federalism
   (2) federalism
   (3) republicanism
   (4) democracy
   (5) colonialism

The Nation Expands

The United States expanded geographically between 1701 and 1850. Under President George Washington, Vermont, Kentucky, and Tennessee were admitted (1791–1796) to the Union; Ohio was admitted (1802) under President Thomas Jefferson. The huge Louisiana Purchase (1803) doubled the size of the country; *Manifest Destiny* became the rallying cry to extend U.S. borders to the Pacific Ocean.

Foreign Affairs In 1812 the United States declared war against Great Britain because of interference with United States trade and aid to the Indians; Britain imposed a blockade. Despite successful military campaigns, the United States lost this unpopular war. As a result of the war, pro-British Federalists lost strength, westward expansion continued, industrialization increased as a result of the British blockade, and a new sense of nationalism arose.

President James Monroe proclaimed through the *Monroe Doctrine* (1823) that European nations would no longer be allowed to colonize the Americas and that the United States would remain neutral in European conflicts. Western expansion continued.

Jacksonian Democracy and the Mexican War

Sectionalism (political, cultural, and economic differences between regions of the country, principally North, South, and West) became a problem. President Andrew Jackson, a *populist* representing the common people, was elected as a result of factional and sectional differences. Jackson opposed a national bank; farmers and crafts people gained a louder voice in government. Under President James Polk the United States annexed Texas (1845), but he was unable to purchase the territory including New Mexico and California. Boundary disputes led the United States to declare war on Mexico; the Treaty of Guadalupe Hidalgo (1848) ending the war resulted in the *Mexican Cession*. The United States gained land that eventually became California, Utah, Nevada, and parts of four other states.

EXPANSION OF THE UNITED STATES, 1783–1853

EXERCISE 4: THE WAR OF 1812

Directions: Choose the best answer for the following question.

Which event contributed to the sense of nationalism in the United States after the War of 1812?

(1) the spirit of Manifest Destiny that caught fire during the early 1800s

(2) the need to manufacture its own goods because of the British naval blockade

(3) the scapegoating of the Federalists as traitors

(4) both 1 and 2

(5) both 2 and 3

Times of Internal Strife

Sectionalism persisted; *tariffs* (taxes on imported goods, favored by the more industrialized North and opposed by the agricultural South and West) were viewed as unequal and unfair. Slavery was a major issue. Conflicting views included *popular sovereignty* (those affected should determine what was best), the acceptance of slavery where it already existed but a ban on slavery in new areas, and the belief of *abolitionists* that slavery was evil and should be banned. The *Dred Scott decision* (1857) worsened relations between North and South when the Supreme Court ruled that a slave was property and could not sue for his freedom in a federal court.

The Nation Goes to War President Abraham Lincoln promised the restriction of slavery to where it already existed, but the southern states feared domination by the North. Eleven southern states seceded from the union to form the Confederate States of America.

The Civil War The Civil War (1861–1865) was fought mostly in the South. The North had a greater population, the means to manufacture goods, excellent transportation, and natural resources. The South had familiarity with battle sites and great confidence in its outstanding military leaders. Lincoln issued the *Emancipation Proclamation* (1862), freeing slaves in the states that had seceded. With General Robert E. Lee's surrender in 1865, the war ended. The enormous task ahead was mending the division between North and South, rebuilding the South, and readmitting the South to the Union.

Reconstruction Lincoln's plan for reuniting the nation included the regaining of citizenship rights and statehood for the South; however, before he could carry out his plan, he was assassinated by a Confederate sympathizer. Andrew Johnson, a Tennesseean, succeeded him but was mistrusted by Congress as being pro-South. He became the only U.S. president to be *impeached* (charged with official misconduct), but he was not convicted and not removed from office. The Thirteenth Amendment to the Constitution (1865) banned slavery. The Fourteenth and Fifteenth Amendments (1868 and 1870) guaranteed citizenship and the right to vote to former slaves. The Congress required southern states to ratify these amendments before they could be readmitted into the Union.

EXERCISE 5: A DIVIDED NATION

Directions: Choose the best answer for each question or statement.

1. A referendum is a political procedure that allows voters to approve or disapprove of a measure proposed by the voters themselves or by the legislature. This method is most similar to which of the following proposed solutions to the issue of slavery?
   (1) abolitionism
   (2) compromise
   (3) popular sovereignty
   (4) secession
   (5) territorial balance

2. The Dred Scott decision is cited as a decisive event leading to the Civil War. The values upheld by the Supreme Court's decision were that
   (1) slavery was inhuman
   (2) states had more rights than people
   (3) new states could permit slavery
   (4) slavery could only be maintained in the South
   (5) human beings could be treated as property

EXERCISE 6: THE VOTE ON SECESSION

Directions: Based on the following map, match the state in the left column with its description in the right column.

_____ 1. Virginia

_____ 2. Texas

_____ 3. Kentucky

(a) As a "border state," it remained in the Union despite being a slave state.

(b) This state split in two over the issue of secession, with the western part loyal to the Union.

(c) The entire state seceded from the Union even though only its eastern part voted to do so.

The Rise of Industrial America

The growth of industry after the Civil War changed the nation's economy. More goods were mass produced at lower cost, and the United States became a world industrial leader by the turn of the century. Factories and city populations grew, and consumer demand encouraged business expansion, new products, and new industries.

Growth of Big Business Rapid, widespread industrialization led to the development of big business, especially the steel, railroad, and oil industries. Work conditions deteriorated while the government followed a *laissez-faire* (noninterference) policy toward business.

Urbanization and Social Change Urbanization is a shift from living in rural areas to the cities. Before industrialization, one-sixth of the American population lived in cities; by 1890 it was one-third. Cities had railway centers to transport people, supplies, and goods. A flood of immigrants (1870–1900) added to an abundant labor supply.

Labor and Progressivism When the health, safety, and comfort of laborers was largely ignored, labor unions were organized to deal with employers. Two early unions were the Knights of Labor (1869) and the American Federation of Labor (1881). Other groups and individuals fought political corruption and tried to improve the quality of life for Americans. Their progressive reforms of the late 1800s and early 1900s included the Sherman Anti-Trust Act, which outlawed monopolies; the Hepburn Act, which gave the Interstate Commerce Commission increased authority to regulate the nation's railroads; the Pure Food and Drug Act, which set standards for the production and sale of foods and drugs; the establishment of the United States Department of Agriculture (USDA), which began inspecting meat; child labor laws; and minimum wage and workers' compensation laws.

EXERCISE 7: GROWTH OF BIG BUSINESS

Directions: Place a check before each of the following actions that represents economic activity *without* government intervention.

_____ **1.** The Federal Communications Commission (FCC) requires AT&T to divest—break up into smaller companies.

_____ **2.** A large company hires and pays unskilled workers whatever the market will bear and is not brought into court for violating the minimum wage law.

_____ **3.** A credit card company charges its customers whatever amount of interest it wants to.

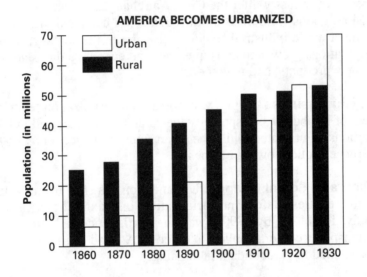

AMERICA BECOMES URBANIZED

EXERCISE 8: AMERICA BECOMES URBANIZED

Directions: Based on the bar graph above, answer the following questions.

1. (a) What was the first decade in which more people lived in urban areas than in rural areas? _____

(b) By 1930, the number of people living in urban areas was approximately how many million? _____

2. The figures in the bar graph support the fact that the United States probably reached half its present population of 248 million (based on the 1990 census) by
   (1) the 1890s
   (2) the 1900s
   (3) the 1910s
   (4) the 1920s
   (5) the 1930s

Becoming a World Power

Its long-standing policy of *isolationism* discouraged the United States from foreign involvements, but its increasing industrial needs demanded foreign markets for its goods. Americans opened trade with Japan in 1854. The United States later joined the big European powers in demanding trading posts in China. The nation had already purchased Alaska (in 1867). In the late 1800s it added Hawaii (annexed in 1893) and a few other small Pacific islands. The nation's continuing trend toward *imperialism* (a policy of gaining control over other regions or countries) increased in the 1890s.

The Spanish-American War The United States supported Cuban rebels who revolted against Spain. The United States battleship *Maine* was sent to protect American citizens in Cuba and exploded. The United States held Spain responsible and declared war against Spain in 1898. In four months, the United States won the war and gained control of Guam, Puerto Rico, and the Philippines.

World War I Nationalist conflicts and European power struggles caused twenty-seven nations to take part in a world war that began in 1914. The Central Powers included Germany, Austria-Hungary, and Turkey. The Allied Powers included Great Britain, France, Russia, and Italy. The United States tried to remain neutral but joined the Allied Powers after German attacks on ships carrying American citizens. The Allied Powers drove back the Central Powers, and the Germans conceded defeat. With the signing of the Treaty of Versailles (1919), a League of Nations was established for world peace. Because of Congressional opposition, the United States did not join the league, contributing to its decline, and the nation returned to a policy of isolationism and a focus on domestic issues.

From Prosperity to Despair President Calvin Coolidge believed in few government regulations, reduced government spending, and lower taxes. The "Roaring Twenties" was a period of prosperity, (investment risks in hope of gain), bootlegging (illegal liquor), and materialism. In 1929 the stock market crashed. Soon businesses failed, and unemployment soared. President Herbert Hoover tried to cope with the economic crisis, but his policy of not interfering in business doomed him to failure. The number of unemployed workers reached 11 million. President Franklin D. Roosevelt was elected on the promise of a "New Deal."

The goals of the New Deal were relief, economic recovery, and reforms to prevent another depression. New programs and agencies, including the social security system and National Recovery Act, changed governmental policy. The economic and emotional climate of the country slowly changed for the better, but full recovery came only with another world war.

EXERCISE 9: THE UNITED STATES BECOMES A WORLD POWER

Directions: Choose the best answer to each of the following questions.

1. Which of the following foreign policy actions in recent times is a direct result of early American imperialist policy?
   (1) America's military support of Israel in the Middle East
   (2) the implicit support of apartheid in South Africa by some large American corporations
   (3) America's establishment of military bases in the Philippines' Subic Bay
   (4) the stationing of American troops in West Germany
   (5) America's patrolling of waters off the Libyan coast

2. From the end of the Civil War until the Spanish-American War in 1898, most Americans were isolationists. Which is the most likely cause of such widespread desire for withdrawal from international concerns?
   (1) the lack of information about events taking place in foreign lands
   (2) the desire to expand U.S. boundaries farther across the continent into Canada and Mexico
   (3) the disillusionment with foreign allies who had refused to take sides during the Civil War
   (4) the nation's preoccupation with reconstruction and industrialization after the Civil War
   (5) the resentment toward the new immigrants flooding the country

EXERCISE 10: WORLD WAR I

Directions: Fill in the following blanks.

The United States became involved in the war in 1917 by joining the side

of the **(1)** _____. The **(2)** _____ formally ended

the war in 1919. Congress did not want the United States to join the

(3) _____. As a result of this sentiment, the United States

adopted its former foreign policy of **(4)** _____.

EXERCISE 11: THE NEW DEAL

Directions: Match the group in the left column with the New Deal legislation it most likely would have supported in the right column.

_____ **1.** unemployed laborers	**(a)** National Industrial Recovery Act
_____ **2.** the elderly	**(b)** Civilian Conservation Corps
_____ **3.** environmentalists	**(c)** Social Security Act

From Isolationism to Superpower

Because of its isolationist policy and the depression, the United States ignored conflicts between a number of countries: Germany's increasing militarism; Japan's aggression toward China; a civil war in Spain; and Italy's invasion of Ethiopia.

World War II With Germany's invasion of Poland (1939), Great Britain and France declared war. Italy and Germany joined with Japan as the Axis powers. With the Japanese attack on Pearl Harbor in 1941, the United States declared war on Japan and Germany and joined the Allied forces, which included Great Britain, the Soviet Union, and France. The global, six-year war resulted in the loss of millions of lives and cost billions of dollars. One month before massive Allied efforts caused Germany to surrender, Roosevelt died.

Harry Truman became the new president and was determined to end the war with Japan quickly by dropping atomic bombs on Hiroshima and Nagasaki. Japan surrendered. The post-war Yalta Agreement provided for the division of Germany into four zones controlled by Great Britain, the Soviet Union, France, and the United States. The United Nations was established as a world organization for peace. Scars remaining from the war include the Holocaust (extermination of six million Jews).

The Cold War President Truman formulated the Truman Doctrine (supporting free peoples resisting internal armed minorities or foreign powers). The containment of communism became a U.S. policy in the years of what became known as the Cold War, a non-military struggle between the Soviet Union and the United States and their respective allies. The Cold War heated up in Korea.

The Korean War After World War II, the Soviet Union and the United States occupied the northern and southern halves of Korea respectively. By 1950, a communist government was established in the North, and armies representing the North and the South were stationed along the border. When North Korea crossed the border and invaded South Korea, President Truman committed U.S. troops and asked for United Nations support. The fighting continued until 1953 when a treaty was signed and the boundary was restored between North and South Korea. Tensions remained.

The Eisenhower Years As the Cold War continued, the United States and the Soviet Union increased their military forces, and both developed the hydrogen bomb. During the 1950s, Senator Joseph McCarthy and other anticommunist extremists used hatred and fear of communism to accuse and ruin many prominent people in government, business, and entertainment.

Economic development and social change marked President Eisenhower's second term. The launching of the first man-made satellite (Sputnik) by the Soviet Union encouraged the United States to enter the space race. The modern civil rights movement began as a result of the U.S. Supreme Court decision *Brown* v. *Board of Education of Topeka*. Many Southern schools resisted the ruling that "separate educational facilities are inherently unequal." An act in 1957 established the Civil Rights Commission to investigate illegal voting requirements.

EXERCISE 12: WORLD WAR II
Directions: Write *T* in the space if the statement is true and *F* if it is false.

_____ **1.** Territorial aggression by the Axis powers was a leading cause of World War II.

_____ **2.** Japan's bombing of Pearl Harbor ended the neutrality of the United States.

_____ **3.** The United Nations is a league of nations determined to defend its members in the event of war.

Recent Decades

Kennedy and Johnson The 1960s began with high hopes as a new young president challenged Americans to work for a brighter future. The decade turned into a turbulent period of racial, social, and political divisions. John F. Kennedy, the first Catholic to be elected president, established the Peace Corps and VISTA (Volunteers in Service to America). Kennedy envisioned a "new frontier" of U.S. manned space flights that would land Americans on the moon before the end of the decade.

In 1961, Kennedy established a blockade to prevent Soviet ships from reaching Cuba, demanding that missile sites in Cuba be dismantled. Not wanting to risk war, Soviet Premier Khrushchev agreed. Kennedy continued Eisenhower's civil rights policies, and the Rev. Martin Luther King, Jr., led nonviolent protests. Kennedy was assassinated in 1963 before many of his social programs became a reality.

President Lyndon Baines Johnson vowed to continue Kennedy's programs. He pushed social legislation through Congress as a basis for his "Great Society." Most significant were the Civil Rights Act (1964), forbidding racial discrimination in public places and where federal funds were used, and the Voting Rights Act (1965), which protected the right of African Americans to vote. American involvement in the Vietnam War escalated in 1963–1968, and public controversy divided Americans. Antiwar protests occurred, and Johnson chose not to seek reelection.

The Nixon Era The Vietnam War continued, including President Richard M. Nixon's ordering of troops into Cambodia. He gradually withdrew troops and negotiated a pullout by 1973. Nixon's policy of *détente* (easing of tensions between nations) helped establish the Strategic Arms Limitation Talks (SALT) agreement (limiting of missiles) with the Soviet Union. He visited the People's Republic of China (1972), and the United States became a major peacekeeping influence. Overshadowing these accomplishments was the Watergate scandal (1972), which forced Nixon to resign to avoid impeachment proceedings. Vice President Gerald Ford finished Nixon's term of office.

Carter Washington "outsider" Jimmy Carter was elected in 1976, and he sought to regain the public's confidence in leadership. He confronted problems that included inflation and increasing oil prices. Triumphs included his role in a peace treaty between Egypt and Israel, improved diplomatic relations with China, a second SALT treaty, and return of control of the Panama Canal to Panama. Damaging was the takeover of the American embassy in Iran and the captivity of American hostages. The release of the hostages came on the inauguration day of President Ronald Reagan.

Reagan-Bush President Ronald Reagan was sixty-nine when elected, conservative, and very popular. Under Reagan, many social programs were cut, with replacements expected by states, local governments, and private industry. Poverty and homelessness increased as unemployment soared to levels not seen since the 1930s depression. Great effort went into anticommunist efforts, including a massive military buildup, and hard-line defense policies prevailed.

Political changes during the administration of President George Bush (1989–1993) included the collapse of communism in Eastern Europe, the Persian Gulf War, and the breakup of the Soviet Union. The United States suffered a deepening recession in the early 1990s, the Gross National Product (GPN) fell, and unemployment remained high. Bush's strength was in foreign affairs, and political challengers focused upon needed economic recovery.

Clinton President Bill Clinton was seen in 1992 as a "New" Democrat, a moderate moving away from "tax-and-spend big government." Promising to be a force for change, he directed his efforts toward the federal deficit, job stimulus, health care and welfare reform, diversity (women and minorities in Cabinet and other appointments), limited economic aid to Russia, and intervention in Bosnia.

EXERCISE 13: RECENT DECADES

Directions: Match the presidents with the events that took place during their administrations.

_____ **1.** John F. Kennedy   **(a)** Watergate scandal

_____ **2.** Lyndon B. Johnson   **(b)** Persian Gulf War

_____ **3.** Richard M. Nixon   **(c)** American hostage crisis (Iran)

_____ **4.** Jimmy Carter   **(d)** Cuban Missile Crisis

_____ **5.** Ronald Reagan   **(e)** massive military buildup

_____ **6.** George Bush   **(f)** Voting Rights Act

3
POLITICAL SCIENCE

Human beings are social animals; therefore, people must live in groups. To maintain order in society, governments with rules and laws are established to meet the needs of the individuals who make up society. Important functions of government include making decisions, resolving conflicts, and providing necessary services. *Political scientists* analyze the organization and management of government within a society.

Types of Political Systems

Several types of political systems exist in the world. The differences among political systems chiefly concern the way the government acquires and uses its authority.

dictatorship—A single leader completely controls the political, social, and economic aspects of life in a country. Historical examples include Adolf Hitler (Germany) and Benito Mussolini (Italy). Modern-day examples include Colonel Muammar Gadhafi (Libya) and Saddam Hussein (Iraq).

monarchy—Power to rule is held by a royal family; power is passed to succeeding generations. In the past, *absolute monarchies* had final say in governmental decision making; today most monarchs are bound by the laws of a constitution and have limited authority. An example is Queen Elizabeth II of England, who rules as ceremonial leader, while governmental decisions are made by Parliament, headed by a prime minister.

democracy—Head of the government is chosen by the people; a leader's decisions must meet the approval of the people. Two types of democracies exist today. In a *pure democracy*, people make the decisions directly, which is impractical with a large population. Pure democracy is usually found only in small towns, for example, town meetings in parts of New England. In a *representative democracy*, the people elect representatives to determine policies and make laws for the entire population. An example is the United States.

oligarchy—Government is by a few leaders who form a group. This form is similar to a dictatorship in that government officials are not elected by the people and often come to power after a revolution. A *junta* (*hoon'-tuh*) is a group of persons controlling a government after a revolutionary seizure of power. Modern-day examples include Communist countries such as the former Soviet Union and the People's Republic of China.

ANSWERS TO EXERCISES IN THIS CHAPTER BEGIN ON PAGE 415.

EXERCISE 1: METHODS OF OBTAINING POWER

Directions: Listed are five ways by which goverment leaders may assume power. Read the definitions and apply them to the questions that follow.

ancestry—The leader comes from a family that has led the country for many generations.

divine right—The leader claims to have been placed in his or her position by God.

conquest—The leader acquires territory through military domination.

revolution—The leader comes to power as a result of an overthrow of the existing political system.

popular vote—The leader is chosen by the vote of the people he or she is to govern.

1. The French, inspired in part by the revolt of the thirteen colonies against England, replaced their monarchy with a republic. The new leader came to power by
   (1) ancestry
   (2) divine right
   (3) conquest
   (4) revolution
   (5) popular vote

2. Czechoslovakia maintained its independence in the 1930s until Hitler's army occupied the small nation and forced it to become part of the Third Reich. Hitler acquired power over Czechoslovakia by
   (1) ancestry
   (2) divine right
   (3) conquest
   (4) revolution
   (5) popular vote

The U.S. Federal Government

The U.S. Constitution is based on the idea of federalism. Under *federalism*, the authority of the government is divided between the states and a central government. The central government is further divided into three branches: the *legislative*, which makes the laws; the *executive*, which carries out the laws; and the *judicial*, which interprets the laws. Under this separation of powers, no one part of government is able to dominate another. Each branch of government is able to exert its authority to prevent another branch from becoming too powerful.

The Legislative Branch:
Maker of Laws

The powers of the legislative branch of the government are outlined in Article One of the Constitution. The U.S. legislature, called the U.S. Congress, is made up of two houses—the House of Representatives and the Senate. The House of Representatives is called the lower house, and the Senate is called the upper house, although their powers are basically equal.

In the House of Representatives, each state's number of representatives is based on its population in relationship to the population of the entire country. Smaller states have fewer representatives than larger states. To determine the correct number of representatives a state should have, a *census*, or counting of the population, occurs every ten years. In the Senate, each state is equally represented with two senators. Representatives are chosen by popular election and serve for two years. Senators are chosen by popular election also, although under the original Constitution they were chosen by the state legislatures. Senators serve six-year terms.

The U.S. Congress has the power to

- levy and collect taxes
- borrow money
- regulate commerce
- coin money
- declare war
- provide and maintain an army and navy

- approve treaties (Senate only)
- impeach the president (House only)
- try an impeached president (Senate only)
- introduce bills other than tax bills
- introduce a revenue or tax bill (House only)
- approve presidential appointments (Senate only)
- admit new states to the Union

These powers are called *enumerated* powers because they are listed in Article One of the U.S. Constitution. In addition to enumerated powers, the Constitution provides for powers that are not listed. The *elastic clause* enables the legislative branch to stretch its authority to meet the needs of specific situations that the authors of the Constitution could not foresee.

EXERCISE 2: LEGISLATIVE REPRESENTATION
Directions: Choose the best answer for each of the questions below.

1. Which of the following states is likely to have the least number of representatives in the House?
   (1) Texas
   (2) New York
   (3) Alaska
   (4) California
   (5) Georgia

2. Although New Jersey is smaller in size than Wyoming and Nevada, it has a larger number of representatives. Based on this fact, which of the following can you infer to be true?
   (1) New Jersey has a dwindling population.
   (2) New Jersey is primarily an urban, industrial state.
   (3) New Jersey is a densely populated state.
   (4) both 1 and 2
   (5) both 2 and 3

EXERCISE 3: THE LEGISLATIVE BRANCH

Directions: Write *C* in the space if the action listed is an example of a power stated in the U.S. Constitution and listed on page 116. Write *E* in the space if it is an example of an application of the elastic clause.

_____ **1.** Congress approved economic sanctions against the apartheid regime of South Africa.

_____ **2.** Congress reformed the nation's tax structure in 1986.

_____ **3.** The Ninety-Ninth Congress introduced legislation to abolish the mandatory retirement age for workers.

The Executive Branch: Enforcer of the Laws

Article Two of the U.S. Constitution outlines the powers of the executive branch of the U.S. government. The executive branch consists of the president, vice president, and all of the agencies and departments that are necessary to administer and enforce the laws of the country. As described in Article Two of the U.S. Constitution, the president

- is commander-in-chief of the armed forces
- has power to grant reprieves and pardons for offenses against the United States
- may appoint judges to the U.S. Supreme Court and ambassadors (with the approval of the Senate)
- may nominate and appoint major executive officers
- may veto (refuse to approve) bills sent by Congress

Vagueness of executive authority has allowed each president to shape the office to his own personality. "Strong" presidents, to some extent, have dominated the legislative branch and have relied less on the advice of their cabinets and direction from Congress. Strong presidents frequently use their veto power. "Weak" presidents, on the other hand, have made the office subordinate to the legislature, have relied more on their cabinets, and have been less authoritative. Generally speaking, however, the office of president has been one of increasing authority.

The president serves for four years and is limited to a maximum of two terms. The vice president serves if the president becomes disabled or dies in office before completing the term. The president and vice president are chosen by popular vote, but the electoral college later officially certifies the results of the popular election. The *electoral college* consists of a group of electors from each state who, a month after the general election, cast votes for the president and vice president. To be officially elected president, a candidate must receive a majority of the electoral votes. Originally established to serve as a check and balance against an unsound decision made by the voters, the electoral college today is a target of much criticism. Many politicians believe that the institution has outlived its usefulness and should be abolished.

In general, the candidate who receives the majority of a state's popular vote almost always receives the state's electoral votes. Only twice has a candidate received the majority of the popular vote but lost the election because of the electoral vote (1876 and 1888 elections).

EXERCISE 4: THE EXECUTIVE BRANCH
Directions: Choose the best answer for each question below.

1. Which of the following early presidents best fits the description of a "strong" president?
   (1) President Madison, a statesman who declared war on Britain in 1812 only after popular demand called for it
   (2) President John Adams, who believed that the governing representatives should be "the rich, the well-born, and the able"
   (3) President Thomas Jefferson, who had qualms about the Louisiana Purchase and opposed the first Bank of the United States on the grounds that the Constitution did not provide for it
   (4) President James Monroe, who advanced the idea of the Monroe Doctrine on the advice of his secretary of state, John Quincy Adams
   (5) President Andrew Jackson, who made unprecedented use of his veto power and who relied little on Congress and his cabinet in making his decisions

2. Originally, the second highest vote-getter in a presidential election automatically became vice president. This was changed later when parties were founded and candidates for president and vice president ran together on a ticket. Which of the following is the best explanation as to why the policy for electing the vice president was changed?
   (1) The Constitution required that candidates for the offices of president and vice president be from the same party.
   (2) The country was better served when the candidates for president and vice president came from different regions of the country.
   (3) Before the system was changed, it was easier to cheat a candidate out of the presidency.
   (4) Too many unqualified candidates for the presidency were running for office; the new system guaranteed the candidates would be better qualified.
   (5) The new system prevented the vice president (who often had opposing political views) from obstructing the president's ability to govern.

The Judicial Branch: Interpreter of the Laws

Article Three of the Constitution describes the Supreme Court of the United States. The purpose of the Supreme Court is to rule on the constitutionality of certain laws passed by Congress, the president, and the states themselves. The authority to decide whether or not a law is in keeping with the spirit of the Constitution is called *judicial review*.

The Supreme Court is composed of nine justices appointed for life by the president (with the approval of the Senate). The head of the court is called the *chief justice*. The judicial branch of the federal government consists of the U.S. Supreme Court, the eleven Circuit Courts of Appeal distributed throughout the country, and approximately ninety federal District Courts. Some of the powers vested in the Supreme Court are the powers to rule on the following: cases involving a state and citizens of another state, controversies between two or more states, cases between citizens of different states, cases between a state and its citizens or between a foreign state and U.S. citizens, conflicts arising on the high seas, and conflicts over patents and copyrights. In carrying out its rulings, a decision is reached when a majority of the justices of the Supreme Court agree.

EXERCISE 5: THE JUDICIAL BRANCH
Directions: Choose the best answer to complete the following statement.

Chief Justice Charles Evans Hughes wrote in 1907, "The Constitution is what the Judges say it is." This quote best defines the Supreme Court's power of
(1) checks and balances
(2) ignoring the decisions made by the legislative branch
(3) being "above the law"
(4) judicial review
(5) judicial supremacy

EXERCISE 6: STATES' VERSUS INDIVIDUALS' RIGHTS
Throughout the history of the U.S. Supreme Court, the court has had to decide whether or not it should preserve and uphold the federal system (which included supporting the authority of the individual states) or uphold the rights of the individual.

Directions: For each of these landmark cases, write *I* if it is a victory for the rights of the individual.

_____ **1.** the case of *Plessy* v. *Ferguson* (1896), in which the Supreme Court upheld a lower-court decision that separate but equal facilities for blacks and whites were correct and legal
_____ **2.** the case of *Roe* v. *Wade* (1973), in which the court ruled that states could not prohibit abortion under certain conditions during the first six months of pregnancy
_____ **3.** the case of *Miranda* v. *Arizona* (1966), in which the court ruled that a person accused of a crime must be informed of his or her rights or any resulting confession would be invalid

System of Checks and Balances

The framers of the Constitution understood that the powers of the three branches had to be balanced so that no one center of power dominated the other two. To prevent this from happening, the U.S. Constitution allows for certain actions by one branch to restrain the activities of another. One such restraint is the ability of the president to refuse approval, or veto, a bill sent from Congress.

However, Congress could still pass the bill into law by a vote of two-thirds of its members. This procedure is called *overriding a veto*. Finally, if the issue is brought to the Supreme Court, the court can declare the law unconstitutional. This happens if the justices conclude that the law contradicts the principles of the Constitution.

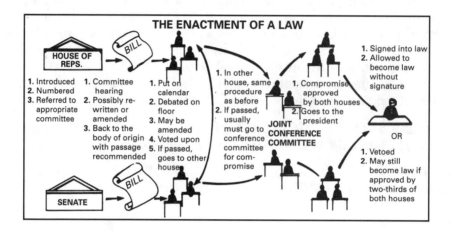

EXERCISE 7: THE ENACTMENT OF A LAW

Directions: Choose the best answer for the following question.
Which statement is best supported by the preceding chart?

(1) Bills justified by the elastic clause in the Constitution must be introduced directly by the president.
(2) Before being sent to the president, a bill must be approved in identical form by both houses of Congress.
(3) A filibuster on certain bills may not take place in either house.
(4) A bill introduced in the Senate may be changed by the House but not the other way around.
(5) The president must sign all bills for them to become law.

EXERCISE 8: SYSTEM OF CHECKS AND BALANCES

Directions: In column I, write the *branch* of government that *exercises* the power described on the left. In column II, write the *branch* of government that is *checked* by the use of the power.

Power	I Who exercises power?	II Who is checked?
1. to appoint federal judges	(a) _____	(b) _____
2. to impeach the president	(a) _____	(b) _____
3. to rule a law unconstitutional	(a) _____	(b) _____

State and Local Governments

State Government

Article Four of the Constitution defines the role of the states. The structure of the state government resembles that of the federal government. The executive authority of the state is the governor. Like the president, the governor has veto power.

The legislative branch, which makes the laws, is composed of two houses in all states except Nebraska. Each state has its own court system, which includes trial courts, appellate courts, and a state supreme court. Also, each state has its own written constitution (most of which are based on the federal model).

The state constitution outlines the powers and duties of the various state officials and agencies. Like the federal system, the fifty states have systems of checks and balances among the three branches of government.

Most criminal codes and civil laws are established by state law. The state also establishes laws for contracts, chartering businesses, and marriage and divorce. Another responsibility of state government is to charter local governments. The powers of municipalities—villages, towns, and cities—are outlined and defined in a charter approved by the state.

EXERCISE 9: POWERS OF STATE GOVERNMENT
Directions: In the spaces provided, write *S* if the power belongs to the states, *F* if it belongs to the federal government, and *B* if it belongs to both.

_____ **1.** vetoing a bill by the chief executive

_____ **2.** declaring war against a foreign country

_____ **3.** establishing a legal age for drinking alcoholic beverages

Local Government

While the structure and organization of the federal and state governments are similar, local governments can be quite different. Local governments are usually one of three types:

mayor-council—mayor elected; council members represent districts
council-manager—council elected; manager hired to oversee operations
commission—commissioners elected to run departments like
    police/fire, public works

All municipalities receive most of the money to operate from local taxes, fees, and service charges.

The U.S. Political System

The voting public has been viewed as holding a range of positions on political issues. These political positions are illustrated as occupying one of five segments of a spectrum. The segments are generally referred to as political labels. To win an election, each political party must obtain the majority of the votes cast. Since most American voters occupy the middle of the spectrum, both political parties must appeal to this group of voters to win.

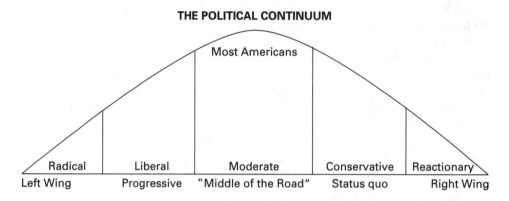

THE POLITICAL CONTINUUM

Most Americans

Radical	Liberal	Moderate	Conservative	Reactionary
Left Wing	Progressive	"Middle of the Road"	Status quo	Right Wing

radical—advocates sweeping changes in laws and methods of government

liberal—advocates political change for progress, especially social improvement

moderate—believes in avoiding extreme changes and measures

conservative—advocates the existing social order and only gradual change

reactionary—resists change and advocates a return to earlier policies

EXERCISE 10: THE POLITICAL SPECTRUM
Directions: Identify the political position of each of the quotes.

An issue in American life that has generated many positions and has divided the population is bilingualism. Many Americans are concerned that we are quickly becoming a bilingual country—the primary and secondary languages being English and Spanish. Americans have varying opinions about the increasing concessions made to our Spanish-speaking minority.

1. "We might as well accept the fact that Hispanic-Americans are here to stay and are significant contributors to our American way of life. Instead of criticizing them for speaking in their native tongue, the government should improve bilingual programs to make it easier for Hispanics to learn English." The speaker is best expressing the opinion of a

   (1) radical   **(2)** liberal   **(3)** moderate   **(4)** conservative   **(5)** reactionary

2. "English has been the primary language here and always will be. I suggest that before Hispanics are granted citizenship or are given jobs, they should be made to pass a test on standard English." The speaker is expressing the opinion of a

   (1) radical   **(2)** liberal   **(3)** moderate   **(4)** conservative   **(5)** reactionary

3. "Unless the laws that treat Mexicans as second-class citizens because of their inability to speak the language are changed immediately, starting tomorrow, Mexicans should stop picking lettuce, washing dishes, and sweeping floors—doing the dirty work at low pay that other Americans think they are above doing." The speaker is expressing the opinion of a

   (1) radical   **(2)** liberal   **(3)** moderate   **(4)** conservative   **(5)** reactionary

Political Parties

A *political party* is a group whose goal is to influence public policy by getting its candidates elected to office. Although the U.S. Constitution makes no provision for political parties, they serve useful functions in our democracy. Political parties define the issues and propose possible solutions for governmental problems. They act as another check in our governmental system of checks and balances by monitoring the policies of the party in power. Parties enable citizens to become involved in the governmental apparatus and help to keep the number of candidates running for public office manageable.

For over a century, there have been two major political parties in the United States—the Democrats and the Republicans. The differences between the Democratic and Republican parties tend to center around domestic, economic, and social issues as well as foreign policy. Most fundamentally, however, the two parties differ in their views of the role of government in solving problems.

In general, the Democratic party favors a strong federal government at the expense of the sovereign rights of the states; advocates government regulation of big business; endorses labor unions; and champions the rights of the disadvantaged and minorities. The Republican party, on the other hand, generally favors stronger state authority at the expense of the federal government; advocates free enterprise; supports checks on labor unions; and believes in maintaining the status quo (keeping things as they are). There are exceptions to these generalizations, of course; and in recent years, the distinctions between the two parties have become increasingly blurred.

EXERCISE 11: POLITICAL PARTIES

Directions: Write *D* in the space provided if the statement generally applies to the Democratic party's philosophy and *R* if it generally applies to the Republican party's philosophy.

_____ **1.** favors having state and local governments solve their own problems

_____ **2.** supports labor unions and the right of their members to strike

_____ **3.** advocates spending large amounts of money for welfare and other social services

Pressure Groups

Once public officials are elected, they are under constant pressure exerted by individuals, businesses, governmental agencies, and others who make up their constituency. *Pressure groups* are organized groups not associated with a political party who actively seek to influence public opinion, policies, and actions. The attempt to influence legislation is called *lobbying*. Lobbyists constantly watch for bills that may affect the group or groups they represent. Political Action Committees, known as PACs, seek to influence public officials directly.

The Electoral Process

Both the Democratic and Republican parties maintain national party headquarters and staffs. Every four years, a national convention is held to nominate a presidential candidate, who must win a majority of delegates either in the primaries and caucuses that precede the nominating convention or at the convention itself. A political *primary* enables members of a party to express their preference for a candidate to run in the general election. In most primary elections, the candidate must receive a *plurality* (more votes than any other candidate) to win. Primaries may be open or closed. In an *open primary* voters need not declare their party affiliations. In a *closed primary* voters must declare whether they are Republicans or Democrats. *Caucuses* are local meetings in a state where party members meet and vote for their preferred candidates.

At the nominating convention, each state sends a designated number of delegates, who are local and state party representatives, to help select the party's nominee. At the end of a week-long forum in which the issues are discussed and speeches are delivered, the delegates vote to choose the party's nominee and to approve the party's platform. The *platform* is a formal declaration of the principles for which the party stands.

After the candidates from each party campaign for office, the general election is held. In the general election, the winner must receive a *majority* of the votes cast in the electoral college. A candidate can win without a majority of the popular votes but must receive a majority in the electoral college. If no such majority results, the election is decided by the House of Representatives. Once elected, public officials are responsible to a *constituency*—the people who elected them to office.

EXERCISE 12: ELECTING A PRESIDENT

Directions: Match each definition on the right with the correct term on the left.

_____ **1.** primary   **(a)** declaration of a party's stand on the issues

_____ **2.** platform   **(b)** the people a public official represents

_____ **3.** constituency   **(c)** party election to select a candidate to run in the general election

EXERCISE 13: THE ELECTORAL PROCESS

Directions: Choose the best answer for the following question.

Based on the definition of a closed primary, which of the following practices is generally true in order for the results to be valid?

(1) Republicans and Democrats alike can vote in any primary they choose.
(2) Voters should declare their party affiliations (Republican or Democrat) and vote in the respective primary.
(3) Voters need not declare whether or not they are Republican or Democrat when they vote in a primary.
(4) Voters should bypass the primary and only vote in the general election.
(5) Voters should not be eligible to vote in primaries; primaries are only for party regulars on the local and state levels.

4
ECONOMICS

There is more to human survival than meeting the needs of food, shelter, and clothing. *Economists* study how a society meets its unlimited material needs with its limited resources. The limitation of resources requires that people make choices about what needs to satisfy.

Societies also must make choices. Every society must answer three basic questions when determining the type of economic system under which it will operate. These questions are

- What should be produced?
- How should it be produced?
- How should the product be distributed?

To answer these questions, each government must first identify its goals and values and then determine what resources are available to produce what the society needs.

Factors of Production

Economists have identified three vital factors of production: natural resources, capital, and labor.

Natural resources are the raw materials needed to produce goods. Trees must be available for the production of wood and paper products. Automobiles can be built only if ore can be mined to make the necessary steel. *Capital*, as it is referred to here, is any equipment, factories, or machines that are used to produce other goods or to provide services. Capital also may be defined as money invested in an enterprise. A sewing machine and an entire lumber mill are examples of capital. *Labor* is made up of the people who do the work. They run the assembly lines, plant the crops, build the buildings, drive the trucks, and sell the merchandise.

History has shown that no matter how carefully and efficiently an economy manages the factors of production, they remain scarce as compared to the ever increasing demands society makes upon them.

ANSWERS TO EXERCISES IN THIS CHAPTER BEGIN ON PAGE 416.

EXERCISE 1: FACTORS OF PRODUCTION
Directions: In each example, write *N* if the factor of production refers to natural resources, *C* if it refers to capital, and *L* if it refers to labor.

_____ **1.** the tools a plumber uses in practicing the trade

_____ **2.** diamonds unearthed from the mines of South Africa

_____ **3.** farmers who plant the spring corn crop

Economics and Government

A nation's system of government often determines the type of economic system under which the nation will operate. For example, the U.S. system of government is founded on the principle of individual freedom. This belief in the importance of individual freedom contributed greatly to the establishment of capitalism as the economic form under which the American economy operates.

Capitalism

Capitalism is an economic system based on the private ownership of the resources of production. Investment decisions are made by the individual or corporation rather than by the government. The production, distribution, and prices of goods and services are determined by competition in a free market. The government intervenes only when necessary to protect the public interest.

Socialism

Under *socialism*, the most important industries and services are publicly and cooperatively owned. These industries, which may be steel production, banking and finance, public transportation, or health, are controlled with the goal of providing equal opportunity for all.

In socialist economies, ownership of private property is permitted; however, owners of businesses, together with the government, decide what goods and services are produced, how they are produced, and who should get them. The economy of Sweden is a socialist economy.

Communism

A third economic order does not permit private ownership of property and the means of production at all. Under *communism*, the government owns the property and distributes the society's goods in accordance with the "common good." The government decides what goods and services are produced and who should get them. Examples are the economies of the People's Republic of China (prior to recent reforms), Cuba, and the former Soviet Union.

None of these three economic systems exists in pure form. That is, no *completely* capitalist, socialist, or communist economy exists in the modern world. In its operation, each of the economic systems incorporates some aspects of another. The term *mixed economy* is used to describe the U.S. economy because some government regulation of private enterprise exists. For example, the Food and Drug Administration ensures that any new medicine or drug that is marketed in the United States has been properly tested before it is sold to the public.

EXERCISE 2: ECONOMIC SYSTEMS AND GOVERNMENTS

Directions: Choose the best answer to complete each of the following statements.

1. The quote "In the area of economics, the government that governs least governs best" best describes the economic system of
   (a) capitalism
   (b) socialism
   (c) communism

MARKET | Capitalism | Socialism | Communism | COMMAND

2. According to the continuum of economic systems, which of the following conclusions may be drawn?
(1) Communism is the best example of the market system.
(2) Capitalism is the best example of the command system.
(3) Socialism is the opposite of capitalism.
(4) Capitalism is the opposite of communism.
(5) Capitalism is better than any other system represented.

Supply and Demand

The foundation of American capitalism is supply and demand. *Supply* is the quantity of goods and services available for sale at all possible prices. *Demand* is the desire to buy the product or service and the ability to pay for it.

Producers or suppliers are in business to make a profit. Therefore, they supply goods and services at a price. They must charge prices high enough to cover their costs for production and earn a profit for themselves. Consumers who are willing and able to buy these goods and services create a demand.

The amount of production (supply) of an item and its price depend on the cost of production and the demand in the marketplace. In general, producers seek the highest possible prices to maximize their profits. Consumers seek the lowest possible prices to keep money in their pockets. These opposing goals of producers and consumers significantly affect prices in the marketplace.

Price and Supply—The Producer's View

In general, the higher the price, the greater the number of companies that supply a product or service. A high-priced item or service that yields a large profit will attract many producers who will compete with one another for a share of the market. A good example of the relationship between price and supply is the running-shoes phenomenon. Consumers—adults and teens— paid higher prices for labels such as Nike and Reebok than they ordinarily might have for other brands. As a result, several competitors entered the market (increasing the supply) seeking to make money on the product. When too many producers compete in the marketplace, however, supply exceeds demand because buyers cannot or will not buy all of the goods offered for sale. As a result, a surplus occurs and prices fall.

Price and Supply—The Consumer's View

From the consumer's viewpoint, the higher the price, the lower the demand; the lower the price, the greater the demand. If prices for running shoes became too high, consumers might stop buying them and revert to wearing off-brands. On the other hand, when prices for an item fall too low and consumer demand exceeds the producer's ability to provide the product, a shortage in supply occurs. As a result, prices rise higher, and in extreme cases, the product is rationed. Under rationing, the quantity of the item sold is restricted.

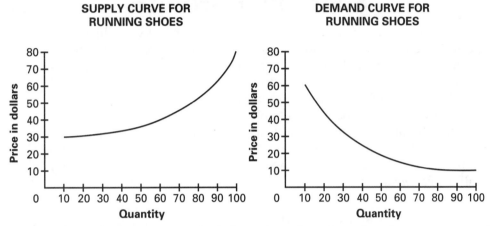

As shown in the graph on the left, as the price of running shoes goes up, the quantity supplied increases. As shown in the graph on the right, as the price of running shoes goes down, the quantity demanded rises.

Supply and Equilibrium

To produce exactly the amount that consumers are willing to buy, producers must determine at what point supply equals demand. Economists call this point the *equilibrium*. Equilibrium occurs when the supply and demand curves intersect. This establishes the market price for a product or service. When the price is greater than the equilibrium, demand falls and there is more of a product or service than people want to buy. This is called a *surplus*. When the price falls below the equilibrium, demand increases, exceeding supply, and a *shortage* in the product or service occurs.

EXERCISE 3: SUPPLY, DEMAND, AND EQUILIBRIUM

Directions: Study the graph and answer the following questions or statements.

1. According to the graph, the market price of these videocassette recorders would be about
   (1) $500
   (2) $400
   (3) $300
   (4) $250
   (5) $200

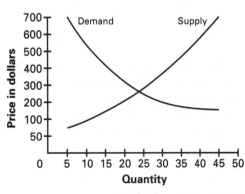

SUPPLY, DEMAND, AND EQUILIBRIUM
Videocassette Recorders

2. If the market price for videocassette recorders fell to $150, what would be the likely result?
   (1) Demand would decrease.
   (2) Supply would remain the same.
   (3) Demand would increase.
   (4) Producers would not be able to satisfy demand.
   (5) The supply would become scarce.

Economic Growth

Economic growth is a major goal of an economic system. In a growing economy, there is an increasing capacity to produce more goods and services. During periods of great economic growth, consumers are increasingly able to buy these goods and services. An economy's growth should occur at a steady and controllable pace.

This process may be likened to blowing up a balloon. If a balloon is inflated too quickly, it may burst; if it is inflated too slowly, it may never reach its full capacity. Similarly, the American economy must grow evenly, or problems will occur. The following diagram illustrates what economists call the *business cycle*.

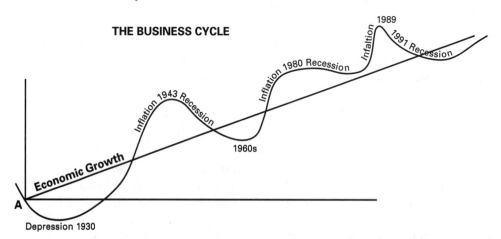

Line A is the goal of economic growth—what economists believe is a healthy level of producing goods and services.

Inflation and Its Effects

When too much money and credit are available and too few goods are available to satisfy demand, the dollar loses its value and the prices of goods increase. The country begins a period of inflation. (Notice the upward slope of the line.)

For consumers to be able to keep pace with the rise in the cost of goods, their wages must increase. For producers to pay the increased wages, they must produce more goods and charge higher prices for them. This chainlike pattern in which wage increases feed on price increases is called an *inflationary spiral*. For inflation to fall, demand must be decreased and credit restricted. However, one result of curbing high inflation is often an economic recession.

Deflation and Its Effects

When too little money and credit are available, and more goods are available than necessary to satisfy demand, the dollar gains value and the prices of goods decrease. Under these circumstances, the economy enters a period of deflation. Because goods remain unsold, producers' profits fall. Falling profits lead to layoffs. Unless the situation is corrected, a recession occurs; if the recession is prolonged, a depression can result. The United States experienced this condition during the Great Depression of the 1930s.

Measurement of Economic Growth

Economic indicators are statistics that show economic experts how the economy is performing. Among the more commonly used economic statistics are stock market trading, unemployment percentages, number of housing starts, and the gross national product (GNP).

One of the most important measurements of economic growth, the *GNP* represents the total value of all goods and services produced in one year. Economists measure GNP in current dollars and again in constant dollars. *Current* dollars indicate the actual dollar value of goods. *Constant* dollars take into account the change in prices over the years because of inflation. In measuring the nation's GNP, economists measure current dollars against constant dollars during a given year. In recent years, economists have used 1987 as the base year with which to compare current GNP dollars.

Money and Monetary Policy

Money is the medium of exchange accepted by a society in payment for goods and services. The nation's money supply consists mainly of coins, bills, and checking and savings deposits. The U.S. Federal Reserve Board is responsible for setting the nation's *monetary policy*—the regulation of the nation's supply of money and credit in order to keep the economy in balance. Through the nation's banking system, the Federal Reserve Board controls the availability of credit to consumers primarily in two ways—by determining the reserve ratio and by setting the discount rate.

The Reserve Ratio

Every lending institution—banks and savings and loan associations—must hold on to a certain amount of its deposits. This amount that cannot be lent out is called the *reserve ratio*. Most banks are members of the nation's Federal Reserve System (the Fed). By controlling the reserve ratio, the Fed determines the amount of money banks are able to lend.

The Discount Rate

A second way in which the Fed influences the nation's economy is through the *discount rate*. The discount rate is the rate of interest the Fed charges member banks to borrow money. Banks make money by charging a higher interest rate on loans than they pay to those who deposit money into checking and savings accounts.

To have more money to meet demand, banks often borrow from the Federal Reserve System. The bank then lends the money to its customers (borrowers) at a higher rate. The Fed adjusts the discount rate to affect the supply of money. For example, if the discount rate is 5 percent, consumer banks might lend it out for 10 percent. Thus, you can see the impact a changing discount rate has on the availability of credit in the U.S. economy.

EXERCISE 4: MONEY AND MONETARY POLICY

Directions: Circle *T* if the statement is true or *F* if it is false.

T F **1.** Purchasing power is increased through the banking system by banks lending funds from deposited money after first setting aside required reserves.

T F **2.** Most banks belong to the Federal Reserve System.

T F **3.** The prime rate is the interest rate the Fed charges member banks to borrow money.

Government and Fiscal Policy

While the U.S. Federal Reserve Board directly influences the supply of money and credit in the economy, the government, through its fiscal policy, also indirectly affects the nation's economic condition. In establishing *fiscal policy*, the president proposes an annual budget to the Congress. As Congress determines what programs are needed, it must also consider how these programs will be funded. Raising taxes is the simplest and most common answer.

Consumers and businesses pay these taxes to the government. The government, in turn, spends the money on programs designed to help the citizens and the country, such as interstate highways, the space program, and the military. By deciding whether to raise or lower taxes and whether to increase or decrease spending, the government is controlling a major part of the money supply.

If the government spends less than it collects in taxes, a *budget surplus* results. If the government spends more than it collects, the condition is called *deficit spending.* A *balanced budget* results when the income from taxes equals the money spent on programs.

EXERCISE 5: FISCAL AND MONETARY POLICY

Directions: Circle the correct answer choice in parentheses.

1. During a recession, to put more money in circulation, the president and Congress should (increase/decrease) government spending while (raising/lowering) taxes.

2. During an inflationary period, the Fed should (increase/decrease) the money in circulation by (raising/lowering) the discount rate while (increasing/decreasing) the reserve ratio.

5
GEOGRAPHY

Geographers study the physical features of the earth and the ways in which humans have adapted to these features. In their investigation of the surfaces and regions of the earth, geographers rely on two basic tools. A *globe* is a spherical representation of the earth that shows the continents, countries, and waterways in their true proportions. Globes are not easily portable, however, so mapmakers draw *maps*, which are flat representations of the earth's regions.

Maps

There are many different types of maps. The following are a few examples:

topographical maps—show physical land features (hills, mountains, plains) of an area
political maps—show borders between countries or states
population maps—illustrate the distribution of people over an area
weather and climate maps—show current or forecasted weather or climates

These and other types of maps can show anything from a small area to the entire world.

Symbols and Legends

So that you can read a map, mapmakers provide symbols and a legend, or key, that tells what the symbols stand for. For example, on a political map, a star usually indicates a state's or nation's capital. On population maps, the number of people who live in a given city is often indicated by the size of the dot that locates the city. (Larger dots indicate cities with large populations; small dots indicate cities with small populations.)

A scale of miles or kilometers is often provided in the legend. The legend on a map scale might read "One inch equals 50 miles." An example of a scale is shown on the next page. You can measure distance with a ruler or with a strip of paper that has a straight edge.

EXERCISE 1: MEASURING DISTANCE

Directions: Study the map and answer the questions that follow.

1. According to the map shown here, approximately how far is Denver from San Francisco? _____

2. Approximately how far is the west coast of California from the eastern boundary of Colorado? _____

Latitude and Longitude

The *equator*, an imaginary line that circles the earth halfway between the poles, divides the earth into two *hemispheres*, or halves. The half of the earth north of the equator is the Northern Hemisphere; the half south of the equator is the Southern Hemisphere. North America, Central America, and a small part of South America lie in the Northern Hemisphere.

The distance from the equator is measured on maps and globes by degrees of latitude. Lines of *latitude* are parallel lines that measure distance north or south of the equator in degrees. The equator is located at 0 degrees latitude, the North Pole at 90 degrees north latitude, and the South Pole at 90 degrees south latitude. Most of the continental United States lies between 25 and 50 degrees north latitude.

Lines of *longitude* are lines that measure distances in degrees east and west of the *prime meridian*, an imaginary line running pole to pole through Greenwich, England, that divides the world into the Eastern and Western Hemispheres. The prime meridian is located at 0 degrees longitude. There are 180 degrees east of the prime meridian and 180 degrees west of it, for a total of 360 degrees around the earth. Most of the United States, including Alaska and Hawaii, lies between 65 and 125 degrees west longitude.

The lines of latitude and longitude cross each other to form what is called a *grid*. To locate a particular place on a globe or map, you must find the point where two lines intersect. The number of degrees of latitude and longitude indicate the location. For example, in the grid diagram below, the island of Madagascar, located off the southeast coast of Africa, is located at approximately 20 degrees south latitude and 45 degrees east longitude.

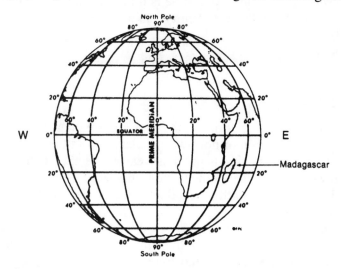

Based on the grid, what continent is found at 50 degrees north latitude and 0 degrees longitude?

[Answer: You should have answered *Europe*. The point where the 50 degree north line of latitude meets the 0 degree line of longitude is the continent of Europe; Europe is located directly north of Africa.]

Time Zones

A *time zone* is a geographical region within which the same standard time is used. To establish time zones for the entire world, geographers have divided the earth into 24 sections, one for each hour of the day. Since the earth is 360 degrees, this means that 15 degrees (360 divided by 24) are equal to one hour of a day. In the 48 contiguous (connected) states of the United States, there are four time zones: Eastern, Central, Mountain, and Pacific, as shown in the following map.

TIME ZONES ACROSS THE UNITED STATES

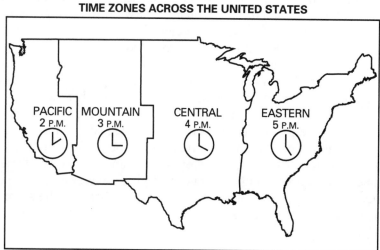

EXERCISE 2: TIME ZONES

Directions: Choose the best answer for each question.

1. According to the map, what time is it in Los Angeles when it is midnight in Philadelphia, Pennsylvania?
   (1) 9:00 A.M.
   (2) 9:00 P.M.
   (3) 3:00 P.M.
   (4) 3:00 A.M.
   (5) 2:00 A.M.

2. The lines marking the four time zones are irregular. All of Indiana except a tiny section of northwest Indiana lies in the Eastern time zone. Which of the following is the most reasonable explanation for why northwest Indiana lies in the Central time zone?
   (1) The people in northwest Indiana voted to be included in the Central time zone.
   (2) The time zones must be evenly divided; in order to obtain an even division of time zones in the United States, part of Indiana was placed in the Central time zone.
   (3) Western Kentucky and western Tennessee, the states south of Indiana, are located in the Central time zone; therefore, northwest Indiana had to comply with the rule.
   (4) Northwest Indiana was once a part of northeast Illinois, which is why the region has a different time zone from the rest of the state.
   (5) Northwest Indiana is considered to be part of Chicago's metropolitan area; therefore, for economic reasons it lies in the same time zone as Chicago.

Topography and Climate

Geographers divide the earth's land into four general landforms: plains, mountains, hills, and plateaus. These land forms are defined by their shape and *elevation* (distance above *sea level*).

Plains typically are areas of flat or gently rolling land (and usually at a low elevation). *Hills* are elevations of less than 1,000 feet that have sides sloping up to flat or rounded tops. *Plateaus* are wide areas of generally flat land at a high elevation. *Mountains* are elevations of over 1,000 feet, with steep inclines on all sides and pointed or rounded tops.

Plains regions have a uniform climate characterized by hot, dry weather during the summer and very cold temperatures during the winter. Because plains are flat, there are no barriers against the cold air that sweeps across them during the winter. Hills and plateaus generally share the climate characteristics of the plains near which they are located, but may be cooler if their elevation is high. Mountains often act as boundaries between different climate regions. The lower slopes of the mountains usually share the climate of the surrounding area, but the higher the elevation, the colder the air gets. The highest mountains are snowcapped because the air around them never rises above freezing.

Mapmakers illustrate the varying heights and shapes of land masses by using ***contour lines***, lines that show elevations in numbers of feet or meters. The closer together the contour lines, the steeper the incline. An example of a contour map follows.

CONTOUR MAP

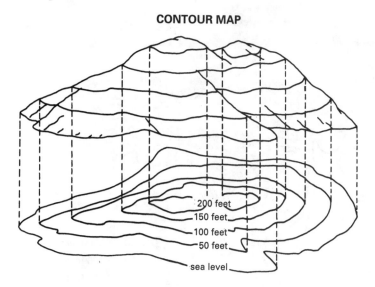

What would this land form be classified as—a hill, plain, mountain, or plateau?

[Answer: Because the land mass is lower than 1,000 feet and has a rounded top, it would be classified as a hill.]

EXERCISE 3: U.S. TOPOGRAPHY

Directions: Choose the best answer for the statement and questions below.

1. Based on its location, which of the following cities in the United States is at the highest altitude?
   (1) Detroit
   (2) Boston
   (3) Denver
   (4) Chicago
   (5) Memphis

2. Low-lying land is often subject to flooding. Land that lies below sea level acts as a bowl that collects water. Which of the following cities best meets this description?
   (1) Las Vegas
   (2) New York City
   (3) New Orleans
   (4) Atlanta
   (5) Phoenix

EXERCISE 4: THE INDIAN SUBCONTINENT
Directions: Study the map and answer the questions that follow.

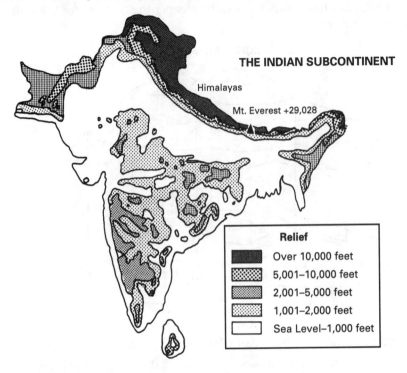

THE INDIAN SUBCONTINENT

Himalayas

Mt. Everest +29,028

Relief

■	Over 10,000 feet
▨	5,001–10,000 feet
▦	2,001–5,000 feet
▨	1,001–2,000 feet
□	Sea Level–1,000 feet

1. What is the highest point in the Himalayas?
   (1) 6,000 feet
   (2) 10,300 feet
   (3) 19,861 feet
   (4) 29,028 feet
   (5) 33,411 feet

2. The majority of the land shown on the map may be generally described as being at an elevation of
   (1) over 10,000 feet
   (2) between 5,000 and 10,000 feet
   (3) between 2,000 and 5,000 feet
   (4) between 1,000 and 2,000 feet
   (5) between sea level and 1,000 feet

TEST 3: SCIENCE

The GED Science Test consists of multiple-choice questions requiring knowledge of basic science concepts. The test emphasizes your ability to think about these concepts. You will not be required to recall isolated facts. Rather, you will read a passage or look at an illustration and answer questions based on it. To answer successfully, you will need to have an understanding of basic science concepts and be able to interpret illustrations and reading passages. You will also have to show that you can understand what you read, apply information to a new situation, analyze relationships among ideas, and make judgments about the material.

How many questions are on the test?

There are 66 multiple-choice questions, and you will be given 95 minutes to complete the test. About two-thirds of the questions will be based on reading passages of up to 250 words each, and one-third will be based on visuals—diagrams, charts, or graphs. Look at the Post-Test at the end of this book as an example.

What's on the test?

The GED Science Test can be broken down into the content areas it covers and the skills it tests: Life Sciences (Biology)—50% and Physical Sciences (Earth Science, Chemistry, and Physics)—50%. Keep in mind that a given question may draw from a number of these subjects. For example, a question on air pollution may draw from material covered in both biology and chemistry.

Also remember that you are being tested on your ability to think through certain ideas and concepts. You will be asked to do more than just find an answer that was given in a passage. Thinking skills that you will be tested on include Understanding Ideas—20%, Applying Ideas—30%, Analyzing Ideas—30%, and Evaluating Ideas—20%.

1
BIOLOGY—THE STUDY OF LIVING THINGS

The scientific study of all life forms is known as *biology*. Biologists are interested in how living things grow, change over time, and interact with one another and their environment. All living things react to stimuli, take in food and grow, eliminate wastes, and reproduce. Let's start with the basic unit of life, the cell.

The Cell, the Basis of Life

The *cell* is the smallest unit of living material capable of carrying on the activities of life. Cells, the "building blocks" of an organism, were first observed in 1665 by Robert Hooke, with the aid of a crudely made microscope. Cells vary widely in size and appearance. It is the number of cells in an organism, however, and not their size, that determines the size of an organism. The cells of a human being and a whale are of equal size. The whale is larger because its genetic pattern dictates that a larger number of cells be produced. An "average" cell measures about 10 micrometers (0.00004 inch) in diameter. This means that a parade of 25,000 typical cells end to end would measure only one inch.

Types of Cells

Two kinds of cells are plant cells and animal cells. The plant cell has a cell wall that protects it, and an animal cell does not. Also, plant cells contain *chloroplasts*, structures active in the food-making process, while animal cells do not. Both plant and animal cells are surrounded by a delicate boundary, the *cell membrane*. The cell membrane preserves the cell by acting as a barrier between it and the outside environment, helps the cell maintain its shape, and regulates molecular traffic passing into and out of the cell.

The following illustration shows the differences between the plant cell and animal cell.

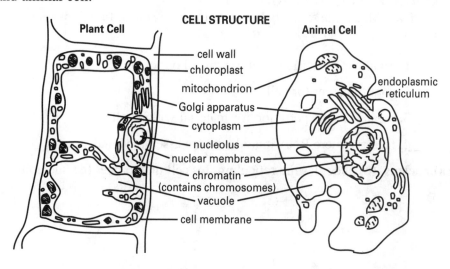

CELL STRUCTURE

Plant Cell

Animal Cell

- cell wall
- chloroplast
- mitochondrion
- Golgi apparatus
- cytoplasm
- nucleolus
- nuclear membrane
- chromatin (contains chromosomes)
- vacuole
- cell membrane

endoplasmic reticulum

Cell Structure

Within the cell membrane is *protoplasm*, a jellylike substance that forms the largest component of the cell. The protoplasm lying between the nuclear membrane and the cell membrane is called *cytoplasm*. A highly specialized and complex structure, the cell has its own control center, transportation system, power plants, factories for making needed materials, and even a reproductive blueprint, or chemical recipe.

Most of the organelles (little organs) performing these functions are located within the cytoplasm. Resembling an intricate tunnel system, the *endoplasmic reticulum* serves as a network for transporting materials from one part of the cell to another or from the cell to the environment. The power plants of the cell are the *mitochondria*, the sites where the cell releases energy for cellular work. Mitochondria are abundant in highly active cells that produce energy for important life processes. For example, more than 1,000 mitochondria have been counted in a single liver cell.

Located in stacks of platelike membranes at one side of the nucleus, the *Golgi apparatus* organelle functions as a packaging plant. Proteins and carbohydrates are gathered together and enclosed in a membranous sac. In gland cells, the Golgi apparatus is responsible for releasing the gland's hormones into the body.

Of all the structures within the cell, the most important is the *nucleus*, the control center of the cell. The nucleus is surrounded by a double nuclear membrane. Pores in the nuclear membrane permit the passage of molecules between the cytoplasm and the nucleus. Within the nucleus are the *chromosomes* and the *nucleolus*. Each chromosome contains several hundred *genes*, which contain *DNA*, a molecular acid that carries instructions on how the organism should develop. While the chromosomes serve as a "chemical recipe" for the cell, the genes might be considered individual ingredients.

The nucleolus is rich in *RNA*, an acid that is essential in the chemical activity of the cell. The nucleolus contains sections of chromosomes that are believed to be important in the manufacture of protein.

ANSWERS TO EXERCISES IN THIS CHAPTER BEGIN ON PAGE 418.

EXERCISE 1: CELL STRUCTURE

Directions: Match the terms below with the mechanical functions they perform.

_____ **1.** regulator of traffic passing into and out of cell

_____ **2.** control center for cell

_____ **3.** means of transportation for material within cell

_____ **4.** factory where RNA ingredients are assembled and stored

(a) nucleus **(b)** endoplasmic reticulum **(c)** cell membrane **(d)** nucleolus

EXERCISE 2: CELLS

Directions: Choose the best answer for each of the following questions.

1. The main purpose of the reading passage is to point out that
   (1) all living things are made of cells
   (2) the nucleus is the control center of the cell
   (3) there are differences between plant and animal cells
   (4) the cell is a highly organized, complex structure with subsystems of its own
   (5) the Golgi apparatus functions as a packaging plant in the cell

2. In plant cells, chloroplasts are active in the chemical processes required to make food. Animal cells have no chloroplasts. Based on this, we can conclude that
   (1) plant cells are more complex than animal cells
   (2) plant cells and not animal cells generate chemical reactions
   (3) animal cells prey upon plant cells as a food source
   (4) animal cells are more complex than plant cells
   (5) animals must obtain food from outside sources

3. According to the passage, mitochondria are the power plants that produce energy for important life processes in the animal cell and are responsible for cellular respiration. What part of a plant cell serves a similar function?
   (1) cell wall
   (2) nucleus
   (3) nucleolus
   (4) chromosome
   (5) chloroplast

Cells and Active Transport

Every cell has a membrane that selectively permits the passage of certain molecules in and out of the cell. The movement of molecules through the cell membrane without any effort on the cell's part is achieved by diffusion. *Diffusion* is the movement of molecules from an area of high concentration to an area of low concentration. Vibrating molecules are propelled away from one another after they collide. It is through this process that odors can fill a large room in a short period of time. Diffusion is important in higher organisms such as the human body. For example, oxygen moves from air sacs in the lungs through cell membranes and into the blood through diffusion.

A cell's cytoplasm contains many substances in varying degrees of concentration. These concentrations differ sharply from those in the fluid surrounding the cell. Such differences are so essential that the cell can die if the differences are not maintained. Given the opportunity, diffusion would quickly eliminate these critical differences. Therefore, the cell must be able to negate, and sometimes even reverse, the process of diffusion. This is accomplished by active transport. During *active transport*, the cell moves materials from an area of low concentration to an area of high concentration. This work requires energy.

EXERCISE 3: CELLS AND ACTIVE TRANSPORT

Directions: In the blank spaces below, supply the words that correctly complete each statement.

1. Diffusion is the movement of molecules from an area of

   _____ concentration to an area of

   _____ concentration.

2. In active transport, materials are moved from an area of

   _____ concentration to an area of

   _____ concentration.

EXERCISE 4: DIFFUSION AND OSMOSIS

Directions: Choose the best answer for each of the following questions.

1. In the human body, the process of diffusion
   (1) allows for concentrations of materials where needed in the body through stockpiling
   (2) regulates blood flow
   (3) allows an even distribution of substances throughout all cells of the body
   (4) comes into play in times of extreme illness
   (5) plays an insignificant role in the body's functioning

2. *Osmosis* may be described as a process by which water in a solution is able to move through the cell membrane from a lower concentration to a higher one in order to maintain balance on either side of the membrane. If the salt solution in blood plasma surrounding red blood cells is higher than the solution inside the cells, which is most likely to occur?
   (1) Water will leave the cell and pass into the blood plasma.
   (2) Water will leave the blood plasma and pass into the cell.
   (3) The cell will shrink because of a loss of water.
   (4) 1 and 2
   (5) 1 and 3

Mitosis—Cell Division

An organism has the capacity to grow. As a cell grows, its cell membrane becomes unable to provide oxygen and nutrients for the interior of the cell and wastes are unable to leave the cell. In addition, a nucleus can control only so much cytoplasm. Therefore, when a cell reaches its limit in size, it must divide, or undergo a process called mitosis.

Mitosis is the process by which cells reproduce themselves by division. In a multicellular organism, mitosis leads to tissue growth and maintenance. In a single-celled organism, mitosis results in two new genetically identical, independent organisms. Mitosis can be divided into four stages or phases, as shown by the following.

Stage 1: Prophase

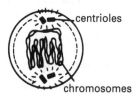

Genetic material in the nucleus is duplicated (doubled). Then, as prophase begins, the nuclear membrane and nucleolus disappear. The genetic material, which has not been easy to view, now becomes evident as long, threadlike bodies, the chromosomes. As prophase continues, centrioles appear at opposite ends of the cells and small fibers start to form between them.

Stage 2: Metaphase

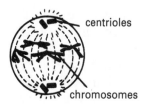

The spindle fibers attach themselves to the genetic material at the center of the chromosomes (centromeres). The chromosomes are now quite thick and visible. They begin to line up at the equator of the cell.

Stage 3: Anaphase

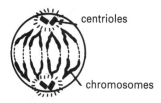

The centromeres divide, and the duplicate pairs of chromosomes separate. The separate pairs then repel each other and move toward the poles of the cell.

Stage 4: Telophase

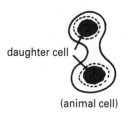

(animal cell)

When the chromosomes arrive at the poles, telophase begins. In telophase, the nuclei reform, the chromosomes gradually become less visible, and the cell separates to form two new cells. The daughter cells are genetically and physically identical to the parent cell except for size.

In single-celled organisms, cell division results in two new individuals. In complex organisms (more than one cell), the new daughter cells form a subsystem of the parent cell. In many organisms, cell reproduction is at its peak while the organism grows. As the organism ages, the process is limited to the replacement of old and damaged cells.

EXERCISE 5: MITOSIS

Directions: Match the phase of mitosis shown on the left with its description shown on the right.

_____ **1.** prophase   **(a)** chromosomes become easily visible

_____ **2.** metaphase   **(b)** chromosomal material lines up at the center of the cell

_____ **3.** anaphase   **(c)** cell divides to form two new cells

_____ **4.** telophase   **(d)** pairs of chromosomes move to opposite poles

Meiosis—Reproductive Cell Division

Each organism has a chromosome number that is characteristic of that organism. For example, all of the cells in the human body contain forty-six chromosomes except for the **gametes** (the reproductive cells). The reproductive cells (sperm and egg) cannot carry the same number of chromosomes as those of other parts of the body. If they did, the offspring that would result from the union of both the egg and the sperm would have twice the normal amount of genetic material after cell division. In animals, this would result in the termination of the embryo early in development. To prevent this, the sex cells undergo meiosis.

In **meiosis** a parent cell undergoes two special types of cell division that result in the production of four gametes (reproductive cells). Each gamete has half the number of chromosomes of the original parent cell. The two stages of meiosis are illustrated below.

MEIOSIS I

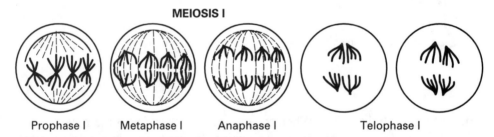

Prophase I   Metaphase I   Anaphase I   Telophase I

The chromosome pairs come together to exchange genes. This process, called **crossing over**, ensures a recombination of genetic material. Later, the pairs separate and one of each pair moves to a new cell. During Telophase I the cytoplasm divides and two daughter cells are formed. Each daughter cell is called a **haploid cell**, a cell that contains half the number of chromosomes of the original parent cell.

MEIOSIS II

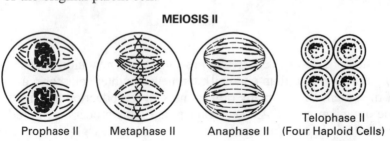

Prophase II   Metaphase II   Anaphase II   Telophase II (Four Haploid Cells)

(NOTE: Only one daughter cell from Meiosis I is shown here.)

In Meiosis II the chromosomal material combines, separates, and moves to new cells, resulting in four reproductive cells. In humans, when two haploid cells (a sperm and egg, each containing twenty-three chromosomes) unite in fertilization, they form a *diploid* cell, a cell containing forty-six chromosomes. The fertilized cell contains forty-six chromosomes, or twenty-three pairs—half from the mother and half from the father.

EXERCISE 6: MEIOSIS

Directions: Number the steps in meiosis in the order in which they occur.

_____ Two new cells divide, resulting in four reproductive cells.

_____ Chromosome pairs come together.

_____ Chromosome pairs separate, and each moves to a new cell.

_____ Chromosomes exchange genes.

EXERCISE 7: CELL DIVISION

Directions: Choose the best answer for each of the following questions.

1. The method of reproduction that provides for the most variety in offspring is
   (1) asexual (nonsexual) reproduction
   (2) mutative reproduction
   (3) sexual reproduction
   (4) cloning
   (5) cellular reproduction

2. Cancer is a condition in which cells that serve no function in the body invade healthy ones. Based on this, we can conclude that malignant cancer cells
   (1) do not reproduce by mitosis
   (2) divide by meiosis
   (3) divide more unpredictably than normal cells
   (4) divide less frequently than benign cells
   (5) are parasites and do not reproduce by division at all

Genetics and Heredity

Heredity is the term used to describe the passing of traits from parents to offspring. *Genetics* is the study of how traits are passed on. *Geneticists*, the scientists who study heredity, have found that hereditary information of an organism is carried by the chromosomes of the cell nucleus.

Genes map out all our inherited traits. For each trait every human receives two genes—one from the mother and one from the father. Genes may be dominant or recessive. The dominant gene will always appear in an offspring, if present. For example, since brown eye color is a dominant trait, 90 percent of human beings have brown eyes. If two dominant genes are inherited, the resulting trait will be a combination of the two inherited characteristics.

Sexual reproduction ensures that the offspring is composed of genetic material from both parents. This genetic material is thoroughly remixed with every fertilization so that, with the exception of identical twins, no two offspring of the same parents are the same genetically.

Gender and Mutations

Whether a mother gives birth to a boy or girl is determined by the "X" and "Y" chromosomes. A person receives two sex chromosomes—one from the father's sperm cell and one from the mother's egg cell. Egg cells contain a single "X" chromosome. Male sperm cells may contain either an "X" or a "Y" chromosome. If two "X" chromosomes unite, a female will result. If the sperm reaching the egg has a "Y" chromosome, a male will be produced. The sperm cells, then, carry the chromosome that determines the **gender** of offspring.

Sometimes a mistake occurs in the genetic makeup of a chromosome during cell duplication. This change in the genes is called a **mutation** and may be passed on to offspring. Two mutations in humans are Down's syndrome, which results in brain damage, and muscular dystrophy, a disease that causes muscles to waste away.

EXERCISE 8: GENETICS AND HEREDITY

Directions: Study the diagram and choose the best answer for the questions that follow.

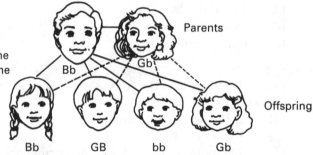

HOW COLOR IS INHERITED
G = Dominant Green Eye Gene
B = Dominant Brown Eye Gene
b = Recessive Blue Eye Gene

Parents

Offspring

Bb   GB   bb   Gb

1. According to the diagram, what percentage of this couple's children might have blue eyes?
   (1) 75 percent
   (2) 50 percent
   (3) 0 percent
   (4) 25 percent
   (5) 100 percent

The following question is not based on the preceding diagram.

2. The Jones family has had four children, all girls. The fifth child born is a boy. This change is the result of
   (1) conception classes taken by the parents
   (2) the timing of the fertility cycles
   (3) the father's contribution of a "Y" chromosome
   (4) the mother's contribution of a "Y" chromosome
   (5) the "law of averages" finally catching up

Growth, Energy, and Living Things

Some of the characteristics that distinguish living things from nonliving things are the capacities for growth, food consumption, and release of energy for cellular work. Important biological processes involved in these functions are the nitrogen cycle, photosynthesis, and cellular respiration.

The Nitrogen Cycle

Nitrogen, which makes up nearly 80 percent of Earth's atmosphere, is an essential ingredient for living tissues. Human beings and other animals depend on plants as a source of nitrogen. Plants cannot manufacture nitrogen themselves, so to obtain it they must depend on other organisms. Free nitrogen, however, cannot be used by organisms, so it must combine with other elements to form *nitrates* that can be used. Plants absorb these nitrates to manufacture *amino acids*, which are essential components of protein needed by living cells. Amino acids are used to manufacture both proteins and nucleic acids that are absorbed by humans.

The conversion of free nitrogen into a combined form is called *nitrogen fixing*. This is best achieved by certain bacteria—microorganisms and decomposers—that live in the soil. These microorganisms live in special sacs, called *nodules*, on the roots of legumes—plants such as alfalfa, peas, and beans. The microorganisms produce *nitrogenase*, an enzyme that is essential to nitrogen fixing. Scientists believe that all of the nitrogen in Earth's atmosphere has been fixed and liberated many times. At any one time, probably only a few pounds of nitrogenase exist on our planet. This small amount, however, is enough to sustain all life on Earth.

EXERCISE 9: THE NITROGEN CYCLE
Directions: Choose the best answer for each of the following questions.

1. Symbiosis describes the relationship between two organisms that are different but that live together for their mutual benefit. The microorganisms that live in the nodules attached to legumes may be described as symbiotic. Another example of a symbiotic relationship would be
   (1) bacteria that can live only in the stomachs of hoofed animals and that help the animals digest food
   (2) bees that make their hives in caves, thereby providing a ready source of food for bears
   (3) soldier ants that live and work together in colonies
   (4) tapeworms that live in the intestines of humans
   (5) scavengers, such as vultures, that feed on the carcasses of dead animals

2. Which of the following farming procedures best illustrates the process of nitrogen fixing?
   (1) rotating a crop of cotton one year with a crop of beets
   (2) irrigating the land with more modern methods
   (3) using more advanced equipment to plow the land
   (4) rotating the planting of cotton one year with a crop of soybeans
   (5) using airplanes to spray the crops with insecticides

Photosynthesis

Plants can live without human beings, but human beings cannot live without plants. Plants provide the oxygen we need to breathe and the nutrients we need to thrive. Green plants are self-sufficient because they are able to make their own food, while humans and lower animals must obtain their food to live.

Photosynthesis is the food-making process by which green plants convert the light from the sun into usable chemical energy. Photosynthesis can be understood as a process involving several steps. The first step is the capture of energy by the plant. In most plants the process of photosynthesis takes place within the ***chloroplasts***, where chlorophyll molecules absorb light. ***Chlorophyll*** is the substance that gives plants their green color. Using the energy that chlorophyll releases from sunlight, the plant splits water into its two components—oxygen and hydrogen. The oxygen is released to the atmosphere, and hydrogen recombines with carbon dioxide to produce carbohydrate molecules (a form of starch) in the plant.

EXERCISE 10: PHOTOSYNTHESIS

Directions: Choose the best answer for each of the following questions.

1. Which of the following may we conclude about plants and the process of photosynthesis?
   (1) Plants that do not possess chlorophyll must use a process other than photosynthesis to produce the energy they need.
   (2) Photosynthesis is used by plants to make energy because it is the simplest method available.
   (3) Plants that do not use the process of photosynthesis are parasites; they must obtain food from another source.
   (4) 1 and 2
   (5) 1 and 3

Question 2 is based on the information in the following passage.

   Some plants have leaves in which chlorophyll is lacking in some parts and is present in others. A coleus plant, with its brightly colored leaves, is one example. In an experiment in which the pigment (color) of the coleus leaf is removed, an iodine solution will identify places where starch is present by turning that part of the leaf brown.

2. Which of the following would you predict to happen to a coleus leaf in such an experiment?
   (1) The areas that turn brown will be areas where the leaf was green originally.
   (2) The leaf would not turn brown at all.
   (3) The areas that turn brown are the areas where the leaf was not green.
   (4) The entire leaf would turn brown.
   (5) Only half the leaf would turn brown.

Cellular Respiration

Cellular respiration is the complex series of chemical reactions by which a cell releases the energy trapped inside glucose molecules. *Glucose*, a form of sugar, is the end product of the process of photosynthesis. The process of cellular respiration, then, is the reverse of photosynthesis. During cellular respiration, cells (plant or animal) break down the glucose so that energy is released for cellular work. Because the energy cannot be free-floating in the cell, it is repackaged and stored. Cellular respiration occurs in three stages, beginning with the breakdown of a molecule of glucose and ending with the energy needed for the cell to perform its work. Energy that is not used is released in the form of heat.

EXERCISE 11: CELLULAR RESPIRATION

Directions: Choose the best answer for each of the following questions.

1. From the information about cellular respiration, we can infer that
   (1) in plants, photosynthesis must always precede cellular respiration
   (2) no relationship exists between photosynthesis and cellular respiration
   (3) photosynthesis and respiration share many processes
   (4) cellular respiration occurs only in animal cells
   (5) plants do not perform cellular work

2. The rate of cellular respiration in humans can be measured by the amount of carbon dioxide exhaled. Which of the following would you expect to be true about the rate of cellular respiration for a group of students who are the same age, height, and weight?
   (1) Africans would have a higher rate of cellular respiration than Asians.
   (2) Boys would have a higher rate of cellular respiration than girls.
   (3) Girls would have a higher rate of cellular respiration than boys.
   (4) Athletes would tend to have higher rates of cellular respiration than nonathletes.
   (5) Nonathletes would have higher rates of cellular respiration than athletes.

3. If you measured the amounts of carbon dioxide exhaled, which of the following populations would be *most effective* in proving your hypothesis in the preceding example?
   (1) by the students immediately after they wake up
   (2) by every student after vigorous exercise
   (3) by one student at rest and another student after vigorous exercise
   (4) by half the students at rest and half the students after vigorous exercise
   (5) by one quarter of the students at rest and one quarter after vigorous exercise

Diversity of Life

The job of categorizing the many different kinds of living things has been made easier by a system of classification.

Classification of Organisms

The classification system for living things moves from the general to the specific. Each downward step in the classification system provides more detail about the organism that is classified. The **kingdom** is the broadest grouping. Within each kingdom, the organisms with the greatest similarities are grouped further into a **phylum**. Below the phylum is the **class**. The class is followed by an **order**, a **family**, a **genus**, and a **species**. The classification of the human (*Homo sapiens*) is illustrated in the following chart.

TAXONOMY OF HUMAN CLASSIFICATION

Category	Taxon	Characteristics
Kingdom	Animalia	Is multicellular, cannot make its own food, is able to move
Phylum	Chordata	Has a notochord (skeletal rod) and hollow nerve cord
Class	Mammalia	Has hair or fur; female secretes milk to nourish young
Order	Primate	Has flattened fingers for grasping, keen vision, poor sense of smell
Family	Hominidae	Walks on two feet, has flat face, eyes facing forward, color vision
Genus	Homo	Has long childhood, large brain, speech ability
Species	Sapiens	Has reduced body hair, high forehead, prominent chin

EXERCISE 12: CLASSIFICATION OF ORGANISMS

Directions: Read the definitions and apply them to the questions that follow. Listed below, from lowest to highest, are the five kingdoms into which all living organisms are classified

kingdom monera—simple one-celled, mobile organism lacking organelles, some of which can produce their own food (example: bacterium) *kingdom protista*—single-celled, mobile organism having a more complex cell structure than monera (example: paramecium)

kingdom fungi—multicellular, lacks chlorophyll, cannot move, obtains food from other organisms (example: mushroom)

kingdom plantae—multicellular, has chlorophyll, produces its own food, has no mobility (example: moss)

kingdom animalia—multicellular, capable of moving by itself and obtaining its own food (example: bird)

1. Streptococcus is a single-celled organism that has no organelles and that occurs in a sequence of chains. It causes strep throat when it invades the throat. In which kingdom would it be classified?
   (1) monera
   (2) protista
   (3) fungi
   (4) plantae
   (5) animalia

2. Mold is a parasite that grows on bread, cheese, or other organic foods. It lacks chlorophyll and obtains nutrients from the host. In which kingdom would it be classified?
   (1) monera
   (2) protista
   (3) fungi
   (4) plantae
   (5) animalia

Evolution and Natural Selection

Among all cultures of human beings, there is some explanation for the origin of humankind. In many cultures, the theory of Divine Creation is the most widely accepted explanation for the origin of Earth and its creatures. This belief holds that a supreme being created the world and its varied forms of life and that all species created remained unchanged since the beginning of time.

A scientific explanation that has wide currency is the theory of *evolution*. Proposed in 1859 by Charles Darwin in *On the Origin of Species*, the theory holds that all forms of life developed gradually (over 600 million years) from different and often much simpler ancestors. These forms of life adapted over the years to meet the demands of their environment. Thus, all lines of descent can be traced back to a common ancestral organism.

As offspring differed from their parents, generations with characteristics that were less and less alike resulted. Ultimately, new species were formed from the diverse offspring because these new characteristics were inheritable. The new characteristics of the offspring are explained by *natural selection* ("survival of the fittest"). Species that are best adapted to the conditions under which they live survive and reproduce; those that are not adapted perish.

EXERCISE 13: EVOLUTION AND NATURAL SELECTION

Directions: Choose the best answer for each question below.

1. An unusual member of the animal kingdom is the duckbill platypus—an animal that has many characteristics of birds, mammals, and reptiles. Found in Australia and Tasmania, the animal has a ducklike bill, has webbed and clawed feet, is covered with thick fur, and reproduces by laying eggs. Which of the following hypotheses related to Darwin's theory of evolution could be applied to the platypus?
   (1) The platypus is the result of the interbreeding of three distinct animal classes.
   (2) The platypus is the earliest living member of the mammalian family.
   (3) The platypus developed independently in a closed environment during the early history of mammals.
   (4) The platypus was not subject to the influences described in Darwin's theory.
   (5) Mammal life originated in Australia and Tasmania hundreds of millions of years ago.

Question 2 refers to the following passage.

Mammals are placed in two groups—*placental* (having a placenta that nourishes the fetus) and *marsupial* (having a pouch in which the young are nourished and carried). Most of the world's marsupials are found on the continent of Australia and the islands nearby, where few placental mammals lived during the early history of the continents.

2. Based on the preceding information about how marsupials differ from placental mammals, we can infer that
   (1) marsupials are less biologically advanced than placental mammals
   (2) placental mammals are more primitive than marsupials
   (3) marsupials cannot survive in areas other than Australia and North America
   (4) marsupials are the oldest forms of life on Earth
   (5) marsupials descended from the reptiles

3. Which of the following mammals best exhibits a physical adaptation to environmental conditions?
   (1) cow
   (2) lion
   (3) mouse
   (4) seal
   (5) bear

Ecology and Ecosystems

The science of *ecology* involves the interrelationship of a living organism with other organisms and with its nonliving environment. The ecologist studies the relationships between the component organisms and their environments. A self-supporting environment is called an *ecosystem*. The photosynthetic producers, the consumers, decomposers, and their environment constitute an ecosystem.

In a typical ecosystem, the primary producers are the green plants that derive their energy from the sun. For example, a rabbit (primary consumer) feeds on the plant; a fox (secondary consumer) preys on the rabbit; a buzzard (tertiary, or third-level, consumer) feeds on the carcass that the fox leaves behind; decomposers (the bacteria and fungi that feed on the scraps left by the buzzard) provide the nitrates necessary for the green plants.

The ecological balance of a community is delicate. The removal of one key element can destroy a system, sometimes permanently. The following passage describes an imbalance in a particular ecosystem.

EXERCISE 14: ECOLOGY AND ECOSYSTEMS

Directions: Read the passage and in the blanks below write the correct element in the ecosystem described in the passage.

At the end of the nineteenth century, ranchers moved onto the grassy Kaibab Plateau in northern Arizona. They were attracted by the fine grazing areas and abundance of deer for hunting. Fearing that the mountain lion, another inhabitant of the region, would prey on the cattle and deer, the ranchers waged a campaign to eradicate the cat from the plateau. They were successful in their effort, and mountain lions disappeared within a few years.

Their success produced catastrophic ecological results, however. Increased numbers of deer, along with herds of cattle that grazed on the land, denuded it. Soon, heavy rains caused major erosion, and the land was reduced to a fraction of its usefulness. This problem has occurred repeatedly where humans have manipulated an ecosystem without considering the possible consequences.

1. primary producer _____

2. primary consumers _____ and

_____

3. secondary consumer _____

4. The destruction of the _____ led to the increase

of grazing by _____ and

_____ , which led to

_____ of the land and its eventual

_____ by heavy rains.

2
EARTH SCIENCE—
THE STUDY OF EARTH

Earth science is the study of the planet Earth and its origin and development. It differs from the life sciences in that it focuses on nonliving rather than living things. Earth science is a very broad field that covers the subjects of astronomy, geology, meteorology, and oceanography.

Astronomy, the Study of Heavenly Bodies

The beginning of any study of Earth generally lies in astronomy. *Astronomers* study the size, movements, and composition of the heavenly bodies. By observing the stars, planets, comets, and other objects in space, astronomers hope to understand how our planet was created and how it evolved. A number of important theories have been advanced to explain the beginning of Earth and the universe in which it lies. Two related theories are the big bang theory and the pulsation theory.

The Big Bang and Pulsation Theories

According to the *big bang theory*, a "cosmic egg" made up of dust and gas containing all the matter in the universe exploded 15 to 20 billion years ago. The basic atoms, elements, and heavenly bodies of the universe were created. This theory is widely accepted because it accounts for the apparent expansion of the universe and the background radiation found in outer space. A refinement of the big bang theory was the development of the *pulsation theory*. According to this theory, the universe will expand to a certain point and then begin to contract. This contraction will continue until the cosmic egg is again achieved, when another "big bang" will create expansion in the universe.

Stars and Galaxies

The big bang theory also explains how stars are formed. According to supporters of the theory, the energy from the bang was so powerful that matter lighter than air remained suspended in space. Eventually, the force of gravity exerted itself; and the matter was drawn, along with helium and hydrogen gases, into dark, cloudlike formations. The gaseous matter became compressed, and the colliding of the compressed particles produced heat. A star developed when the temperature reached 15 million degrees centigrade—the temperature at which nuclear reactions begin.

The lifetime of a star ranges from a few hundred thousand years to billions of years. Most stars eventually use up their supply of hydrogen, contract to a smaller size, and then explode. The explosion results in clouds of dust and gas. Some stars eventually contract to *black holes*—stars of very small size that have gravitational fields so strong that not even light escapes from them.

Most stars exist within a very large formation called a *galaxy*. Hundreds of millions of galaxies are believed to exist in the universe. The stars of a very distant galaxy may be so closely packed together that we can see them only as a blur of light rather than as individual stars.

Our galaxy, the Milky Way, is a spiral galaxy, as are 80 percent of all galaxies. The Milky Way is composed of at least 100 billion stars and enough matter, in the form of dust and gas, to create millions of additional suns. The following illustration shows the Milky Way Galaxy.

THE MILKY WAY GALAXY

ANSWERS TO EXERCISES IN THIS CHAPTER BEGIN ON PAGE 419.

EXERCISE 1: STARS AND GALAXIES

Directions: Number the steps of star formation in the correct sequence, with *1* representing the first step and *4* the last.

_____ Heat is produced by the colliding of molecules.

_____ Fifteen million degrees centigrade is reached, and visible light is emitted.

_____ Dust and gas move throughout the universe.

_____ Gas and dust become compressed because of gravitational forces.

The Sun and the Solar System

Despite the importance of the Sun as the star at the center of our solar system, it is really only an "average" star when compared to others in our galaxy. It is average in age (4 to 5 billion years old), size (860,000 miles in diameter), and heat intensity (surface temperature about 6,000 degrees centigrade).

Other members of the solar system include the nine planets, seven of which have one or more satellites (moons), and 1,600 large asteroids located between Mars and Jupiter. The inner planets (Mercury, Venus, Earth, and Mars) are small, with high densities and few satellites. The outer planets (Jupiter, Saturn, Uranus, and Neptune) are large gas giants and have many moons. Pluto is so far away that all we can tell is that it is not similar to other outer planets.

The planets are believed to have begun as clumps of matter within the dust cloud that formed the Sun. They were too small to achieve the conditions needed to become stars. Instead, they cooled and became the planets as we know them. Our space probes have reached all except the most distant outer planets, and it appears that Earth is the only inhabited body in our solar system. The following illustration shows our solar system.

OUR SOLAR SYSTEM

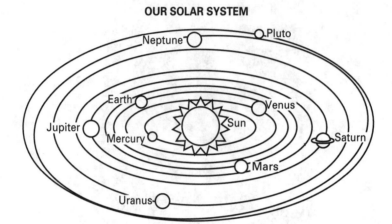

EXERCISE 2: THE SOLAR SYSTEM
Directions: Choose the best answer for the question below.

The "Goldilocks problem" in astronomy (in which one of Earth's neighboring planets is too hot to support life and another is too cold to support life) applies to which two planets?
(1) Pluto and Neptune
(2) Mars and Saturn
(3) Mercury and Venus
(4) Venus and Mars
(5) Jupiter and Uranus

EXERCISE 3: THE PLANETS
Directions: Based on the information in the table, complete each of the following statements by writing the name of the correct planet in the blank.

Planet	Length of Year	Length of Day	Number of Satellites	Distance from Sun (miles)
Mercury	88 days	58 days	0	36 million
Venus	225 days	243 days	0	67 million
Earth	365.26 days	23.9 hours	1	93 million
Mars	686.98 days	24.6 hours	2	142 million

1. The length of the day is approximately the same

on _____ and _____.

2. Of the planets listed, you would "age" at the fastest rate on

_____.

3. Mars takes a little more than three times longer to revolve around the

Sun than _____.

Geology, the Study of Earth's Formation

The occurrence of natural disasters is evidence that Earth is changing constantly. *Geologists* study the features of Earth and how they affect its development. In this century alone, geologists have made significant, revolutionary discoveries, including the formulation of the theory of plate tectonics, a theory that explains the development of mountains and ocean trenches and the occurrence of earthquakes and volcanic eruptions.

Continental Drift and Plate Tectonics

Scientists have long observed that accurately drawn maps of Africa and South America suggest that the two continents once fit together. Based on this observation, geologists formulated the ***theory of continental drift:*** the formation of all seven continents into a supercontinent millions of years ago. It broke apart and split into the land masses that are recognized today as the seven continents.

Despite this appearance of the continents as an interlocking puzzle, scientists could not explain why the continents drifted apart. The ***theory of plate tectonics***, advanced in the 1960s, provided an explanation of the phenomenon. According to the theory, Earth is made up of the crust, mantle, outer core, and inner core, as depicted in the following picture.

EARTH'S STRUCTURE

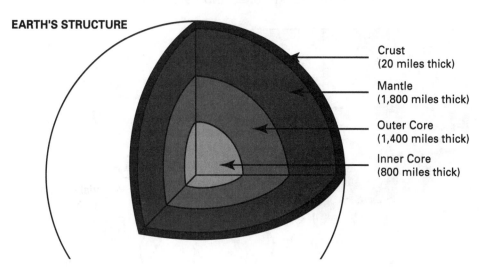

Crust
(20 miles thick)

Mantle
(1,800 miles thick)

Outer Core
(1,400 miles thick)

Inner Core
(800 miles thick)

The crust and upper mantle are made up of about twenty plates. These plates may be likened to plates floating on the surface of water in a vast sink. They move very slowly—approximately one-half to four inches per year. Attached to the surface of these plates are the continents and the ocean floor. As the plates slowly move, they carry the continents with them. Geologists believe that the plates move because currents of partially molten rock in the mantle carry them.

This motion of the plates provides explanations. When two plates collide, one plate piles atop another, forming a mountain. When one plate is forced down into the mantle of another, a trench occurs. A volcano is created when the heat beneath the surface of Earth melts the plate material that was forced into the trench and sends the molten rock to the surface. An earthquake is formed by the shifting and breaking of the surface rocks when two plates slide past each other.

The vibrations caused by the slippage of plates are called *seismic waves*. The strength of these waves is measured by a device called a seismograph and then rated on the Richter scale. Earthquakes measuring more than 4.5 on the Richter scale are considered potentially dangerous.

EXERCISE 4: PLATE TECTONICS
Directions: Choose the best answer for the following question.

According to the passage, the theory of plate tectonics helps explain which of the following?
(1) the Earth's gravitational pull
(2) earthquakes, volcanoes, and mountains
(3) the theory of continental drift
(4) 1 and 2
(5) 2 and 3

EXERCISE 5: EARTHQUAKES
Directions: Choose the best answer for the question below, based on the following map.

U. S. EARTHQUAKE ZONES AND SEISMIC RISK

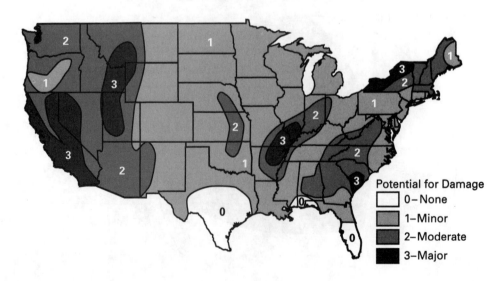

Potential for Damage
	0–None
	1–Minor
	2–Moderate
	3–Major

Which of the following statements about earthquakes is supported by the map?

(1) California is the only state in which residents might expect major earthquake damage.

(2) Texas and Florida are the only states that do not have to worry about earthquakes.

(3) The potential for moderate to major earthquake damage is greatest on the West Coast.

(4) Most of the continental United States is not affected by earthquakes.

(5) Earthquakes are the most dangerous phenomenon on Earth.

EXERCISE 6: CONTINENTAL DRIFT

Directions: Read the following passage and choose the best answer for the question.

> Ascension Island is a small volcanic island located in the south Atlantic halfway between Africa and South America. It is a famous breeding ground for sea turtles. Giant green turtles each year swim 2,000 miles from the coast of South America to lay their eggs on Ascension Island. This phenomenon has puzzled scientists for years.

Which of the following geological hypotheses best explains the behavior of the giant sea turtles?

(1) Ascension Island is the only place in the world where turtle eggs can survive.

(2) Predators, like alligators that live on the coast of South America, eat turtle eggs, forcing the sea turtles to migrate.

(3) The turtles laid their eggs on Ascension Island millions of years ago before the continents of Africa and South America became separated.

(4) 1 and 2

(5) 2 and 3

Geologic Time

You might consider fifty years to be a long time. In geology, however, fifty years is not very long, since geologic time extends back nearly five billion years, when geologists believe Earth was formed. We owe our concept of **absolute time**—time not influenced by arbitrary human reference points—to geology. Geologists are able to fix periods of time by studying the rocks found in Earth's crust. These rocks serve as records of time.

The rocks found in Earth's crust are of three types, described according to their origins. **Igneous rocks** are formed when molten rock (magma) hardens. Just below igneous rock are **metamorphic** rocks, which have been changed by high pressure and temperature within the crust. The rocks that undergo metamorphosis are mainly igneous rocks. **Sedimentary** rocks are deposited near Earth's surface by wind, water, and ice. In sedimentary rock, the oldest layers are on the bottom and the youngest are on the top.

Instruments for Measuring Time

How do we determine which rocks are older than others? In **radiometric measurement**, geologists measure the rate of radioactive decay in the minerals found in the rock. Over the last century, scientists have learned that radioactive substances will change, or decay, into nonradioactive substances over a period of time. This method is valid for matter up to 50,000 years in age. Radiometric dating works well with samples of igneous and sedimentary rocks because it measures the radioactivity of minerals created when the rocks were formed. For metamorphic rock, however, the age of the original rock and the age of metamorphism are difficult to pinpoint.

The principle of **faunal succession** is also used to determine the age of sedimentary rock. Geologists examine the types of animal fossils found in layers of sedimentary rock. Igneous and metamorphic rock rarely contain fossils. Scientists have found that certain layers of rock will contain certain kinds of fossils, no matter where in the world the rock is located. Moreover, scientists have found that certain fossils are always found at lower layers than others, indicating that a sequence exists to the evolution of organisms.

EXERCISE 7: MEASURING GEOLOGIC TIME

Directions: Choose the best answer for each of the following questions.

1. Based on the information in the preceding passage, which correctly describes the placement of the three types of rocks?
   - **(1)** Igneous is located at the surface, metamorphic in the middle, and sedimentary on the bottom.
   - **(2)** Sedimentary is located at the surface, metamorphic in the middle, and igneous at the bottom.
   - **(3)** Metamorphic is located at the surface, sedimentary in the middle, and igneous at the bottom.
   - **(4)** Igneous is located at the surface, sedimentary in the middle, and metamorphic at the bottom.
   - **(5)** Sedimentary is located at the surface, igneous in the middle, and metamorphic at the bottom.

2. Trilobite fossils are found at a depth of 18 meters in a rock bed, and coral fossils are found at 14 meters. Which of the following is likely to be true about each organism?
   - **(1)** Coral is older than trilobites.
   - **(2)** Coral and trilobites are the same age.
   - **(3)** Coral and trilobites share a common ancestry.
   - **(4)** Trilobites are more advanced than corals.
   - **(5)** Trilobites are older than corals.

Minerals and Rocks

Minerals are the building blocks of rocks. A **mineral** is a natural, inorganic solid with a specific composition and structure. All specimens of a given mineral share certain physical properties. Some physical properties of minerals are crystalline form, hardness, color, and cleavage (the way they break).

More than 95 percent of Earth's crust is made up of the minerals formed from the elements oxygen and silicon. The following chart shows the eight main elements, including their percent of the crust's weight and volume.

Element	Percent of Crust's Mass (weight)	Percent of Crust's Volume (space)
Oxygen	46.71	94.24
Silicon	27.69	0.51
Aluminum	8.07	0.44
Iron	5.05	0.37
Calcium	3.65	1.04
Sodium	2.75	1.21
Potassium	2.58	1.85
Magnesium	2.08	0.27

EXERCISE 8: MINERALS AND ROCKS
Directions: Choose the best answer for the questions below.

1. According to the information in the table, which element represents less of the crust's weight but occupies over three times the space of silicon, a major component of the crust?
   (1) sodium
   (2) calcium
   (3) potassium
   (4) magnesium
   (5) iron

2. Which of the following best explains why oxygen, a gas, is the largest component of Earth's crust?
   (1) Oxygen gives Earth's crust its lightness.
   (2) Oxygen is the most abundant element in the world.
   (3) Oxygen is found in plants, and plants are significant parts of Earth's crust.
   (4) Oxygen is needed to sustain all life on Earth.
   (5) Oxygen is capable of combining with most of the elements in Earth's crust.

The Changing Earth

Erosion is the wearing away of Earth's surface through gravity, wind, ice, and water. Erosion has occurred throughout time and will continue as long as dry land exists. The pull of *gravity* makes surface material move downward. Downslope movements may be rapid or very slow. They may involve only the surface material, or they may involve the bedrock underneath. Houses built on hills can contribute to soil movements because the weight of the homes may add to the gravitational force. *Wind* contributes to the erosional process by carrying surface material from one location to another.

Glaciers, huge sheets of ice that can move slowly over land, pick up and carry rocks and soil with them. When they pass through river valleys, they deepen them. Mountain glaciers, coupled with the downward force of gravity, create avalanches that can cause great erosional damage.

Of all the erosional agents, running water is the most powerful. Rivers, working with the force of gravity, are devastating in their erosional impact. The action of rivers flowing against the land has formed gorges as large as the Grand Canyon. As rivers erode land, they carry deposits with them. *Deltas* are formed at the mouths of rivers that empty into a lake or ocean. The soil that is carried along a river and deposited at its mouth is the richest and most fertile of all soils. The Nile and Mississippi rivers have formed deltas that are noted for their rich soil, making these regions highly desirable for agriculture.

EXERCISE 9: THE CHANGING EARTH
Directions: Choose the best answer for the following question.

Which of the following procedures followed by a farmer is not related directly to preventing erosion?
(1) planting grass in gullies to act as a filler
(2) planting crops in alternate rows (strip farming)
(3) contour plowing around a hill
(4) planting new trees to replace those that die
(5) planting more seeds than are necessary to yield a bountiful crop

Oceanography, the Study of Earth's Oceans

Observed from space, Earth has been described as a big blue marble. The one feature that contributes to this description is water covering nearly 71 percent of Earth's surface. Earth scientists who study large bodies of water are called *oceanographers*. Inventions such as sonar (an underwater ranging device), deep-diving submarines, and remote-control cameras have aided in our exploration of the oceans.

From their studies oceanographers have made many discoveries that help them to understand and explain phenomena. For example, the theory of plate tectonics was further substantiated by the finding that a ridge encircling the globe lies under the ocean—the *oceanic ridge*. This ridge circles the globe like the seam of a baseball. Numerous openings have been photographed along the crest of this ridge. Evidence from the pictures provided the basis for the theory that magma forces itself up from the ridges, pushes the ocean plates apart, cools, and forms new rock that becomes part of the ocean plate.

The Oceans' Beginning

Oceanographers are not sure how Earth's oceans began. Many believe they were formed by the release of water bound up in rocks of Earth's interior. Evidence from some of the most ancient sedimentary rocks suggests that the original sediments forming the rocks were deposited in water. Scientists do know that the volume of water covering Earth is affected by the formation of glaciers and the melting of huge blocks of ice covering Earth's surface. The graph below illustrates the change in sea level during the past 20,000 years. (Glaciers covered much of Earth 20,000 years ago.)

EXERCISE 10: CHANGE IN SEA LEVEL

Directions: Choose the best answer for each of the following question.

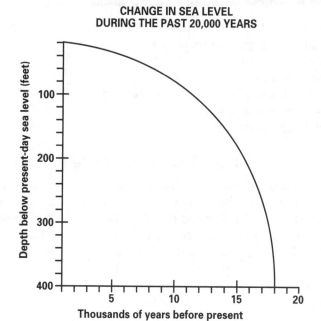

Based on the graph, Earth's sea level was at its lowest approximately
(1) 1,000 years ago
(2) 5,000 years ago
(3) 10,000 years ago
(4) 15,000 years ago
(5) 18,000 years ago

EXERCISE 11: THE OCEANS' BEGINNING

Directions: Choose the best answer for the questions below.

DISTRIBUTION OF WATER ON EARTH	
Type of Water	**Relative % of abundance**
Seawater	86.5
Lakes, rivers	0.03
Continental Ice	1.3
Water vapor in atmosphere	0.001
Water in sediments and sedimentary rocks	12.2

1. Which of the following sources yields the smallest amount of water throughout Earth?
   (1) seawater
   (2) lakes and rivers
   (3) continental ice
   (4) water vapor in the atmosphere
   (5) water in sediments and sedimentary rocks

2. The presence of 12 percent of water in sediments and in sedimentary rocks lends support to the theory of
   (1) continental drift
   (2) plate tectonics
   (3) how Earth's sea level has risen over time
   (4) the origin of the oceans
   (5) faunal succession

The Oceans' Tides

One phenomenon of the oceans that can be easily observed is the occurrence of tides. *Tides* result from the rising and falling of the ocean's surface caused by the gravitational pull of the Sun and the Moon on Earth. The Moon is the most dominant factor in causing tides because of its closeness to Earth.

When the Moon is directly overhead, the ocean beneath it tends to bulge up, causing a tide. On the opposite side of Earth, the oceans experience a lesser bulge. As Earth rotates once every twenty-four hours, it experiences two high tides and two low tides. The position of the Moon in relation to the Sun and Earth determines the period and height of the tides. *Spring tides* are tides of greater-than-average range. *Neap tides* are tides of smaller-than-average range. The illustration in the exercise below shows a spring tide and a neap tide.

EXERCISE 12: THE OCEANS' TIDES
Directions: Choose the best answer for the following questions.

SPRING AND NEAP TIDES

1. Spring tides are tides of greater-than-average range. During which two phases of the Moon is the gravitational pull of the Moon together with the Sun likely to be greatest, causing a spring tide?

A. last quarter—when the Moon is to the left side of Earth, as shown
B. full moon—when Earth is between the Sun and the Moon
C. first quarter—when the Moon is to the right side of Earth
D. new moon—when the Moon is between Earth and the Sun

(1) A and B
(2) A and C
(3) A and D
(4) B and C
(5) B and D

Question 2 is based on the following explanation:

Syzygy (siz' uh gee) is the term that describes a rare alignment of the Sun, Moon, and Earth that causes extraordinarily high tides. This phenomenon occurred during the period from December 30, 1986, to January 4, 1987. It aggravated the severe storms that occurred along the Atlantic Coast. Three coinciding events occurred during this five-day period.

A. The Moon's orbit was closest to Earth—about 223,000 miles instead of 240,000 miles.
B. The Moon was directly between Earth and the Sun, causing a new moon.
C. Earth's orbit was the closest to the Sun—91½ million miles, instead of the normal 93 million miles.

2. Conditions under which the Moon's orbit is farthest from Earth, Earth is between the Sun and the Moon, and Earth's orbit is farthest from the Sun would likely result in
(1) the same effect as syzygy
(2) unusually low tides
(3) neap tides
(4) spring tides
(5) unusually high tides

Meteorology, the Study of Earth's Atmosphere

Meteorologists study Earth's atmosphere to understand and predict the weather. The *atmosphere* is the invisible layer of air that envelops Earth. Scientists believe that it is primarily because of our atmosphere that life exists on Earth and not on neighboring planets such as Mars and Venus. The atmosphere is not one distinct air mass that surrounds Earth; it is composed of several layers of air that begin at specific altitude ranges.

Meteorologists have identified four layers of Earth's atmosphere. In ascending order (from lowest to highest) they are the troposphere, stratosphere, ionosphere, and exosphere. The *troposphere* lies closest to

Earth. It extends upward about seven to ten miles. Earth's weather occurs in this layer of the atmosphere, and it contains almost all of the clouds. The *tropopause* is the boundary where the troposphere ends and the stratosphere begins. The *stratosphere* begins somewhere between seven and ten miles and extends upward about thirty miles. It is a uniform layer of air with little vertical air movement. Airplane travel in this layer is generally smooth and visibility always clear.

Above the stratosphere, the *ionosphere* extends upward about 300 miles. The air in the ionosphere is extremely thin, and air particles are electrified. Through the ionosphere, radio waves are transmitted great distances around Earth. The *exosphere* is the highest layer of the atmosphere. It is characterized by extreme heat during the day when the Sun's direct rays reach it and extreme cold at night when it is shielded from the Sun's direct rays.

EXERCISE 13: LAYERS OF EARTH'S ATMOSPHERE

Directions: Choose the best answer for each of the following questions after reading the passage below and studying the accompanying diagram.

At different altitudes of Earth's atmosphere, we are able to observe different phenomena. Also, scientists are able to use different technologies to explore and understand Earth and the regions in outer space.

1. *Noctilucent* clouds, spectacular clouds that can be seen only at dusk, appear shortly after sunset. At which atmospheric level are these clouds visible?
   (1) exosphere
   (2) troposphere
   (3) stratosphere
   (4) ionosphere
   (5) tropopause

2. "D" layer radio waves that are transmitted around the world may be found at
   (1) the upper range of the stratosphere
   (2) the lower range of the stratosphere
   (3) the lower range of the ionosphere
   (4) the upper range of the ionosphere
   (5) the upper range of the troposphere

3. The illustration suggests that the peak of Mt. Everest
   (1) is at times hidden by clouds
   (2) extends beyond the tropopause
   (3) lies in the troposphere
   (4) 1 and 2
   (5) 1 and 3

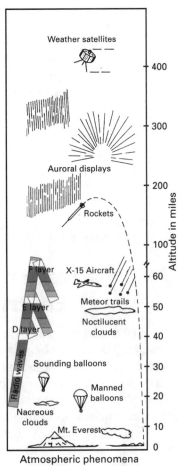

Atmospheric phenomena and observation tools

EXERCISE 14: OZONE IN THE ATMOSPHERE

Directions: Read the following passage and choose the best answer for the question that follows.

Ozone, a corrosive, pungent, and toxic gas, occurs in the atmosphere when the Sun's ultraviolet rays cause ionization in oxygen atoms. Ozone is beneficial to us because it absorbs ultraviolet rays, preventing these lethal wavelengths from reaching Earth's surface. At lower levels in Earth's atmosphere, however, especially in large urban areas, ozone can be created from a chemical reaction involving solar heat and the exhaust from cars. The chief ingredient of smog, this form of ozone is harmful to humans and can cause difficulty in breathing.

The harmful form of ozone that can be seen as smog is formed in the
(1) exosphere
(2) troposphere
(3) stratosphere
(4) ionosphere
(5) tropopause

The Water Cycle

In predicting the weather, meteorologists must consider not just the air surrounding us but also how it interacts with the water that covers Earth's surface. The atmosphere and the **hydrosphere** (the watery portion of Earth) create the **water cycle**. This cycle helps to explain precipitation, an important element in our weather.

The Sun is a key link in the chain of events that makes up the water cycle. The Sun radiates heat, which daily evaporates millions of tons of water from Earth's oceans, lakes, rivers, and streams into the air. As moist air rises, it slowly cools. Finally, it cools so much that the humidity (water vapor in the air) reaches 100 percent. At this point, the water vapor condenses and clouds form. Depending on the temperature and other conditions, either rain or snow falls as precipitation when the clouds can't hold all of the water. The rain or snow eventually flows to the ocean, and the cycle is completed again. The following illustration shows the water cycle.

THE WATER CYCLE

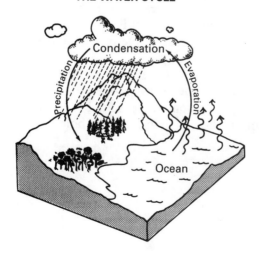

EXERCISE 15: THE WATER CYCLE

Directions: Number the steps 1–5 (first to last) of the water cycle in the correct sequence.

_____ Rain or snow returns water to the ocean.

_____ Condensation occurs, forming clouds.

_____ The Sun radiates heat.

_____ Precipitation in the form of rain or snow occurs.

_____ Water evaporates into the atmosphere.

EXERCISE 16: HUMIDITY

Directions: Read the passage and answer the questions that follow.

Humidity is the amount of water vapor in the air at a given time. At warm temperatures, the air can hold more moisture than it can at cold temperatures. *Relative humidity* is the amount of vapor the air is holding expressed as a percentage of the amount the air is capable of holding. For example, at 86 degrees Fahrenheit, the air can hold a maximum of 30.4 grams of water per cubic meter. If the air at the same temperature is holding only 15.2 grams of water, then the relative humidity is 50 percent. At the point when the air becomes saturated (exceeds the most water vapor it can hold), it releases water vapor in the form of dew (condensation) or precipitation.

1. If the air at 61 degrees is holding the maximum amount of moisture that it can, and the temperature suddenly drops to 45 degrees, what is likely to be the result?
   (1) The air will become saturated with water vapor.
   (2) Precipitation will be released in the form of rain.
   (3) Precipitation will be released in the form of hail.
   (4) 1 and 2
   (5) 1 and 3

2. During subfreezing days in many parts of the country, the indoor relative humidity decreases when homes are heated. Furniture and skin dry out, and static electricity increases. For health reasons, doctors recommend the use of humidifiers. Which of the following best explains the lack of humidity in the air indoors?
   (1) The amount of water vapor in the air goes down.
   (2) The water vapor in the air evaporates.
   (3) The water vapor present in the air at lower temperatures is less than the amount that heated indoor air can hold.
   (4) 1 and 2
   (5) 2 and 3

Air Masses, Fronts, and Weather

Another key element in determining Earth's weather is an air mass. Cold air masses tend to be unstable and turbulent and move faster than warm air masses. The clouds that are formed by cold air masses are *cumulus clouds*, puffy, cottonlike clouds. During warm weather, when cold air masses bring precipitation, it is likely to be in the form of thundershowers. Warm air masses are usually stable, and the wind that accompanies them is steady. Clouds that are formed by warm air masses are *stratus clouds*, low-lying, level clouds that in warm weather bring precipitation in the form of drizzle.

A *front* occurs when two air masses collide and a boundary between the two masses form. The weather for the land below is affected. Fronts may be either weak or strong. Strong fronts generally bring precipitation. When cold air acts like a plow and pushes warm air back, a *cold front* forms. If the cold air retreats, and the warm air pushes it away, a *warm front* occurs. Sometimes, the boundary between the two air masses does not move, and the front becomes stationary. *Stationary fronts* bring conditions similar to those brought by warm fronts. However, precipitation that results is usually milder and lasts longer.

EXERCISE 17: AIR MASSES, FRONTS, AND WEATHER
Directions: Choose the best answer for the following questions.

1. Which of the following changes in the weather can occur when a strong warm air mass displaces a cold air mass?
   (1) Cumulus clouds may form, winds become gusty, and thunderstorms may result.
   (2) Stratus clouds may form, winds may become steady, and drizzling occurs.
   (3) Stratus clouds may form, winds become turbulent, and thunderstorms may result.
   (4) Cumulus clouds may form, winds become steady, and thunderstorms may result.
   (5) The sky remains cloudless, and no winds or precipitation occurs.

2. Based on the preceding passage, which of the following has *no* relation to the action of fronts in causing weather changes?
   (1) the temperature of the air mass
   (2) the speed at which the air mass moves
   (3) the strength of the air mass
   (4) the stability of the winds that accompany the air mass
   (5) the direction in which the air mass moves

3
CHEMISTRY—
THE STUDY OF MATTER

Chemistry is the branch of science that concerns the composition, structure, properties, and changes of matter. *Matter* is any substance that occupies space and has mass. Your chair, desk, table, and the air you breathe are composed of matter. Matter exists in four states—as solids, liquids, gases, and as plasma, an ionized gas of which the Sun is made.

The Atom, the Basis of Matter

In chemistry, atoms are the building blocks for matter. The *atom* is the smallest particle of an element that has the properties of that element. An *element* is a substance that occurs in nature and that cannot be broken down into a simpler substance. Nearly one hundred fundamental substances known as elements are known to occur in nature. A few elements have been produced synthetically by humans. Atoms form molecules. A *molecule* is the smallest part of a compound that can exist by itself. A molecule consists of two or more atoms joined together chemically.

In the early nineteenth century, only a few elements were known to exist. According to the theory of John Dalton, an atom cannot be made, destroyed, or divided; and atoms of the same element are alike. This became known as the *atomic theory*. Later physicists discovered that the nucleus of an atom can be split by bombarding it with neutrons, a process known as *nuclear fission*.

A Russian chemist, Dmitri Mendeleyev, constructed the *periodic table* by which he calculated the atomic weights of the different elements. The elements are identified by symbols taken largely from Latin names for the elements. The weights of all the other elements are based on the weight (mass) of hydrogen, the lightest known element. Hydrogen was given the atomic mass of 1 and assigned the atomic number 1. An atom of oxygen, an abundant gas on Earth, has a mass 16 times that of a hydrogen atom; therefore, oxygen was given an atomic mass of 16. Oxygen is the eighth lightest element and is assigned the atomic number 8. Dalton's and Mendeleyev's discoveries were the most significant in the field of chemistry since that of Lavoisier, a French chemist who identified oxygen as the key element that supports combustion. An example of the periodic table is illustrated on page 176.

Atomic Structure

Scientists have learned a great deal about atoms since Dalton's time. For example, an atom is composed of a nucleus with one or more electrons surrounding it. The *nucleus*, located in the center of the atom, is made up of protons and neutrons. A *proton* is a positively charged particle. An element's atomic number is determined by the number of protons it has. Since hydrogen has only one proton in its nucleus, it has an atomic number of 1. A **neutron** has a mass nearly equal to a proton's but has no charge at all. The nucleus has a positive charge determined by the number of protons it contains. The nucleus provides the mass number for an element.

An **electron** is a negatively charged particle. Electrons occupy an orbit, or shell, that surrounds the nucleus. Each shell can hold only a fixed number of electrons. It is the number of shells that distinguishes one element from another. The greater the number of shells with orbiting electrons an element has, the greater its atomic number. The following illustration shows the structure of an atom.

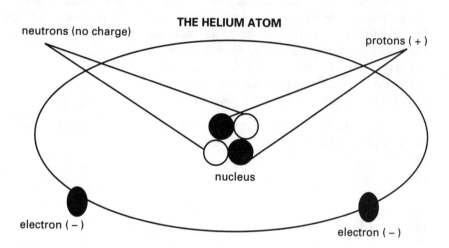

THE HELIUM ATOM

neutrons (no charge)

protons (+)

nucleus

electron (–)

electron (–)

ANSWERS TO EXERCISES IN THIS CHAPTER BEGIN ON PAGE 421.

EXERCISE 1: ATOMIC STRUCTURE

Directions: Match the terms below with the correct description by writing the correct letter of the term in the space provided.

_____ 1. the second lightest element; contains two protons in its nucleus

(a) oxygen

_____ 2. a negatively charged particle

(b) neutron

_____ 3. the part of an atom that determines element's mass

(c) proton

_____ 4. a particle that has no charge

(d) helium

_____ 5. a positively charged particle

(e) electron

_____ 6. an element containing eight protons in its nucleus

(f) nucleus

EXERCISE 2: NUCLEAR ENERGY

Directions: Read the passage below and choose the best answer for each of the following questions. You may need to refer to the periodic table shown on page 176.

Nuclear energy may be released in two ways. Nuclear fission involves the splitting of the nucleus of a heavy chemical element by bombardment with neutrons. Nuclear *fusion* involves the uniting of two nuclei of an element at high temperatures and pressure to form the nucleus of a new, heavier element.

1. Based on the information in the passage and the atomic masses shown in the periodic table, energy from nuclear fusion would be released when
   (1) uranium nuclei are fused to make plutonium
   (2) hydrogen nuclei are fused to make oxygen
   (3) oxygen nuclei are fused to make helium
   (4) hydrogen nuclei are fused to make helium
   (5) helium nuclei are fused to make hydrogen

2. Energy from nuclear fission would be released in the splitting of the nucleus of which element?
   (1) plutonium
   (2) hydrogen
   (3) oxygen
   (4) 1 and 2
   (5) 1 and 3

EXERCISE 3: ISOTOPIC ELEMENTS

Directions: Read the passage and table below and choose the best answer for the statements that follow.

Sometimes the number of neutrons in the atom of an element varies. This can affect the mass number of an element. For example, the element carbon has six protons in its nucleus, but it can also have as few as six or as many as seven neutrons in its nucleus. An element that can vary in the number of neutrons in its nucleus is described as being *isotopic*. Thus, two isotopes of carbon exist—carbon 12 and carbon 13, and they have different chemical properties. Of the two, carbon 12 is the more common.

Element	Atomic Number	Mass Number
Hydrogen	1	1.01
Helium	2	4.00
Lithium	3	6.94
Beryllium	4	9.01
Boron	5	10.81

1. The only element in the preceding chart that could have an isotope of mass number 6 and whose two nuclei might be fused to form carbon 12 would be

(1) hydrogen
(2) helium
(3) lithium
(4) beryllium
(5) boron

2. Deuterium and tritium are two isotopes that have mass numbers of 2 and 3, respectively. Of the two isotopes, tritium is especially radioactive. Based on the preceding chart, you could infer that these elements used in nuclear fusion are different forms of

(1) hydrogen
(2) helium
(3) lithium
(4) beryllium
(5) boron

Elements and Periodicity

The periodic table (shown on the following page) organizes elements based on their atomic and physical properties. The table relates the properties of the elements to their atomic numbers. Elements in the same row (across) have the same number of shells containing a varying number of electrons. Elements in the same column (down) have the same number of electrons in their outermost shell.

In classifying elements according to physical properties, scientists consider color, odor, taste, density, boiling point, solubility (ability to dissolve), malleability (capability of being shaped by beating), and hardness. Out of these properties arose the three broad groupings that chemists have used to categorize all of the elements—metals, nonmetals, and metalloids.

Metals conduct heat and electricity well, melt at high temperatures, and have a high density and brilliant luster. Examples are sodium, gold, and aluminum. *Nonmetals* melt at low temperatures, have low luster, are less dense than metals, and are poor conductors of heat and electricity. Examples are carbon, sulfur, and oxygen. *Metalloids* have properties of metals and nonmetals. Examples are antimony and arsenic.

According to the periodic law, as the atomic number increases for elements in a column, similar properties occur regularly and to a greater degree. For example, the metals with the atomic numbers 3, 11, and 19—lithium, sodium, and potassium—are all chemically active metals. In many cases, the greater the atomic number, the higher the degree of certain properties. While the second member of this group, sodium, is chemically active, rubidium, the fourth member, is so highly active that it bursts into flame upon exposure to air.

THE PERIODIC TABLE OF THE ELEMENTS

6 — Atomic Number
C — Symbol

Name
Carbon
Mass Number (number of protons and neutrons)
12

1 H Hydrogen 1																		2 He Helium 4
3 Li Lithium 7	4 Be Beryllium 9											5 B Boron 11	6 C Carbon 12	7 N Nitrogen 14	8 O Oxygen 16	9 F Fluorine 19	10 Ne Neon 20
11 Na Sodium 23	12 Mg Magnesium 24											13 Al Aluminum 27	14 Si Silicon 28	15 P Phosphorus 31	16 S Sulfur 32	17 Cl Chlorine 35	18 Ar Argon 40
19 K Potassium 39	20 Ca Calcium 40	21 Sc Scandium 45	22 Ti Titanium 48	23 V Vanadium 51	24 Cr Chromium 52	25 Mn Manganese 55	26 Fe Iron 56	27 Co Cobalt 59	28 Ni Nickel 59	29 Cu Copper 64	30 Zn Zinc 65	31 Ga Gallium 70	32 Ge Germanium 73	33 As Arsenic 75	34 Se Selenium 79	35 Br Bromine 80	36 Kr Krypton 84
37 Rb Rubidium 85	38 Sr Strontium 88	39 Y Yttrium 89	40 Zr Zirconium 91	41 Nb Niobium 93	42 Mo Molybdenum 96	43 Tc Technetium 98	44 Ru Ruthenium 101	45 Rh Rhodium 103	46 Pd Palladium 106	47 Ag Silver 108	48 Cd Cadmium 112	49 In Indium 115	50 Sn Tin 119	51 Sb Antimony 122	52 Te Tellurium 128	53 I Iodine 127	54 Xe Xenon 131
55 Cs Cesium 133	56 Ba Barium 137	57 La Lanthanum 139	72 Hf Hafnium 178	73 Ta Tantalum 181	74 W Tungsten 184	75 Re Rhenium 186	76 Os Osmium 190	77 Ir Iridium 192	78 Pt Platinum 195	79 Au Gold 197	80 Hg Mercury 201	81 Ti Thallium 204	82 Pb Lead 207	83 Bi Bismuth 209	84 Po Polonium 209	85 At Astatine 210	86 Rn Radon 222
87 Fr Francium 223	88 Ra Radium 226	89 Ac Actinium 227	104 Unq Unnilquadium 260	105 Unp Unnilpentium 262	106 Unh Unnilhexium 263	107 Uns Unnilseptium 262	108 Uno Unniloctium 265	109 Une Unnilennium 266	110 Uun Unununium								

Rare Earth Elements

Lanthanide Series	58 Ce Cerium 140	59 Pr Praseodymium 141	60 Nd Neodymium 144	61 Pm Promethium 145	62 Sm Samarium 150	63 Eu Europium 152	64 Gd Gadolinium 157	65 Tb Terbium 159	66 Dy Dysprosium 163	67 Ho Holmium 165	68 Er Erbium 167	69 Tm Thulium 169	70 Yb Ytterbium 173	71 Lu Lutetium 175
Actinide Series	90 Th Thorium 232	91 Pa Protactinium 231	92 U Uranium 238	93 Np Neptunium 237	94 Pu Plutonium 244	95 Am Americium 243	96 Cm Curium 247	97 Bk Berkelium 247	98 Cf Californium 251	99 Es Einsteinium 252	100 Fm Fermium 257	101 Md Mendelevium 258	102 No Nobelium 259	103 Lr Lawrencium 260

EXERCISE 4: ELEMENTS AND PERIODICITY

Directions: Choose the best answer for each of the following questions.

1. The metals copper, silver, and gold are in the same family (column), having atomic numbers of 29, 47, and 79, respectively. According to the principle of periodic law, of the three metals, gold would have the highest degree of which physical property?
   (1) value
   (2) rarity
   (3) volatility
   (4) malleability
   (5) scarcity

2. Radon is in the same family as helium, neon, argon, krypton, and xenon. Which of the following facts would help you to determine that radon has a greater density than the other elements in the same family?
   (1) Radon is found in the ground while the others are not.
   (2) Radon has a higher atomic number than the other elements in its family.
   (3) Radon poses potential health problems for people in areas where great concentrations are found in the ground.
   (4) 1 and 2
   (5) 2 and 3

Elements and Chemical Reactions

Each chemical reaction has two components. A ***reactant*** is the substance or substances that enter into the reaction. The ***product*** is the substance or substances that result from the reaction. A chemical reaction may be either a ***combination reaction***, in which two elements or substances are combined, or a ***decomposition reaction***, in which an element or substance is broken down.

Chemical reactions are written in a shorthand called a ***chemical equation***. A chemical formula uses symbols for elements and shows the number of atoms for each element of a substance. For example, the chemical reaction that produces water would be written:

$$2H_2 + O_2 \longrightarrow 2H_2O$$

When you read a chemical equation, the large number tells how many molecules (structures containing more than one atom) are present. When only a single molecule or atom is present, the number 1 is not written. The smaller subscript number tells how many atoms of an element are present in each molecule.

The equation for water says that two molecules of hydrogen gas (H_2) plus one molecule of oxygen gas (O_2) combine to form two molecules of water (H_2O). Notice that one molecule of hydrogen gas (H_2) contains two atoms of hydrogen, and one molecule of oxygen gas (O_2) contains two atoms of oxygen. Each molecule of water (H_2O) contains two atoms of hydrogen and one atom of oxygen.

The chemical reaction in which one atom of carbon unites with two atoms of oxygen to form carbon dioxide would be written:

$$C + O_2 \longrightarrow CO_2$$

This equation says that one molecule of carbon plus one molecule of oxygen (two atoms of oxygen) combine to form one molecule of carbon dioxide (CO_2).

All chemical reactions are governed by the *law of conservation of matter*. This law holds that matter can neither be created nor destroyed in a chemical reaction. A chemical equation adheres to this law; it shows the same number of atoms on both sides of the arrow for each element involved in a reaction. For example, the following chemical reaction occurs when methane gas (CH_4) is burned with oxygen:

$$CH_4 + 2O_2 \longrightarrow CO_2 + 2H_2O$$

Methane gas burns with oxygen to form carbon dioxide and water vapor; specifically, one molecule of carbon dioxide and two molecules of water. Notice that the reaction begins with one carbon atom (C) and ends with one carbon atom (C). The reaction begins with four hydrogen atoms (H_4) and ends with four hydrogen atoms ($2H_2$, or $2 \times 2 = 4$). The reaction begins with four oxygen atoms ($2O_2 = 2 \times 2 = 4$) and ends with 4 oxygen atoms ($O_2 + 2O = 4$). When the number of atoms of each element is equal on both sides of the equation, we say that the equation is *balanced*.

EXERCISE 5: BALANCED EQUATIONS
Directions: Identify each of the following equations as either balanced or unbalanced by writing B or U in the space provided.

_____ **1.** $N_2 + O_2 \longrightarrow 2NO$

_____ **2.** $Fe + HCl \longrightarrow FeCl_3 + H_2$

_____ **3.** $2H + O \longrightarrow H_2O$

EXERCISE 6: CHEMICAL REACTIONS
Directions: Choose the best answer for each of the following questions.

1. The chemical reaction that gives soda pop (a carbonated beverage) its fizz results from dissolving a molecule of carbon dioxide into a molecule of water. Which of the following represents the chemical equation for the process?
   (1) $CO_3 + H_2O \longrightarrow H_2CO_4$
   (2) $CO_2 + H_2O \longrightarrow H_2CO_3$
   (3) $CO + H_2O \longrightarrow H_2CO_2$
   (4) $CO_2 + H_2O \longrightarrow H_2CO_2$
   (5) $CO + 2H_2O \longrightarrow H_4CO_2$

2. The reactants and products of a chemical reaction
   (1) always double in mass
   (2) must always balance
   (3) never equal each other in mass
   (4) always need a catalyst
   (5) must triple themselves to balance

Question 3 refers to the following passage.

A ***physical change*** does not produce a new substance. For example, when you saw wood or dissolve salt in water you are not changing the chemical composition of the substances. However, a new substance is formed when a ***chemical change*** takes place. Some common chemical changes include the burning of wood and the rusting of metal on a car.

In an experiment concerning physical and chemical changes, you add 10 g of copper sulfate to 100 ml of water. You heat the solution over a low flame and stir. After the solution cools, you place a piece of aluminum foil in the copper sulfate solution. After 24 hours, the solution has changed from deep blue to a very light blue, and the aluminum has acquired a deep copper coating.

3. Which of the following pieces of information would you need to prove that a chemical change had occurred?
   (1) whether the copper sulfate solution had been heated
   (2) whether the solution had been stirred
   (3) whether twenty-four hours had passed
   (4) whether the aluminum had acquired a copper coat
   (5) whether the aluminum was breakable

Elements in Combination

Compounds are formed when two or more elements combine in a chemical reaction. The resulting product usually has different properties from either of the component elements. Compounds, when formed, can be broken down into simpler substances only by chemical action. For example, water, the most commonly known compound, is composed of two atoms of hydrogen and one atom of oxygen. When water is subjected to extreme temperatures, it can be reduced to its component elements—hydrogen and oxygen—and its liquid characteristic is lost.

Mixtures are substances that are formed when two or more elements or compounds are mixed in different proportions. The resulting product retains the properties of the combining elements. In most mixtures the combining ingredients can be separated easily. For example, gunpowder is a mixture of charcoal (a form of carbon), sulfur, and potassium nitrate (a compound of potassium and nitrogen). When mixed, the three ingredients form gunpowder, a highly explosive substance. These three ingredients can be identified by their different colors in this mixture.

When a solid, liquid, or gaseous substance is dissolved in a liquid, a homogeneous *solution* is formed. The substance that is dissolved into the liquid is called the *solute*. The liquid in which the substance is dissolved is called the *solvent*. An *aqueous* solution features water as the solvent. A *tincture* has alcohol as the solvent, such as the antiseptic tincture of iodine. Sometimes a solution is formed when a substance is dissolved in a gas or solid.

When metals are combined in varying proportions, they often form *alloys.* In an alloy, each metal dissolves into the other at high temperatures. Common examples of alloys are brass (copper and zinc), bronze (copper, tin, and other elements), and steel (iron, carbon, and other elements). An *amalgam* is formed when a metal is dissolved into mercury, a liquid metal. Amalgams are used chiefly in making tooth cements.

EXERCISE 7: TYPES OF SUBSTANCES

Directions: Choose the best answer to the questions that follow.

1. Table salt—sodium chloride, one of the most common substances occurring in nature—is best classified as
  (1) a compound
  (2) a mixture
  (3) a solution
  (4) an alloy
  (5) an amalgam

2. Air is composed of nitrogen (78 percent), oxygen (21 percent), argon (0.93 percent), carbon dioxide (0.03 percent), and other gases (0.04 percent). Air may be *best* described as
  (1) a compound
  (2) a mixture
  (3) a solution
  (4) an alloy
  (5) an amalgam

Chemical Bonding

When compounds are made, a bond is formed between two or more elements. A *bond* is a force that holds together two atoms, two ions (electrically charged particles), two molecules, or a combination of these. Bonding may result from either the transfer or the sharing of electrons between atoms.

When electrons are transferred from one atom to another, an *ionic bond* is formed. In the following example, an ionic bond is formed when an electron from a sodium atom is transferred to the outermost shell of a chlorine atom. The result is the common compound table salt.

SODIUM AND CHLORINE ATOMS   **SODIUM CHLORIDE**

● = electron in Na

○ = electron in Cl

The Na electron has tranferred over to the Cl atom.

In the preceding example, both sodium and chlorine are electrically neutral (have no charge); however, when the sodium atom loses its electron, it becomes positively charged. Opposite charges attract, forming a bond. Ionic compounds such as salt typically have high melting and boiling points, are flammable, conduct electricity when dissolved in water, and exist as solids at room temperatures.

When two or more different atoms of elements share electrons to form a molecule, a *covalent* bond is formed. For example, two atoms of hydrogen are bonded to one atom of oxygen to form the compound water.

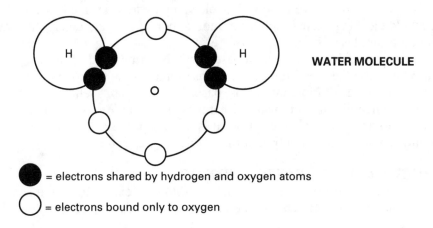

WATER MOLECULE

● = electrons shared by hydrogen and oxygen atoms

○ = electrons bound only to oxygen

In covalent bonding, the outermost shell of the element with the greatest number of electrons is filled to capacity at eight electrons. Once the combining element achieves eight electrons in its outermost ring, it cannot combine with another element. Covalent compounds such as water typically have low melting and boiling points, are nonflammable, have poor conductivity, and exist as gases and liquids.

EXERCISE 8: COMPOUNDS AND CHEMICAL BONDING
Directions: Choose the best answer for each of the following questions.

1. In ionic bonding, atoms are held together by
   (1) sharing electrons
   (2) transferring electrons
   (3) chemical attraction
   (4) temperature
   (5) magnetic fields

2. In covalent bonding, atoms are held together by
   (1) sharing electrons
   (2) transferring electrons
   (3) chemical attraction
   (4) temperature
   (5) magnetic fields

Acids, Bases, and Salts

Many compounds that result from ionic and covalent bonding are categorized as acids or bases. An *acid* is a covalent compound that produces hydrogen ions when dissolved in water. Acids have a sour taste. Common acids are acetic acid (the main component of vinegar), citric acid (found in citrus fruits), lactic acid (found in milk), and hydrochloric acid (a component of stomach acid used in digestion).

A *base* is a compound that forms hydroxide ions when dissolved in water. Bases are able to take a proton from an acid or to give up an unshared pair of electrons to an acid. Bases are described as alkaline because they dissolve in water and have a slippery feel. Many hydroxides are bases. Household cleaning agents such as ammonia, borax, lye, and detergents are common examples of bases.

When an acid combines with a base, a salt is formed and water is released because the metal found in the base replaces the hydrogen contained in the acid. Inorganic acids, bases, and inorganic salts can conduct electricity when dissolved in water. Chemists apply the *litmus test* to a substance to determine whether or not it is an acid or base. An acid turns blue litmus paper red, and a base turns red litmus paper blue.

EXERCISE 9: ACIDS, BASES, AND SALTS

Directions: The questions are based on the following explanation and scale. Read the information and choose the best answer for each question.

The designation pH (*potential for Hydrogen-ion formation*) is a value by which certain substances are classified according to acidity or alkalinity. The pH scale ranges from 0 to 14, with the value 7 representing neutrality. The pH scale is illustrated below.

pH SCALE

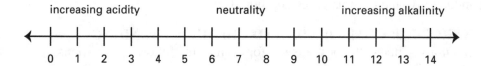

1. According to the pH scale, acetic acid, a very mild acid, would most likely be found between
   (1) 7 and 8
   (2) 0 and 1
   (3) 2 and 3
   (4) 4 and 5
   (5) 10 and 1

2. Based on the pH scale, water would be found
   (1) between O and 1
   (2) between 3 and 4
   (3) at 7
   (4) at 14
   (5) between 5 and 6

3. Which of the following could be used to prove that a substance is an acid?

(1) The substance has a pH above 7.

(2) The substance is sour or caustic.

(3) It neutralizes a base to form a salt and water.

(4) 1 and 2

(5) 2 and 3

EXERCISE 10: A CAR BATTERY

Directions: Read the passage below and answer the questions.

Acids, bases, and inorganic salts (salts obtained from nonliving things) are effective conductors of electricity. The common car battery demonstrates an electric current generated by the chemical action between an acid and a metal. In a car battery, pure lead (the negative post) and lead dioxide (the positive post) are submerged in sulfuric acid (the conductor). Distilled water is added periodically to maintain the proper level of the sulfuric acid. The pure lead loses two electrons when it reacts with the sulfuric acid—the acid changes the lead to lead dioxide. At the same time, the positive post containing lead dioxide gains two electrons and changes the sulfuric acid that it is submerged in to lead sulfate (a salt) and water. The current that makes the car start results from the flow of electrons from the lead dioxide to the lead through the sulfuric acid to the starter switch, all of which makes a complete circuit. A diagram of a car battery is shown below.

CAR BATTERY

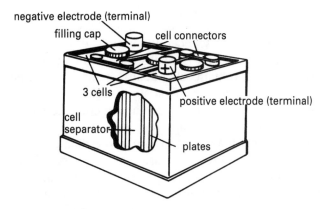

1. An *electrolyte* is an inorganic compound that will conduct an electric current when dissolved in water. What is an electrolyte in the preceding example?

(1) lead dioxide

(2) sulfuric acid

(3) distilled water

(4) 1 and 2

(5) 2 and 3

2. A substance is *oxidized* when it loses electrons. In the preceding example, which of the following compounds is oxidized?
(1) lead
(2) lead dioxide
(3) lead sulfate
(4) water
(5) sulfuric acid

3. The substances that oxidize and reduce other substances are called *oxidizing agents* and *reducing agents*. In the preceding example, the oxidizing and reducing agents, in correct order, are
(1) lead dioxide and water
(2) sulfuric acid and lead dioxide
(3) lead and sulfuric acid
(4) lead sulfate and lead dioxide
(5) sulfuric acid and water

4. Which of the following can you conclude to be true when a battery is discharged and can no longer generate a current?
(1) The sulfuric acid can no longer oxidize the lead.
(2) The lead dioxide can no longer reduce the sulfuric acid.
(3) The battery has run out of sulfuric acid.
(4) 1 and 2
(5) 1 and 3

Reaction Rate, Catalysts, and Equilibrium

Chemical reactions occur at different rates determined by the conditions under which reactions occur. Sugar dissolves more quickly in hot water than in cold. White phosphorus bursts into flame when exposed to the air. Reactions such as these may be speeded up or slowed down when another substance is introduced. A *catalyst* is a substance that increases the rate of a chemical reaction but itself remains chemically unchanged. Some catalysts have a negative effect. A negative catalyst slows down the chemical reaction. Negative catalysts are often inhibitors, such as the chemicals used in undercoating a car to retard the rusting process.

A given set of reactants may react to form more than one product. Often, the by-products react to form the original reactants. When the rate of forward reaction balances the rate of reverse reaction, *chemical equilibrium* occurs. For example, the carbon monoxide in car exhaust enters the atmosphere and reacts with oxygen to form carbon dioxide. The carbon dioxide is broken down by sunlight into the original reactant—carbon monoxide. This reaction represents chemical equilibrium because the reaction reverses itself. Chemical reactions such as these create a cycle.

EXERCISE 11: REACTION RATE, CATALYSTS, AND EQUILIBRIUM

Directions: Choose the best answer for the following questions.

1. Lipase is an enzyme produced by the liver that helps in the digestion of fats by speeding up the rate at which lipids (fats) are changed into fatty acids and glycerol. Based on this description, we can conclude that an enzyme is
   (1) a product in a chemical reaction
   (2) a negative catalyst
   (3) a biological catalyst
   (4) both 1 and 2
   (5) both 1 and 3

2. Which of the following processes illustrates chemical equilibrium?
   (1) bonding
   (2) photosynthesis
   (3) respiration
   (4) 1 and 2 together
   (5) 2 and 3 together

4
PHYSICS—THE STUDY OF HOW MATTER BEHAVES

Physics concerns the forces that cause matter to behave as it does in our world. The scope of physics is so broad that other branches of science cannot be fully understood without some knowledge of its basic laws. A *force* shows the presence of *energy* (the capacity to do work) in an environment. The area of physics that deals with forces, energy, and their effect on bodies is *mechanics*.

Mechanics

The study of mechanics was one of the first sciences developed. Ancient Greek philosopher and scientist Aristotle theorized that heavy bodies fall faster than light bodies. This theory was proved false in the early seventeenth century by Italian scientist and mathematician Galileo, who dropped items of different weights from the Leaning Tower of Pisa. The force acting upon the objects was not fully understood, however, until Sir Isaac Newton, an Englishman, formulated laws of gravity and motion that explained how different forces act on objects.

The Force of Gravity

Gravity, the most commonly experienced of all forces in nature, was first proposed by Newton when he observed the motion of an apple falling from a tree. He developed the *law of universal gravitation*, which holds that every body having a mass exerts an attractive force on every other body having a mass in the universe. The strength of the force depends on the masses of the objects and the distance between them. (*Mass* is the measure of the amount of matter in an object.) Thus, the apple's falling to earth illustrates the gravitational pull (attraction) of the larger Earth on the smaller apple. The law also explains how the planets, attracted by the much larger Sun, remain in their orbits as they revolve around it.

Newton's Three Laws of Motion

According to the *law of inertia*, a body remains at rest or continues in a state of uniform motion unless a force acts on it. For example, when you drive a car and suddenly jam on the brakes, you continue to move forward. This is because your body's tendency is to remain in the same state of uniform motion (moving forward). The brakes were applied to the car, so its uniform motion was changed.

The *law of applied force* holds that a body's change in speed and direction is proportional to the amount of force applied to it. For example, the vanes on a windmill, which move by the force of the wind, will accelerate according to the speed and direction of the wind that drives them.

The *law of action and reaction*, maintains that for every action there is an equal but opposite reaction force. For example, a gun's muzzle kicks backward when a bullet is discharged from it.

EXERCISE 1: LAWS OF FORCE AND MOTION

Directions: In the space provided, write *G* if the example illustrates Newton's law of universal gravitation, *I* if it applies to the law of inertia, *AF* if it applies to the law of applied force, and *AR* if it applies to the law of action and reaction.

_____ **1.** A jet, upon landing, lowers the flaps on its wings. The flaps create drag, a force that reduces lift and helps the plane to slow down.

_____ **2.** A rocket is propelled upward by the powerful downward discharge of exhaust gases.

_____ **3.** A bullet discharged into the air eventually falls to the ground.

_____ **4.** A pendulum in a grandfather clock, once set in motion, continues to swing, thereby regulating the clock's movement.

EXERCISE 2: THE FORCE OF GRAVITY

Directions: Read the paragraph below and answer the question that follows.

An astronaut weighs in before blast-off. He weighs only a fraction of his original weight when he steps on a scale on the moon. Journeying to Jupiter, he finds that his weight has increased several times over his original weight.

These changes in weight may be explained *best* by

(1) the amount of force each planet produced as the astronaut weighed himself
(2) the distance from the Sun of the planetary bodies on which he weighed himself
(3) changes in the atmospheric pressure on the different heavenly bodies
(4) the amount of calories consumed during the flight
(5) the duration of time that elapsed between weigh-ins

Work, Energy, and Power

In physics, **work** occurs when a force succeeds in moving an object it acts upon. For example, a person who lifts a fifty-pound weight one foot off the floor is performing work. For work to be performed, the movement of the object must be in the same direction as the force—in this case vertical. Work may be expressed as any force unit times any distance unit and may be written as follows: $W = F \times D$.

The amount of work done is the amount of force multiplied by the distance moved. In the preceding example, fifty foot-pounds of work is done when fifty pounds are lifted one foot: 50 lb × 1 ft = 50 ft lbs.

Energy is required to do work. In the example above, muscular energy is illustrated in the form of a body that is capable of doing work. **Kinetic energy** is energy possessed by a body in motion, such as a moving train.

Potential energy is energy that is stored or is available for use by a body. For example, coal has potential energy that is released only when it is burned. A boulder positioned on a hilltop has potential energy; after it is pushed, its potential energy becomes kinetic.

Power is the rate at which work is done. Power is generally measured in horsepower, which is equal to 550 foot-pounds per second or 33,000 foot-pounds per minute.

The Law of Conservation of Energy

The *law of conservation of energy* holds that all the energy of the universe is conserved. The capacity for energy to do work can be changed from one kind to another, but it cannot be lost. This principle can be illustrated in the following example of energy generated from a waterfall.

Water possesses *potential energy*. When water moves rapidly in a downward motion, drawn by the pull of gravity, the potential energy is changed into *kinetic energy*. Kinetic energy from a waterfall can be harnessed to power a turbine, a rotary engine, creating *rotational energy*. This rotational energy is sufficient to generate *electrical energy*, which in turn is converted into *light* and *heat* energy, which we use in our home. The initial potential energy was changed into five different forms.

EXERCISE 3: FORMS OF ENERGY
Directions: In the space provided, write *K* if the example demonstrates kinetic energy and *P* if it demonstrates potential energy.

_____ **1.** a strong west wind blowing across a region

_____ **2.** a stick of unlit dynamite

EXERCISE 4: TYPES OF ENERGY
Directions: Defined below are five types of energy that can perform work. Read the definitions and apply them to the questions that follow.

nuclear energy—from splitting an atom or fusing more than one atom
chemical energy—from the reaction of two or more substances combining with one another
electrical energy—from an electric current
solar energy—from the Sun's heat
steam energy—from steam pressure

1. Energy that results from the fission of uranium-235 nuclei that is used to generate electrical power is
   (1) nuclear energy
   (2) chemical energy
   (3) electrical energy
   (4) solar energy
   (5) steam energy

2. Energy that results from the ignition of a gas and air mixture and that powers a car is

(1) nuclear energy
(2) chemical energy
(3) electrical energy
(4) solar energy
(5) steam energy

Simple Machines

A *machine* is a device that transmits or multiplies force. It operates on the principle of a little force being applied through a great distance and a great resistance being overcome through a short distance. The wheelbarrow, the crowbar, the pulley, and the inclined plane are simple machines. Complex machines are made of more than one simple machine. A *lever* is a simple machine used to perform work by lifting a great weight. A lever is just a bar that is free to pivot on its support (called a *fulcrum*). Through the use of a lever, for example, a one-thousand-pound weight can be lifted with relatively little effort (force).

THE LEVER—A SIMPLE MACHINE

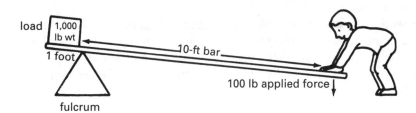

The illustration above shows that it would take 100 pounds of force for a person to lift a 1,000-pound weight positioned 1 foot from the fulcrum when the lever bar is 10 feet long. This may be expressed as follows:

$$1,000 \text{ lb} \times 1 \text{ ft} = 100 \text{ lb} \times 10 \text{ ft}$$

In this case, a relatively small force (100 lb) applied at a great distance from the object (10 ft) is able to overcome great resistance (1,000 lb). According to this principle, the greater the distance between the fulcrum and the applied force, the less force required to perform the work.

EXERCISE 5: SIMPLE MACHINES
Directions: Choose the best answer for the following question.

According to the principle that a little force applied through a great distance can overcome great resistance, which is likely to happen if the lever bar in the preceding illustration is increased to 20 feet in length and the weight remains at the end of the bar?

(1) The effort to lift the weight would increase to 150 pounds of applied force.
(2) The effort to lift the weight would remain at 100 pounds of applied force.
(3) The effort would be decreased by half, to 50 pounds of applied force.
(4) The resistance of the weight would double.
(5) The resistance of the weight would triple.

The Nature of Heat and Energy

Today we know that heat, the result of the random motion of molecules, is nothing more than energy itself. One theory of physics that has contributed greatly to our understanding of the phenomenon of heat is kinetic theory, a basic theory that explains how different states of matter can exist.

The Kinetic Theory of Matter

According to the *kinetic theory of matter*, matter exists in three states—as solids, liquids, or gases. A fourth state, *plasma*, is an ionized gas; the Sun is made up of plasma. The form, or phase, of matter is determined by the motion of the molecules within it.

Solids are composed of atoms or molecules in limited motion. These atoms or molecules are in direct contact with one another, allowing for little or no space available for random movement. The attractive forces of the particles keep the solid intact and give the solid its definite shape and structure.

In *liquids*, individual atoms or molecules are able to move past one another into new positions, giving this form of matter its fluidity. Cohesive forces hold liquids intact.

Gases are substances in which the individual atoms or molecules are in constant random motion. The motion, or kinetic energy, increases along with an increase in temperature. Molecules are unable to hold together, and this property gives gases the ability to flow or spread out to fill the container in which they are placed.

Heat, Temperature, and the States of Matter

The state of matter depends on its heat content. *Temperature* is a measure of heat intensity. The change from one state of matter to another involves the addition or subtraction of a certain amount of heat per gram of substance. For example, at 32 degrees Fahrenheit, water, a liquid, changes to ice, a solid. Above 32 degrees Fahrenheit, the ice changes to water, a liquid. Above 212 degrees Fahrenheit (the boiling point of water), it changes to steam, a gaseous state. Impurities in water affect its freezing point.

Certain materials expand when their temperature is raised and shrink when it is lowered. Liquids expand more noticeably than solids, but gases expand even more. The mercury thermometer employs this principle.

Temperature can be measured in degrees centigrade or degrees Fahrenheit. On the centigrade (or Celsius) scale, 0 degrees represents the freezing point of water, and 100 degrees is the boiling point. On the Fahrenheit scale, 32 degrees represents the freezing point of water, and 212 degrees is the boiling point. While temperature is measured in degrees by thermometer, heat is measured by the calorie or British Thermal Unit (BTU). A *calorie* is the amount of heat needed to raise one gram of water one degree centigrade. The BTU is the amount of heat required to raise one pound of water 1 degree Fahrenheit.

EXERCISE 6: KINETIC THEORY OF MATTER

Directions: In the space provided, write *T* if the statement is true or *F* if it is false.

_____ **1.** There is more rigid molecular structure in a solid than in a gas.

_____ **2.** An increase in temperature decreases the molecular motion of a gas.

_____ **3.** Molecules moving past each other in a liquid give it fluidity.

EXERCISE 7: HEAT AND TEMPERATURE

Directions: Read the passage below and answer the question that follows.

> Different materials expand at different degrees of temperature change and in different percentages of their length, volume, or surface. Buckling can occur when a material such as asphalt used for road surfaces reacts to changes in temperature, causing potholes. This is one of the reasons for the widespread use of reinforced concrete on road surfaces and in high-rise apartment construction.

The widespread use of reinforced concrete in construction suggests that
(1) concrete and steel expand and contract at nearly the same temperatures
(2) reinforced concrete expands at temperatures much higher than ordinary asphalt and does not buckle
(3) reinforced concrete does not expand and contract at all
(4) 1 and 2
(5) 2 and 3

The Nature of Waves

A *wave* is a periodic or harmonic disturbance in space or through a medium (water, for instance) by which energy is transmitted. Water, sound, and light all travel in waves. The illumination a lamp provides comes from light waves (a form of electromagnetic waves); the music emanating from a stereo comes from sound waves; the powers to preserve food and warm it come from electromagnetic waves; the power that transmits signals to a TV set comes from radio waves (another form of electromagnetic waves); and the energy that gives a waterbed its soothing motion comes from water waves.

Types and Properties of Waves

Waves transmit energy in different ways, and all phases of matter transmit waves. An example of a solid transmitting wave energy is an earthquake that takes place when rocks are under pressure and snap or slide into new positions. Waves that are felt and seen in water are examples of a liquid transmitting wave energy. Gases also transmit wave energy, as in an explosion, when heat, sound, and light waves are generated.

A *longitudinal* wave is one in which the particles of the medium move back and forth in the same direction as the wave itself moves. An example of a longitudinal wave is a sound wave that occurs when a tuning fork is tapped. In a **transverse** wave the particles of the medium move at right angles to the direction of the wave's movement. An example is a pebble tossed into a still pond. Light travels in transverse waves.

A **crest** is the point of highest displacement in a wave, and the **trough** is the point of lowest displacement. Crests and troughs are easily visible in water waves. **Wavelength** is defined as the distance between two successive wave crests or two successive wave troughs. Wave **frequency** is the number of wave crests that pass a given point per second. Therefore, the shorter the wavelength, the higher the wave frequency. In fact, a wave's speed equals the wavelength times the wave frequency.

SOUND WAVE

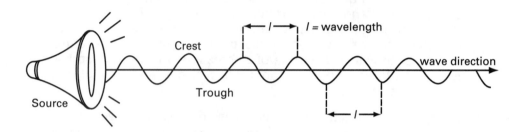

Sound Waves

Sound waves, as illustrated above, are longitudinal waves. A musical pitch, or tone, is heard when there is a definite frequency to a wave. The lower the frequency, the lower the tone. For example, the frequency of a bass speaker in a stereo is lower than a tweeter, or high-frequency speaker.

A sound wave is a wave of compression. It begins at a source such as a horn speaker. The speaker vibrates, compressing the air in front of it, and, like a spring, pushes it away. As the wave passes, the air molecules are forced together. The sensation of hearing results when these waves strike the eardrum. Sound waves can travel through solids, liquids, and gases. In fact, the human body can be a medium for sound waves. Ultrasonic waves, very high-pitched waves, are used in medicine today.

EXERCISE 8: WAVE TYPES
Directions: In the space provided, write L if the statement is an example of a longitudinal wave and T if it is an example of a transverse wave.

_____ **1.** a wave that can be seen when a loose rope held end to end is jerked at one end

_____ **2.** the hum created when an arrow is released from a bow

_____ **3.** waves that appear on the surface of the ocean

EXERCISE 9: PROPERTIES OF WAVES

Directions: Look at the illustration below and answer the question that follows.

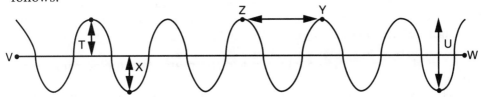

According to the illustration above, which points could be used to measure wavelength?

(1) T and Y
(2) X and Y
(3) Z and Y
(4) V and W
(5) T, X, and U

The Nature of Light

Physicists define *light* as a form of electromagnetic energy that stimulates sensitive cells of the retina of the human eye to cause perception of vision. Electromagnetic energy can be expressed in wavelength ranges along a continuum, or spectrum. Light occupies the center of a spectrum that ranges from the low end (gamma rays) to the high end (radio waves). The other rays that occupy the electromagnetic spectrum are x-rays, ultraviolet rays, and infrared rays. Ultraviolet rays are invisible and are chiefly responsible for sunburn and tan. Heat-emitting objects, such as the sun or a radiator, send out infrared rays that can be detected only by certain sensitive instruments.

THE ELECTROMAGNETIC SPECTRUM

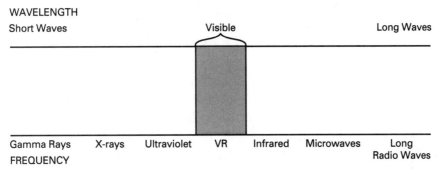

The visible rays of the spectrum are recognized by the human eye as color. In order, these colors are red, orange, yellow, green, blue, indigo (deep blue), and violet. The shortest wavelengths that we can see are those we call violet; the longest ones we call red.

Two theories about the nature of light exist. These seemingly opposing theories really just focus on different properties of light. According to the *wave theory of light*, light is a luminous energy emitted by a light source and travels through space as a transverse wave. According to the *particle theory of light*, light energy is both radiated (transmitted) and absorbed as tiny packets, or bundles, and not as continuous waves. Atoms and molecules are able to emit or absorb light energy in specific amounts.

EXERCISE 10: THE PHOTOELECTRIC PRINCIPLE

Directions: Read the passage below and answer the question that follows.

The electric eye, or photoelectric cell, is a mechanism used to open and close a garage door when a beam of light is activated or broken. The principle of the electric eye is based on the photoelectric effect. The photoelectric effect occurs when a beam of light strikes certain metals, causing electrons to be knocked out of the metal, producing an electric current.

This is how it happens: Light falling on the inside of a bulb coated with an active substance causes electrons to be emitted. The electrons are attracted to a positively charged electrode positioned in the center of the bulb like a filament. An electric current results when the electrons (negatively charged particles) are attracted to the positively charged particles of the electrode. It is observed that electrons will be knocked loose only when a certain light energy is reached. The current can then be controlled by changes in light intensity. It appears that electrons are able to absorb only a certain amount of light at one time. When light shines on the electric eye, a current is established and the door moves. When the beam of light is broken, the door stops.

The principle of the electric eye acts to
(1) support the wave theory of light that light comes only from a luminous source
(2) dispute the belief that all light exists only as a continuous wave
(3) support the particle theory of light, which states that light energy is transmitted in packets and bundles and not as waves
(4) 1 and 2
(5) 2 and 3

Properties of Light Waves

Following is a summary of the properties of light waves:

reflection—the angular return of a light wave that occurs when it strikes a shiny surface (example: light bouncing off a mirror)

refraction—the apparent bending of light waves as they pass from one medium to another (example: straw looking broken in a glass of water)

diffraction—the bending of light waves according to their wavelengths as they pass near the edge of an obstacle or through a small opening (example: "rainbow" pattern on a compact disc held edgewise toward white light)

interference—the altering of brightness of light rays that occurs when they interfere with each other, causing reinforcement and cancellation (example: holding thumb and finger together and looking through the opening at a bright light)

polarization—the restriction of light waves to a particular plane, horizontal or vertical (example: the dimming effect of polaroid sunglasses)

EXERCISE 11: PROPERTIES OF LIGHT WAVES
Directions: Defined on page 194 are five changes that light waves can
undergo. Apply the definitions to the questions that follow.

1. A coin lying at the bottom of a pool is located at a different point from
   where the eye perceives it to be. The light rays from the coin bend as
   they pass from water to air. This demonstrates
   (1) reflection
   (2) refraction
   (3) diffraction
   (4) interference
   (5) polarization

2. Rays of light striking a polished piece of chrome appear to bounce off its
   surface. This demonstrates
   (1) reflection
   (2) refraction
   (3) diffraction
   (4) interference
   (5) polarization

The Nature of Electricity

Electricity is another invisible but vital form of energy that we often
take for granted. The more urbanized we become, the more dependent on
electricity we are. Nuclear energy, despite its potential hazards, has emerged
as an important source for generating electrical power. Physicists define
electricity as a form of energy that results from the flow of loose electrons—
electrons weakly bound to atoms. Electricity is closely related to the
attractive force, magnetism.

Magnetism and Electrical Charges

The points of attraction at opposite ends of a magnet are called its *poles*.
Magnets have a north and a south pole (also called positive and negative).
The opposite poles of two different magnets will attract each other.
Correspondingly, similar poles (two north or south poles) will repel each
other. The space around magnets is called a *magnetic field*. Only a few
natural and manmade materials can be magnetized—iron, steel, nickel,
cobalt, and some alloys. A magnet is illustrated below.

MAGNET AND LINES OF FORCE

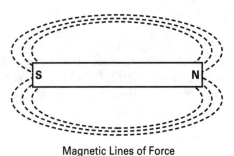

Magnetic Lines of Force

Every magnetic substance contains *domains*, groups of molecules with attractive forces. Before a substance is magnetized, these domains are arranged randomly so that the field of one domain is canceled out by the field of another. When the substance is magnetized, the domains line up parallel to the lines of force, with all north poles facing the same direction. This makes a permanent magnet out of a material in which the domains are too weak to disarrange themselves.

In most elements, the atoms possess a slight magnetic field because of their spinning electrons. However, the fields cancel each other out because the atoms rotate and spin in different directions. In a magnet, whole groups of atoms line up in one direction and increase each other's magnetic effect rather than cancel it out. These magnetic concentrations are called *magnetic domains*.

MAGNETIZED AND UNMAGNETIZED IRON ATOMS

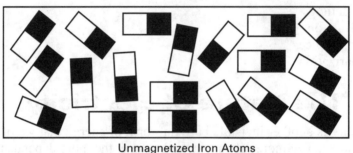

Unmagnetized Iron Atoms

N ▢▨ S—Domain

Magnetized Iron Atoms

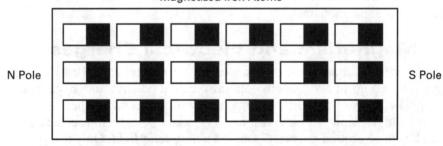

N Pole   S Pole

Static Electricity and Magnetism

Static electricity is a stationary electrical charge caused by the friction of two objects, one positively charged and the other negatively charged. Static electricity operates on the same principle as magnetism. The rubbing of the carpet by your shoes causes your body to become electrified. The shock you feel is caused by your negatively charged body being neutralized by the positive charge of the object you touch. Upon contact, your body is no longer charged. Static electricity is stored and does not move. The charged object must be brought into contact with another object that has an opposite charge for electrical shock to occur.

EXERCISE 12: ELECTRICITY AND MAGNETISM

Directions: Choose the best answer for the questions below. The first question is based on the following paragraph.

Earth itself is surrounded by a magnetic field. This may be because of strong electric currents in Earth's core and the rotation of Earth. The north magnetic pole is located in Canada; the south magnetic pole is in nearly the opposite location, near Antarctica. The strong magnetic attraction of these poles tends to align the needle of a compass in a northerly-southerly direction.

1. Based on the preceding passage, a compass will tell direction because
   (1) the whole Earth acts as a magnet
   (2) the Chinese discovered the magnetic poles
   (3) the Greeks discovered the magnetic poles
   (4) large iron deposits are located in Canada
   (5) the magnetic attraction of Earth is increasing

2. Which of the following would be attracted to either pole of a magnet?
   (1) a piece of aluminum
   (2) a piece of brass
   (3) a piece of tin
   (4) an unmagnetized piece of cobalt
   (5) a magnetized piece of cobalt

Electric Currents

Early scientists who experimented with electric charges found that charges could move easily through certain materials called *conductors* (such as metal, salt solutions, acids, and hot gases). Other materials (such as rubber) found not to conduct charges at all are called *insulators*.

An *electric current* is created by an electric charge in motion. In a solid conductor, such as wire, the current is a stream of moving electrons. In a liquid or gas, the current may be positively and negatively charged atoms, or ions.

An electric current flowing through a solid conductor can be compared to the flow of water through pipes. An electric current moves slowly—about a hundredth of an inch per second. Lights come on instantly when a switch is turned on because the wires are always filled with electrons just as a water pipe is always filled with water.

Electromagnets

An *electromagnet* is a core of soft magnetic material surrounded by a coil of wire. An electric current is passed through the wire to magnetize the core when a switch is flicked or a button pushed. The device then has the power to attract iron objects. When the switch is turned off, the attraction is broken. Electromagnets are used in radios and in ordinary doorbells.

EXERCISE 13: CONDUCTORS AND INSULATORS

Directions: In the blanks below, write *C* if the material is a conductor of electricity and *I* if it is an insulator.

_____ 1. leather

_____ 2. silver

_____ 3. wood

_____ 4. salt water

_____ 5. plastic

EXERCISE 14: ELECTROMAGNETS

Directions: Choose the best answer for the following question.

A radio with a strong electromagnet would not be placed near the navigation instruments on a plane or ship because
(1) the radio wouldn't work because of electrical interference
(2) the radio couldn't be heard clearly because of static
(3) the accuracy of the compass would be affected by the magnetic field established by the radio's electromagnet
(4) the radio's electromagnet would cause all the navigation instruments to malfunction
(5) the radio would draw too much electrical energy, causing the electrical system of the ship or plane to discharge

TEST 4: LITERATURE AND THE ARTS

The GED Literature and the Arts Test consists of prose passages of approximately 200 to 400 words, poetry passages of approximately 8 to 25 lines, and drama excerpts. Each passage is followed by multiple-choice questions that require you to interpret selections from popular literature, classical literature, and commentaries about literature and the arts. You will need to understand what you read, apply information to a new situation, and analyze elements of style and structure in passages.

How many questions are on the test?

There are 45 multiple-choice questions, and you will be given 65 minutes to complete the test. Each passage on the literature test is preceded by a purpose question. This question is not a title for the passage. Rather, it is intended to help you focus your reading of the piece. Look at the Post-Test in this book as an example.

What's on the test?

The GED Literature and the Arts Test can be broken down into the content areas it covers and the skills it tests. The following subjects make up the content of the test: Popular Literature—50%, Classical Literature—25%, and Commentaries about Literature and the Arts—25%. Also, remember that you are being tested on the following thinking skills: Understanding Ideas (Literal and Inferential Comprehension)—60%, Applying Ideas—15%, and Analyzing Ideas—25%.

1
INTERPRETING PROSE FICTION

The fiction passages presented on the Literature and the Arts Test are taken from either novels or short stories and usually present imaginary people and events that imitate life. Novels and short stories are written in *prose*—ordinary spoken language—and share common literary devices and techniques. Although many elements in fiction are common to both the novel and the short story, there are basic differences between the two forms.

The Novel and the Short Story

The *novel* is a long, book-length story. Often, the novelist writes a story that involves several characters and the events in their lives. A skillful novelist brings together characters, their adventures, and their struggles and weaves them into one main plot.

The *short story* is also a work that deals with imaginary characters, locations, or events; but the story is much shorter than a novel. Moreover, a short story usually focuses on fewer characters and on one event. By narrowing the focus, the short-story writer achieves a single effect. A good short-story writer gets to the point and quickly develops believable characters and events. The writer has limited space in which to create a work of art. Edgar Allan Poe, one of America's earliest and best short-story writers, believed that a short story should be read in one sitting. This is hours, not the days or weeks it might take to read a novel.

Although novels and short stories are developed around fictional characters, the events that occur may sometimes be based on fact. This is especially true in historical novels. For example, *Gone with the Wind*, one of the most popular novels of this century, describes events in the American Civil War.

The basic elements of fiction are illustrated in the puzzle below.

BASIC ELEMENTS OF FICTION
The Novel and Short Story

Setting When and where the story takes place	**Plot** What happens in the Story	**Characterization** Who is in the story
	Theme What the story means	
Style and Language What makes the writing unique	**Point of View** Who tells the story	**Tone** What the author's attitude is

Setting: When and Where the Story Takes Place

The *setting* of a short story or novel is the time (time of day or year), place, conditions, and atmosphere in which the action occurs. Some authors are very direct about revealing their settings. They state early in a work exactly when and where the story is happening:

Examples: He rode into St. Louis at high noon in August 1875.
The vehicle completed its orbit before landing on the lunar surface. It was A.D. 2021.

Inferring Time and Place

In many stories, the time and place are not directly stated. The reader needs to read between the lines, or look for clues, to identify a specific time and place. Read the following paragraph to infer setting. Underline all the clues that suggest *time* (when the action takes place) and *location* (where the action takes place).

> James saddled the pony and led the new pet around to the side of the porch. He stopped and tied the reins to the tractor so that he could attach a big red bow to the bridle.
> Yesterday, he'd bought the saddle, reins and bridle, and the bow at the department store over in Helena. He'd planned well for this surprise.
> The sun had barely risen when Angie, barefoot and still dressed in her nightgown, ran out of the old screen door and heard her father say, "Happy tenth birthday, honey!"

1. Does the action take place in a city or on a farm? What details act as clues?
2. Does the action take place in the 1860s or 1960s? What details act as clues?
3. Does the action take place in the early morning or the late evening? What details act as clues?
4. Does the action take place in Montana or in New Jersey? What details act as clues?

[Answers: The action takes place on a farm. Clues are *tractor, barn, saddled the pony,* and *over in Helena.* Tractors and department stores did not exist in the 1860s, so you can assume that the action takes place in the *1960s.* It takes place in early morning. Clues are *The sun had barely risen* and *Angie, barefoot and still dressed in her nightgown.* The location of the story is Montana (*Helena*).]

Atmosphere as Part of Setting

An important part of setting is *atmosphere*—the sensations and emotions associated with details of the physical setting. For example, if a story opens with a nighttime setting, a thunderstorm, a castle, and a man approaching the door, the author is creating an atmosphere of mystery or suspense. On the other hand, if a story opens with early morning as the setting and children playing happily in a playground, the atmosphere is lighthearted.

EXERCISE 1: ATMOSPHERE AS PART OF SETTING

Directions: Read the passage below and indicate which details help you determine the atmosphere of fear.

HOW DOES THIS MAN FEEL?

I've got to hide, he told himself. His chest heaved as he waited, crouching in a dark corner of the vestibule. He was tired of running and dodging. Either he had to find a place to hide, or he had to surrender. A police car swished by through the rain, its siren rising sharply. They're looking for me all over. . . . He crept to the door and squinted through the fogged plate glass. He stiffened as the siren rose and died in the distance.

Yes, he had to hide, but where?

He gritted his teeth. Then a sudden movement in the street caught his attention. . . .

—Excerpted from "The Man Who Lived Underground"
by Richard Wright

Characterization: Who Is in the Story

Characters are the fictional people in a novel or short story. *Characterization* is the method by which a writer creates fictional people who seem lifelike and believable. Writers may use any of these different methods to create character: describing the character and his or her actions, revealing the character's speech patterns, revealing what other characters say about the character, and revealing the character's unspoken thoughts.

Dialogue as an Element of Characterization

Dialogue is conversation among characters in a story. Quoting what a character says allows authors to reveal a character's attitudes, feelings, and true personality in the character's own words rather than through descriptions alone. In novels and short stories, quotation marks are placed around each speaker's exact words. Usually an author will provide transitions like *he said* and *she replied* to indicate when a character is speaking. The following sentences illustrate the difference between a restatement of a person's words and a speaker's exact words.

Restatement: She told me that she would call me for an appointment.
Exact words: "I will call you for an appointment," she said.

In longer conversations, *he said* and *she asked* may not be used in each sentence. Notice that the speakers are identified only once in this passage:

"May I help you?" inquired the eager car salesman.
"I'm looking for a used car, but I can't spend much money," Jill replied.
"I'm sure we can find something in your price range! Step over here, please. I'll show you our newer models. We have some beauties. . . ."
"Uh, I don't have much money—only a few hundred dollars."
"Well, . . . step this way to some of our older economy cars."

Plot: What Happens in the Story

The events that occur in a story make up the *plot*. The plot events occur in some time order or logical sequence. To practice comprehension of sequence, arrange the plot events below in numerical order. Notice the cause-and-effect relationship between events.

_____ **a.** Then, a small crafts shop was for sale, so we decided to make our move.

_____ **b.** For years, my sisters and I discussed owning our own business.

_____ **c.** We contacted a real estate agent about purchasing the shop.

_____ **d.** With pride, we stood with our families outside of our new shop as the workmen hoisted the sign that read "Pins and Needles."

_____ **e.** First, I read articles about developing a "cottage industry" as we considered opening a store in one of our homes.

[Answers: **a.** 3, **b.** 1, **c.** 4, **d.** 5, and **e.** 2]

Flashback as an Element of Plot

An author may choose to present events out of order. One such popular technique is called *flashback*. For example, a novel or film may present a voice saying, "It all began fifteen years ago when the couple met. . . ." The story then shifts to another scene, fifteen years earlier. The events progress in order until, by the end of the story, the characters have returned to the time and place of the opening scene.

Parts of a Plot

The events that make up a plot may be grouped and labeled according to their function in a story. The diagram illustrates the four basic parts of a plot: exposition, conflict, climax, and resolution.

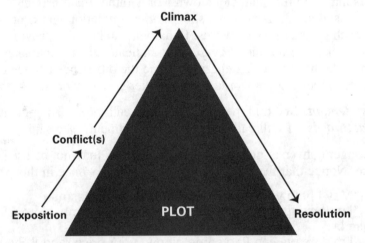

Exposition refers to background information that "sets the stage" for a story. *Conflict*, or friction between opposing characters or forces, is the basis of every plot. Most stories and novels are centered around one of the following conflicts:

Individual vs. self—inner struggles characters suffer while trying to decide what to do—change jobs, get divorced, have children, tell someone the truth about something

Individual vs. another—disagreements between characters

Individual vs. society—struggles against the rules, conventions, or pressures of living with other humans

Individual vs. nature and other forces—struggles against forces beyond a character's control, such as an earthquake or other natural disaster, or an abstraction like evil

Another element of plot is *climax*, the point of highest intensity in the plot. The climax of a story occurs when the conflict comes to a head. For example, the climax of many westerns occurs when the hero and villain meet face-to-face in a gun duel. The climax does not always occur at the very end of the story, but it usually occurs in the last part. All of the events and conflicts involving characters must be evident before they can lead to the climax. Mystery stories have very obvious climaxes. All of the clues come together to provide the answer to "Whodunit?" Following the climax, all of the loose ends are tied together, and readers learn the outcome of the conflict, or *resolution* (also usually the story's ending).

Point of View: Who Tells the Story

When you read fiction, ask yourself through whose eyes, or *point of view*, the story is being told. An author can choose from a variety of ways to tell a story. For example, if you were to write a story about a basketball game, you might choose the point of view of the coach, a fan, the guard of the leading team, or a player sitting on the bench.

The point of view from which a story is told is important because the reader has to identify with, or "get into the skin of," the character. For this reason, most authors tell their story through the eyes of the *main character*, the character whom the action affects most. Only the thoughts of the main character are revealed when the author chooses this point of view.

A writer, having decided who is to tell, or *narrate*, the story, may relate the events in first person or third person. In *first-person narration,* the word *I* is used, and the narrator speaks directly to the reader. In his famous novel *The Adventures of Huckleberry Finn,* Mark Twain made Huck Finn the narrator of the story. Huck is the main character, and the story is told through his words.

In *third-person narration*, the story is told by an "outsider" (not involved in the action). The main character is referred to as *he* or *she*. There are several different approaches to the third-person point of view, depending on how much the author wants readers—and the main character—to know.

The passage on page 206 is from an Ernest Hemingway short story, "The Short Happy Life of Francis Macomber." Hemingway describes the hunter's activities and the lion's thoughts as the animal is shot. You can tell that the story is told in the third person because Hemingway uses *he* to refer to both Macomber and the lion.

EXERCISE 2: DETERMINING POINT OF VIEW

Directions: Underline each noun (e.g., *Macomber*) or pronoun (e.g., *he*, *his*, or *them*) that represents a person or people. Circle each noun or pronoun that refers to the lion. The first three are done for you.

HOW DOES THE LION FEEL?

Macomber stepped out of the curved opening at the side of the front seat, onto the step and down onto the ground. The lion still stood looking majestically and coolly toward this object that his eyes only showed in silhouette, bulking like some super-rhino. There was no man smell carried toward him and he watched the object [jeep], moving his great head a little from side to side. Then watching the object, not afraid, but hesitating before going down the bank to drink with such a thing opposite him, he saw a man figure detach itself from it and he turned his heavy head and swung away toward the cover of the trees as he heard a cracking crash and felt the slam of a .30-06 220-grain solid bullet that bit his flank and ripped in sudden hot scalding nausea through his stomach. He trotted, heavy, big-footed, swinging wounded full-bellied, through the trees toward the tall grass and cover, and the crash came again to go past him ripping the air apart. Then it crashed again and he felt the blow as it hit his lower ribs and ripped on through, blood sudden hot and frothy in his mouth, and he galloped toward the high grass where he could crouch and not be seen and make them bring the crashing thing close enough so he could make a rush and get the man that held it.

Theme: What the Story Means

Behind all of the action in a story or movie is the writer's or director's purpose. The creator of a work wants it to have meaning for the audience. The main idea, or *theme*, may be an insight into life, a viewpoint about a social issue, a new view of an old problem, or positive or negative looks into human nature.

In successfully written fiction, as in effective films, the theme is rarely stated directly. Instead, it is implied or suggested. The reader or viewer is expected to interpret the meaning from all elements presented. For example, since the early 1950s, many science fiction writers and filmmakers have given us stories about aliens landing on our planet. A typical plot involves the aliens trying to take over Earth. One human being usually leads a rebellion against them. The theme is fear of the unknown.

EXERCISE 3: INFERRING THEME

Directions: Read the passage below and choose the best answer to each question that follows.

WHAT CONCERNS MISS STRANGEWORTH?

After thinking for a minute, she decided that she would like to write another letter, perhaps to go to Mrs. Harper, to follow up the ones she had already mailed. She selected a green sheet this time and wrote quickly: HAVE YOU FOUND OUT YET WHAT THEY WERE ALL LAUGHING ABOUT AFTER YOU LEFT THE BRIDGE CLUB ON THURSDAY? OR IS THE WIFE REALLY ALWAYS THE LAST ONE TO KNOW?

Miss Strangeworth never concerned herself with facts; her letters all dealt with the more negotiable stuff of suspicion. Mr. Lewis would never have imagined for a minute that his grandson might be lifting petty cash from the store register if he had not had one of Miss Strangeworth's letters. Miss Chandler, the librarian, and Linda Stewart's parents would have gone unsuspectingly ahead with their lives, never aware of possible evil lurking nearby, if Miss Strangeworth had not sent letters opening their eyes. Miss Strangeworth would have been genuinely shocked if there *had* been anything between Linda Stewart and the Harris boy, but as long as evil existed unchecked in the world, it was Miss Strangeworth's duty to keep her town alert to it.

—Excerpted from "The Possibility of Evil" by Shirley Jackson

1. The conflict of this passage is between Miss Strangeworth and
   (1) nature
   (2) Mrs. Harper
   (3) herself
   (4) society
   (5) imaginary evil

2. The theme of the passage is best stated in which of these ways?
   (1) It is a citizen's duty to judge the behavior of others.
   (2) What people don't know won't hurt them.
   (3) Regardless of their intentions, some people create pain for others.
   (4) Knowing all the facts is not important when making accusations.
   (5) One should not join organizations if one has something to hide.

Tone and Style
Tone: What the Author's Attitude Is

The *tone* of a novel or short story is the overall attitude that an author conveys toward his or her subject. When listening to a person speak, you can infer the person's attitude by the sound of his or her voice. The tone tells you whether the person means to be sarcastic or serious or funny. When reading, you must infer the author's tone.

An author's choice of words and phrasing reflects his or her attitude. What tone is presented in the paragraph below? Write a few words that describe the tone of this passage.

Our first-born son, "Matt the Mouth," was a wild, oversized, constantly hungry toddler. As he grew, he seemed to dwarf all other children around him. His first word was *cake*, and his first step was taken toward the refrigerator! How that kid loved to eat!

[Answer: You might have written *funny, humorous, comical, light, nostalgic,* or *mocking*. The author is a parent looking back on a son whose eating habits were memorable. The tone is not one of sadness or resentment, but one of fond yet humorous memories of "Matt the Mouth."]

EXERCISE 4: TONE AND CHARACTERIZATION

Directions: Read the passage below and answer the questions that follow.

WHAT IS THE AUTHOR'S TONE?

Her doctor had told Julian's mother that she must lose twenty pounds on account of her blood pressure, so on Wednesday nights Julian had to take her downtown on the bus for a reducing class at the Y. The reducing class was designed for working girls over fifty, who weighed 165 to 200 pounds. His mother was one of the slimmer ones, but she said ladies did not tell their age or weight. She would not ride the buses by herself at night since they had been integrated, and because the reducing class was one of her few pleasures, necessary for her health, and *free,* she said Julian could at least put himself out to take her, considering all she did for him. Julian did not like to consider all she did for him, but every Wednesday night he braced himself and took her.

—Excerpted from "Everything That Rises Must Converge" by
Flannery O'Connor

1. "[S]he said Julian could at least put himself out to take her [to her class], considering all she did for him. Julian did not like to consider all she did for him, but every Wednesday night he braced himself and took her." If the author read these lines, how would her voice sound?
   (1) gentle and tolerant
   (2) angry and bitter
   (3) tragic and depressed
   (4) sarcastic and funny
   (5) sweet and resigned

2. The author's attitude is most likely that people like Julian's mother are
   (1) to be laughed at or ridiculed
   (2) to be respected for their high ideals
   (3) to be tolerated and sympathized with
   (4) absolutely wrong in their outlook on life
   (5) morally superior to all other people

Style and Language: What Makes the Writing Unique

Style refers to the author's unique use of the language—the choice and arrangement of words. An author's style may contain long, complex sentences, it may contain everyday spoken language, or it may contain dialect.

Dialect as an Element of Style

Dialect is the pattern of speech characteristic of a certain region. In the United States, we can sometimes tell if people are from the Deep South or New England just by their accents. Regional expressions, word choices, and pronunciations contribute to dialect. Writers of fiction may have their characters speak in dialects. Below are two examples of how the dialect of an area and time period are used in novels. The first example is from

Nathaniel Hawthorne's *The Scarlet Letter*. The characters are Puritans living around Boston in the 1600s.

> "Pearl! Little Pearl!" cried he, after a moment's pause; then, suppressing his voice, "Hester! Hester Prynne! Are you there?"
>
> "Yes; it is Hester Prynne!" she replied, in a tone of surprise; and the minister heard her footsteps approaching from the sidewalk, along which she had been passing, "It is I, and my little Pearl."
>
> "Whence come you, Hester?" asked the minister. "What sent you hither?"

Notice words such as *whence* ("from where") and *hither* ("here").

The next passage is from Zora Neale Hurston's 1937 novel *Their Eyes Were Watching God.* It is written in a dialect that was spoken by some rural, southern African-Americans of the time.

> "What she doin' coming back here in dem overhalls? Can't she find no dress to put on?—Where's dat blue satin dress she left here in?—Where all dat money her husband took and died and left her?—What dat ole forty year ole 'oman doin' wid her hair swingin' down her bak lak some young gal?—Where she left dat young lad of a boy she went off here wid?"

Types of Styles

Authors who publish many works often become known and appreciated for their styles as well as their themes and characters. Hemingway, for example, is known for a terse writing style of few words. On the other hand, Charles Dickens is known for a narrative style characterized by long sentences and vivid descriptions. Edgar Allan Poe used short sentences, the repetition of words, and many dashes, exclamation points, and italics to add emotion and suspense to his stories. He opens "The Tell-Tale Heart" with: "True!—nervous—very, very dreadfully nervous I had been and am! but why *will* you say that I am mad?"

EXERCISE 5: IDENTIFYING AN AUTHOR'S STYLE

Directions: Read the passage below. Underline all descriptions and images that appeal to your senses: sight, smell, taste, touch, and especially hearing.

WHAT IMAGES DOES THE WRITER CALL TO MIND?

The soprano screak of carriage wheels punished my ear. Sun, seeping through the blinds, filled the bedroom with a sulphurous light. I didn't know how long I had slept, but I felt one big twitch of exhaustion.

The twin bed next to mine was empty and unmade.

At seven I had heard my mother get up, slip into her clothes and tiptoe out of the room. Then the buzz of the orange squeezer sounded from downstairs, and the smell of coffee and bacon filtered under my door. Then the sink water ran from the tap and dishes clinked as my mother dried them and put them back in the cupboard.

Then the front door opened and shut. Then the car door opened and shut, and the motor went broom-broom and, edging off with a crunch of gravel, faded into the distance.

—Excerpted from *The Bell Jar* by Sylvia Plath

Figures of Speech as an Element of Style

Figures of speech are not meant to be taken literally. They are expressive ways of describing. You hear figures of speech in spoken English every day. In fiction writing, figurative language is used to create vivid pictures and original descriptions. There are many kinds of figures of speech. In literature, especially in poetry, you can find specific figures of speech called *similes*, *metaphors*, and *personification*. A brief explanation of each follows:

A *simile* (sim' uh lee) is a comparison that shows a likeness between two unlike things. A simile is introduced by the words *like*, *than*, or *as*.

Examples: Her hair was like woven straw.
　　　　　 She is colder than ice.
　　　　　 Bill is as strong as an ox.

A *metaphor* (met' uh for) is a comparison that does not contain *like*, *than*, or *as*. A metaphor implies that one thing *is* something else.

Examples: The path was a ribbon of moonlight.
　　　　　 All the world is a stage.

Personification (per sahn' uh fuh kay' shun) attributes some human activity or quality to an animal or thing.

Examples: The sun smiled down on me.
　　　　　 The leaves awoke and greeted the season.

How to Read Fiction on Your Own

While your examination of each element of fiction contributes to your understanding, it is the *whole*, not its *parts*, that represents a work of art. Use the tips that follow to guide your reading of literature.

TIPS ON READING FICTION

As you read a story, ask yourself:

- What is the setting?
- What is the atmosphere?
- Who are the characters?
- Are they named or described?
- What is the plot?
- What is the conflict?
- From whose point of view is the story told?
- What are clues to the theme?
- What is the author's style like?
- What is the author's tone?

About Prose Fiction: Commentary

Sometimes it is useful to read literary criticism *about* fiction. **Criticism** is the art of evaluating and analyzing a work of art or literature. A **critic** is a person who expresses an opinion about or who comments on a work of art or literature. Critics are also known as **reviewers**, persons who review works of literature or art.

Writers of literary criticism analyze a particular work by discussing setting, plot, characterization, theme, tone, and style and language. Critics read works of fiction, poetry, drama, and nonfiction. They ask such questions as "How did the author create the story?" and "Was the author successful in achieving her goal?"

A critic may write general commentary about fiction and nonfiction in a newspaper or magazine column that appears regularly. A critic may also write reviews of movies, television programs, theater performances, art exhibits, live or recorded musical performances, or dance.

Nearly one-fourth of the questions on the Literature and the Arts Test will deal with commentary. **Commentary** is writing *about* literature and the arts—published comments, reviews, and criticism.

EXERCISE 6: COMMENTARY ABOUT FICTION

Directions: Below is a brief review of a novel which tells a little about the author and his or her career, major events in the plot of the book, and the reviewer's opinion of the book. Read the review and answer the questions that follow.

History Repeats Itself
by Anne Whitehouse
A Review of *The Last Room* by Elean Thomas
Virago/Trafalgar Square, paper, $13.95

The Last Room, the Jamaican writer Elean Thomas's first novel, is about two generations of mothers and daughters. Valerie Barton, nicknamed Putus ("meaning sweet and special"), is the only child and bright hope of her parents. As her mother says, "You wi be the one who bruk dem slavery chain fi-ever." But Putus's father dies, her mother remarries, and the girl is sent away. Befriended by an older man, she becomes pregnant. Young and naive, she does not realize at first that her condition means the death of her hopes. History repeats itself when Putus leaves her own daughter, Icylane, behind in Jamaica to join a man in England whom she will marry. Eighteen years pass. The story continues through Icy, now a civil servant, who goes to England to seek out the mother who abandoned her and who is said to be ill. Throughout the novel, Ms. Thomas makes generous use of dialect, and a glossary of Jamaican terms is provided. Her storytelling only falters with the somewhat disconcerting break between the stories of Putus and Icy; one wants to follow Putus's life as a young woman instead of returning to her decades later, when she has only the remnants of her anger and pride. Nevertheless, *The Last Room* is an affecting novel about hope and disillusionment, expectation and failure.

1. What is the reviewer's opinion of the story?
   (1) Its dialect is confusing.
   (2) The focus should remain on Putus.
   (3) Icy is the book's best character.
   (4) The characters should remain in Jamaica.
   (5) The story falters because it's set in England.

2. Which statement best sums up the reviewer's opinion of the author?
   (1) She is a good storyteller.
   (2) She is a beginning writer.
   (3) Her writing is confusing.
   (4) She doesn't know Jamaica.
   (5) She doesn't know England.

3. Which of the following categories does *The Last Room* most likely fall into?
   (1) humorous writing
   (2) detective-mystery
   (3) science fiction
   (4) real-life drama
   (5) light romance

2
INTERPRETING POETRY

Poetry expresses ideas and emotions in a tightly controlled and structured way. Simply put, poetry is the best words in their best order. Poetry is compressed. *Imagery* (word pictures that appeal to the five senses) and figures of speech enable the poet to convey ideas in just a few words.

Some poems are written in rhyme, the repetition of a sound at the end of two or more words, like *say* and *hay*. Sound and rhythm, the "beat," arouse feelings and evoke thoughts. All of these characteristics of poetry make it a distinct form of literature. On the Literature and the Arts Test, you will be expected to demonstrate your understanding of a poem's meaning. You should be able to read a poem, spend a few minutes interpreting it, and answer the questions about the theme.

ANSWERS TO EXERCISES IN THIS CHAPTER BEGIN ON PAGE 426.

EXERCISE 1: INTERPRETING TWO POEMS
Directions: Read each poem aloud and answer the questions that follow.

WHAT ARE THE POETS SAYING AND HOW ARE THEY SAYING IT?

Oh, When I Was in Love with You

Oh, when I was in love with you,
    Then I was clean and brave,
And miles around the wonder grew
    How well did I behave.

And now the fancy passes by,
    And nothing will remain,
And miles around they'll say that I
    Am quite myself again.

—A. E. Housman

Sonnet 43

How do I love thee? Let me count the ways.
I love thee to the depth and breadth and height
My soul can reach, when feeling out of sight
For the ends of Being and ideal Grace.
I love thee to the level of every day's
Most quiet need, by sun and candlelight.
I love thee freely, as men strive for Right;
I love thee purely, as they turn from Praise.
I love thee with the passion put to use
In my old griefs, and with my childhood's faith.
I love thee with a love I seemed to lose
With my lost saints—I love thee with the breath,
Smiles, tears, of all my life!—and, if God choose,
I shall but love thee better after death.

—Elizabeth Barrett Browning

1. The theme of both poems involves
   (**1**) separation
   (**2**) love that is not returned
   (**3**) beauty
   (**4**) romantic love
   (**5**) love for one's fellow human being

2. A technique common to both poems is the use of
   (**1**) personification
   (**2**) imagery
   (**3**) rhyme
   (**4**) simile
   (**5**) metaphor

TIPS ON READING POETRY

1. Read the title as a clue to the meaning.

2. Read the whole poem to get the general ideas and mood.

3. Ask yourself: What is this about? What is the poet saying? What does the poem mean? What is the theme?

4. Reread the poem using the punctuation as a guide. (Stop where there's a period or other end mark, not at the end of a line.)

5. Notice how lines are grouped together and if lines are repeated. What is the poet stressing by repeating words and lines?

6. Notice the language used and unusual word choices, comparisons, imagery, and figures of speech.

7. Read the poem aloud so you can hear it, especially if words rhyme.

8. Summarize in your own words what the poem is saying to understand the poem's tone and theme.

The Shape of Poetry

The structure and form of poetry distinguish it from other types of literature. Many poets choose a highly structured format, in which they shape their ideas using rhyme, rhythm, and stanzas. A *stanza* is a group of lines that work together to express an idea. A new stanza signals that a new idea is being introduced in a poem. Often, stanzas are separated by a blank space. The following poem by Dorothy Parker contains two stanzas:

On Being a Woman

stanza 1
> Why is it, when I am in Rome,
> I'd give an eye to be at home
> But when on native earth I be,
> My soul is sick for Italy?

stanza 2
> And why with you, my love, my lord,
> Am I spectacularly bored,
> Yet do you up and leave me—then
> I scream to have you back again?

When you sing a song, you may sing a verse, a chorus, the second verse, the same chorus, the third verse, a chorus, etc. A *verse* is any piece of poetry that is arranged in a pattern. Many songs were poems before they were set to music. An example is "The Battle Hymn of the Republic," by Julia Ward Howe. The term *free verse* refers to verses without a regular rhythmic pattern and usually without rhyme. Much of today's poetry is free verse.

Capitalization and Punctuation

In poetry, as in prose, a comma or a dash means "pause." A period means "stop." If the poem contains capitalization and punctuation, it should be read in sentences, not just one line at a time. Sometimes the reader may have to run two or more lines together. For example, in the poem "History," which follows, lines 2–4 are read "Morning sunlight lengthened in spears across the linoleum floor." The use of capital letters in poetry can vary. Sometimes a poet capitalizes each line. Sometimes a poet capitalizes a word for emphasis.

EXERCISE 2: THE SHAPE OF POETRY
Directions: Read aloud the poem below and answer the questions that follow. Notice the capitalization and punctuation as you read.

HISTORY

Grandma lit the stove.
Morning sunlight
Lengthened in spears
Across the linoleum floor.
Wrapped in a shawl,
Her eyes small
With sleep,
She sliced papas,
Pounded chiles
With a stone
Brought from Guadalajara.

After
Grandpa left for work,
She hosed down
The walk her sons paved
And in the shade
Of a chinaberry,
Unearthed her
Secret cigar box
Of brought coins
And bills, counted them
In English,
Then in Spanish,
And buried them elsewhere.
Later, back
From the market,
Where no one saw her,
She pulled out

Pepper and beet, spines
Of asparagus
From her blouse,
Tiny chocolates
From under a paisley bandana,
And smiled.

That was the '50s,
And Grandma in her 50s
A face streaked
From cutting grapes
And boxing plums
I remember her insides
Were washed of tapeworm,
Her arms swelled into knobs
Of small growths—
Her second son
Dropped from a ladder
And was dust.
And yet I do not know
The sorrows
That sent her praying
In the dark of a closet,
The tear that fell
At night
When she touched
Loose skin
Of belly and breasts.
I do not know why

Her face shines
Or what goes beyond this shine,
Only the stories
That pulled her
From Taxco to San Joaquin,

Delano to Westside,
The places
In which we all begin.

—Gary Soto

1. There are eleven lines in the first stanza. How many *sentences* are there? (Notice periods.)

2. In which stanza is she happier? Give the clue word that indicates this mood.

3. Who is the narrator in this poem?

The Sound of Poetry

Poets rely on many devices, including rhyme, rhythm, and alliteration to communicate their messages to readers. Babies and toddlers may be introduced to the literature of their native language through nursery rhymes. *Rhyme* is the repetition, in two or more words, of the stressed vowel sound and of the syllables that follow that sound.

Examples: Hickory-dickory-*dock*, the mouse ran up the *clock*.
Jack and *Jill* went up the *hill*.

Just as word choices produce a desired effect in poetry, so does the beat, or rhythm, of a poem. In poetry, *rhythm* is the rise and fall of stressed words and syllables. If the rhythm is regular, or ordered strictly, the poem is said to have *meter*.

The repetition of consonant sounds, usually at the beginning of words, is *alliteration*. "Peter Piper picked a peck of pickled peppers" is an example of alliteration. Nursery rhymes contain much alliteration, and advertising slogans and jingles incorporate this technique frequently.

EXERCISE 3: THE SOUND OF POETRY
Directions: Read the poem and answer the questions that follow. Notice (1) the absence of capitalization, (2) the rhythm, and (3) alliteration of the sounds made by the letters *m, s,* and *b.*

maggie and milly and molly and may

maggie and milly and molly and may
went down to the beach (to play one day)

and maggie discovered a shell that sang
so sweetly she couldn't remember her troubles, and

5 milly befriended a stranded star
whose rays five languid fingers were;

and molly was chased by a horrible thing
which raced sideways while blowing bubbles: and

may came home with a smooth round stone
10 as small as a world and as large as alone.

For whatever we lose (like a you or a me)
it's always ourselves we find in the sea

—e. e. cummings

1. List at least two different examples of alliteration:

(1) _____

(2) _____

2. Cummings uses rhyme in this poem. In lines 5–6 *star* and *were* do not rhyme. Which other pairs of lines do not rhyme?

3. Lines 11–12, which read "For whatever we lose (like a you or a me) / it's always ourselves we find in the sea," contain the theme of the poem. In these lines, the author is expressing which of the following ideas?
(1) The sea is a source of life and death.
(2) The sea is the best place for a person to reflect about life.
(3) Everybody does not have the same respect for the sea.
(4) The sea and its surroundings can give people a fresh view on life.
(5) The sea represents all of our moods.

Words That Stand for Sounds

Most poetry is written to be read aloud. As the poet writes the words, he or she is aware of the sound of the poem. Many poets use "sound words" to enhance the imagery and message of their poetry. The term ***onomatopoeia*** (ahn' uh mah' tuh pee' uh) refers to the use of words that imitate sounds. Sound-imitating words include *buzz*, *screech*, *boom*, *crash*, and *whisper*.

EXERCISE 4: WORDS THAT STAND FOR SOUNDS
Directions: Carl Sandburg wrote the following poem in 1920. Notice how the "sounds" of the poem imitate the sounds of a jazz band. Answer the questions that follow.

WHAT JAZZ SOUNDS CAN YOU HEAR?
Jazz Fantasia

Drum on your drums, batter on your banjos, sob on the long cool winding saxophones. Go to it, O jazzmen.

Sling your knuckles on the bottoms of the happy tin pans, let your trombones ooze, and go husha-husha-hush with the slippery sandpaper.

Moan like an autumn wind high in the lonesome treetops, moan soft like you wanted somebody terrible, cry like a racing car slipping away from a motorcycle-cop bang-bang! you jazzmen, bang altogether drums, traps, banjos, horns, tin cans—make two people fight on the top of a stairway and scratch each other's eyes in a clinch tumbling down the stairs.

Can the rough stuff. . . . Now a Mississippi steamboat pushes up the night river with a hoo-hoo-hoo-oo . . . and the green lanterns calling to the high soft white stars . . . a red moon rides on the humps of the low river hills. . . . Go to it, O jazzmen.

1. Sandburg uses alliteration to establish a rhythm in the first stanza. Which words illustrate alliteration?
   (1) *long* and *cool*
   (2) *sob* and *winding*
   (3) *to* and *it*
   (4) *O* and *jazzmen*
   (5) *batter* and *banjos*

2. One figurative device that Sandburg uses in the third stanza is both a simile *and* an example of personification. Which of the following descriptions represents both of these?
   (1) "high in the lonesome treetops"
   (2) "like a racing car slipping away from a motorcycle-cop"
   (3) "Moan like an autumn wind"
   (4) "make two people fight on the top of a stairway"
   (5) "bang altogether drums, traps, banjos, horns, tin cans"

Interpreting Meaning

When you interpret a poem, you rephrase it, putting the poem into your own thoughts and words. You may simply change words around to make a statement more understandable to you. You may guess at the poet's main purpose and ask yourself, *Why is the poet using this comparison?* or *Why does the poet say this?*

Read the following poem, "My Papa's Waltz," by Theodore Roethke. Then read it again, a stanza at a time. Write a sentence or two summarizing each stanza in your own words. After you write *your* interpretation, read the interpretation provided at the end of the poem. You may or may not agree with the interpretation.

My Papa's Waltz

The whisky on your breath
Could make a small boy dizzy;
But I hung on like death:
Such waltzing was not easy.

We romped until the pans
Slid from the kitchen shelf;
My mother's countenance
Could not unfrown itself.

The hand that held my wrist
Was battered on one knuckle;
At every step you missed
My right ear scraped a buckle.

You beat time on my head
With a palm caked hard by dirt,
Then waltzed me off to bed
Still clinging to your shirt.

Interpretation of stanza 1: A man is remembering his father. His father must have been drinking before he began dancing with his son.

Interpretation of stanza 2: The son remembers dancing wildly around the kitchen while his mother watched disapprovingly.

Interpretation of stanza 3: The son remembers being small enough to notice the battered knuckle of his father and to remember the pain of his ear scraping against his father's belt buckle each time his father stumbled.

Interpretation of stanza 4: His father was dirty from working hard; his hands were still dirty as they danced. The son held on to his father as they waltzed.

EXERCISE 5: INFERRING MEANING

Directions: In the blanks below the poem, indicate the line numbers and key words that support the inferences.

Strength

That strong right hand that
once balanced our
young sons near the sky,
once tossed bales of
5 straw each August,
once pitched no-hitters
after Sunday picnics,
once tenderly stroked
my once-auburn hair . . .

10 That hand
now crudely arches to grasp
a bamboo cane and
now trembles as you reverently
bow your feeble body in prayer
15 and give thanks for the years
of that strong right hand.

Inferences	Line Numbers	Key Words
1. The man is a father.	_____	_____
2. The man was athletic.	_____	_____
3. The man is now elderly.	_____	_____

Inferring Mood

Mood is very important in poetry. When a poet creates a poem, the words chosen help present an overall feeling. The mood may be humorous and light, or somber and serious. Within a poem, the mood sometimes changes. Read the following song from the musical *Cats*. As you read, identify the mood of each part. Circle the word that most accurately describes the mood of each stanza.

Memory

Midnight, not a sound from the pavement.
Has the moon lost her memory?
She is smiling alone.
In the lamp light the withered leaves
    collect at my feet
And the wind begins to moan.

1. (**a**) optimistic
   (**b**) lonely
   (**c**) eager

Memory. All alone in the moonlight
I can smile at the old days.
I was beautiful then.
I remember the time
    I knew what happiness was,
Let the memory live again. . . .

2. (**a**) nostalgic
   (**b**) humorous
   (**c**) afraid

Daylight. I must wait for the sunrise
I must think of a new life
And I mustn't give in.
When the dawn comes
    tonight will be a memory, too
And a new day will begin. . . .

3. (**a**) depressed
   (**b**) sarcastic
   (**c**) hopeful

Touch me. It's so easy to leave me
All alone with the memory
Of my days in the sun.
If you touch me you'll understand
 what happiness is.
Look, a new day has begun.

4. (a) regretful
  (b) content
  (c) confused

[Answers: **1. (b)** *lonely* (moon smiling alone and the wind moaning),
2. (a) *nostalgic* (cat smiling and remembering), **3. (c)** *hopeful* (daylight
and a new day), **4. (b)** *content* (new day has begun)]

The Language of Poetry
Imagery

A poet relies on readers' abilities to create images or pictures in their
minds from the words on a page. For this reason, the poet must choose the
perfect word to convey a thought. When a poem appeals to your senses and
enables you to imagine a scene, the poem is rich in ***imagery***.

> *Example:* The noisy raindrops hit the car's hood like thousands
>   of thumbtacks.

Can you "see" the raindrops and "hear" the metallic sound made as they hit
the car's hood?

Personification

Personification is a form of imagery in which human activities or
qualities are attributed to an animal or a thing. In other words, a nonhuman
thing comes "alive" as it is given human abilities. Carl Sandburg used
personification to immortalize a city in his famous poem "Chicago." Notice
that he addresses the city as a person. Here are the opening lines.

Chicago

Hog Butcher for the World,
Tool Maker, Stacker of Wheat,
Player with Railroads and the Nation's Freight Handler;
Stormy, husky, brawling,
City of the Big Shoulders:

The names he calls the city in the first three lines refer to the commerce and
industry Chicago was known for. Chicago is personified—made human—
when the poet refers to it as "stormy, husky, brawling / City of the big
shoulders."

In the following poem, underline all examples of personification. In what
ways is the town human?

Steel Town

August skies accept
your belch of refuse
and ashes are excreted
high above new grass that
timidly borders
your concrete veins,

pulsating to sustain the hectic tempo
of days that too soon expire.
Your structure ages, breathing lessens,
and you remain
a body
with no soul.

[Answers: You should have underlined *belch*, *excreted*, *timidly*, *veins*, *pulsating*, *expire*, *ages*, *breathing*, and *body with no soul*. The poet writes as if the town possesses the human abilities to live and die.]

EXERCISE 6: THE LANGUAGE OF POETRY
Directions: Write *imagery* if a line evokes an image or *personification* if it attributes a human quality to an inanimate object.

Line 1: Midnight, not a sound from the pavement. _____

Line 2: Has the moon lost her memory? _____

Line 3: She [the moon] is smiling alone. _____

Simile and Metaphor

A *simile* is a comparison of two unlike things. A simile includes the word *like*, *than*, or *as*. Poet Robert Frost uses similes in the following poem, "Design." Underline the four similes.

Design
I found a dimpled spider, fat and white,
On a white heal-all,[1] holding up a moth
Like a white piece of rigid satin cloth—
Assorted characters of death and blight
Mixed ready to begin the morning right,
Like the ingredients of a witches' broth—
A snow-drop spider, a flower like a froth,
And dead wings carried like a paper kite.
What had that flower to do with being white,
The wayside blue and innocent heal-all?
What brought the kindred spider to that height,
Then steered the white moth thither in the night?
What but design of darkness to appall?—
If design govern in a thing so small.

[1] A *heal-all* is a type of plant.

[Answers: You should have underlined these similes: "a moth / Like a white piece of rigid satin cloth"; "Like the ingredients of a witches' broth"; "a flower like a froth"; and "dead wings carried like a paper kite."]

A *metaphor* is an implied or suggested comparison between two things. A metaphor does not contain *like*, *than*, or *as*. With a metaphor, one thing is the second thing to which it is being compared.

Example: The day was an unwritten journal page waiting to be filled.

This metaphor presents an image of a blank paper—the day—ready for activities. The day *is* an unwritten journal page.

In this opening stanza of "An Indian Summer Day on the Prairie," by Vachel Lindsay, there are three metaphors. What three comparisons are made?

The sun is a huntress young,
The sun is a red, red joy,

The sun is an Indian girl,
Of the tribe of the Illinois.

[Answer: The poet compares the sun to a huntress, joy, and an Indian girl. The reader gets a different image of the sun and an idea of the prairie setting.]

EXERCISE 7: MORE PRACTICE IN INTERPRETING A POEM

WHAT IS THE POET SAYING ABOUT DEATH?
Because I Could Not Stop for Death

1

Because I could not stop for Death,
He kindly stopped for me;
The carriage held but just ourselves
And Immortality.

2

We slowly drove, he knew no haste,
And I had put away
My labor, and my leisure too,
For his civility.

3

We passed the school where children
    played
At wrestling in a ring;
We passed the fields of gazing grain,
We passed the setting sun.

4

We paused before a house that
    seemed
A swelling of the ground;
The roof was scarcely visible,
The cornice but a mound.

5

Since then 'tis centuries; but each
Feels shorter than the day
I first surmised the horses' heads
Were toward eternity.

—Emily Dickinson

1. Match the stanza on the left with the images on the right by writing the correct letter in the space provided.

_____ **Stanza 1**   **(a)** images of a school yard, farm, land, dusk

_____ **Stanza 2**   **(b)** the narrator riding in a carriage with two others

_____ **Stanza 3**   **(c)** a slow ride as the narrator accepts her fate

_____ **Stanza 4**   **(d)** the narrator remembering the day of the carriage ride, hundreds of years before

_____ **Stanza 5**   **(e)** the carriage pausing at a gravesite

2. The poet capitalizes the words *Death* and *Immortality* to illustrate that
   (1) death is a major theme
   (2) they are the chief concerns of a person's life
   (3) they are characters in the poem
   (4) the two words are opponents, one fighting the other
   (5) they are two unexplainable concepts that people must deal with

3. From the last stanza, one can infer that the speaker in the poem
   (1) knows when she is going to die
   (2) feels time moves too slowly
   (3) never looks back at the past
   (4) enjoys carriage rides
   (5) believes in eternal life

About Poetry: Commentary

Below is a sample review of a poetry collection. The review is written by a literary critic whose purpose is to evaluate a volume of poetry. You might see a review of poetry in a literary magazine or the literature section of a news magazine or newspaper.

WHAT IS THE CRITIC'S OPINION?
Whispered Secrets by Ann Fox Chandonnet, Denise Lassaw, Eleanor Limmer, and Joanne Townsend
Sedna Press, $10
Reviewed by Stephen C. Levi

Whispered Secrets was a book long in coming and well worth the wait. In fact, it is unexpectedly refreshing. Allow this reviewer to explain. Sedna Press, as the foreword explains, takes its name from the Eskimo goddess, Sedna, whose father severed her fingers and then allowed her to sink into the sea. There she created all of the marine life on which the Eskimos lived as well as all storms at sea. She was thus both creator and destroyer.

With such a publishing imprint and four women poets, I was prepared for another manhating, how-I-hurt collection of poetry by bitter women. I was pleasantly surprised. As a unit, the poems form a spear of opinion thrusting forward with a single theme: a woman's personal ownership of herself achieved through self-knowledge and coming to terms with herself and her surroundings. More basically put, the poems carry the message that wealth of spirit comes from knowledge of oneself and understanding that the slings and arrows of outrageous fortune are often gifts which make us stronger.

Further, the four women present their points of view separately. Each poet adds her own special direction of philosophical travel yet, at the same time, collimates [runs parallel] with the bent of the other three. In the end, the collection holds together well and delivers the message clearly.

EXERCISE 8: COMMENTARY ON POETRY
Directions: Choose the best answer for each of the questions.

1. Which of the following statements would the reviewer agree with?
   (1) Women's poetry is almost always objective.
   (2) Hardships can help us face up to our lives.
   (3) Publishers need to have interesting imprints.
   (4) Women poets should always write in groups.
   (5) The goddess Sedna is not a subject for a poem.

2. The reviewer states, "*Whispered Secrets* was a book long in coming and well worth the wait." What is another way of saying the same thing?
   (1) The time put into the book shows in the excellence of the writing.
   (2) The writers took much too long to write the book.
   (3) Readers had to wait a long time to read the book.
   (4) The book would be better if it had come out earlier.
   (5) Waiting for the book made people expect too much.

3
INTERPRETING DRAMA

Drama is the form of literature designed to be performed in the theater by actors taking on the roles of characters. In many cases, drama closely imitates life because the actors confront real-life situations and come to grips with real-life problems.

The requirements for interpreting drama on the GED Test are similar to those for interpreting prose fiction and poetry. It is not difficult to read a play; however, you must be able to "see" the action. You must use your imagination and picture the action taking place. You need to read carefully to infer setting, characterization, and theme. Words in parentheses—stage directions—are not meant to be read aloud. They are directions to the actors and explanations of "what's happening" as the actors speak.

How Drama Differs from Other Forms of Literature

Although drama has much in common with poetry and fiction, each of the three forms of literature treats its subject differently. Illustrated below are differences in the way each form of literature treats the same subject—a marriage proposal.

Prose: The young couple, John and Mary, went for a midnight boat ride on the Mississippi River. John gave Mary a diamond ring, and she accepted his proposal of marriage.

Poetry: Lovers in the moonlight
Aboard the *Delta Miss*
Exchanged a ring and promises
And sealed them with a kiss.

Drama: [*John and Mary board the* Delta Miss *for a midnight cruise.*]

JOHN: [*Embracing Mary*] I love you. [*He gives her a package.*]

MARY: [*Surprised*] What's this?

JOHN: It's a symbol of our future together—if you agree to marry me next month.

MARY: [*Opening the package and seeing a diamond ring*] Oh, John!

JOHN: [*Slipping the ring on her finger*] Don't ever take it off.

MARY: No . . . [*flustered*] I mean yes! I mean no, I won't take it off. . . . Yes, I'll marry you. [*They kiss.*]

Dialogue

In a play, as in other forms of literature, *dialogue* is conversation between characters. When reading dialogue in a novel or short story, it is sometimes difficult to keep track of who is talking because the speakers are not always identified. In reading drama, however, there are clues to help you keep track of who is speaking.

Clue #1: The speakers are identified in each line that is delivered. The names and the use of the colon (:) let you know who's speaking. When only two people are speaking, it is easy to follow, but when three or more characters get involved, you must read more carefully and be aware of which speaker is responding to which other characters.

Clue #2: Punctuation marks are used to begin and end a character's speech. Notice the end marks, especially for questions (?) and exclamations (!). Punctuation is used in drama to show volume of voice and emotion. Dashes (—) and ellipses (. . .) are also used to show pauses. Dashes are used to show a break in thought, while ellipses indicate that there is a pause in the words or that one character is being interrupted by another character.

Clue #3: Line spacing between lines of dialogue indicates who's speaking. A more obvious and visual clue that indicates when a different speaker is talking is the "white space" between lines of dialogue.

ANSWERS TO EXERCISES IN THIS CHAPTER BEGIN ON PAGE 427.

EXERCISE 1: DIALOGUE AND PUNCTUATION
Directions: Read the dialogue below, noticing the punctuation. Then answer the questions that follow.

> [*The scene begins in a nineteenth-century parlor as Catherine, Edward and Victoria's daughter, enters with tea.*]
>
> CATHERINE: Would you like some tea and . . .
> EDWARD: Not now—Can't you see we're talking?
> VICTORIA: *You're* talking—I'm not!
> EDWARD: Oh—a little irritable, are we?
> VICTORIA: No—just bored—with you. . . .
> CATHERINE: [*Mumbling*] I'm leaving. [*She exits.*]

In the space below, write the name of the character that correctly completes each statement.

1. Catherine interrupts _____.

2. _____ is rude to Catherine.

3. Victoria is upset with _____.

EXERCISE 2: INFERRING MOOD FROM DIALOGUE
Directions: Choose the best answer to the question that follows.

The mood of this scene may *best* be described as
(1) tense
(2) happy
(3) suspenseful
(4) nostalgic
(5) humorous

Stage Directions

Stage directions are used to assist the actors and director in interpreting the writer's intentions and purpose and to help the reader follow the imagined actions. In the previous brief scene, the stage directions are "[*The scene begins in a nineteenth-century parlor as Catherine, Edward and Victoria's daughter, enters with tea.*]"; "[*Mumbling*]"; and "[*She exits.*]." Notice that the playwright inserts the directions within and between the dialogue. The stage directions tell the reader who Catherine is and why she leaves. A play excerpt in this chapter requires you to follow the action as well as the words.

From Idea to Production

The ancient Greeks sat on a hillside to watch plays; today we turn on our television sets, see movies, or attend live productions. To appreciate a play, movie, or TV drama fully, it helps to know how drama is created by a writer (playwright or dramatist). Usually, it is written to be performed rather than to communicate directly to *readers*. It takes the work of many different people with different talents and skills to put on a performance. Costumers, set designers, makeup artists, and many others contribute.

When playwrights or screenplay writers create a script, they visualize their final work as a performance. The producer, who finances the production, chooses a director who will effectively present the raw material—the script. The director casts actors and actresses who fit the characters the writers have created.

Structure of Drama

A play is composed of *acts*— the major divisions of a dramatic work. Acts are composed of scenes. *Scenes* show an action that occurs in one place among characters.

A *prologue* begins and an *epilogue* ends classical drama. Because there was no scenery in early drama, an actor would come on stage and introduce the play by explaining the setting and some of the plot. He would also deliver a summary poem or speech at the end of the play. Although the prologue and epilogue are not as common in drama today, some television dramas and movies use them to help the audience understand the plot.

Shakespeare developed and refined the structure of drama as we know it today. He presented his plots in five acts. These acts are subdivided into numbered scenes. The diagram below shows the relationship between the acts and the corresponding elements of a traditional plot.

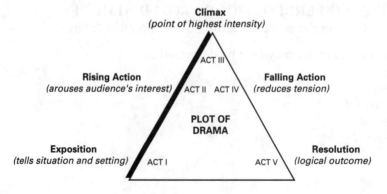

Climax
(point of highest intensity)

ACT III

Rising Action
(arouses audience's interest)   ACT II   ACT IV   **Falling Action**
(reduces tension)

PLOT OF DRAMA

Exposition
(tells situation and setting)   ACT I

ACT V   **Resolution**
(logical outcome)

Elements of Drama

Plot, setting, character, and theme are elements that apply to drama. The plot in drama is tightly structured; as in a short story, there is *exposition* that orients the audience to the dramatic situation and setting. The *rising action* is made up of all of the events that create suspense and arouse the audience's interest. All of these events and conflicts lead to the *climax*, the point of highest intensity in the play. The *falling action* may be brief. The conclusion or *resolution* is the logical outcome of the plot. As in fiction, the resolution ties up all of the loose ends of the plot.

Characterization

Since characters in plays are intended to be brought to life by actors before a live audience, they are not developed in exactly the same ways as characters in novels and stories. How can you interpret character? One way is by listening to the character's dialogue and watching his or her facial expressions and mannerisms. Another way to interpret character is to be aware of the motivation for the character's actions.

Dialogue and Nonverbal Communication

In drama, personalities are revealed by what characters say. Dialogue carries greater responsibility for getting the author's point across in drama than in fiction. In drama, character is also revealed by the actor's *nonverbal communication*—mannerisms, tone of voice, facial expression, and costume.

Motivation

In drama, a character's behavior is based on his or her *motivation*— the reasons for the character's actions. Actors who perform the roles of characters ask themselves, *What is my motivation? What are my character's reasons for acting this way?* Below is an excerpt of a play about the relationship between a mother and daughter. They are having a discussion in which much is revealed about their personalities, backgrounds, and conflicts. In order to infer mood, character, and form, you must rely on your understanding of dialogue.

EXERCISE 3: UNDERSTANDING CHARACTER
Directions: Read the passage below and answer the questions that follow.

WHAT ARE THE CHARACTERS' PERSONALITIES?

MAMA: Nothing I ever did was good enough for you, and I want to know why.

JESSIE: That's not true.

MAMA: And I want to know why you've lived here this long feeling the way you do.

JESSIE: You have no earthly idea how I feel.

MAMA: Well how could I? You're real far back there, Jessie.

JESSIE: Back where?

MAMA: What's it like over there, where you are? Do people always say the right thing or get whatever they want, or what?

JESSIE: What are you talking about?

MAMA: Why do you read the newspaper? Why don't you wear that sweater I made for you? Do you remember how I used to look, or am I just any old woman now? When you have a fit do you see stars, or what? How did you fall off the horse, really? Why did Cecil leave you? Where did you put my old glasses?

JESSIE: They're in the bottom drawer of your dresser in an old Milk of Magnesia box. Cecil left because he made me choose between him and smoking.

MAMA: Jessie, I know he wasn't that dumb.

JESSIE: I never understood why he hated it so much when it's so good. Smoking is the only thing I know that's always just what you think it's going to be. Just like it was the last time and right there when you want it and real quiet.

MAMA: Your fits made him sick, and you know it.

JESSIE: Say seizures, not fits. Seizures.

MAMA: It's the same thing. A seizure in the hospital is a fit at home.

JESSIE: They didn't bother him at all. Except he did feel responsible for it. It was his idea to go horseback riding that day. It was his idea I could do anything if I just made up my mind to. I fell off the horse because I didn't know how to hold on. Cecil left for pretty much the same reason.

—Excerpted from *'night, Mother* by Marsha Norman

1. The relationship between the mother and daughter seems to suffer from
   (1) Jessie's dependence on Mama
   (2) Mama's dependence on Jessie
   (3) a lack of communication
   (4) Jessie's resentment of her mother
   (5) Mama's hatred of Cecil, Jessie's husband

2. Mama may best be described as
   (1) understanding
   (2) vengeful
   (3) supportive
   (4) critical
   (5) selfish

3. The mood that this excerpt conveys is one of
   (1) despair
   (2) happiness
   (3) suspense
   (4) tension
   (5) doubt

EXERCISE 4: SUPPORTING FACTS AND INFERENCES

Directions: Below is a list of facts and inferences made about Jessie's character. In the spaces provided, write the key words from the passage that support each fact or inference.

1. Jessie is separated from Cecil. _____

_____

2. Jessie is confused about what her mother wants to know. _____

_____

3. Mama doesn't believe Jessie's story of how she fell off the horse. _____

_____

EXERCISE 5: INTERPRETING A SCENE FROM A PLAY

Directions: Read the passage below and answer the questions that follow.

WHAT PROBLEM IS BEING DISCUSSED BY ALICE AND GENE?

ALICE: I'm doing a lot for my kids. I don't expect them to pay me back at the other end. [*Gene wanders around, thinking, scuffing the grass.*] I'm sure we could find a full-time housekeeper. He can afford it.

GENE: He'd never agree.

ALICE: It's that or finding a home. [*Gene frowns.*] Sidney's folks like where they are. Also, we might as well face it, his mind's going. Sooner or later, we'll have to think about powers of attorney, perhaps committing him to an institution.

GENE: It's all so ugly.

ALICE: [*smiling*] Yes, my gentle Gene, a lot of life is.

GENE: Now, look, don't go trying to make me out some soft-hearted . . . [*He can't find the word.*] I know life is ugly.

ALICE: Yes, I think you know it. You've lived through a great deal of ugliness. But you work like a Trojan to deny it, to make it not so. [*after a moment, not arguing*] He kicked me out. He said he never wanted to see me again. He broke Mother's heart over that for years. He was mean, unloving. He beat you when you were a kid. . . . You've hated and feared him all your adult life. . . .

GENE: [*cutting in*] Still he's my father, and a man. And what's happening to him appalls me as a man.

ALICE: We have a practical problem here.

GENE: It's not as simple as all that.

ALICE: To me it is. I don't understand this mystical haze you're casting over it. I'm going to talk to him tomorrow, after the session with the lawyer, about a housekeeper. [*Gene reacts but says nothing.*] Just let me handle it. He can visit us, and we can take turns coming to visit him. Now, I'll do the dirty work. Only when he turns to you, don't give in.

GENE: I can't tell you how ashamed I feel . . . not to say with open arms, "Poppa, come live with me . . . I love you, Poppa, and I want to take care of you." . . . I need to love him. I've always wanted to love him. [*He drops his arms and wanders off.*]

—Excerpted from *I Never Sang for My Father*
by Robert Anderson

1. The relationship between Alice and Gene is
   (1) husband and wife
   (2) nurse and doctor
   (3) sister and brother
   (4) close friends
   (5) mother and son

2. Alice would agree with which of the following statements?
   (1) All children should care for their elderly parents.
   (2) Nursing homes are for people who have no children.
   (3) The best situation for the elderly is staying in their own houses.
   (4) Children should get powers of attorney before placing parents in institutions.
   (5) Elderly parents should not expect their children to take care of them.

3. Gene exhibits all of the following emotions *except*
   (1) depression
   (2) relief
   (3) disgust
   (4) shame
   (5) frustration

4. Gene's last speech reveals Gene's
   (1) acceptance of his father's love
   (2) anger with Alice's negative attitude
   (3) eagerness to visit his father and offer to care for him
   (4) guilt that he doesn't love his father
   (5) inability to make decisions that affect his future

EXERCISE 6: INTERPRETING A FILM REVIEW

Directions: On the Reading Literature and the Arts Test, you may be required to answer questions about commentary on a film or play. Read the review below and answer the questions that follow.

HOW DOES *THE LAST TYCOON* PORTRAY HOLLYWOOD?
Film Review of *The Last Tycoon*

F. Scott Fitzgerald, author of *The Great Gatsby*, has been called the "Poet of the Jazz Age," the 1920s. But he also had something important to say about Hollywood's Golden Age, the 1930s—and he said it in his last book, *The Last Tycoon*. He showed Hollywood
5 as a kind of company town and the heads of studios as absolute rulers. Critic Edmund Wilson has called *The Last Tycoon* the best book ever written about moviemaking.

Somehow, director Elia Kazan and Harold Pinter (who wrote the screenplay) have managed to turn *The Last Tycoon* into a
10 fascinating low-key film. It couldn't have been easy. Fitzgerald died in 1940, leaving only six finished chapters of *The Last Tycoon*. He left notes for some possible endings, and the one Pinter and Kazan chose may not please everybody.

The time is 1933, the place a big Hollywood studio, like MGM.
15 Monroe Stahr (Robert De Niro) is the studio production head. Fitzgerald meant Stahr to be based on the late Irving Thalberg, MGM's creative "Boy Wonder." Like Thalberg, Stahr is a human dynamo. He controls every stage of filmmaking. He shows actors how to act, screenwriters how to write, and the studio boss (Robert
20 Mitchum) how to run things.

But Stahr himself is a flawed human being. He sees life as a movie and people as shadows. He even tries to "cast" Kathleen (Ingrid Boulting), the girl he loves, as a reincarnation of his dead wife. But real life keeps getting into the act. People refuse to stay in
25 the roles he has chosen for them. The writers he thinks of as children are ready to strike. His boss resents his arrogance and looks for a way to get rid of him.

The Last Tycoon won't please Hollywood Boosters, but Fitzgerald fans should like it. It pays respect to his work and to his last troubled years as a screenwriter in Hollywood.

1. Lines 8–10, "Elia Kazan and Harold Pinter have managed to turn *The Last Tycoon* into a fascinating low-key film," illustrate the writer's attitude toward Kazan and Pinter, which is one of
(1) ridicule
(2) admiration
(3) envy
(4) indifference
(5) disgust

2. Lines 21–22 offer support for the statement that Stahr
(1) is a man with character flaws
(2) is like Irving Thalberg, the "Boy Wonder"
(3) is energetic and thoughtful
(4) treats writers as children
(5) heads all aspects of production

3. "*The Last Tycoon* won't please Hollywood Boosters" implies
that the film will
  (1) be unpopular with most film critics
  (2) be successful as a money-making film
  (3) not win Academy Awards
  (4) offend Fitzgerald's survivors
  (5) offend the producers of Hollywood films

WRITE YOUR OWN FILM REVIEW

The Artists: Read the credits.

1. Director:

2. Actors/Actresses:

  (stars)

  (supporting)

3. Writer and composer of musical score:

The Film Itself

4. In a paragraph or two, what is the plot of the movie?

5. Are the actors' and actresses' portrayals believable?

6. What do you like about the film?

7. What do you dislike about the film and would like to see
  improved?

8. What is the film's message or theme?

9. Who would this film most likely appeal to?

10. Rate the film on a scale of 0 to 5 (0 for poor, 5 for excellent).

4
INTERPRETING NONFICTION

If you read a daily newspaper or articles in *People*, *Newsweek*, *Sports Illustrated*, *Ebony*, or *Better Homes and Gardens*, you read nonfiction. Articles or books explaining how to diet, strip furniture, or buy a car are also nonfiction. *Nonfiction* is literature that is *not* fiction; it is based on fact. The nonfiction author writes about actual people, events, and ideas. The author's purpose may be to inform, instruct, entertain, record, examine, persuade, or analyze.

Types of Nonfiction

Nonfiction appears in several forms and covers every conceivable subject. To organize such a wide range of material, libraries use the Dewey decimal system or the Library of Congress system in categorizing their books. Forms of nonfiction include biographies, autobiographies, articles, essays, and speeches. A description and example from each category is represented in this chapter.

Biography—About People

Biography, a popular form of nonfiction, is a factual book or sketch that records the life of an individual. Biographies are written about historical figures, politicians, sports figures, current and past celebrities, major writers and literary figures, and others. Biographers report major events in a person's life and interpret their meaning. A biography is often meant to entertain as well as to educate. Traditionally, biographies were written after someone's death, as a tribute. But today, more and more biographies are written about people who are still alive.

ANSWERS TO EXERCISES IN THIS CHAPTER BEGIN ON PAGE 428.

EXERCISE 1: BIOGRAPHY
Directions: Read the biographical sketch below of a famous essayist and answer the questions that follow.

WHO WAS HENRY DAVID THOREAU?

Henry David Thoreau was born in Concord, Massachusetts, in 1817. He graduated from Harvard in 1837. The week he graduated, he heard a speech by Ralph Waldo Emerson and became a follower of the famous essayist and poet. Thoreau tried teaching but resigned after objections to his refusal to use corporal punishment; teachers were expected to hit students. In 1839, Thoreau, on a vacation from teaching, journeyed down the Concord River with his brother. The trip resulted in his first book, *A Week on the Concord and Merrimack Rivers*. He and his brother also opened a private school, where he introduced the idea of field trips to study nature.

Philosopher and writer Ralph Waldo Emerson encouraged Thoreau to keep a daily journal and to write poetry and essays. On July 4,1845, Thoreau began his famous "experiment in living" at Walden Pond. He lived in a cabin in the woods.

He wrote, "I went to the woods because I wished to live deliberately. . . ." The journal entries he wrote while living at Walden Pond were later published and became an American nonfiction classic, *Walden*.

Known as an individualist and nonconformist, someone who did not always go along with the rest of society, Thoreau also wrote the essay "On the Duty of Civil Disobedience." [See page 238.] The essay was written as a result of his one-day imprisonment for refusing to pay a poll tax that helped fund the United States' war with Mexico. He also opposed slavery and did much in 1859 to publicize abolitionist John Brown as a martyr. Thoreau died of tuberculosis in Concord in 1862.

His works, especially "On the Duty of Civil Disobedience," were later read by Mahatma Gandhi of India and Martin Luther King, Jr. Thoreau's ideas of civil disobedience and passive resistance were practiced by both Gandhi and King in their protests against their respective governments. Today, Thoreau is viewed as one of the great thinkers and writers in American history.

1. It is significant that Thoreau moved to Walden Pond on July 4, 1845, because
  (1) it was his summer vacation from teaching
  (2) he wanted to attract worldwide attention to his cause
  (3) the pond was beautiful in July
  (4) he was hiding from the law
  (5) it was the anniversary of the nation's independence

2. In *Walden*, Thoreau writes, "I went to the woods because I wished to live deliberately, to front only the essential facts of life, and see if I could not learn what it had to teach, and not, when I came to die, discover that I had not lived." If you were to follow Thoreau's advice, you would
  (1) live and work in New York City
  (2) get involved in national politics
  (3) live away from civilization
  (4) take time out to ponder the meaning and beauty of life
  (5) become a stockbroker and make as much money as possible

3. According to the biographical sketch, Thoreau's most influential work is
  (1) the essay "On the Duty of Civil Disobedience"
  (2) the book *A Week on the Concord and Merrimack Rivers*
  (3) the book *Walden*
  (4) his journals
  (5) his poetry

4. Civil disobedience may best be described as
  (1) disregarding all laws passed by one's government
  (2) nonviolent resistance to unjust laws
  (3) breaking any law that one does not like
  (4) living one's life as a free spirit
  (5) a violent attempt to overthrow one's government

Oral History—Word of Mouth

Not all biographical works document the life of a famous or distinguished individual. Studs Terkel's book *Hard Times* records facts and impressions about the lives of many different "common people" who were affected by the Great Depression of the 1930s. Many times, nonfiction authors interview their sources, then summarize the interview in their own words. Here, Terkel reports both his questions to Cesar Chavez, the former head of the United Farm Workers of America, and Chavez's responses.

EXERCISE 2: ORAL HISTORY

Directions: Read the passage below and answer the questions that follow.

WHAT DOES CHAVEZ REMEMBER ABOUT THE DEPRESSION?

[*Chavez*] We had been poor, but we knew every night there was a bed *there* and that *this* was our room. There was a kitchen. It was sort of a settled life, and we had chickens and hogs, eggs and all those things. But that all of a sudden changed. When you're small, you can't figure these things out. You know something's not right and you don't like it, but you don't question it and you don't let that get you down. You sort of just continue to move.

But this had quite an impact on my father. He had been used to owning the land and all of a sudden there was no more land. What I heard . . . what I made out of conversations between my mother and my father—things like, we'll work this season and then we'll get enough money and we'll go and buy a piece of land in Arizona. Things like that. Became like a habit. He never gave up hope that some day he would come back and get a little piece of land.

I can understand very, very well this feeling. These conversations were sort of melancholy. I guess my brothers and my sisters could also see this very sad look on my father's face.

[Terkel] *That piece of land he wanted . . . ?*

[Chavez] No, never. It never happened. He stopped talking about that some years ago. The drive for land, it's a very powerful drive.

When we moved to California, we would work after school. Sometimes we wouldn't go. "Following the crops," we missed much school. Trying to get enough money to stay alive the following winter, the whole family picking apricots, walnuts, prunes. We were pretty new, we had never been migratory workers.

Write *T* if a statement is true or *F* if it is false.

_____ **1.** Chavez is very bitter about his experience.

_____ **2.** According to Chavez, children keep going along even when they do not understand what's happening.

_____ **3.** Being a migrant worker affected Chavez's opportunity to get a good education.

_____ **4.** The Great Depression did not greatly affect Chavez's family.

Autobiography—About You

Only *you* can write your autobiography, the story of your own life. *Autobiography* is a *self*-biography. Many writers of autobiographies are not professional writers but notable individuals telling their own stories. Notable autobiographies include *Anne Frank: The Diary of a Young Girl,* the diary of a young Jewish girl who hid from the Nazis in World War II; *Out of Africa,* the autobiography of Isak Dinesen, which was the basis for the film of the same title; and *The Autobiography of Malcolm X* which served as the basis for Spike Lee's film about Malcolm X. Autobiographies are also known as *memoirs.*

Like authors of fiction, authors of nonfiction exhibit particular styles. Autobiographies, especially, tend to be written in a less formal style because the writers are revealing the personal details of their lives. In the passage below, Dick Gregory, writer, comedian, and social activist, uses many sentence fragments—quick images to set the mood. Notice his style and the effects he achieves.

EXERCISE 3: AUTOBIOGRAPHY
Directions: Read the passage below and answer the questions that follow.

HOW DOES DICK GREGORY FEEL ABOUT SCHOOL?

The teacher thought I was stupid. Couldn't spell, couldn't read, couldn't do arithmetic. Just stupid. Teachers were never interested in finding out that you couldn't concentrate because you were so hungry, because you hadn't had any breakfast. All you could think about was noontime, would it ever come? Maybe you could sneak into the cloakroom and steal a bite of some kid's lunch out of a coat pocket. A bite of something. Paste. You can't really make a meal of paste, or put it on bread for a sandwich, but sometimes I'd scoop a few spoonfuls out of the paste jar in the back of the room. Pregnant people get strange tastes. I was pregnant with poverty. Pregnant with dirt and pregnant with smells that made people turn away, pregnant with cold and pregnant with shoes that were never bought for me, pregnant with five other people in my bed and no Daddy in the next room, and pregnant with hunger. Paste doesn't taste too bad when you're hungry.

The teacher thought I was a troublemaker. All she saw from the front of the room was a little black boy who squirmed in his idiot's seat and made noises and poked the kids around him. I guess she couldn't see a kid who made noises because he wanted someone to know he was there.

—Excerpted from "Not Poor, Just Broke" in
Nigger—An Autobiography

1. From the author's point of view, the teacher was all of the
   following *except*
   (1) unaware of his hunger
   (2) insensitive to his real needs
   (3) aware of his disruptive behavior
   (4) uninterested in him
   (5) understanding of his problems

2. Cesar Chavez and Dick Gregory were alike in that both men
   (1) lived in fatherless homes
   (2) had their early education interrupted
   (3) had no brothers or sisters
   (4) made names for themselves despite their childhood poverty
   (5) had no faith at all in adults

3. The title of the chapter from which the excerpt comes is, "Not Poor, Just Broke." This title suggests that Gregory
   (1) wasn't poor; he'd just spent his lunch money
   (2) was used to poverty, so it didn't bother him
   (3) supposes that being poor is the same thing as being broke
   (4) believes being broke is better than being poor
   (5) thinks those who are called poor by others don't necessarily consider themselves to be poor

Journals and Letters

Diaries and journals are daily records of personal activities, events, or reflections. When people write their autobiographies, they may refer to their diaries or journals as sources of material. Ralph Waldo Emerson referred to his journals as his "savings banks" in which he deposited his thoughts. Below is an entry from one of his journals.

EXERCISE 4: JOURNAL ENTRIES
Directions: Read the passage and answer the questions that follow.

WHAT IS EMERSON'S ATTITUDE TOWARD LIFE?

November 11, 1842 [age thirty-nine]

Do not be too timid and squeamish about your actions. All life is an experiment. The more experiments you make the better. What if they are a little coarse, and you may get your coat soiled or torn? What if you do fail, and get fairly rolled in the dirt once or twice? Up again you shall never be so afraid of a tumble.

1. Based on the quotation above, with which of the following statements about life might Emerson agree?
   (1) Life is one big bowl of cherries.
   (2) Life is a precious gift not to be wasted.
   (3) Life is one big rat race.
   (4) Life isn't fair.
   (5) Life is a risk; to risk is to be alive.

2. Which of the following occupations is the best expression of Emerson's beliefs?
   (1) philosopher
   (2) writer
   (3) astronaut
   (4) physician
   (5) historian

Article—Just the Facts, Please

An *article* is a short nonfiction piece, often appearing in a newspaper or magazine. The writer presents facts, usually in an objective manner. *Feature articles* are special attractions that cover topics that have high reader interest. An article may instruct readers in how to do something, or it may be simply entertaining. Reading a major daily newspaper regularly will allow you to practice your reading and comprehension skills as well as enjoy interesting nonfiction. Use the newspaper index to guide you to the articles and learn the differences between objective and subjective reporting.

Essay—One Person's View

An *essay* is a nonfiction work in which an author presents a personal viewpoint on a subject. Traditionally, an essay is a formal piece of writing, an expository piece that "exposes" and analyzes a subject.

Below is an excerpt from a well-known formal essay, "On the Duty of Civil Disobedience," by Henry David Thoreau. Remember that the essay was written after Thoreau was jailed for refusing to pay a poll tax that he viewed as support for the Mexican War. The essay is personal in that Thoreau uses it to explain his views; it is serious in tone, and the vocabulary is somewhat more difficult than today's prose. The ideas put forth in this excerpt of the long essay were shared by civil rights leaders of the 1960s and 1970s, the Nazi-resisters of the 1930s and 1940s, and others.

EXERCISE 5: THE FORMAL ESSAY
Directions: Read the passage below and answer the questions that follow.

WHAT IS THE PURPOSE OF GOVERNMENT?

I heartily accept the motto,—"That government is best which governs least;" and I should like to see it acted up to more rapidly and systematically. Carried out, it finally amounts to this, which also I believe,—"That government is best which governs not at all;" and when men are prepared for it, that will be the kind of government which they will have. Government is at best but an expedient; but most governments are usually, and all governments are sometimes, inexpedient. The objections which have been brought against a standing army, and they are many and weighty, and deserve to prevail, may also at last be brought against a standing government. The standing army is only an arm of the standing government. The government itself, which is only the mode which the people have chosen to execute their will, is equally liable to be abused and perverted before the people can act through it. Witness the present Mexican war, the work of comparatively a few individuals using the standing government as their tool; for, in the outset, the people would not have consented to this measure.

This American government,—what is it but a tradition, though a recent one, endeavoring to transmit itself unimpaired to posterity, but each instant losing some of its integrity? It has not the vitality and force of a single living man; for a single man can bend it to his will. It is a sort of wooden gun to the people themselves; and, if ever they should use it in earnest as a real one against each other, it will surely split. . . .

1. The title of the essay implies that a citizen
   (1) is disloyal for disobeying laws
   (2) should serve in the army
   (3) should appreciate U.S. citizenship
   (4) is obligated to break an unjust law
   (5) must vote in all elections

2. In the line "The government itself, which is only the mode which the people have chosen to execute their will," the word *execute* is used to mean
   (1) capital punishment of criminals
   (2) kill during a war
   (3) carry out; perform
   (4) ignore the wishes of
   (5) create; originate

3. Thoreau's interpretation of "government" is that the government
   (1) is the people themselves
   (2) is made up of knowledgeable leaders
   (3) is a tool of the standing army
   (4) should give fewer freedoms to its citizens
   (5) encourages individual liberty

EXERCISE 6: COMPARING AND CONTRASTING STYLES

Style, the author's unique use of language to express an idea, distinguishes a formal from an informal essay. Below are two essays about computers. One is written with a light approach—a conversation between a customer and an airline worker. The other is a discussion of the danger of computers in the workplace. Note the differences in style and approach.

Directions: Read each passage and answer the questions that follow.

Passage I

HOW DOES THE WRITER FEEL ABOUT COMPUTERS?

The most frightening words in the English language are, "Our computer is down." You hear it more and more as you go about trying to conduct your business.

The other day I was at the airport attempting to buy a ticket to Washington and the attendant said, "I'm sorry, I can't sell you a ticket. Our computer is down."

"What do you mean your computer is down? Is it depressed?"

"No, it can't be depressed. That's why it's down."

"So if your computer is down just write me out a ticket."

"I can't write you out a ticket. The computer is the only one allowed to issue tickets for the plane." I looked down the counter, and every passenger agent was just standing there drinking coffee and staring into a blank screen. "What do all you people do?"

"We give the computer the information about your trip, and then it tells us whether you can fly with us or not."

"So when it goes down, you go down with it."

"That's very good, sir. I haven't heard it put that way before."

"How long will the computer be down?" I wanted to know.

"I have no idea. Sometimes it's down for ten minutes, sometimes for two hours. There is no way we can find out without asking the computer, and since it's down it won't answer us."

—Excerpted from "The Computer Is Down" by Art Buchwald

1. All of the following elements of style are found in this passage *except*
   (1) exaggerated circumstances
   (2) first-person narration
   (3) long, explanatory paragraphs
   (4) dialogue
   (5) sarcasm

2. "There is no way we can find out without asking the computer, and since it's down it won't answer us." This statement reveals the airline agent's
   (1) irritation with the customer
   (2) creativity
   (3) ability to deal with crises
   (4) total dependence on the computer
   (5) seniority of position

Passage 2

WHAT IS THIS WRITER'S OPINION OF COMPUTERS?

The millions of people on the bottom levels of electronic hierarchies [computer networks that connect managers with workers] are increasingly likely to spend their days in an isolated no-man's-land, subservient to intelligent information systems that report their progress to unseen supervisors far away. Because computers measure quantity better than quality, such systems tend to reward employees who work faster more than those who work better. There's a sharp rise in loneliness and disconnection as individuals blindly forge ahead. Service people on the telephone or at a cash register curtly terminate attempts at idle conversation because their performance is being electronically monitored. Once judged on their ability to communicate with customers or troubleshoot unexpected situations, they're now evaluated by the number of transactions they complete in a shift or the number of keystrokes required to draft a document. In these "electronic sweatshops," the computers are running the people, not the other way around.

—Excerpted from "The Dark Side of the Boom" by Mary S. Glucksman

3. The tone of this passage, as compared to Passage 1, is more
   (1) humorous
   (2) satirical
   (3) conversational
   (4) serious
   (5) informal

4. The main idea, or point, of the excerpt is that electronic offices are
   (1) the wave of the future
   (2) an improvement over old-time offices
   (3) causing psychological problems in workers
   (4) increasing American productivity
   (5) helping people develop their ability to troubleshoot

5. Both authors would agree with which of the following statements?
   (1) We would be better off without computers.
   (2) The airline industry would be safer without computers.
   (3) Computers are a necessary part of human life.
   (4) People should control computers rather than letting computers control them.
   (5) The government should control all computers.

Speech—Telling It Like It Is

Essays embrace a variety of tones, styles, language, and themes. A *speech*, a *spoken* communication about a topic, is similar to the essay in organization. The speaker should have an interesting introduction, support for the main idea, and a strong conclusion. Because speeches are considered to be nonfiction, they can be analyzed by examining tone, style, message, and purpose.

Notable speeches include Abraham Lincoln's "Gettysburg Address," John F. Kennedy's "Inaugural Address," and Martin Luther King, Jr.'s "I Have a Dream." King's speech has been publicized, taped, and widely recognized as instrumental in the civil rights movement.

EXERCISE 7: PRACTICE INTERPRETING A SPEECH

Directions: Read the excerpt from John F. Kennedy's "Inaugural Address" and answer the questions that follow.

WHAT DOES THE PRESIDENT ASK OF HIS FELLOW CITIZENS?

In your hands, my fellow citizens, more than mine, will rest the final success or failure of our course. Since this country was founded, each generation of Americans has been summoned to give testimony to its national loyalty. The graves of young Americans who answered the call to service surround the globe.

Now the trumpet summons us again—not as a call to bear arms, though arms we need; not as a call to battle, though embattled we are; but a call to bear the burden of a long twilight struggle, year in and year out, "rejoicing in hope, patient in tribulation," a struggle against the common enemies of man: tyranny, poverty, disease, and war itself.

Can we forge against these enemies a grand and global alliance, North and South, East and West, that can assure a more fruitful life for all mankind? Will you join me in this historic effort?

In the long history of the world, only a few generations have been granted the role of defending freedom in its hour of maximum danger. I do not shrink from this responsibility; I welcome it. I do not believe that any of us would exchange places with any other people or any other generation. The energy, the faith, the devotion which we bring to this endeavor will light our country and all who serve it, and the glow from that fire can truly light the world.

And so, my fellow Americans, ask not what your country can do for you; ask what you can do for your country.

My fellow citizens of the world, ask not what America will do for you, but what together we can do for the freedom of man.

1. The tone of the speech can best be characterized as
   (1) sarcastic
   (2) light-hearted
   (3) angry
   (4) uplifting
   (5) sad

2. One of the purposes of the speech is to motivate listeners to
   (1) preserve the right to bear arms
   (2) enlist in the armed services
   (3) serve their country
   (4) take an oath swearing to their national loyalty
   (5) prepare themselves for battle

3. The speech is characterized by all of the following stylistic devices *except*
   (1) a standard, predictable rhythm and the use of rhyme
   (2) the use of the personal pronouns *we* and *us* to build rapport with listeners
   (3) catchy turns of phrase in which subjects and objects are inverted
   (4) the repetition of key words
   (5) questions that invite readers to answer "yes" silently

The Style and Language of Commentary

Commentary is a form of nonfiction in which the writer comments about literature and the arts: film, television, dance, music, art, and theater. A person who writes commentary—a critic—evaluates a work of art and assesses the work's strengths and weaknesses. Because a critic or reviewer is both describing and analyzing a work of art, the style and language of commentary is often highly descriptive. The reader of commentary must be able to analyze style as well as tone to evaluate the reviewer's judgment about a work of art.

Reading on Two Levels

To understand literary criticism, you must be able to read on two levels. First, you must understand facts about both the work of art and its creator. Then, you have to understand the critic's opinions.

Ask yourself these questions:

1. What does the critic say about the author or the author's abilities?

2. What does the critic like about the literary work? What does the critic dislike about the work? Which words communicate the critic's feelings about the work?

3. What statements are based on facts about the work? What statements are based on the critic's opinion or personal reaction to the work?

4. Does the critic recommend the work? Does the critic recognize the literary value of the work?

EXERCISE 8: INTERPRETING A BOOK REVIEW
Directions: Read the following review of a novel and answer the questions that follow.

A Review of *Looking for Bobby*
by Gloria Norris, Knopf, $15.95

The narrator of this often funny novel, Marianne, is a Mississippi woman just awakening to the fact that although her husband is rich and handsome and practically perfect, their marriage was a mistake. She runs off to New York City, hoping to find her first cousin Bobby. Once when they were children and she was lost on a fox hunting trip, Bobby found her and said, "Even if you were a thousand miles away, I would still be close to you and know what you're thinking. No matter what happens, when we grow up, I'll always be there right by you. All you ever have to do is think about me and I'll be close." The descriptions of Marianne's courtship and marriage, her talkative mother-in-law, and the New Orleans scenes are all wonderful. But problems mount, even for a sympathetic reader, when Marianne, in New York, learns that Bobby has switched from selling stocks to directing a play off-Broadway. A producer's lunch at Sardi's is preposterous, and Bobby and his much discussed charisma become equally unbelievable. Nothing that he does makes him appear to the reader as magnetic as he seems to everyone in the book. Then, thanks to Bobby, Marianne gets into show business and becomes a successful agent. She also bumps into him in Mexico and learns his secret. What she finds out about his past isn't all that surprising—a good therapist ought to be able to straighten him out in a couple of weeks. Norris, who has had several short stories published, is skillful at creating eccentric, oversized characters, but they are a lot more fun in the Deep South than when she wedges them into the tritely portrayed showbiz worlds of New York or Hollywood.

Directions: Write a (+) in the blank if the following statement is a positive opinion, (–) if the statement is a negative opinion, and *F* if the statement is only a fact about the novel's plot.

_____ **1.** "The narrator of this often funny novel, Marianne, . . ."

_____ **2.** "But problems mount, even for a sympathetic reader, when Marianne, in New York, learns that Bobby has switched from selling stocks to directing a play off-Broadway."

_____ **3.** "She also bumps into him in Mexico and learns his secret."

EXERCISE 9: INTERPRETING A REVIEW OF A NOVEL

Directions: Choose the best answer to each question below.

1. The critic says, "Norris, who has had several short stories published, is skillful at creating eccentric, oversized characters." In this quotation, the term *oversized* means
  (1) large; overweight
  (2) too many characters for the length of the book
  (3) inappropriate; out of place
  (4) bossy; overbearing; rude
  (5) memorable; unique

2. The critic would agree with which of the following statements?
  (1) Norris should write short stories, not novels.
  (2) A major flaw in the novel is the way the New York scenes are written.
  (3) The most exciting scenes in the novel are set in Mexico.
  (4) *Looking for Bobby* is an exceptionally well-written novel.
  (5) The character of Marianne should be better developed.

Interpreting Other Forms of Commentary

The following three reviews are commentaries on music, art, and television. As you read each review, look for specific qualities of the work that each critic is evaluating. Ask yourself: What facts about the work itself does the critic include? Does the critic like or dislike this work? Why? What does the critic say about the background of the artist? What is the critic's style? How does he or she present the message?

EXERCISE 10: INTERPRETING MUSICAL COMMENTARY

Directions: Read the music review below and answer the questions that follow.

WHO IS WYNTON MARSALIS, AND WHAT DOES THIS CRITIC THINK OF HIM?
Review of *Hot House Flowers* by Wynton Marsalis
(A Four Star Review) ★★★★

Jazz history can be traced through the arrival of precociously talented trumpet players who revolutionize the way jazz is perceived, both by the public and by the musicians who play it. King

Oliver, Louis Armstrong, Roy Eldridge, Dizzy Gillespie, Clifford Brown, Miles Davis, Lee Morgan and Lester Bowie, among others, came on the scene and turned everything upside down by forging new directions or simply making obvious something that had been overlooked. Though he has only made three albums as a leader, Wynton Marsalis has already joined this elite, at least by reputation.

Part of what distinguishes Marsalis is that he has seemingly assimilated jazz history at the tender age of twenty-three. At this point only his beautiful tone and impressive technique are his own, for he has chosen to work, for the most part, in familiar styles. Therein may lie the key to his genius. Marsalis has avoided the trap so many young players fall into of trying to be different just for the sake of being different. Marsalis obviously relishes drawing comparisons to Miles Davis of the fifties on "Melancholis." His specialty is acknowledging such a debt, then playing in such a way as to make it totally an expression of himself. The fact that Wynton Marsalis is also an accomplished classical player may explain in part his understanding of how a tradition can be nurtured rather than just copied.

1. This review reveals the critic's
    (1) dislike of young musicians
    (2) admiration and appreciation of Marsalis
    (3) bias against older, familiar jazz styles
    (4) lack of knowledge about classical jazz musicians
    (5) belief that classical music is better than jazz

2. The reviewer states, "a tradition can be nurtured rather than just copied." This statement supports the critic's belief that a musician should
    (1) ignore other musicians in his rise to fame
    (2) improve, not just repeat, the art
    (3) reject all musicians of the past
    (4) experiment with all types of music
    (5) record the music of previous artists

EXERCISE 11: INTERPRETING A PAINTING
Directions: Read the art review below and answer the questions that follow.

WHAT DOES THE CRITIC SEE IN WYETH'S WORK?
A Review of Artist Andrew Wyeth and His Work
by Frieda Davenport

We can take photographs to "freeze moments" in our memories. We do not consider ourselves artists, for we use the camera to capture the memory for us. When we see a painting which freezes a moment and gives meaning to it, we know art.

Andrew Wyeth, one of the most popular American artists of our time, has the ability to capture moments on canvas. His temperas and watercolors present natural colors—earth tones of browns, greys, and muted shades of pink. He uses white as no other artist has.

Wyeth's subjects and landscapes are rural. His compositions reflect a thoughtful simplicity, as if he has created "impressionistic" photographs. Not only is a landscape captured but a subject against a horizon, old farmhouses, bruised buckets, torn lace curtains, and window frames.

To learn about Wyeth is to see one of his paintings—*Christina's World* (1948)—his most well-known work. Christina, an actual friend of his, is in a crawling position with her back to the observer. She leans into, perhaps yearning for, a farmhouse on the horizon. Centered on the painting and on the horizon is an out-shed, a barn, which is to the left of the house.

The three focal points—the girl, the barn, and the farmhouse—are "balanced" on a grassy, barren field. The "plainness" is characteristic of Wyeth. Each time we look at the painting, we are drawn to Christina, the "center" of the painting and of her world.

Wyeth is often categorized as an American Realist, but to label artists is to limit our views of their accomplishments. The simplicity of Wyeth's work discourages complexity of thought, and we are left to thoroughly enjoy the moment that he creates for us.

1. The review discusses all of the following *except*
  (1) the popularity of the artist
  (2) the types of paints and techniques used
  (3) the artist's preference in colors
  (4) a specific painting
  (5) the price of one of Wyeth's paintings

2. The quality that the critic likes most in *Christina's World* is Wyeth's
  (1) accuracy
  (2) colors
  (3) simplicity
  (4) complexity
  (5) portrayal of the 1940s

Interpreting a Television Review

In many reviews, the critic reacts to one book, film, or work of art. However, criticism may discuss trends or characteristics of one type of art. The following television review presents views about the nature of TV programming. As you read, look for statements of fact and statements of opinion. Remember that most reviews are persuasive essays. The critic's purpose is illustrated with details and examples. Notice this critic's style, tone, and use of language.

EXERCISE 12: INTERPRETING A TELEVISION REVIEW

Directions: Read the television review below and answer the questions that follow.

HOW DOES THE REVIEWER RATE THE "ALL-TIME BEST" SITCOMS?
"M★A★S★H"

Where "Lucy" created a new comic form for TV, and "All in the Family" used social issues for comic fodder, "M★A★S★H" did what only the greatest—the classic—comedies do: mix hilarity and tragedy, often in equal measure. "M★A★S★H" made us laugh till we cried. And though its anti-war message occasionally got heavy-handed, it was never at the expense of laughter or character. Like all great sitcoms, it succeeded mainly by exploring, indeed celebrating, the chemistry between the characters. The last episode of "M★A★S★H" was the most-watched program in TV history for good reason. Yes, the final episode of "Cheers" may yet rival it, but "M★A★S★H" has an underriding urgency to its comedy—it's about life, death, war, and the redeeming grace of humor—that makes it, in our eyes, the best sitcom in history.

1. If you were retitling the review, which of the following titles would you choose?
   (1) Keeping It All in the Family
   (2) How "Lucy" Changed Our Viewing
   (3) Watching the Last of the Best
   (4) Is TV Getting Better or Worse?
   (5) Laughing and Crying with a Classic

2. The reviewer would agree that a sitcom that hopes to become the best in history must
   (1) contain very powerful anti-war messages
   (2) have strong relationships among characters
   (3) closely follow the comic form of the "Lucy" show
   (4) use "All in the Family" as a writing blueprint
   (5) use humor to cover up the tragedy in a story

3. What is the tone of the review?
   (1) appreciative
   (2) questioning
   (3) uncomplimentary
   (4) irresolute
   (5) sarcastic

TEST 5: MATHEMATICS

The GED Mathematics Test consists of multiple-choice questions. Almost all of the questions will be either word problems or based on some graph or other illustration. These math items will test not only your ability to do arithmetic, algebra, and geometry, but also your problem-solving skills. To answer successfully, you will need to estimate the answer, go through several steps to solve a problem, and select only the information needed to solve the problem. Sometimes you will need to determine that not enough information is given to get an answer.

How many questions are on the test?

There are approximately 56 problems, and you will be given 90 minutes to complete the test. About one-third of the items will be based on diagrams, charts, or graphs. Some of the questions will appear in item sets—a passage or drawing that is followed by 2 or more problems. Some of the problems will not require any computation. Instead, you will have to determine how a problem could be set up to solve it.

What's on the test?

The GED Mathematics Test can be broken down into the content areas it covers and the skills it tests. The following subjects make up the content of the test: Arithmetic (Measurement, Number Relationships, Data Analysis)—50%; Algebra—30%; Geometry—20%.

What can help me prepare for the test?

The following are some specific suggestions to help you:

1. To learn a new skill, go over the example problems carefully. Try to do the example problems yourself.
2. Learn the rules that are summarized in the boxes in each section. Then try to say the rules out loud and explain how to use them.
3. Check each exercise with the answer key starting on page 431. You need to know right away if you are grasping the skills.
4. Use all of the problem-solving strategies that are provided in this section. In particular, you will find that drawing a picture with the information and estimating an answer will often help you understand a problem that seems confusing.
5. Do your practice work in pencil. Carefully write down all the information that you need to solve a problem.

Getting Rid of "Math Anxiety"

Many people feel that they are just "not good in math." If this is true of you, listed below are some ideas that will help.

1. Accept the fact that although you have some math anxiety, most other people do too.
2. Math requires logic, but often intuition comes first. Don't be afraid to use the ideas that pop into your mind.

3. You can be creative. Solving a problem in a way that's different from what is given in the book is fine, too.
4. Estimating answers is helpful with many problems.
5. Use all the tools at hand—your fingers, paper, pencil, pictures— whatever works for you.
6. Have confidence in yourself and your ability to learn math concepts and try new approaches.

Reviewing Whole Numbers and Problem Solving

Most of the problems on the Mathematics Test are word problems. Basic to solving all word problems is a good, strong foundation in math facts, mainly the multiplication tables and the addition facts. Your ability to work with decimals, fractions, and other math skills will determine how quickly and accurately you can do these computations. If you feel you need to review addition, subtraction, multiplication or division, see Contemporary's other GED preparation books (listed on page xv).

1
DECIMALS

Maxine's normal temperature is 98.6°. When she had the flu, it rose to 102.4°.

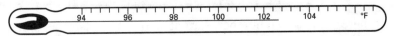

Elena has a new job working as a receptionist. She is paid $6.55 an hour and makes $245.63 a week.

Numbers like 98.6, 102.4, and 245.63 are *decimals*. These everyday decimals are already familiar to you. To fully understand and use decimals, it is important to learn about place values first.

Using Decimals

In our number system, we have ten digits: 0, 1, 2, 3, 4, 5, 6, 7, 8, 9. We use these digits to write every number. The place that a digit occupies in a number tells us the value of the digit. This means that each digit has a *place value.* We can use the chart below to read the place value of numbers. The whole numbers are to the left of the *decimal point.* The decimals, which are parts of a whole, are to the right of the decimal point. Decimals are also called *decimal fractions*. The places to the right of the decimal point are called *decimal places*. Notice that the names of the decimal places end in *th*.

Billions	Hundred Millions	Ten Millions	Millions	Hundred Thousands	Ten Thousands	Thousands	Hundreds	Tens	Ones	and	Tenths	Hundredths	Thousandths	Ten-Thousandths	Hundred-Thousandths	Millionths
							3	2	6	●	7	5				

▶ **TIP:** We use the decimal point to separate the whole-number places and the decimal places. The point is read as "and."

In the number 326.75, the 3 is in the hundreds place, 2 is in the tens place, 6 is in the ones place, 7 is in the tenths place, and 5 is in the hundredths place. The number 326.75 has two decimal places. The number is read as "326 and 75-hundredths." The .75 is read as "75-hundredths" because we give the entire decimal the name of the last decimal place it occupies. This is also why we read $326.75 as "326 dollars and 75 cents."

> **READING DECIMALS**
> 1. Read the whole part first.
> 2. Say "and" for the decimal point.
> 3. Read the decimal part.
> 4. Say the place name of the last digit.

▶ **TIP:** If there is no whole number, start at step 3. For instance, .008 is read as "eight-thousandths."

Zeros in Decimals

The zero is very important in writing and reading decimal numbers. To see how important zeros are, read the names of each of the mixed decimals below. *Mixed decimals* combine whole numbers with decimal fractions.

12.5   12.05   12.005

The three numbers are read as "12 and 5-tenths," "12 and 5-hundredths," and "12 and 5-thousandths." The only digits used to write these numbers are 0, 1, 2, and 5. The actual value of the number depends on the place value of each digit. The zeros in the second two numbers "hold" the number 5 in a specified decimal place—the hundredths place in 12.05 and the thousandths place in 12.005.

ANSWERS TO EXERCISES IN THIS CHAPTER BEGIN ON PAGE 431.

EXERCISE 1: READING DECIMALS
Directions: Circle the number on each line that matches the written value. Remember that the word *and* stands for the decimal point.

1. five-hundredths   500   .05   .5
2. one hundred and two-thousandths   102.00   100.2   100.002
3. Write the following in number form:
   (a) seven-tenths
   (b) two thousand and eight-hundredths
   (c) three hundred five and fifty-six thousandths
   (d) sixty-five ten-thousandths

Comparing and Ordering Decimals

Sometimes we need to compare decimals to see which one is larger. This is when adding zeros *after* the last decimal digit is most useful. It is easier to compare numbers that have the same number of decimal places. Adding zeros to the right of the last decimal digit does not change the value of a number. For example, 12.5, 12.50, and 12.500 all have the same value. To compare .14 and .126, first add a zero to .14 to make it .140. Now both .126 and .140 are expressed in thousandths and have the same number of decimal places:

.14 = .140   .126 = .126

You can now see that 126-thousandths is smaller than 140-thousandths because 126 is less than 140.

Example: Put 4.8, 4.12, 4.2, and 4.1003 in order from the *smallest to the largest.*

STEP 1. Write in zeros so that each number has the same number of decimal places. Then number the mixed decimals in order from the *smallest to the largest.*

4.8	= 4.8000	4th
4.12	= 4.1200	2nd
4.2	= 4.2000	3rd
4.1003	= 4.1003	1st

STEP 2. Using your ranking system, put the *original numbers* in order from smallest to largest.

1st	4.1003
2nd	4.12
3rd	4.2
4th	4.8

EXERCISE 2: COMPARING DECIMALS
Directions: Solve each problem.

1. Select the larger number in each pair.
   (a) .005; .05 (b) 4.10; 4.01 (c) .7; .68 (d) .5; .51 (e) 1.033; 1.03
2. Sarah has to pile these crates in order from the *heaviest on the bottom to the lightest on the top.* What would be the correct order in which to pile the crates? (List their weights from bottom to top.)

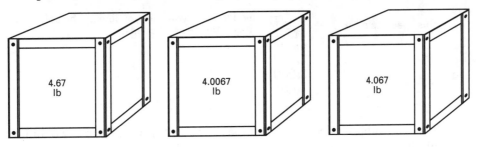

4.67
lb

4.0067
lb

4.067
lb

Rounding Decimals

We might solve a problem involving money and get an answer like $25.128. Since our money is expressed in hundredths, we must round off the answer to dollars and cents. Following are the steps we use to round off the answer.

Example: Round off $25.128 to the nearest cent.

STEP 1. Underline the place value to which you are rounding.

$25.1<u>2</u>8

STEP 2. Identify the digit to the right of the place to which you are rounding.

$25.1<u>2</u>8 ← number to the right

STEP 3. (a) If this digit is 5 or more, increase the digit in the place to which you are rounding by 1 and drop the digits to the right.
(b) If this digit is less than 5, keep the same digit in the place to which you are rounding and drop the digits to the right.

$25.1<u>2</u>8 ← 5 or more
+ 1
―――――
$25.13

EXERCISE 3: ROUNDING DECIMALS

Directions: Solve each problem.

1. A $\frac{3}{8}$ inch drill bit has a diameter of .375 inches. What is the size of the drill bit to the nearest hundredth inch?
2. The width of a boat is 8.275 feet. What is the width to the nearest tenth of a foot?
3. Juanita's temperature was 101.68 degrees. What was her temperature to the nearest degree?

Adding and Subtracting Decimals

There are three basic rules to follow:

> **ADDING AND SUBTRACTING DECIMALS**
> 1. Line up the decimal points.
> 2. Add or subtract the numbers.
> 3. Bring the decimal point straight down.

Example 1:   Add 2.1, .48, 38, and .005.

Read this space as a zero. ⟶ ⎤　　Filled in zeros will help you line up the columns.
　　　　　　　　　　　　　　⌄⌄ Line up the decimal points.

$$
\begin{array}{r}
2.100 \\
.480 \\
38.000 \\
+ \quad .005 \\
\hline
40.585
\end{array}
$$

When you subtract decimals, you may have to fill in zeros to get enough decimal places.

Example 2:   Subtract .0856 from 12.1.

$$
\begin{array}{r}
12.1 \\
- \quad .0856 \\
\end{array}
\qquad
\begin{array}{r}
^{0\,9\,9\,1} \\
12.1000 \\
- \quad .0856 \\
\hline
12.0144
\end{array}
\;\longleftarrow \text{Filled in zeros are necessary.}
$$

EXERCISE 4: ADDING AND SUBTRACTING DECIMALS

Directions: Solve each problem.

1. Add 5.9, 2.46, 6, 3.07, and .48.
2. Subtract 5.2 from 43.
3. Find the distance around the field shown. All distances are in meters.

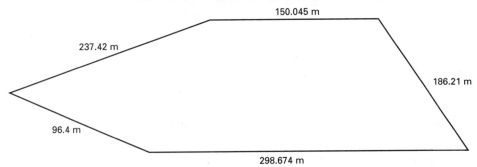

150.045 m

237.42 m

186.21 m

96.4 m

298.674 m

4. Can you balance a checkbook? At the beginning of the week, your balance was $472.24. During the week, you wrote checks for $42.87, $5.93, $10, $17.48, and $38.40. What is your new balance?

Part of a service order is shown below. Use the information given to answer question 5.

LAKE MARINE SERVICE		Date: 8/12		Name: Kim Yang	
Qty.	**Part**	**Amount**	**Work Performed**	**Labor Charge**	
1	Gear Lube	17 50	1. Winterize	70 00	
1	Grease	4 95	2. Weld skeg	90 00	
1	Oil	6 00	3. Repair ladder	n/c	
1	Gas	13 44			
3	Antifreeze	60 75			
			Total Labor	160 00	
			Total Parts		
			Tax	2 63	
	Total		**Invoice Total**		

5. What is the invoice total for Mr. Yang's boat?

Multiplying and Dividing Decimals

Decimals are multiplied the same way as whole numbers, and then the decimal point is placed in the answer. There are three rules for multiplying decimals.

MULTIPLYING DECIMALS

1. Multiply the two numbers as whole numbers, ignoring the decimal points.
2. Find the total number of decimal places in the numbers being multiplied.
3. Count the total number of decimal places in the answer, starting from the right, and place the point there.

Example 1:   Multiply 3.2 and 4.05.

$$
\begin{array}{r}
4.05 \\
\times\ \ 3.2 \\
\hline
810 \\
12\ 15 \\
\hline
12.960
\end{array}
$$

4.05 two decimal places
× 3.2 one decimal place

12.960 = 12.96 total of three decimal places
(You can drop the last zero.)

Example 2:   28 × .06

$$
\begin{array}{r}
28 \\
\times\ .06 \\
\hline
1.68
\end{array}
$$

28 no decimal places
× .06 two decimal places
1.68 total of two decimal places

Example 3 shows putting zeros at the beginning of the answer to have enough decimal places.

Example 3:   .043 × .0056

$$
\begin{array}{r}
.0056 \\
\times\ .043 \\
\hline
168 \\
224 \\
\hline
2408
\end{array}
$$

.0056 4 decimal places
× .043 3 decimal places

2408 You need a total of 7 decimal places.

In this case, put three zeros at the beginning of the number: **.0002408**

▶ **TIP:** Notice that it is easier to multiply if you put the longer number on top.

Dividing Decimals

How many $.59 hamburgers can you buy for $8.00? To answer this question, you have to divide decimals. There are two basic types of decimal division: (1) division of decimals by whole numbers and (2) division of decimals by decimals. Let's look at examples of each type.

DIVIDING DECIMALS BY WHOLE NUMBERS
1. Divide as though both numbers were whole numbers.
2. Divide by the number that follows the division sign (÷).
3. Place the decimal point in the answer directly above the decimal point in the dividend.

Example 1 shows how to divide a decimal by a whole number.

Example 1:   36.48 ÷ 4 ⌐ Place decimal point directly above the decimal point in the dividend.

$$\begin{array}{r} 9.12 \\ 4\overline{)36.48} \\ -36 \\ \hline 04 \\ -4 \\ \hline 08 \\ -8 \\ \hline 0 \end{array}$$

As Example 2 shows, some whole-number problems require you to add a decimal point and zeros.

Example 2:   12 ÷ 25 ⌐ Place decimal point directly above and zeros below.

$$\begin{array}{r} .48 \\ 25\overline{)12.00} \\ 10\,0 \\ \hline 2\,00 \\ 2\,00 \\ \hline 0 \end{array}$$

Example 3 shows a problem that often causes difficulty. If the first whole number in the divisor doesn't divide into the first number after a decimal point, you *must* put in a zero before continuing your division.

Example 3:   .35 ÷ 7

⌐ Put in the zero after the decimal point.

$$\begin{array}{r} .05 \\ 7\overline{)\,.35} \end{array}$$

Dividing By a Decimal

To divide a decimal by a decimal, you have to change the divisor into a whole number. Because you do this, you also have to move the decimal point in the dividend the same number of places.

Example 1:   4.864 ÷ .32

⌐ Place the decimal point directly above the decimal point in the dividend.

Move the decimal → point two places to the right.

← Move the decimal point two places to the right.

$$\begin{array}{r} 15.2 \\ .32\overline{)4.86\,4} \\ -3\,2 \\ \hline 1\,66 \\ -1\,60 \\ \hline 6\,4 \\ -6\,4 \\ \hline 0 \end{array}$$

Sometimes, you will have to add zeros to move the decimal point.

Example 2: 25 ÷ .125

$$
\begin{array}{r}
200. \\
.125\overline{)25.000} \\
-25\ 0 \\
\hline
00 \\
-\ 0 \\
\hline
0 \\
-\ 0 \\
\hline
0
\end{array}
$$

Move the decimal → point three places to the right.

← Add three zeros and move the decimal point three places to the right.

DIVIDING A DECIMAL BY A DECIMAL

1. Move the decimal point in the divisor all the way to the right.
2. Move the decimal point in the dividend the same number of places to the right.
3. Place the decimal point in the answer directly above the decimal point in the dividend.
4. Divide as though both numbers were whole numbers.

▶ **TIP:** The easy way to multiply or divide by multiples of 10 (10, 100, 1000, etc.) is simply to move the decimal point. When you multiply, you move the decimal point to the right. When you divide, you move it to the left. In either case, the decimal point moves as many places as there are zeros in the multiple of ten. (As the examples show, you add zeros when necessary.)

Examples: .13 × 1000 = 130   9.5 ÷ 100 = .095

       3   3   2   2
     zeros places   zeros places

EXERCISE 5: MULTIPLYING AND DIVIDING DECIMALS

Directions: Solve each problem.

1. Multiply .342 × 1.5.
2. Multiply $6.50 × 3.5.
3. Divide 6.005 by .05.
4. .012 ÷ 3
5. 472 × 10,000
6. 456.12 ÷ 100

7. At the store, Mike bought a 3.5-pound package of chicken at $1.19 a pound and 2 gallons of milk at $2.30 a gallon. Which expression shows what Mike paid?
   - **(1)** (3.5 + 1.19) + (2 + 2.30)
   - **(2)** (3.5 + 2) + (1.19 + 2.30)
   - **(3)** (3.5 × 1.19) + (2 × 2.30)
   - **(4)** 2.5(1.19 + 2.30)
   - **(5)** 2(1.19 + 2.30)

Estimating for Problem Solving

Estimating is a handy tool to use in solving decimal problems. If a problem involves decimals, reread the problem and replace the mixed decimals with whole numbers. This will help you see how to solve the problem. After choosing the correct operations to use, work the problem with the original decimal numbers if an exact answer is necessary.

Example: What is the cost of 12.8 gallons of gasoline at $1.19 per gallon?

   Estimation: What is the cost of 13 gallons of gasoline at $1 per gallon? Using whole numbers helps us to see we should multiply 1 × 13, which equals 13. Our answer in the original problem should be about $13. The actual answer rounds off to $15.23.

EXERCISE 6: ESTIMATING

Directions: Estimate the answers to the following problems.

1. If a bushel of apples cost $8.95, what will ten bushels cost?
   estimation _____

2. How many streamers, each 1.75 feet long, can be cut from a roll of crepe paper 36 feet long?
   estimation _____

EXERCISE 7: DECIMAL WORD PROBLEMS

Directions: Use estimation to help you solve the problems. Sometimes you may need to find the exact amount.

1. You are building a bookcase with shelves that are 3.2 feet long. How many complete shelves can be cut from a 12-foot board?
   (1) 2   **(2)** 3   **(3)** 4   **(4)** 5   **(5)** not enough information is given

2. The carat is a unit of measure used to weigh precious stones. It equals 3.086 grains. How many grains does a 2.8-carat diamond weigh?

(1) 3.086   (2) 5.886   (3) 8.6408   (4) 86.408   (5) 8640.8

Question 3 is based on the table below.

Employee No.	Regular Pay	Overtime Pay	Gross Earnings	Social Security Tax (FICA)	Federal Income Tax (FIT)	Total of Deductions	Net Pay
24	237.25	117		26.48	71.26		
35	339.45	71.25		26.93	82.14		
17	265.72	168.75		27.03	86.90		

3. Find the net pay for employee 17 after deductions are taken out.

(1) $113.93   (2) $320.54   (3) $434.47   (4) $548.40

(5) not enough information is given

4. The odometer of your sports car read 7353.2 miles at the start of a trip. When you returned it, it read 8747.6 miles, and you had used 86.4 gallons of gasoline. How many miles per gallon did you get? (Round off to the nearest tenth.)

(1) 1.6   (2) 16.1   (3) 16.2   (4) 18.6   (5) 1394.4

2
FRACTIONS

Forms of Fractions

Fractions represent a part of a whole. The top number is called the *numerator*, and the bottom number is called the *denominator*.

$$\frac{5}{8}$$

5 *numerator*
tells how many parts you have

8 *denominator*
tells how many parts a whole is divided into

This circle is divided into 8 parts. $\frac{5}{8}$ of this circle is shaded. $\frac{3}{8}$ is not.

There are many types of fractions that you will use in your work:

Proper fractions: The numerator is smaller than the denominator. $\frac{1}{2}, \frac{2}{5}, \frac{1}{7}, \frac{3}{9}$

Improper fractions: The numerator is the same as or larger than the denominator. $\frac{5}{4}, \frac{3}{2}, \frac{7}{3}, \frac{5}{5}$

Like fractions: Fractions have the same denominator. $\frac{1}{8}, \frac{3}{8}, \frac{6}{8}, \frac{5}{8}$

Unlike fractions: Fractions have different denominators. $\frac{1}{4}, \frac{7}{8}, \frac{3}{5}, \frac{9}{2}$

Mixed numbers: Combines a whole number and a proper fraction. $2\frac{1}{3}, 3\frac{1}{4}, 6\frac{1}{5}$

ANSWERS TO EXERCISES IN THIS CHAPTER BEGIN ON PAGE 432.

EXERCISE 1: TYPES OF FRACTIONS
Directions: Based on the information above, name each group of fractions below. (Some groups will have two names.)

1. $\frac{2}{3}, \frac{5}{3}, \frac{1}{3}, \frac{7}{3}$ ――――――――――

2. $1\frac{3}{4}, 7\frac{1}{5}, 2\frac{1}{8}$ ――――――――――

3. $\frac{1}{2}, \frac{1}{4}, \frac{2}{5}, \frac{3}{7}$ ――――――――――

Raising and Reducing Fractions

To use fractions easily, you must be able to *raise* a fraction to higher terms or to *reduce* a fraction to lower terms. In either case, you are changing both the numerator and the denominator of the fraction. When you do either, you are finding an *equivalent fraction*—a fraction that has the same value. For example, a half-dollar has the same value as two quarters. As equivalent fractions, these can be written as $\frac{1}{2} = \frac{2}{4}$. This relationship can also be shown in pictures.

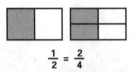

$$\frac{1}{2} = \frac{2}{4}$$

TO RAISE A FRACTION TO HIGHER TERMS
Multiply both the numerator and the denominator by the same number. You will obtain an equivalent fraction.

Example 1: $\dfrac{5\,(\times\,2) = 10}{8\,(\times\,2) = 16}$

TO REDUCE A FRACTION TO LOWER TERMS
Divide both the numerator and the denominator by the same number. You will obtain an equivalent fraction. (Hint: Look for a number that divides evenly into both.)

Example 2: $\dfrac{12\,(\div\,4) = 3}{16\,(\div\,4) = 4}$

A fraction is in the *lowest terms* if there is no whole number that will divide evenly into both numerator and denominator. For example, $\frac{3}{8}$ is already in lowest terms because there is no whole number other than 1 that divides evenly into 3 and 8. Fraction answers should always be reduced to lowest terms. In fact, all fraction answers for the Mathematics Test will be given in lowest terms.

EXERCISE 2: RAISING AND REDUCING FRACTIONS
Directions: Solve each problem.

1. Raise each fraction to higher terms as indicated.
   (a) $\dfrac{3\,(\times\,3)}{8\,(\times\,3)} = \dfrac{}{24}$ (b) $\dfrac{6}{7} = \dfrac{}{28}$

2. Reduce each fraction to lower terms as indicated.
   (a) $\dfrac{12\,(\div\,4)}{16\,(\div\,4)} = \dfrac{}{4}$ (b) $\dfrac{30}{42} = \dfrac{}{7}$

3. Reduce each of the following fractions to the lowest terms.
   (a) $\dfrac{6}{8}$ (b) $\dfrac{25}{30}$

Relating Fractions and Decimals

In many arithmetic problems, you will work with both fractions and decimals. Each fraction can be expressed as a decimal, and vice versa. You can think of decimals as fractions with denominators in multiples of 10: 10, 100, 1000, and so on.

For example: one decimal place $= \dfrac{}{10}$

two decimal places $= \dfrac{}{100}$

three decimal places $\dfrac{}{1000}$

Therefore, $.1 = \dfrac{1}{10}$ and $.03 = \dfrac{3}{100}$. Let's review the methods of changing from decimals to fractions and fractions to decimals.

Example 1: Change .75 to a fraction.

STEP 1. Write the number 75 without a decimal point as a numerator. $\dfrac{75}{}$

STEP 2. Write 100, the value of the last decimal place as a denominator. $\dfrac{75}{100}$

Example 2: Change .039 to a fraction. This can be reduced to $\frac{3}{4}$

$.039 = \dfrac{39}{1000}$ ← number without decimal point
  ← three decimal places are thousandths

CHANGING A DECIMAL TO A FRACTION

1. Write the number without the decimal point. This is your numerator.
2. Make the denominator the value of the last place value in the decimal.

To change a fraction to a decimal, divide the numerator by the denominator. You can do this because a fraction bar also indicates division. In other words, $\frac{5}{8}$ can mean $5 \div 8$ or $8\overline{)5}$.

Example 1:

$$\frac{5}{8} = 8\overline{)5.000} = .625$$
$$\begin{array}{r} -48 \\ \hline 20 \\ -16 \\ \hline 40 \\ -40 \\ \hline 0 \end{array}$$

Example 2:

$$\frac{2}{3} = 3\overline{)2.00} = .66\tfrac{2}{3}$$
$$\begin{array}{r} -18 \\ \hline 20 \\ -18 \\ \hline 2 \end{array}$$

▶ TIP: Example 2 is a repeating decimal. After two decimal places, you can bring up the remainder to be part of a fraction. If necessary, you can round off decimals; for example, $.66\tfrac{2}{3} = .67$.

EXERCISE 3: CHANGING FRACTIONS TO DECIMALS

Directions: Solve each problem.

1. Change the following decimals to fractions. Reduce if necessary.

    (a) $.07 = \dfrac{}{100}$ **(b)** $.32$ **(c)** 3.1

2. Change the following fractions to decimals. Write a fractional remainder after two decimal places.

    (a) $\dfrac{3}{8}$ **(b)** $\dfrac{4}{3}$ **(c)** $\dfrac{5}{6}$

Relating Mixed Numbers and Improper Fractions

In your work with fractions, you will have to change mixed numbers to improper fractions, and vice versa.

Example 1:   Change $3\frac{7}{8}$ to an improper fraction.

    STEP 1.   Multiply the whole number by the denominator. $(3 \times 8) = 24$

    STEP 2.   Add that to the numerator of the fraction. $24 + 7 = 31$

    STEP 3.   Write the sum over the original denominator. $3\frac{7}{8} = \frac{31}{8}$

Example 2:   Change $\frac{11}{5}$ to a mixed number.

    STEP 1.   Divide the denominator into the numerator.

$$\frac{11}{5} = 5\overline{)11} \begin{array}{r} 2 \\ \hline \end{array}$$
$$\begin{array}{r} -10 \\ \hline 1 \end{array}$$

    STEP 2.   Put the remainder over the denominator.

$$\frac{11}{5} = 5\overline{)11} \begin{array}{r} 2\frac{1}{5} \\ \hline \end{array}$$
$$\begin{array}{r} -10 \\ \hline 1 \end{array}$$

EXERCISE 4: CHANGING IMPROPER FRACTIONS AND MIXED NUMBERS

Directions: Solve each problem.

1. Change the following to improper fractions.
   (a) $12\frac{1}{4}$ **(b)** $6\frac{2}{3}$
2. Change the following to whole or mixed numbers.
   (a) $\frac{9}{9}$ **(b)** $\frac{17}{5}$

Comparing Numbers
The Number Line

The number line is similar to a ruler except that it has no beginning or end. We indicate this by putting arrows at both ends of the line. We can say that all numbers are represented on this line even though it would be impossible to try to label all of them. Note that the numbers get larger as you go to the right on the line.

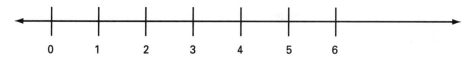

Whole numbers as well as mixed numbers can be represented on the number line.

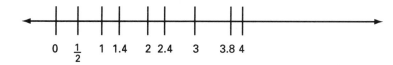

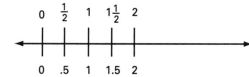 As the illustration shows, the same points can indicate equal fractions and decimals. For example, $1\frac{1}{2}$ has the same value as 1.5.

We can use the number line to compare numbers and show their order. If we are given two numbers, then one of three statements must be true:

1. The two numbers are equal.
2. The first is larger than the second.
3. The first is smaller than the second.

There are symbols to indicate these relationships:

Symbol	Meaning	Example
=	is equal to	4 = 4
>	is greater than	7 > 3
<	is less than	2 < 9

▶ **TIP:** The "arrow" always points to the smaller number.

Comparing Decimals

When you compare decimals, make sure you have the same number of decimal places in each number. Attach as many zeros as needed after the last number in the decimal. Remember that adding zeros to the end of a decimal number does *not* change its value.

Example: Compare .064 and .06.

.064 has 3 decimal places   .064   ←Both now have 3 decimal places.

.06 has 2 decimal places   .060   ┘

Now both numbers are expressed in thousandths.
Because 64 > 60, .064 > .060. So .064 > .06.

Comparing Fractions

To compare fractions, we must make sure that they have the same denominator. This is called the ***common denominator.*** For instance, we can compare $\frac{3}{16}$ and $\frac{11}{16}$. We know $\frac{11}{16} > \frac{3}{16}$ because 11 is greater than 3. If the fractions that you are comparing have different denominators, you must find a common denominator.

Example 1:   Which is larger, $\frac{5}{8}$ or $\frac{1}{2}$?

STEP 1.   Look at the larger denominator. If it is evenly divisible by the smaller denominator, use the larger one as the common denominator. $\frac{5}{8}$ $\frac{1}{2}$

STEP 2.   Write both fractions with the same denominator. Change one fraction to higher terms. $\frac{5}{8} = \frac{5}{8}$

$$\frac{1\ (\times 4)}{2\ (\times 4)} = \frac{4}{8}$$

STEP 3.   Compare and determine which is larger. $\frac{5}{8} > \frac{4}{8}$, so

$$\frac{5}{8} > \frac{1}{2}$$

In some cases, the smaller denominator will not divide into the larger. You can multiply them together if they are small enough to get a reasonable common denominator.

Example 2:   Which is larger, $\frac{2}{3}$ or $\frac{3}{4}$?

STEP 1.   Multiply the denominators to get a common denominator. $3 \times 4 = 12$

STEP. 2.   Give them both the same denominator. In this case, it will be 12.

Multiply $\frac{2}{3}$ by 4 and $\frac{3}{4}$ by 3. $\dfrac{2\ (\times 4) =\ 8}{3\ (\times 4) =\ 12}$

$$\dfrac{3\ (\times 3) =\ 9}{4\ (\times 3) =\ 12}$$

STEP 3.   Compare the fractions. $\frac{9}{12} > \frac{8}{12}$, so

$\frac{3}{4}$ is larger than $\frac{2}{3}$.

In other cases, the common denominator you get by multiplying might be too large to work with. In this case, find multiples of both denominators. Use the smallest multiple they have in common as the common denominator.

Example 3:   Which is larger, $\frac{5}{12}$ or $\frac{3}{10}$?

STEP 1.   Find multiples of both denominators.   12: 12, 24, 36, 48, 60
The smallest multiple of both will be   10: 10, 20, 30, 40, 50, 60
the common denominator.

STEP 2.   Raise both fractions to higher terms. $\frac{5\ (\times 5)}{12\ (\times 5)} = \frac{25}{60}$
Divide the denominators into 60 to
find which numbers to multiply
the fractions by: $\frac{3\ (\times 6)}{10\ (\times 6)} = \frac{18}{60}$
$60 \div 12 = 5$ and $60 \div 10 = 6$.

STEP 3.   Compare the fractions. $\frac{25}{60} > \frac{18}{60}$, so

$\frac{5}{12}$ is greater than $\frac{3}{10}$.

TO FIND A COMMON DENOMINATOR

Look at the larger denominator.
1. Is it divisible by the other denominator? If so, use the larger number as the common denominator.
2. If not, try multiplying the denominators together.
3. If multiplying results in a very large common denominator, try multiples of both denominators until you can find a common multiple.

Comparing Fractions and Decimals

We can compare fractions and decimals, but we must first change the decimal to a fraction or the fraction to a decimal.

Example: Compare $\frac{7}{8}$ and .75.

STEP 1.   Change $\frac{7}{8}$ to a decimal. $\frac{7}{8} = 8\overline{)7.000}$ (.875)

STEP 2.   Write .75 with 3 decimal places
because .875 has 3 decimal places.   .75 = .750
.875 > .750, so

STEP 3.   Compare. $\frac{7}{8}$ is greater than .75.

EXERCISE 5: COMPARING NUMBERS

Directions: Solve each problem.

1. Which of the following is larger?
   (a) $\frac{7}{8}$ or $\frac{3}{5}$ (b) $\frac{2}{3}$ or $\frac{4}{9}$

2. Compare by using the symbol $>$, $<$, or $=$. For example, $6 \boxed{<} 9$.

   (a) $3 \ \square\ 8$ (d) $\frac{9}{9} \ \square\ \frac{2}{2}$

   (b) $\frac{3}{4} \ \square\ \frac{2}{3}$ (e) $.07 \ \square\ .0873$

   (c) $2\frac{3}{8} \ \square\ \frac{5}{2}$

Operations with Fractions
Adding and Subtracting Fractions

When you are asked to add or subtract fractions or mixed numbers, you must be sure that the fractions have common denominators. If they don't, then rewrite the fractions with common denominators before adding or subtracting.

Example 1: Add $\frac{3}{8}$ and $\frac{1}{8}$.

     STEP 1.   Since the denominators are the same, add the numerators.

     STEP 2.   Reduce the answer.

$$\begin{array}{r} \frac{3}{8} \\ + \frac{1}{8} \\ \hline \frac{4}{8} \end{array} \quad \begin{array}{l} (\div 4) \\ (\div 4) \end{array} = \frac{1}{2}$$

Example 2: Add $\frac{1}{10}$ and $\frac{3}{5}$.

     STEP 1.   Find the common denominator and equivalent fractions.

     STEP 2.   Add the numerators.

$$\begin{array}{l} \frac{1}{10} \qquad\qquad = \frac{1}{10} \\ + \frac{3}{5} \ (\times 2) = \frac{6}{10} \\ \hline \qquad\qquad\qquad \frac{7}{10} \end{array}$$

Example 3: $\frac{2}{3} + \frac{1}{6} + \frac{3}{4}$

     STEP 1.   Find the common denominator for all numbers.

     STEP 2.   Add the numerators and put them over the denominator.

     STEP 3.   Change the improper fraction to a mixed number.

$$\begin{array}{l} \frac{2}{3} = \frac{8}{12} \\ \frac{1}{6} = \frac{2}{12} \\ + \frac{3}{4} = \frac{9}{12} \\ \hline \qquad \frac{19}{12} = 1\frac{7}{12} \end{array}$$

1. Be sure all fractions have common denominators.
2. Add the numerators.
3. Put the total over the common denominator and be sure the answer is in lowest terms.

You follow the same method for adding mixed numbers. Add the fractions first in case you need to combine your fraction total with the whole numbers.

Example 4: Jorge bought $1\frac{3}{4}$ pounds of chicken and $6\frac{2}{3}$ pounds of ground beef for the picnic. How much did he buy altogether?

STEP 1. Find the common denominator: 12.

STEP 2. Add the fractions. Simplify the improper fraction $\frac{17}{12}$ to the mixed number $1\frac{5}{12}$.

$$1\frac{3}{4} = 1\frac{9}{12}$$
$$+ 6\frac{2}{3} = 6\frac{8}{12}$$
$$7\frac{17}{12} = 7 + 1\frac{5}{12} = 8\frac{5}{12}$$

STEP 3. Add $1\frac{5}{12}$ to 7 to get $8\frac{5}{12}$.

1. Be sure fractional parts have common denominators.
2. Add the fractional parts. Simplify to a mixed number if necessary.
3. Add the whole numbers.
4. Be sure your answer is in lowest terms.

The process of subtracting fractions is similar to adding fractions.

Example 5: $\frac{7}{16} - \frac{3}{16}$

$$\frac{7}{16}$$
$$-\frac{3}{16}$$
$$\frac{4}{16} = \frac{1}{4}$$

Example 6: Take $\frac{3}{8}$ from $\frac{11}{12}$.

$$\frac{11}{12} = \frac{22}{24}$$
$$-\frac{3}{8} = \frac{9}{24}$$
$$\frac{13}{24}$$

1. Be sure the fractions have common denominators.
2. Subtract the numerators.
3. Put the difference over the common denominator.
4. Be sure the answer is in lowest terms.

One difference between adding and subtracting mixed numbers is that you might have to regroup to be able to subtract.

Example 7: Miriam needs to lose $9\frac{1}{4}$ pounds. She has already lost $5\frac{3}{4}$ pounds. How much does she have left to lose?

STEP 1. When you write the problem, you see that you can't take $\frac{3}{4}$ from $\frac{1}{4}$. You must regroup. Take 1 from 9. Since 1 can also be written as $\frac{4}{4}$, rewrite the 9 as $8\frac{4}{4}$.

$$9\frac{1}{4} = 8\frac{4}{4} + \frac{1}{4} = 8\frac{5}{4}$$
$$-5\frac{3}{4} \qquad\qquad -5\frac{3}{4}$$
$$\rule{4cm}{0.4pt}$$
$$3\frac{2}{4} = 3\frac{1}{2} \text{ pounds}$$

STEP 2. Add the numerators to get $\frac{5}{4}$.

STEP 3. Subtract the fractions and whole numbers. Reduce the fraction.

▶ **TIP:** To decide how to rewrite a 1 that you regroup, look at the denominator of the fraction being subtracted. For example, if you are subtracting $\frac{3}{8}$, write the 1 as $\frac{8}{8}$, or if you are subtracting $\frac{5}{6}$, write the 1 as $\frac{6}{6}$.

TO SUBTRACT MIXED NUMBERS

1. Whether or not you need to regroup, be sure that the fractions have common denominators.
2. Subtract the fractions. If you have to regroup 1 from a whole number, convert it to an improper fraction with the same denominator, adding the numerator of the original fraction (if there is one).
3. Subtract the whole number.

EXERCISE 6: ADDING AND SUBTRACTING FRACTIONS
Directions: Solve each problem.

1. $\frac{2}{3}$ $+ \frac{1}{4}$

2. $3\frac{7}{8}$ $2\frac{5}{6}$ $+ 3\frac{1}{3}$

3. $\frac{9}{10}$ $- \frac{3}{10}$

4. $\frac{4}{5}$ $- \frac{1}{2}$

5. $25\frac{1}{6}$ $- 11\frac{1}{2}$

6. 10 $- 3\frac{2}{17}$

Multiplying Fractions

There is no need for common denominators when you multiply and divide. In some cases, you will just multiply straight across, multiplying numerator by numerator and denominator by denominator.

Example 1: $\frac{3}{4} \times \frac{1}{2} = \frac{3}{8}$

Other problems can be solved more easily by *canceling*, reducing a numerator and a denominator divisible by the same factor.

Example 2: $\frac{6}{15} \times \frac{5}{12}$

$\frac{6}{15} \times \frac{5^1}{12}$

STEP 1. The 15 and the 5 can be divided by 5.

$\frac{6}{3\cancel{15}} \times \frac{\cancel{5}^1}{12}$

STEP 2. The 6 and the 12 can be divided by 6.

$\frac{\cancel{6}^1}{3\cancel{3}} \times \frac{\cancel{5}^1}{\cancel{12}_2} = \frac{1}{6}$

STEP 3. Multiply straight across. If necessary, reduce the answer.

```
┌─────────────────────────────────────────────────────┐
│              TO MULTIPLY FRACTIONS                   │
│  1. Reduce numerators and denominators by canceling. │
│  2. Multiply straight across.                        │
│  3. Be sure your answer is reduced to lowest terms.  │
└─────────────────────────────────────────────────────┘
```

You can also cancel with three fractions. Sometimes you have to "jump" over the middle number.

Example 3: $\frac{3}{8} \times \frac{4}{7} \times \frac{5}{9}$

STEP 1. Divide both the 3 and the 9 by 3.

$\frac{\cancel{3}}{8} \times \frac{4}{7} \times \frac{5}{\cancel{9}_3}$

STEP 2. Divide both the 4 and the 8 by 4.

$\frac{\cancel{3}}{\cancel{8}_2} \times \frac{\cancel{4}^1}{7} \times \frac{5}{\cancel{9}_3} = \frac{5}{42}$

STEP 3. Multiply straight across.

Example 4 shows a case that involves multiplying mixed numbers.

Example 4: Sarah usually jogs $2\frac{1}{3}$ miles daily. She jogged the full distance on 3 days and $\frac{1}{2}$ the distance on another day. How many miles did she jog in all?

STEP 1. Change all mixed numbers to improper fractions.

$2\frac{1}{3} \times 3\frac{1}{2} = \frac{7}{3} \times \frac{7}{2}$

STEP 2. Multiply and change the improper fraction back to mixed numbers.

$\frac{7}{3} \times \frac{7}{2} = \frac{49}{6} = 8\frac{1}{6}$

```
┌─────────────────────────────────────────────────────┐
│            TO MULTIPLY MIXED NUMBERS                 │
│  1. Change mixed numbers to improper fractions.      │
│  2. Reduce numbers divisible by the same number by   │
│     canceling.                                       │
│  3. Multiply straight across.                        │
│  4. Be sure your answer is reduced to lowest terms.  │
└─────────────────────────────────────────────────────┘
```

EXERCISE 7: MULTIPLYING FRACTIONS

Directions: Solve each problem.

1. $\frac{3}{8} \times \frac{2}{15} \times \frac{6}{7}$ 3. $2\frac{1}{2} \times 2\frac{1}{3}$

2. $8\frac{1}{6} \times 4$ 4. $2\frac{3}{4} \times \frac{6}{7}$

Dividing Fractions

Division is the opposite operation of multiplication. For instance, when we divide a number by 2, we are actually multiplying by $\frac{1}{2}$.

$$12 \div 2 = \frac{^6\cancel{12}}{1} \times \frac{1}{\cancel{2}_1} = \frac{6}{1} = 6$$

The fraction $\frac{1}{2}$ is called the **reciprocal** of 2. Two numbers whose product is 1 are reciprocals. Because $5 \times \frac{1}{5} = 1$, the numbers 5 and $\frac{1}{5}$ are reciprocals. To find the reciprocal of a number, you merely invert it, which means you turn it over.

To divide a fraction, use the following method.

Example 1: Divide $\frac{7}{8}$ by $\frac{3}{4}$.

   STEP 1.   Multiply the first fraction by the reciprocal of the second. $\frac{7}{8} \div \frac{3}{4} = \frac{7}{8} \times \frac{4}{3}$

   STEP 2.   Multiply across and change the improper fraction to a mixed number. $\frac{7}{\cancel{8}_2} \times \frac{\cancel{4}^1}{3} = \frac{7}{6} = 1\frac{1}{6}$

To divide a mixed number, first change any mixed numbers to improper fractions.

Example 2: What is $4\frac{2}{3} \div 1\frac{1}{2}$?

   STEP 1.   Change both mixed numbers to improper fractions. $\frac{14}{3} \div \frac{3}{2}$

   STEP 2.   Multiply the first fraction by the reciprocal of the second and change improper fractions back to mixed numbers. $\frac{14}{3} \times \frac{2}{3} = \frac{28}{9} = 3\frac{1}{9}$

TO DIVIDE FRACTIONS OR MIXED NUMBERS

1. Change mixed numbers to improper fractions.
2. Multiply the first fraction by the reciprocal of the second.
3. Change any improper fractions back to mixed numbers.

EXERCISE 8: DIVIDING FRACTIONS

Directions: Solve each problem.

1. $\frac{2}{5} \div 4$ **2.** $\frac{3}{7} \div \frac{6}{35}$ **3.** $9 \div 2\frac{1}{2}$

Simplifying Fraction Problems

The best way to simplify fraction word problems is to restate the problem using whole numbers.

▶ **TIP:** You can always look for key words or basic concepts that indicate the operation to use. A frequently used key word in fraction problems is *of.* A problem may ask you to find $\frac{1}{2}$ of something or $\frac{2}{3}$ of something. When you find a part of something, you multiply.

Example: An upholstery cleaner schedules $1\frac{1}{2}$ hour appointments for each couch to be cleaned. If he works $7\frac{1}{2}$ hours, how many couches will he clean?

Restated, replacing fractions with whole numbers: "A cleaner schedules 2-hour appointments for each couch. If he works 8 hours, how many couches will he clean?"

Solution: After restating the problem, it seems more obvious that it is a division problem — the cleaner is splitting his day into smaller segments. Therefore, we would choose to use division in the original problem.

$$7\frac{1}{2} \div 1\frac{1}{2} = \frac{15}{2} \div \frac{3}{2} \qquad \frac{\cancel{15}^{5}}{\cancel{2}_{1}} \times \frac{\cancel{2}^{1}}{\cancel{3}_{1}} = 5$$

The cleaner will clean 5 couches.

▶ **TIP:** Be sure that the amount that is being divided up comes first in a division problem. In the example above, the $7\frac{1}{2}$-hour period was being divided into $1\frac{1}{2}$-hour segments.

Item Sets

An item set refers to a lot of information given in a paragraph or two or in an illustration. Then several questions (usually 3–5) based on that information will follow.

▶ **TIP:** The key to solving a question based on an item set is choosing only the information needed to answer that particular question.

EXERCISE 9: ITEM SETS

Directions: Write the information needed for each problem and then solve the problem. Questions 1–3 are based on the picture below.

The owner of a campground is planning to add two new roads, Birch Trail and Pine Way. The campground area is $\frac{7}{8}$ mile wide and $\frac{19}{20}$ mile deep.

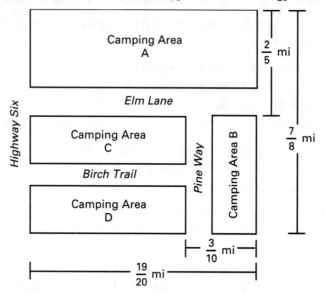

1. What is the length of Pine Way?
   Information needed: _____
   (1) $\frac{1}{8}$ mile **(2)** $\frac{7}{20}$ mile **(3)** $\frac{19}{40}$ mile **(4)** $1\frac{11}{40}$ miles **(5)** $1\frac{2}{3}$ miles

2. What is the total length of the two new roads?
   Information needed: _____
   (1) $\frac{19}{40}$ mile **(2)** $\frac{13}{20}$ mile **(3)** $\frac{21}{23}$ mile **(4)** $1\frac{1}{8}$ miles **(5)** $1\frac{1}{4}$ miles

3. How wide is Elm Lane?
   Information needed: _____
   (1) $\frac{1}{5}$ mile **(2)** $\frac{2}{5}$ mile **(3)** $\frac{19}{40}$ mile **(4)** $\frac{19}{20}$ mile
   (5) not enough information is given

3
RATIO AND PROPORTION

Ratio

A *ratio* is a mathematical way of comparing two quantities. An example is "Six out of every eight students saw the concert." If the ratio compares two quantities with different units, it is called a *rate*. For example, 55 *miles per hour* is a rate. Whether we call the comparison a ratio or a rate, it can be written as a fraction, as a comparison using the word *to*, or as a comparison using a colon. You can set up a ratio whenever you are comparing two numbers.

Example 1: Six out of eight students saw the concert.

The ratio is: 6 to 8 *or* 6:8 *or* $\frac{6}{8}$
$\frac{6}{8}$ can be reduced to $\frac{3}{4}$

Example 2: "I drove 55 miles per hour."

The rate is: 55 miles to 1 hour *or* 55:1 *or* $\frac{55}{1}$

The word *per* often tells you to set up a ratio. This ratio is a rate because it compares two different units: *miles* to *hours*.

▶ **TIP:** In a ratio, unlike a fraction, the number 1 is kept in the denominator.

ANSWERS TO EXERCISES IN THIS CHAPTER BEGIN ON PAGE 433.

EXERCISE 1: RATIO
Directions: Write each comparison as a ratio or a rate in fraction form. Be sure to reduce each fraction completely.

1. 30 minutes to 1 hour
2. 3 pounds of meat for 4 people
3. 88 feet in 8 seconds
4. $80 for 12 boards

EXERCISE 2: APPLICATION OF RATIOS

Directions: Solve each problem.

    Questions 1 and 2 are based on the information in the table below. Write each ratio as a fraction to compare the expenses.

PAINTERS' WEEKLY WORK EXPENSES				TOTAL
Tools $25	**Supplies** $120	**Transportation** $40	**Telephone** $15	$200

1. Compare the cost of supplies to total expenses.
2. The total expenses are how many times greater than the expense for transportation?
3. You own 300 shares of Consolidated Merchants stock and receive a dividend of $729. What is the dividend per share?

Proportion

    A ***proportion*** is a statement that two ratios (fractions) are equal. The arithmetic statement $\frac{7}{8} = \frac{14}{16}$ is an example of a proportion. In words, it means "7 is to 8 as 14 is to 16." A proportion is true if the ***cross products*** are equal. Cross products are the numbers that are at opposite corners of the equivalent fractions.

Example 1:

$$\frac{7}{8} \rightleftarrows = \rightleftarrows \frac{14}{16}$$

$$\underbrace{7 \times 16}_{112} = \underbrace{8 \times 14}_{112} \quad \text{7 × 16 and 8 × 14 are cross products.}$$

    A useful type of proportion is one in which one of the ratios is not completely known. The missing number is represented by a letter. Example 2 shows how to solve for the letter.

Example 2:   If 3 apples cost 50 cents, find the cost of 15 apples at the same rate. You can write a proportion to represent this.

STEP 1.   Set up the proportion where *c* represents the unknown cost of the apples.

$$\frac{3 \text{ apples}}{\$.50} = \frac{15 \text{ apples}}{c}$$
$$\frac{3}{.50} = \frac{15}{c}$$

STEP 2.   Cross multiply the two given numbers. $15 \times .50 = \$7.50$

STEP 3.   Divide that answer by the number that is left.

$$\$7.50 \div 3 = \$2.50$$
$$c = \$2.50$$

Therefore, if 3 apples cost 50 cents, 15 apples cost $2.50.

$$\frac{3}{\$.50} = \frac{15}{\$2.50}$$

We know this is true because the cross products are equal.

$$3 \times \$2.50 = 15 \times \$.50$$
$$\$7.50 = \$7.50$$

TO SOLVE A PROPORTION
1. Cross multiply two given numbers.
2. Divide that answer by the number that is left in the proportion.

You can also represent the operations to solve a proportion in the following way.

1. Write the proportion.

2. Write the multiplication above a fraction bar.
   Remember that a fraction bar also means "divided by."

3. Write the remaining number under the fraction bar.

4. Solve by multiplying the top and dividing by the bottom.

$$\frac{b}{8} = \frac{5}{20}$$

$$\frac{8 \times 5}{}$$

$$\frac{8 \times 5}{20}$$

$$\frac{40}{20} = 2$$

EXERCISE 3: SOLVING PROPORTIONS

Directions: Solve the following proportions for the missing element in each.

1. $\frac{2}{5} = \frac{m}{10}$

2. $\frac{x}{7} = \frac{3}{21}$

3. $\frac{5}{y} = \frac{15}{20}$

Application of Proportion

Proportion has a great many applications. If a problem compares two types of quantities and asks for a missing factor, you should consider using a proportion to solve the problem.

Example: If a baseball player hits 10 home runs in the first 45 games, at the same rate how many home runs can he expect to hit during the 162-game season?

STEP 1. Gather the given information and identify unknown quantity.

STEP 2. Write a proportion, keeping the labels in the same part of both ratios.

STEP 3. Solve.

10 home runs in 45 games.
h home runs in 162 games.

$$\frac{10 \text{ home runs}}{45 \text{ games}} = \frac{h}{162 \text{ games}}$$

$$\frac{162 \times 10}{45} = \frac{1620}{45} = 36$$

The player can expect to hit 36 home runs in 162 games.

EXERCISE 4: APPLICATION OF PROPORTION

Directions: Solve each problem.

1. The picture to the right is to be enlarged. If the width of the enlargement will be 8 inches, how deep will it be?

2. At Foster's Department Store, the ratio of managers to sales people is 2:9. If Foster's currently has 180 salespeople, how many managers are there?

3. Two pancakes contain 120 calories. Ellen had a stack of 7 pancakes. How many calories did she have?

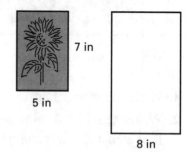

7 in

5 in

8 in

4
PERCENTS

What Are Percents?

Percents, like decimals and fractions, are ways of writing parts of a whole. A percent is a part of a whole that has been divided into 100 equal pieces. Therefore, *percent* means "per hundred."

A percent is written as a number with the sign %. For example, the number 50% means the same as $\frac{50}{100}$ or .50. When you work with percents, you may have to change them to an equivalent decimal or fraction. The chart below shows the relationship among percents, fractions, and decimals.

Percent	Fraction	Decimal
1%	$\frac{1}{100}$	.01
5%	$\frac{5}{100} = \frac{1}{20}$	.05
10%	$\frac{10}{100} = \frac{1}{10}$	.10
25%	$\frac{25}{100} = \frac{1}{4}$	.25
$33\frac{1}{3}\%$	$\frac{33\frac{1}{3}}{100} = \frac{1}{3}$	$.33\frac{1}{3}$
50%	$\frac{50}{100} = \frac{1}{2}$	.50
$66\frac{2}{3}\%$	$\frac{66\frac{2}{3}}{100} = \frac{2}{3}$	$.66\frac{2}{3}$
75%	$\frac{75}{100} = \frac{3}{4}$	.75
100%	$\frac{100}{100} = 1$	1.00

▶ **TIP:** Since 100% is one whole, then anything less than 100% is less than one whole. For example, 75% of a quantity is a part of the quantity.

Changing to Fractions and Decimals

Many problems require a change back and forth from fractions to decimals to percents. To change a percent to a fraction or decimal, remember what % means: percent means "per hundred."

% means " $\times \frac{1}{100}$," and % means " $\times$ .01."

Example 1: Change 13% to an equivalent fraction and to an equivalent decimal.

To a fraction: $13 \times \frac{1}{100} = \frac{13}{1} \times \frac{1}{100} = \frac{13}{100}$

To a decimal: $13 \times .01 = .13$

▶ **TIP:** You will notice that multiplying by .01 moves the decimal point 2 places to the left. $13\% = .13. = .13$

Example 2: Change the following to an equivalent fraction and an equivalent decimal. Be sure to reduce fractions to lowest terms.

80% *To a fraction:* $80 \times \frac{1}{100} = \frac{\overset{4}{\cancel{80}}}{1} \times \frac{1}{\cancel{100}_{5}} = \frac{4}{5}$

   To a decimal: $80 \times .01 = .80$ or $.8$

$33\frac{1}{3}\%$ *To a fraction:* $33\frac{1}{3} \times \frac{1}{100} = \frac{\overset{1}{\cancel{100}}}{3} \times \frac{1}{\cancel{100}_{1}} = \frac{1}{3}$

   To a decimal: $33\frac{1}{3} \times .01 = .33\frac{1}{3}$

150% *To a mixed number:* $150 \times \frac{1}{100} = \frac{\overset{3}{\cancel{150}}}{1} \times \frac{1}{\cancel{100}_{2}} = \frac{3}{2} = 1\frac{1}{2}$

   To a decimal: $150 \times .01 = 1.50$ or 1.5

Some percents can be written like this: .6%. This means "six-tenths of one percent" and is less than 1%.

Example 3: Write .6% as a fraction and as a decimal.

As a fraction: First write the decimal part as a fraction. Then, multiply by $\frac{1}{100}$.

$$.6 = \frac{6}{10} = \frac{3}{5}$$
$$\frac{3}{5} \times \frac{1}{100} = \frac{3}{500}$$

As a decimal: Just write the decimal part and multiply by .01. $.6 \times .01 = .006$

▶ TIP: Always read a decimal carefully for its meaning. Anything over 100% is *more than one whole*. For example, 200% is the same as 2 times a whole. Thus 200% of 6 is 12.

Any proper fraction or decimal followed by % means *less than 1%*. For example, $\frac{3}{4}\%$ means "three-quarters of one percent," and .75% means "seventy-five hundredths of one percent," *not* 75%.

EXERCISE 1: CHANGING TO FRACTIONS AND DECIMALS

Directions: Change each percent to an equivalent fraction *and* an equivalent decimal.

1. 87%   **3.** 12.5%   **5.** $\frac{1}{2}$%

2. $66\frac{2}{3}$%   **4.** 18%

CHANGING TO PERCENTS
- To change a fraction to a percent, multiply by 100 and attach a % sign.
- To change a decimal to a percent, multiply by 100 and attach a % sign.

Example 1:   Change $\frac{7}{8}$ to a percent.

$$\frac{7}{8} \times 100 = \frac{7}{8} \times \frac{100}{1} = \frac{700}{8} = 87\frac{1}{2} = 87\frac{1}{2}\%$$

Example 2:   Change .3 to a percent.

$$.3 \times 100 = 30 = 30\%$$

Example 3:   Change the mixed number 2.04 to an equivalent percent.

$$\frac{2.04}{1} \times \frac{100}{1} = \frac{204}{1} = 204 = 204\%$$

EXERCISE 2: CHANGING TO PERCENTS

Directions: Change the following numbers to equivalent percents.

1. $\frac{3}{8}$ **3.** .625

2. 4.5   **4.** $2\frac{1}{4}$

Using Proportions

A percent word problem can be solved by setting up a proportion. We call this the "*part* over *whole*" method. The proportion below shows how to set up one of these problems.

$$\frac{\text{PART}}{\text{WHOLE}} = \frac{\text{\% (PART)}}{100\% \text{ (WHOLE)}}$$

You may also see it shown this way:

part	%
whole	100

In the example of 25%, the proportion would look like this:

part $\longrightarrow$ $\frac{25}{100} = \frac{25\%}{100\%}$ $\longleftarrow$ percent (part)

whole $\longrightarrow$ $\longleftarrow$ always 100%

This proportion shows that the relationship of a part to a whole is the same as the relationship of a percent to 100%. To solve a percent word problem, you must read the problem carefully and first decide whether you are looking for the *percent, part*, or *whole*. Use an *n* for the number you are trying to find. Remember, the 100 on the bottom right *never* changes.

Example 1:   Find 40% of 120.

   Solution: We are looking for a missing PART.

the missing part $\longrightarrow$ $\dfrac{n}{120} = \dfrac{40}{100}$ $\nwarrow$ percent part
   whole $\longrightarrow$ $\swarrow$ always 100

Cross multiply: $120 \times 40 = 4800$
   Divide: $4800 \div 100 = 48$

The missing number is 48. 40% of 120 is 48.

▶ **TIP:**   Sometimes, to find a percent, it may be easier just to change the percent to a decimal or fraction and multiply. For example, to find 40% of 120: $120 \times .40 = 48$, and $120 \times \frac{2}{5} = 48$.

Example 2:   18 is what percent of 72?

   Solution: We are looking for the PERCENT.

part $\longrightarrow$ $\dfrac{18}{72} = \dfrac{n}{100}$ $\nwarrow$ the missing percent
   whole $\longrightarrow$ $\swarrow$ always 100

Cross multiply: $18 \times 100 = 1800$
   Divide: $1800 \div 72 + 25$

The number is 25%. 18 is 25% of 72.

Example 3:   120% of what number is 60?

   Solution: We are looking for the WHOLE.

part $\longrightarrow$ $\dfrac{60}{n} = \dfrac{120}{100}$ $\nwarrow$ percent
the missing whole $\longrightarrow$ $\swarrow$ always 100

Cross multiply: $60 \times 100 = 6000$
   Divide: $6000 \div 120 = 50$

The missing number is 50. 120% of 50 is 60.

   Notice that in Example 3 the part (60) is larger than the whole (50). This is because the percent is 120%, which is more than 100%.

EXERCISE 3: PERCENT PROBLEMS

Directions: Write down which you are looking for, part, whole, or percent. Then solve each problem.

1. Find 4% of 30.

2. 10 is 2.5% of what number?

3. What percent of $340 is $30.60?

4. $\frac{1}{2}$% of 62 is what number?

Percent Word Problems

Special types of percent problems are finding interest, discounts, and repayments of loans. In general, percent word problems are multi-step problems. You know, of course, that you always multiply and then divide after you have set up a proportion. However, you may also have to perform some addition or subtraction to get a final answer.

Example 1: To pass her science test, Amy must get 75% of the problems correct. Out of 80 questions, how many must she get right to pass?

Given: 75% — the percent

80 — the whole test

Look for: *n* — the number to get right (the part)

The proportion for this problem reads:

$$\text{part} \rightarrow \frac{n}{80} = \frac{75}{100} \leftarrow \text{percent}$$
$$\text{whole} \rightarrow \qquad\qquad \leftarrow \text{always 100}$$

Example 2: Erica is charged 21% in finance charges for the unpaid balance on her credit cards. If her bank tells her she owes $42 in finance charges, what is her unpaid balance?

The proportion for this problem is:

$$\text{finance charge} \rightarrow \frac{42}{n} = \frac{21}{100} \leftarrow \text{percent}$$
$$\text{balance} \rightarrow \qquad\qquad \leftarrow \text{always 100}$$

EXERCISE 4: PERCENT WORD PROBLEMS

Directions: Solve each problem.

1. Jesse takes home $2100 a month. He saves 12% of his earnings, and he spends $420 a month for rent. How much does Jesse save each month?

2. Mrs. Rogers put 15% down on her new car. If the down payment was $1800, how much did the car cost?

3. A political campaign conducted a poll to determine how the candidate was doing. The results were as follows. What percent of the voters was undecided?

Allen	Gault	Undecided
200	120	180

4. Employees at Todd's Musicmart get a 20% discount on all purchases. If Hosea buys three cassettes at $7.49 each, what will he have to pay after his employee discount?

Interest Problems

If you borrow or invest money, you will be dealing with an ***interest rate*** that is expressed as a percent. Interest rates are calculated on an annual basis. Thus, if the loan is longer or shorter than one year, the amount of interest per year must be multiplied by the length of time.

The length of time of the loan must always be expressed as one year or a part of the year. If the time is given in months, write the months as a fraction comparing the given number of months to 12 months.

For example, 9 months $= \frac{9 \text{ months}}{12 \text{ months}} = \frac{3}{4}$ year

If the time is given in days, change it to a fraction of a year by comparing the given number of days to 360 (approximately the number of days in a year).

For example, $120 \text{ days} = \frac{120 \text{ days}}{360 \text{ days}} = \frac{1}{3} \text{ year}$

Example 1: To expand one of its factory-outlet stores, a towel manufacturer secures a $2\frac{1}{2}$-year loan for \$35,000 at an annual interest rate of 7%. How much interest will the manufacturer pay on the loan?

STEP 1. Find the interest for 1 year. $\qquad \frac{n}{35,000} = \frac{7}{100}$

STEP 2. Cross multiply and divide. $\qquad \frac{35,000 \times 7}{100} = 2450$

STEP 3. Find the interest for $2\frac{1}{2}$ years. $\qquad 2450 \times 2\frac{1}{2} = \$6125$

Example 2: Mrs. Barnes borrowed \$4000 for 3 years. Find the amount she repaid if the annual rate of interest was 9%.

STEP 1. Find the interest for 1 year. $\qquad \frac{n}{4000} = \frac{9}{100}$

$\qquad \frac{9 \times 4000}{100} = \frac{36,000}{100} = 360$

STEP 2. Find the interest for 3 years. $\qquad 360 \times 3 = 1080$

STEP 3. Find the amount she repaid. $\qquad 4000 + 1080 = \$5080$

▶ **TIP:** Some interest problems require you to find only the interest, and others require you to find the total amount of the loan or investment. The total is the amount that you borrowed plus the interest. You must read problems carefully to make sure you understand whether you are being asked for the *interest* or the *amount to pay back,* as in Example 2.

SOLVING INTEREST PROBLEMS

1. Set up a proportion and solve it for the interest.

$$\frac{\text{Interest}}{\text{Original Amount}} = \frac{\text{Percent}}{100}$$

2. To find the total interest, multiply the interest by the length of time of the loan.
3. To find the total amount of the loan or investment, add the original amount to the total interest.

▶ **TIP:** A common way to find interest is to use the formula $I = prt$, where $p = \text{principal}$, $r = \text{rate}$, and $t = \text{time}$.

EXERCISE 5: INTEREST PROBLEMS
Directions: Solve each problem.

1. To take advantage of a closeout sale, a motel owner borrows $31,000 to buy 124 color television sets. The loan is for 90 days at an annual interest rate of 12.5%. Find the total amount to be repaid.

   (1) $968.75   **(2)** $3,875   **(3)** $31,968.75   **(4)** $34,875
   (5) not enough information is provided

2. Which expression shows how you find the interest on $1500 at $8\frac{1}{2}$% for one year?

   (1) $\dfrac{1500 \times 8\frac{1}{2}}{100}$ **(2)** $\dfrac{1500 \times 100}{8\frac{1}{2}}$ **(3)** $\dfrac{1500}{100 \div 8\frac{1}{2}}$ **(4)** $\dfrac{100}{1500 \times 8\frac{1}{2}}$ **(5)** $\dfrac{100}{1500 \div 8\frac{1}{2}}$

3. Alex borrowed some money for one year at a rate of 8%. If he paid $360 in interest that year, how much did he borrow?

   (1) $28.80   **(2)** $288   **(3)** $2,880   **(4)** $4,500   **(5)** $36,000

5
MEASUREMENT

Standard Measurement

The units of measurement below are the ones used most often in the United States. They are often referred to as the *standard* or *American* units of measure.

Standard Measurement

Units of Length			Units of Weight		
12 inches (in)	= 1 foot (ft)		2000 pounds (lb)	= 1 ton (T)	
3 feet	= 1 yard (yd)		16 ounces	= 1 pound	
36 inches	= 1 yard				
5280 feet	= 1 mile (mi)		*Units of Time*		
			12 months (mo)	= 1 year (yr)	
Units of Capacity			52 weeks (wk)	= 1 year	
4 quarts (qt)	= 1 gallon (gal)		365 days (da)	= 1 year	
2 pints (pt)	= 1 quart		7 days	= 1 week	
2 cups (c)	= 1 pint		24 hours (hr)	= 1 day	
8 ounces (oz)	= 1 cup		60 minutes (min)	= 1 hour	
			60 seconds (sec)	= 1 minute	

Converting Units

In solving measurement problems, it is often convenient to change the units of measure. This is called making a *conversion*. There are two types of conversions: from a large unit to a smaller unit or from a smaller unit to a larger unit. The following table will be useful in converting units.

CONVERTING UNITS		
To change a large unit to a smaller unit	Multiply $\times$	This is because we want *more* of the smaller unit.
To change a small unit to a larger unit	Divide $\div$	This is because we want *fewer* of the larger unit.

Example 1: Change 7 feet to inches.

Because we are changing from feet (a large unit) to inches (a small unit), we multiply. (Recall: 12 inches = 1 foot.)

$$\begin{array}{r} 12 \text{ inches} \\ \times\ 7 \\ \hline 84 \text{ inches} \end{array}$$

Example 2: Change 6 tons to pounds.

Because we are changing from a large unit to a smaller unit, we multiply. (Recall: 2000 pounds = 1 ton.)

$$\begin{array}{r} 2000 \text{ pounds} \\ \times\ \ \ 6 \\ \hline 12{,}000 \text{ pounds} \end{array}$$

Example 3: Change 48 ounces to pints.

Because we are changing from a smaller unit (ounces) to a larger unit (pints), we divide.

(Recall: 8 ounces = 1 cup, and 2 cups = 1 pint.)

Before dividing to find the number of pints, we must find the number of ounces in a pint.

First, multiply 8 ounces by 2 cups to get 16 ounces in a pint. $\qquad$ $8 \times 2 = 16$

Then, divide 48 ounces by 16 ounces. $\qquad$ $48 \div 16 = 3$

There are 3 pints in 48 ounces.

ANSWERS TO EXERCISES IN THIS CHAPTER BEGIN ON PAGE 435.

EXERCISE 1: CONVERSIONS
Directions: Make the conversions in the following problems.

1. 96 hours = _____days
2. 20 quarts = _____gallons
3. 2 days = _____minutes
4. If Pike's Peak is 14,110 feet high, what is its elevation in miles (to the nearest tenth)?

Basic Operations with Measurements

We often need to add, subtract, multiply, or divide measurements. Let's review these skills.

Example 1: Add 3 pounds 8 ounces to 15 ounces.

$$\begin{array}{r} 3 \text{ lb} \quad 8 \text{ oz} \\ + \qquad 15 \text{ oz} \\ \hline 3 \text{ lb} \, 23 \text{ oz} \end{array}$$ Be sure to add ounces to ounces.

Because 23 ounces is more than 16 ounces (1 pound), simplify it by dividing by 16.

$$\begin{array}{r} 1 \text{ r } 7 = 1 \text{ lb } 7 \text{ oz} \\ 16 \overline{)23} \\ -\ 16 \\ \hline 7 \end{array}$$

3 pounds 23 ounces = 3 pounds + 1 pound 7 ounces = 4 pounds 7 ounces

Example 2: Take 5 pounds 7 ounces from 8 pounds 12 ounces.

$$\begin{array}{r} 8 \text{ lb} \quad 12 \text{ oz} \\ -\ 5 \text{ lb} \quad 7 \text{ oz} \\ \hline 3 \text{ lb} \quad 5 \text{ oz} \end{array}$$ Subtract ounces from ounces.
Then subtract pounds from pounds.

Example 3: Multiply 4 feet 8 inches by 3.

$$\begin{array}{r} 4 \text{ ft} \quad 8 \text{ in} \\ \times \qquad 3 \\ \hline 12 \text{ ft } 24 \text{ in} \end{array}$$ Multiply 3 by 8 inches, then multiply 3 by 4 feet.

12 ft 24 in ← Since 12 inches = 1 foot, simplify the answer.

12 ft 24 in = 12 ft + 2 ft = 14 ft

Example 4:   Divide 2 quarts 5 ounces by 3.

$$\begin{array}{r} 0 \text{ qt} \quad 23 \text{ oz} = 1 \text{ qt} \quad 7 \text{ oz} \\ \hline 3) \overline{2 \text{ qt} \quad 5 \text{ oz}} \\ -0 \\ \hline \end{array}$$

2 qt = 64 oz   ← 3 will not go into 2 quarts. Change 2 quarts to 64 ounces.

+ 5 oz   ← Add 5 ounces to 64 ounces. Then divide by three.

69 oz ÷ 3 = 23 oz = 1 qt 7 oz

BASIC OPERATIONS WITH MEASUREMENTS	
ADDITION	1. Add like units. 2. Write the answer in simplest form.
SUBTRACTION	1. Subtract like units. 2. Regroup units when necessary. 3. Write the answer in simplest form.
MULTIPLICATION	1. Multiply like units if units are involved. 2. Write the answer in simplest form.
DIVISION	1. Divide into the larger unit first. 2. Change the remainder to the smaller unit and add that to any other smaller units. 3. Then divide into the smaller unit. 4. Be sure your answer is in simplest form.

EXERCISE 2: BASIC OPERATIONS WITH MEASUREMENT

Directions: In the following practice problems, add, subtract, multiply, or divide as indicated. Be sure the final answer is in simplest form. For example, an answer of 15 inches should be changed to 1 foot 3 inches.

1. 22 feet 6 inches ÷ 3
2. 5 hours 20 minutes ÷ 8
3. What is the difference in weight of two boxes of cereal, one weighing 1 pound 4 ounces and the other weighing 13 ounces?
4. At a price of $415 per ounce, which of the following represents the value of 1 pound 3 ounces of gold?
   (1) 3($415)   (2) 16($415)   (3) 3 + 16 + $415   (4) 19($415)   (5) $\frac{\$415}{19}$
5. Shane has a part-time job at the local hardware store. He earns $5 per hour. Last week he worked the following times: Monday, 2 hours 30 minutes; Wednesday, 3 hours; Friday, 4 hours 45 minutes; Saturday, 7 hours 15 minutes; and Sunday, 4 hours. How much was he paid last week?
   (1) $28   (2) $66   (3) $72   (4) $86   (5) $107.50

The Metric System

The *metric system* is an international measuring system used to simplify trade and commerce among nations. The basic unit of measure of length is the *meter*. One meter is a little longer than a yard. The basic unit of weight is the *gram*. A paper clip weighs approximately one gram. A more practical comparison to our American system is the kilogram, which is about 2 pounds. The basic liquid measure is a *liter*. A liter has slightly more capacity than a quart.

All units are derived from the basic units of meter (length), gram (weight), and liter (liquid). Prefixes are added to the basic unit to indicate the amount of each unit. For example, the prefix *centi* means one-hundredth; therefore, one centimeter is one-hundredth of a meter, one centigram is one-

PREFIX	MEANING
kilo	1000
hecto	100
deca	10
BASIC UNIT	
deci	$\frac{1}{10}$ (.1)
centi	$\frac{1}{100}$ (.01)
milli	$\frac{1}{1000}$ (.001)

hundredth of a gram, and one centiliter is one-hundredth of a liter.

The diagram below relates the metric prefixes to the decimal system that you already know.

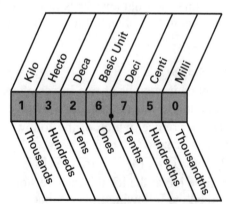

The charts below show the most common units of metric measure.

LENGTH
1 kilometer (km) = 1000 m
1 meter (m) = 1 m
1 centimeter (cm) = .01 m
1 millimeter (mm) = .001 m

WEIGHT
1 kilogram (kg) = 1000 g
1 gram (g) = 1 g
1 milligram (mg) = $\frac{1}{1000}$ g (.001 g)

CAPACITY
1 kiloliter (kl) = 1000 l
1 liter (l) = 1 l
1 milliliter (ml) = $\frac{1}{1000}$ l (.001 l)

Conversion in the Metric System

Conversions between units involve moving the decimal point to the right or left.

The diagram below represents the prefixes from larger to smaller.

| kilo | hecto | deca | unit | deci | centi | milli |

Example 1: Change 420 meters to kilometers.

STEP 1. Recognize that meters to kilometers is going from a smaller unit to a larger. (1000 meters = 1 kilometer) Draw the arrow to show that.

kilometers ⟵————— meters
left (÷)

STEP 2. Since kilo means "thousand," move 3 places.

km hm dam m dm cm mm

420 = .420

Example 2: Convert 4.2 kilograms to grams.

kg hg dag g dg cg mg
3 moves right

4.2 kg = 4.200 g = 4200 g
3 moves right

Example 3: Convert 4 meters 48 centimeters to centimeters.

First, change 4 meters to centimeters.

km hm dam m dm cm mm   4 m = 4.00 cm = 400 cm
2 moves right

Then, add.   400 cm + 48 cm = 448 cm

TO CHANGE METRIC UNITS

1. List the units from largest to smallest.
2. Put a mark at the starting unit.
3. Move by units to the new unit and count the moves right or left.
4. Move the decimal point the same number of places in the same direction.

EXERCISE 3: METRIC MEASUREMENT

Directions: Convert to the units shown.

1. Find the total length of the shaft illustrated below in meters.

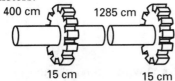

400 cm   1285 cm

15 cm   15 cm

2. The recommended dosage of vitamin C is 857 *milligrams* per day. How many *grams* of vitamin C will Max take in one week if he takes the recommended dosage?

3. If the speed limit sign in Canada reads 80 kilometers per hour and the speed limit sign in some areas of the United States reads 55 miles per hour, which country allows motorists to drive at a faster speed? (1 kilometer = .621 mile)

SPEED LIMIT 80 KPH   SPEED LIMIT 55 MPH

4. Terry competed in a 1000-meter speed skating race; how many kilometers did he skate?

5. Which expression can be used to find the cost of .75 kilogram of cheese at the price of $6.40 per kilogram?

(1) $\frac{\$6.40}{.75}$

(2) $.75 \times \$6.40$

(3) $\frac{\$6.40}{2}$

(4) $.75 + \$6.40$

(5) $\$6.40 - .75$

Special Topics in Measurement
Money Problems

Let's look at a few problems that require calculations involving money. You will be using the formula $c = nr$. A *formula* uses letters to represent rules for finding different quantities or measurements. When you work with formulas, you can substitute different numbers for the letters. To find the total cost (c), multiply the number of units (n) by the cost per unit (r). This is written as $c = nr$. (Two letters next to each other in a formula indicate that the two quantities have to be multiplied.)

Example: Margaret bought the following groceries on May 15: $1\frac{1}{2}$ dozen apples at $1.69 per dozen, 2 dozen eggs at 84¢ per dozen, 2 boxes of bran flakes at $3.15 each, 1 pound of margarine at $1.58 per pound, and 3 cans of soup at 79¢ per can. How much change did Margaret receive from a twenty-dollar bill?

STEP 1. Use the formula $c = nr$ to find the total cost of each item she bought. Then add to find the total cost of the purchases.

Apples: $1\frac{1}{2} \times 1.69 =$
$1.5 \times 1.69 =$
$2.535 = \$2.54$
Eggs: $2 \times .84 = 1.68$
Bran Flakes: $2 \times 3.15 = 6.30$
Margarine: $1 \times 1.58 = 1.58$
Soup: $3 \times .79 = \underline{+2.37}$
Total $\$14.47$

STEP 2. Subtract to find the change from $20.

$\$20.00$
$\underline{- \ 14.47}$
$\$5.53$

▶ **TIP:** Always round money to the hundredths place. In general, we round upward as opposed to downward.

EXERCISE 4: MONEY PROBLEMS
Directions: Solve each problem.

1. Mr. Barnes stocked his garden supply stores with 2 tons of sand in 50-pound bags for $138 per ton. If he sells the entire order of bags of sand for $5.95 per bag, what will be his profit?

(1) $3.19   (2) $69   (3) $200   (4) $276   (5) $470.40

2. You need 48 feet of molding to finish decorating the family room. What is the cost of the molding if each 1-yard length costs 98 cents?

(1) $3.92 **(2)** $15.68 **(3)** $47.04 **(4)** $392.00 **(5)** $470.00

3. A famous-brand multisymptom cold reliever costs $6.48 for 36 capsules. The generic equivalent costs $4.32 for 36 capsules. How much money do you save per dose using the generic medicine if each dose is 2 capsules?

(1) $.06 **(2)** $.12 **(3)** $.18 **(4)** $1.08 **(5)** $2.16

Time Problems

Many jobs require you to punch in on a time clock when you arrive at work and punch out when you leave. The time card will record a starting time and an ending time.

TIME CLOCK

A.M. means "hours between midnight and noon."

P.M. means "hours between noon and midnight."

Numbers on the left of the colon are hours. **3:30** Numbers on the right of the colon are minutes.

Example 1: Tina worked overtime on Thursday. She started at 7:30 A.M. and ended at 6:45 P.M. How long did she work?

STEP 1: Find her morning hours >

$$\begin{array}{r} {}^{1\ 1\ 60} \\ \cancel{12}\text{:}\cancel{00} \\ -\ 7\text{:}30 \\ \hline 4\text{:}30 \end{array}$$ — Borrow 60 minutes from the hours

4:30 or 4 hr 30 min

STEP 2. Find her afternoon hours.

Noon to 6:45 is 6 hours 45 minutes.

STEP 3: Add the total hours.

$$\begin{array}{r} 4\text{:}30 \\ +\ 6\text{:}45 \\ \hline 10\text{:}75 \end{array} = 11\text{:}15$$ — Because 75 minutes is more than 60 minutes (one hour), we simplify that to 1 hour and 15 minutes and add it to 10 hours.

11:15 can be written as *11 hr 15 min* or $11\frac{15}{60} = 11\frac{1}{4}$ hr.

HOW TO CALCULATE TIME

1. Find the number of morning hours.
2. Find the number of evening hours.
3. Add the morning hours and evening hours. Be sure to simplify your answer.

EXERCISE 5: TIME PROBLEMS
Directions: Solve each problem.

1. Roger works the lunch shift from 10:00 A.M. to 2:30 P.M. Monday through Friday each week at $8.00 per hour. Which expression shows how much he earns every four weeks?

   (1) $4\frac{1}{2} + 8 + 5 + 4$

   (2) $(4\frac{1}{2} \times 8) + (5 \times 4)$

   (3) $4\frac{1}{2} \times 8 \times 5 \times 4$

   (4) $4\frac{1}{2}(8 + 5 + 4)$

   (5) $4\frac{1}{2} \times 8$

   Questions 2–4 refer to the time card below:

MARSHALL MANUFACTURING					
NAME: Tom Wolper SS# 000-45-0000					
Date	5/20	5/21	5/22	5/23	5/24
From	8:00 A.M.	8:00 A.M.	8:00 A.M.	8:00 A.M.	8:00 A.M.
To	4:00 P.M.	5:30 P.M.	6:45 P.M.	4:00 P.M.	4:30 P.M.
Total Regular Hours _____ at $7.85					
Overtime Hours _____at $12.00 (over 40 hours)					

2. According to his time card, Tom Wolper worked the week of 5/20 to 5/24. How many overtime hours (any time more than the straight eight-hour shift) did he work that week?
   (1) $3\frac{3}{4}$ (2) 4   (3) $4\frac{1}{4}$ (4) $4\frac{1}{2}$ (5) $4\frac{3}{4}$

3. What is Tom's full pay before deductions? (Include regular hours and overtime hours.)
   (1) $57   (2) $314   (3) $351   (4) $371   (5) $537

4. If state withholding tax is 1%, federal withholding tax is 25%, and social security tax (FICA) is 7%, how much will Tom's take-home pay be after these deductions?
   (1) $122.43   (2) $155.82   (3) $215.18   (4) $248.57   (5) $493.43

5. An airplane travels 960 miles per hour. Which expression tells how far it travels in twenty minutes?
   (1) 960×20 (2) $960 \times \frac{1}{3}$ (3) $\frac{960}{20}$ (4) $\frac{3}{960}$ (5) $\frac{(\frac{1}{3})}{960}$

Reading and Interpreting Scales and Meters

Scale Drawings

A *map* is a drawing of land area. When a map is drawn to scale (in proportion to the land it represents), a *key* is given so you may calculate distances on the map. A key has the information about the ratio for that particular drawing. You can use the scale to set up a proportion to find a distance. Let's look at the local map below. Answer the following questions while referring to the map. Notice the scale of miles at the top of the map.

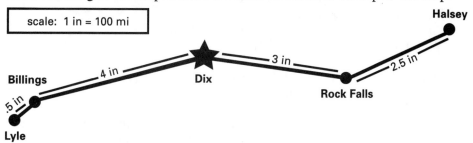

scale: 1 in = 100 mi

Halsey · 2.5 in · Rock Falls · 3 in · Dix · 4 in · Billings · .5 in · Lyle

Example: If the distance from Halsey to Rock Falls on the map is 2.5 inches, what is the actual distance between Halsey and Rock Falls?

The ratio is 1 inch to 100 miles. If the distance on the map between Halsey and Rock Falls is 2.5 inches, we can set up the following proportion to solve the problem. Notice that we are using a proportion to compare two things (inches to miles).

$$\frac{1 \text{ in}}{100 \text{ mi}} = \frac{2.5 \text{ in}}{n \text{ mi}}$$

Cross multiply: $100 \times 2.5 = 250$

Divide: $250 \div 1 = 250$

Reading Meters

Meters are devices used to measure time, speed, distance, and energy used. You might recognize some meters as a speedometer, barometer, or thermometer. Meters give us information to solve problems. Let's look at an example.

The Electric Meter

Appliances such as refrigerators, fans, radios, TVs, and dishwashers require electricity. The electric meter is the instrument that measures the amount of electricity used in kilowatt-hours (kwh). The numbers above the dial indicate one complete round around the dial. Notice that the numbers may go in different directions around the dial.

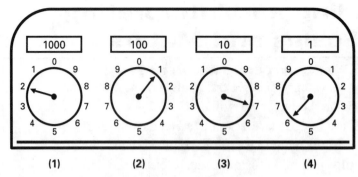

Dial (1) measures the number of 1000 kwh.

Dial (2) measures the number of 100 kwh.

Dial (3) measures the number of 10 kwh.

Dial (4) measures the number of 1 kwh.

(1)　　　(2)　　　(3)　　　(4)

Example:　Read the meter above.

Start reading the dials with the left dial. If the pointer is between two numbers, read the *smaller* of the two numbers. Reading the meter above, you get $\boxed{2176}$.

Dial (1) 2	$2 \times 1000 =$	2000
Dial (2) 1	$1 \times 100\ =$	100
Dial (3) 7	$7 \times 10\ \ =$	70
Dial (4) 6	$6 \times 1\ \ \ =$	6
Total kwh used:		2176

EXERCISE 6: SCALES AND METERS

Directions: Solve each problem.

1. What is the scale for a map in which 2000 miles is represented by 10 inches?
   (1) 1 in = 2 mi　　**(2)** 1 in = 20 mi　　**(3)** 1 in = 200 mi
   (4) 1 in = $\frac{1}{2}$ mi　　**(5)** 1 in = 100 mi

2. Emma's last reading on her electric meter was 3843 kwh. Her new reading is indicated on the meter shown below. If the charge is 12.5 cents per kwh, what is Emma's new electric bill?

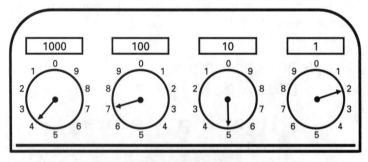

KILOWATT-HOURS

(1) $113.63　　**(2)** $909　　**(3)** $2,020　　**(4)** $2,562.50　　**(5)** $11,362.50

6
GRAPHS, STATISTICS, AND PROBABILITY

Graphs, charts, and statistical tables help us organize information. When you are presented with material that has been organized for you, you must carefully study the details such as the title, subtitle, column and row headings, key (if shown), and type of information given. We call this interpreting the **data**. Statistics is the study of data. With statistics, you organize the data and then draw a conclusion based on them.

Mean and Median

Two common types of statistical problems ask you to find the mean or median of a set of data. The **mean** is the average of the numbers. To find the average, you add the data and then divide by the number of pieces of data.

For instance, Brenda bowled 132, 147, and 108 at the bowling alley last night. To find her mean (average) score, you add: $132 + 147 + 108 = 387$ and then divide by 3 (the number of scores): $387 \div 3 = 129$. Therefore, her average, or mean, bowling score is 129.

The **median** of a set of data is found by arranging the numbers from the smallest to largest and then choosing the middle number in the arrangement. That middle number is the median. You would arrange Brenda's three bowling scores to read 108, 132, 147. The middle score is 132, so the median is 132.

TO FIND THE AVERAGE OR MEAN

1. Add the numbers.
2. Divide by the number of numbers.

TO FIND THE MEDIAN

1. Put the numbers in order from lowest to highest.
2. Choose the middle number. (If there are two middle numbers, find the average of the two numbers.)

Example: To get information on the number of evening diners at her Shamrock Inn, Shannon accumulated the following information for the first 17 days of March. What is the median of the number of diners?

35, 37, 43, 28, 32, 38, 45, 21, 26, 27, 44, 46, 29, 39, 42, 86, 117

The median is 38, while the mean (average) is 43.24.

In this case, the median of 38 is a better representation of the normal amount of diners. The average is thrown off by the large crowds on the 17th day, St. Patrick's Day. The median is often used when the mean does not give a true picture because of a few unusually high or low scores.

EXERCISE 1: MEAN AND MEDIAN

Directions: Solve each problem. *Questions 1 and 2* are based on the information below. Round your answers to the nearest whole number.

The scorekeeper for the Union Town basketball team recorded the results of the last six games.

Date	Opponent	Union Town vs. Opponent
12/4	Hinkley	48 to 37
12/6	Barton	45 to 63
12/10	Angel Park	53 to 42
12/12	Eagle Rock	72 to 24
12/18	Bennett	68 to 44
12/20	Alton	74 to 51

1. What is the average number of points scored by the opponents?
2. What is the median score scored by Union Town?
3. The prices of identical winter jackets at five local stores are $48.95, $39.95, $44.80, $52.25, and $42.88. What is the median price of that jacket?

Graphs

Graphs and charts are useful ways of simplifying complicated information by putting it in picture form. We can often understand an entire situation with only a quick look at a graph. By organizing data visually, graphs and charts help us interpret, compare, and analyze numbers.

Circle Graphs

The circle in a *circle graph* represents a whole quantity.

The circle at the right represents all of the business expenses of Hampton Products, a small family business. If you add all the sections in the circle, the total is 100%.

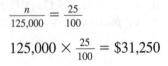

HAMPTON PRODUCTS BUSINESS EXPENSES

Rent and Utilities 25%
Salaries 55%
Insurance 10%
Supplies and Equipment 7%
Miscellaneous 3%

Example: If Hampton Products' business expenses totaled $125,000 last year, how much were the expenses for rent and utilities? We see from the graph that rent and utilities account for 25% of the total. We need to find 25% of $125,000.

$$\frac{n}{125,000} = \frac{25}{100}$$

$$125,000 \times \frac{25}{100} = \$31,250$$

EXERCISE 2: CIRCLE GRAPHS

Directions: Solve each problem.

Questions 1–3 are based on the graph at the right.

DISTRIBUTION OF A YEARLY INCOME OF $32,000

1. What is the average *monthly* expense for rent?
2. How much is spent on clothing during the year?
   (1) $320   **(2)** $480   **(3)** $800   **(4)** $3200
   (5) not enough information is given
3. What is the ratio of savings to entire income?
   (1) 1 to 10   **(2)** 10 to 1   **(3)** 10 to 32   **(4)** 32 to 10
   (5) not enough information is given

Bar Graphs

A *bar graph* is an excellent way of comparing amounts. In the bar graph below, compare income with expenses for a particular year.

EXERCISE 3: BAR GRAPHS

Directions: Use the following graph to answer the questions.

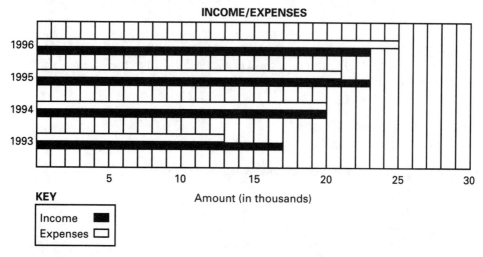

1. What was the average of expenses for the years 1993–1996?
2. In 1995, what was the difference between income and expenses?
   (1) $200   **(2)** $2,000   **(3)** $20,000   **(4)** $21,000   **(5)** $23,000

Line Graphs

Line graphs are used to show trends or patterns. On a line graph, each point relates two values. One is the value on the vertical (↕) axis at the left side, and the other is the value on the horizontal (⟷) axis at the bottom.

As you look at the line graph at the right, notice the following:

1. The title tells what the graph is about.

2. The vertical scale is labeled on the left side of the graph. Each line is an increase of 5°. The horizontal scale is labeled on the bottom of the graph. Each line is an increase of 1 hour.

3. The line shows the following trend: the temperature rose until 11:00 A.M., then remained steady until noon. Then the temperature fell.

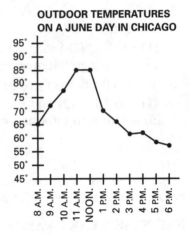

OUTDOOR TEMPERATURES
ON A JUNE DAY IN CHICAGO

You can also use a line graph to compare two different trends. Below is an example of this. One trend is shown with a solid line; the other is shown with a broken line. When a graph uses two or more lines, you can compare information from the lines.

EXERCISE 4: LINE GRAPHS

Directions: Use the graph below to answer questions 1–4 on page 301.

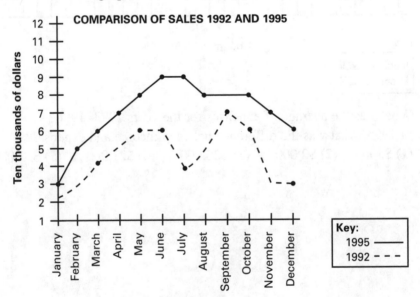

COMPARISON OF SALES 1992 AND 1995

Key:
1995 ———
1992 - - -

1. The title tells us that the graph compares _____ in _____(year) and _____ (year).
2. The vertical scale is labeled in _____.
3. In June of 1992, sales were about _____.
4. The graph shows that both 1992 and 1995 had seasonal highs and lows. In general, 1995 produced considerably _____ sales all year long.

EXERCISE 5: MIXED GRAPH PRACTICE

Directions: Solve each problem.

Questions 1–3 are based on the circle graph at the right.

DISTRIBUTION OF EARNINGS

1. If you make $25,000 per year, what is your annual contribution to social security?
2. If you wanted to have take-home pay of $20,000, how much would your actual earnings have to be?
3. One year, Mike earned $24,000. The deductions from his paycheck were federal tax, FICA, and state tax. What was his yearly take-home pay?

Questions 4–6 refer to the bar graph at the right.

4. What is the difference in height between the Empire State Building and the Sears Tower?
5. The World Trade Center is how many times as tall as the Washington Monument?
6. What is the median height of these six structures?

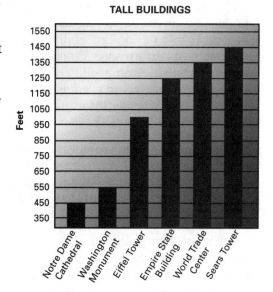

TALL BUILDINGS

Questions 7 and 8 refer to the line graph below.

CONCERT ATTENDANCE SUMMER 1996

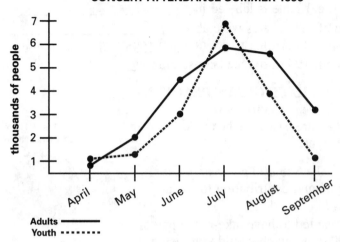

Adults ———
Youth ········

7. In which months was youth attendance higher than that for adults?
8. If adult tickets were $8.50 and youth tickets were $5.75, what were the receipts for the concerts held in August?

Probability

Probability can be called the language of uncertainty. The weather reporter says there is a 40% chance of rain today, but we still don't know if it's going to rain or not. Probability helps us predict the future based on analyzing past performance. Probability can be expressed as a fraction, a ratio, or a percent. A probability of 0 means an event cannot occur. A probability of 1 means an event is sure to happen. Numbers between 0 and 1 (fractions) show whether the event is closer to 0 (closer to not happening) or closer to 1 (more likely to happen).

Let's use a game spinner to illustrate probability. Assume that the wheel is perfectly balanced and that there is an even chance it will stop on any color. Each spin of the wheel is an ***event***. The color it stops at is an ***outcome*** of the event.

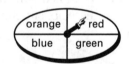

There are four possible outcomes when you spin this wheel: red, blue, green, and orange. A successful event occurs when you spin the wheel and get the color you want. The probability of success is the ratio of the number of successes of an event to the number of possible outcomes of that event. You can express probability in the following fraction or ratio form. Remember, this can also be a percent.

$$\text{Probability} = \frac{\text{Number of Successful Outcomes}}{\text{Number of Possible Outcomes}}$$

Using the spinning wheel, the probability of stopping at red would be $\frac{1}{4}$. While there are four possible outcomes (red, blue, green, or orange), there is only one successful outcome (red). The probability of $\frac{1}{4}$ can also be written as 25%, so you can say there is a 25% chance of landing on red.

Again, using the spinning wheel, find the probability of landing on *either* red *or* green. Now there are two possible outcomes that would be successful. The probability is:

$\frac{2}{4}$ number of successes
number of possibilities

You can reduce $\frac{2}{4}$ to $\frac{1}{2}$. Thus, the probability of landing on red or green is $\frac{1}{2}$, or 50%.

Probability of 0 or 1

A probability of 0 or 0% means an event will *not* take place. Using the same spinning wheel, the probability of landing on purple is 0 because the number of successful outcomes of purple on this wheel is 0. So we would have $\frac{0}{4} = 0$. There is 0% chance of landing on purple.

A probability of 1 or 100% means an event is *certain* to happen. Let's use the spinning wheel to find the probability of landing on red, green, blue, or orange. The number of successful outcomes is 4, and the number of possible outcomes is 4. Now we have $\frac{4}{4} = 1$.

EXERCISE 6: PROBABILITY
Directions: Solve each problem.

1. If a single card is picked from a deck of 52 playing cards, what is the probability that it is the ace of spades?
2. From the same deck of 52 cards, what is the probability of drawing a heart? Give your answer as a percent.
   (*Hint:* There are 13 cards in each suit.)

Questions 3–5 refer to the number cube below. Consider the roll of a single number cube that has six faces as shown.

3. What is the probability of rolling a 5?
   (1) $\frac{1}{6}$ **(2)** $\frac{1}{5}$ **(3)** $\frac{1}{3}$ **(4)** $\frac{1}{2}$ **(5)** $\frac{5}{6}$
4. What is the probability of rolling an even number?
   (1) $16\frac{2}{3}\%$ **(2)** 20%   **(3)** 30%   **(4)** $33\frac{1}{3}\%$ **(5)** 50%
5. What is the probability of rolling a number greater than 6?
   (1) 0   **(2)** $\frac{1}{6}$ **(3)** $\frac{1}{3}$ **(4)** $\frac{1}{2}$ **(5)** 1
6. You flip a coin nine times, and each time it lands on heads. What is the probability it will land on heads the tenth time you flip it?
   (1) $\frac{1}{9}$ **(2)** $\frac{1}{10}$ **(3)** $\frac{1}{2}$ **(4)** $\frac{9}{10}$ **(5)** not enough information is given

Dependent Probability

Suppose a box contains two green balls and three red balls. If one ball is drawn from the box, the probability of drawing a green ball is $\frac{2}{5}$ and the probability of drawing a red ball is $\frac{3}{5}$. If you do not replace the ball drawn, there are now only four balls in the box. The probability for the drawing of the next ball now depends on which ball you drew the first time.

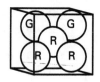

Possibility 1: You Drew a Green Ball

If you drew a *green* ball on the first draw, the box now contains one green ball and three red balls. In this situation, the probability of next drawing a green ball is now $\frac{1}{4}$ and the probability of drawing a red ball is $\frac{3}{4}$.

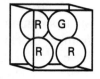

Possibility 2: You Drew a Red Ball

If you drew a *red* ball on the first draw, the box now contains two green balls and two red balls. The probability of drawing a green ball is now $\frac{2}{4}$ or $\frac{1}{2}$, and the probability of drawing a red ball is now $\frac{2}{4}$ or $\frac{1}{2}$.

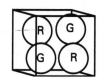

We see that the second draw *depends* on the first draw. This is an example of ***dependent probability.***

EXERCISE 7: DEPENDENT PROBABILITY

Directions: Solve each problem.

Questions 1 and 2 are based on the following situation. Express your answers as fractions. Draw a picture if necessary to help you find the probabilities.

Two cards are drawn in succession from a deck of 52 playing cards without the first card being replaced.

1. If the first card drawn was an ace, what is the probability that the second card is also an ace?
2. What is the probability that the second card drawn is an ace if the first card drawn was not an ace?

Questions 3 and 4 are based on the following situation. Express your answers as fractions.

A change purse contains 3 nickels, 4 dimes, and 2 quarters.

3. What is the probability that the first coin taken from the purse will be a quarter?
4. If the first coin taken from the purse was a nickel, what is the probability that the next coin will be a quarter?

7
NUMERATION

Numeration is the study of number relationships. In this chapter, we'll review powers, roots, and the order of operations. We'll look at the use of formulas and substitution. We'll also look at number patterns, properties of numbers, ordering numbers, and scientific notation.

Powers and Roots
Powers

When a number is multiplied by itself, we say that it is **squared**. We show that with a small 2 placed to the upper right of the number. For example, $7^2 = 7 \times 7 = 49$. This means seven squared is 7 times 7, which is 49.

In the expression 7^2, the two is called the **power** or **exponent**, and the seven is called the **base**. It is best to think of the exponent as an instruction. The exponent tells you what to do with the base. When the exponent is 2, the base is squared, and we multiply the base by itself.

Examples: $\quad 3^2 = 3 \times 3 = 9 \qquad\qquad (\frac{1}{3})^2 = \frac{1}{3} \times \frac{1}{3} = \frac{1}{9}$

Sometimes the exponent is a number other than 2. The exponent tells how many times to multiply the base by itself. For example:

$$3^4 = 3 \times 3 \times 3 \times 3 = 81 \qquad (\frac{1}{2})^3 = \frac{1}{2} \times \frac{1}{2} \times \frac{1}{2} = \frac{1}{8}$$

SPECIAL RULES ABOUT POWERS
1. The number 1 to any power is 1. $\qquad 1^5 = 1 \times 1 \times 1 \times 1 \times 1 = 1$
2. Any number to the first power is that number. $\qquad 6^1 = 6$
3. Any number to the zero power is 1. $\qquad 14^0 = 1$

ANSWERS TO EXERCISES IN THIS CHAPTER BEGIN ON PAGE 438.

EXERCISE 1: POWERS
Directions: For each number below, multiply the base by itself the number of times indicated by its exponent.

1. 5^2

2. 9^3

3. $(\frac{3}{4})^3$

4. 1^{10}

5. 4^0

6. $(.2)^3$

7. 0^2

Square Roots

The operation opposite of squaring a number is finding the **square root** of a number. For instance, $5^2 = 25$, so $\sqrt{25} = 5$. The $\sqrt{}$ symbol is called the **radical symbol**, and it means to find the square root of the number underneath the radical. $\sqrt{36}$ is read, "the square root of 36." Being familiar with perfect squares makes many square roots relatively easy to find. For instance, $\sqrt{100} = 10$ because $10^2 = 100$. $\sqrt{49} = 7$ and $\sqrt{4} = 2$.

If you need to find the square root of a number that is not a perfect square, you can simplify the square root. For instance, $\sqrt{75}$ can be expressed as $\sqrt{25 \times 3} = \sqrt{25} \times \sqrt{3} = 5\sqrt{3}$. You choose 25 and 3 because 25 is a perfect square, and you can find its square root.

EXERCISE 2: SIMPLIFYING SQUARE ROOTS
Directions: Simplify the following square roots.

1. $\sqrt{48}$ **2.** $\sqrt{8}$ **3.** $\sqrt{27}$

Approximating Square Roots

Calculators and tables of square roots can help us find the square roots of unfamiliar numbers. If a table or calculator is not available, **approximation** is helpful. For example, let's find the square root of 75. To find $\sqrt{75}$, we look at the perfect squares closest to 75. Those are 64 and 81.

$\sqrt{64} = 8$
$\sqrt{75}$ Notice that $\sqrt{75}$ is between $\sqrt{64}$ and $\sqrt{81}$.
$\sqrt{81} = 9$

Therefore, $\sqrt{75}$ is between 8 and 9. Because 75 is closer to 81 than to 64, $\sqrt{75}$ is closer to 9. Approximate the answer to be 8.7.

EXERCISE 3: SQUARE ROOTS
Directions: This is a mixture of square root problems. When finding the square root of a perfect square, give the exact answer. When finding the square root of a number that is not a perfect square, give either an approximate answer or a simplified answer.

1. $\sqrt{81}$ **3.** $\sqrt{28}$ **5.** $\sqrt{10}$ **7.** $\sqrt{225}$

2. $\sqrt{1}$ **4.** $\sqrt{52}$ **6.** $\sqrt{16}$

Order of Operations

The following is a series of steps called the *order of operations*.

THE ORDER OF OPERATIONS

First: Perform all powers and roots as they appear from left to right.

Second: Perform all multiplication and division as they appear from left to right.

Third: Perform all addition and subtraction as they appear from left to right.

Example: $16 - 4 \times 2 + 2^4 \div 8$

STEP 1.   Raise the number with an exponent to the power indicated.

STEP 2.   Multiply and divide. $16 - \underbrace{4 \times 2} + \underbrace{16 \div 8}$

STEP 3.   Add and subtract. $16 - (8 + 2)$

$$16 - 10 = 6$$

▶ **TIP:** If you do not follow the order of operations, you will *not* get the right answer. For example, in the problem $8 + 2 \times 2$, you should get $8 + 4$ or 12. If you simply worked from left to right, you would *incorrectly* get $8 + 2$ or $10 \times 2 = 20$.

EXERCISE 4: ORDER OF OPERATIONS

Directions: Simplify the following expressions.

1. $7 - 5 + 3 - 5$

2. $8 + 3 \times 5$

3. $6 + 21 \div 3 - 5$

4. $4 + 3^3 + 3 \times 2 - 2^2$

Parentheses

You will always follow the preceding order of operations when you evaluate an arithmetic expression. However, if a pair of parentheses ( ) is used in the expression, do the work within the parentheses first.

Now our order of operations is

First: Do all work inside parentheses or above and below a fraction bar.

Second: Evaluate powers and square roots.

Third: Multiply and divide.

Fourth: Add and subtract.

Example 1: $4 \times (3 + 5)$

$4 \times \underbrace{(3 + 5)}$ ◄——— Do work inside parenthesis first

$4 \times \quad 8 \quad = 32$

Example 2: $(8^2 + 3) \times (5 + 4)$

Do first ——► $\underbrace{(8^2 + 3)} \times (5 + 4)$

Do these next ——► $\underbrace{(64 + 3)} \times \underbrace{(5 + 4)}$

Now multiply ——► $\quad 67 \quad \times \quad 9 \quad = 603$

Example 3:

Do all work above and below fraction bar $\dfrac{10 - 4}{4 - 2}$

Fraction bar means divide $\dfrac{6}{2} = 3$

Formulas

Letters of the alphabet are often used to represent numbers that you need to find. For instance, you may remember the distance formula $d = rt$. The letters d, r, and t are used to represent numbers for distance *(d)*, rate *(r)*, and time *(t)*. Letters used this way are called **unknowns** or **variables**. This use of letters helps us express general relationships about numbers.

Formulas are a way of showing these general relationships. Some common formulas that help us are the area of a circle $(A = \pi r^2)$, the perimeter of a rectangle *(P = 2l + 2w)*, and the Pythagorean theorem $(c^2 = a^2 + b^2)$. The GED Mathematics Test will include a page of formulas that will help you solve some problems on the test. As you read a particular problem, *you* will have to decide which formula will help you solve it. You should become familiar with the formulas on page 26.

Evaluating Formulas

When you replace letters with numbers in a formula, you **substitute** numbers for letters. When you perform mathematical operations on the substituted values, you are **evaluating** a formula.

In evaluating formulas, it is very important to follow this order of operations:
1. Solve any expressions in parentheses or above or below a fraction bar.
2. Evaluate powers and roots.
3. Multiply and divide.
4. Add and subtract.

Example: Find the volume of a rectangular box whose length is 7 inches, width is 5 inches, and height is 3 inches.

STEP 1. Find the appropriate formula on the formulas page.

$V = lwh$

STEP 2. Substitute the values given.

$V = (7)(5)(3)$

STEP 3. Multiply. Notice that the parentheses indicate multiplication.

$V = 105$ cubic meters

EXERCISE 5: EVALUATING FORMULAS

Directions: Select the appropriate formula from the formulas page. Substitute the numbers in the problem and evaluate the formulas. The units of your answers are given in parentheses.

1. Find the volume of a cube if one side (s) is 5 inches. (cubic inches)

2. Find the simple interest if the principal (p) is $800 at ($r$) 12% annually for 3 years (t). (dollars)

3. Find the area of a circle where $\pi \cong 3.14$ and the radius (r) is 3 inches. (square inches)

4. Find the perimeter of a rectangle if the length (l) is 14 feet and the width (w) is 2 yards. (feet)

Scientific Notation

Our number system is based on multiples of ten. *Scientific notation* uses this idea of a base 10 to give us a shortened method of writing extremely large or extremely small numbers. The notation is used a lot in science, but we are seeing it more often in everyday life as we use calculators and computers.

We can also express fractional powers of ten using negative exponents. The negative sign is used to indicate the reciprocal. (The reciprocal of 10 is $\frac{1}{10}$.) For instance, $10^{-1} = \frac{1}{10} = .1$.

Let's look at some powers of ten using positive and negative exponents:

$10^0 = 1$

$10^1 = 10$ $10^{-1} = \frac{1}{10} = .1$

$10^2 = 100$ $10^{-2} = \frac{1}{10^2} = \frac{1}{100}$ or $.01$

$10^3 = 1000$ $10^{-3} = \frac{1}{10^3} = \frac{1}{1000}$ or $.001$

$10^4 = 10,000$ $10^{-4} = \frac{1}{10^4} = \frac{1}{10,000}$ or $.0001$

WRITING A NUMBER IN SCIENTIFIC NOTATION

1. Represent the number as a number or a mixed decimal between 1 and 10.
2. Write a multiplication sign and represent the number's value to the correct power of 10.

You can use scientific notation to write some numbers in shortened form. Simply count the number of positions that the decimal point must be moved to determine the power of 10 to use. The power of 10 is positive for whole numbers and negative for decimals.

Example 1: Express 86,200,000 in scientific notation. (The original decimal point is understood to be at the end of the number.)

STEP 1. Represent the number as a mixed decimal between 1 and 10. Insert the decimal point between 8 and 62 to get 8.62.

$$86,200,000 = 8.62 \times 10^?$$

STEP 2. Count the number of places the decimal point moved to get from 86,200,000 to 8.62. Since the point moved 7 places to the left, the power of 10 is 7.

$$86,200,000 = 8.62 \times 10^7$$
7 places left

Example 2: Express .00098 in scientific notation.

STEP 1. Represent the number as a mixed decimal between 1 and 10.

$$.00098 = 9.8 \times 10^{-4}$$

Insert the decimal point between 9 and 8 to get 9.8.   4 places right

STEP 2. Count the number of places the decimal moved to get from .00098 to 9.8. Since the point moved 4 places to the right, the power of 10 is -4.

EXERCISE 6: SCIENTIFIC NOTATION

Directions: Express each of the numbers below in scientific notation.

1. .0082
2. 38,200

Each number below is written in scientific notation. Find the actual value.

3. 1.624×10^3
4. 3.12×10^{-1}

8
GEOMETRY

Geometry is the study of shapes and the relationships among them. The geometry that you are required to know for the Mathematics Test is fundamental and practical. You will not be asked to "prove" theorems as you would in a formal geometry class. Instead, you will review the basic concepts in geometry and apply them to everyday situations.

Angles

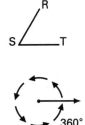

An *angle* is formed when two lines intersect. The point of intersection is called the *vertex* of the angle. On the angle here, point *S* is the vertex. The two sides are *ST* and *SR*.

An angle is named with a small angle symbol ∠ and three points—two on the ends of the angle and one at the vertex: ∠ *RST*. Sometimes, we just name the angle by its vertex, such as ∠ *S*.

An angle is measured in *degrees*. The symbol for degrees is a familiar one from weather reports, such as 72°.

One complete revolution around a point is 360°. One-fourth of a revolution is 90°. A 90° angle, called a *right angle*, is often used in construction. You can often recognize a right angle because of the small square drawn in the vertex. When two intersecting lines meet at right angles, we say they are *perpendicular lines*. The symbol for perpendicular lines is ⊥ .

Special Pairs of Angles

The Mathematics Test will give information about angles and then ask you to use your understanding of their relationships. Let's look at some rules that apply to certain pairs of angles.

Complementary angles are two angles whose sum is 90°. That means the two angles together make a right angle. A 60° angle and a 30° angle are complements of each other because their sums is 90°.

Example 1:   What is the complement of a 53° angle?

Solution: 90° − 53° = 37°

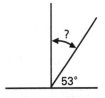

Supplementary angles are two angles whose sum is 180°. When the two angles are placed side by side, their sides form a straight line. A 110° angle is the supplement of a 70° angle because their sum is 180°.

Example 2:   What is the supplement of a 30° angle?

Solution: 180° − 30° = 150°

Vertical angles are formed when two lines intersect. The pair of angles opposite each other are equal. In the picture at the right, ∠ *ABC* and ∠ *DBE* are vertical angles. Therefore, ∠ *ABC* is equal to ∠ *DBE*. We write this as ∠ *ABC* = ∠ *DBE*. ∠ *ABD* and ∠ *CBE* are also vertical angles; therefore, ∠ *ABD* = ∠ *CBE*. Sometimes, as in Example 3, you may be given a pair of intersecting lines and the measurement of one angle. From that one angle, you can find the measure of the other angles.

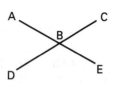

Example 3:   Find the measure of ∠ *EFG*.

   Solution: ∠ *EFG* and ∠ *HFJ* are vertical angles and, therefore, equal. ∠ *EFG* = 130°

Example 4:   Find the measure of ∠ *GFJ*.

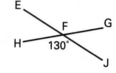

   STEP 1.   Notice that ∠ *GFJ* is the supplement to ∠ *EFG*. Together, they are on a straight line that equals 180°.

   STEP 2.   Subtract the angle you know from 180°.
   180° − 130° = 50°
   ∠ *GFJ* = 50°

Sometimes, angles are merely parts of a picture in a problem. Knowing these angle relationships (complementary, supplementary, and vertical) can help you solve the problem if you look for a pair of angles formed by intersecting lines.

Example 5:   Find the measure of the angle indicated.

   The ladder forms a supplementary angle with the ground.

   To find the missing angle, subtract 45° from 180°.

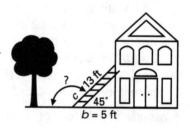

   Solution: 180° − 45° = 135°

ANSWERS TO EXERCISES IN THIS CHAPTER BEGIN ON PAGE 439.

EXERCISE 1: PAIRS OF ANGLES
Directions: Solve each problem.
   Use the picture to answer *questions 1–3*.

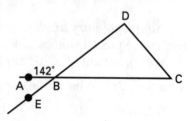

1. Find the measure of ∠ *DBC*.
2. Find the measure of ∠ *ABE*.
3. Find the measure of ∠ *EBC*.
4. Two pieces of a puzzle fit together to form a right angle. If one piece has an angle of 52°, what is the angle of the complementary piece?

Triangles

Triangles are the basis of land measurement. Triangles are used in science, navigation, and building construction. Astronomers use triangles to find out how far stars are from Earth. We also find important uses for triangles in maps, scale drawings, and architectural plans.

What Are Triangles?

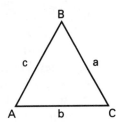

A *triangle* is a closed, three-sided figure. The point where the sides meet is called a *vertex*. At each vertex, we find an angle. The figure on the right is called triangle ABC, written △ *ABC*. It has three angles: ∠ *A*, ∠ *B*, ∠ *C*. The triangle has three sides labeled *a, b, c*. We can name a side by using a single letter or by using the letters representing the angles at the endpoints. For example, another name for side *a* is *BC*, for side *b* is *AC*, and for side *c* is *AB*.

The three angles of every triangle add up to 180°. So we say ∠ *A* + ∠ *B* + ∠ *C* = 180°. Use this fact to find the measure of the third angle of a triangle when the measure of the first two angles is known, as in the following example.

Example: Find ∠ *C* in the triangle.

STEP 1. First, add the measures of the two known angles.

$$40° + 100° = 140°$$

STEP 2. Then, subtract the sum from 180°.

$$180° - 140° = 40°$$

EXERCISE 2: ANGLES IN TRIANGLES

Directions: Find the measurement of the missing angle in each of the following triangles.

1.

2.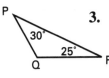

3.

4.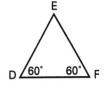

Types of Triangles

Triangles may be named according to the length of their sides. A triangle may be referred to as *scalene, isosceles*, or *equilateral*.

- A *scalene* triangle has no equal sides and no equal angles. In the figure at right, △ *ABC* is scalene. Side *AB* is not equal to side *BC* or to side *AC*.

- An *isosceles* triangle has two equal sides and two equal angles. In △ *DEF* in the figure at right, *DF* is the **base** of the triangle, *DE* and *EF* are the **legs** of the triangle, ∠ *D* and ∠ *F* are the **base angles**, and ∠ *E* is the **vertex angle**. Because *DE* = *EF*, the triangle is isosceles. The two base angles are equal; ∠ *D* = ∠ *F*.

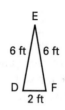

- An *equilateral* triangle has three equal sides and three equal angles. Because the three angles of the triangle must add up to 180°, each angle must be 60°. △ *PQR* is equilateral because *PQ* = *QR* = *PR*. It is also true that ∠ *P* = ∠ *Q* = ∠ *R*. (An equilateral triangle is sometimes referred to as an *equiangular* triangle.)

- A right triangle is a special type of triangle that is often used in geometry problems. A *right triangle* has one right angle of 90°. We can recognize right triangles because the right angle looks like a corner. The small box in the corner indicates a right triangle. In △ *XYZ* at right, ∠ *X* is the right angle. The side opposite the right angle (*YZ*) is called the *hypotenuse.*

EXERCISE 3: TYPES OF TRIANGLES
Directions: Solve each problem.

1. Name each triangle as either a scalene, isosceles, equilateral, or right triangle.

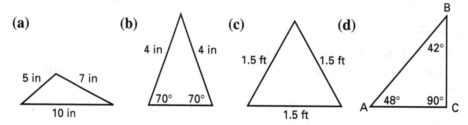

(a) 5 in 7 in 10 in

(b) 4 in 4 in 70° 70°

(c) 1.5 ft 1.5 ft 1.5 ft

(d) B 42° A 48° 90° C

2. In isosceles triangle *ABC*, the base angles are each 52°. Find the measure of the third angle.

3. A right triangle contains a 60° angle. What is the measure of the third angle?

Similar Triangles

Similar triangles are figures that have the same shape. We often use similar figures to find hard-to-measure lengths, such as the distance across a lake or the height of a building. *Similar triangles* are two triangles whose *corresponding angles* are equal and whose *corresponding sides* are in proportion.

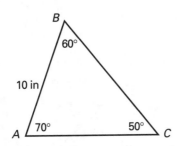

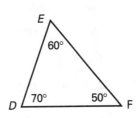

Look at △ *ABC* and △ *DEF*. They are similar triangles because they have the same shape. We can see that corresponding angles are equal. ∠ *A* = ∠ *D*, ∠ *B* = ∠ *E*, and ∠ *C* = ∠ *F*. Therefore, the two triangles are not the same size, but their sides are in proportion. We write this relationship as

$$\frac{AB}{DE} = \frac{BC}{EF} = \frac{AC}{DF}$$

Example 1: On a sunny day, the village inspector used similar triangles to find the height of a flagpole without climbing it. She found that her 6-foot-tall co-worker cast a 10-foot shadow at the same time the flagpole cast a 40-foot shadow. How tall is the flagpole?

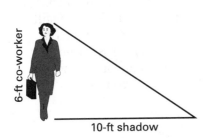

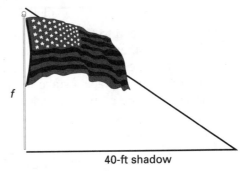

STEP 1. Notice that the co-worker and the flagpole are at right angles to the ground. Set up a proportion.

$$\frac{\text{flagpole}}{\text{co-worker}} = \frac{\text{flagpole's shadow}}{\text{co-worker's shadow}}$$

STEP 2. Fill in the numbers from the problem. Let *f* stand for the flagpole.

$$\frac{f}{6} = \frac{40}{10}$$

STEP 3. Cross multiply and divide.

$$f = \frac{6 \times 40}{10} = \frac{240}{10} = 24 \text{ ft}$$

▶ **TIP:** Always look for similar triangles when you are comparing two triangles.

SOLVING SIMILAR TRIANGLE PROBLEMS

1. Look for two triangles that have the same shape. Be sure the triangles are similar. Corresponding angles must be equal.
2. Redraw the triangles if necessary to show the corresponding sides and angles.
3. Set up and solve a proportion to find the missing length.

EXERCISE 4: SIMILAR TRIANGLES

Directions: Solve each problem.

1. $\triangle ABC$ is similar to $\triangle DEF$. Find *DF*.

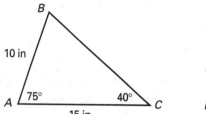

2. An oak tree along a parkway casts an 18-foot shadow at the same time an 8-foot traffic light casts a 12-foot shadow. Find the height of the tree.

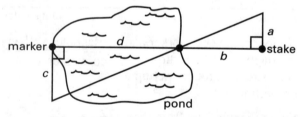

3. Suppose we need to find the distance *d* across a pond but are unable to swim to the other side and measure the distance directly. We can still find the distance. Find a marker on one side of the pond. On the other side of the pond, place a stake in the ground directly across from the marker. Measure a given distance *c* on a line perpendicular to the line determined by the marker and the stake. Then form two triangles as in the sketch below.

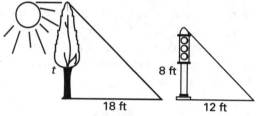

(a) With these measures, what would you do first to determine the distance, *d*?

(b) Find the distance across the pond if $a = 2$ feet, $b = 6$ feet, and $c = 50$ feet.

The Pythagorean Theorem

Although the *Pythagorean theorem* was developed by the Greek mathematician Pythagoras in about 500 B.C., it is still widely used today. Since the rule applies only to right triangles, the problem has to include a 90° angle or the right angle symbol ⌐ for the Pythagorean theorem to apply. In a right triangle, the side opposite the right angle is called the *hypotenuse*, and the other two sides are called the *legs* of the triangle.

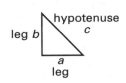

leg *b* hypotenuse *c*

leg *a*

The Pythagorean theorem states that in a right triangle the square of the hypotenuse equals the sum of the squares of the legs. According to the diagram, the Pythagorean theorem is written $c^2 = a^2 + b^2$. This is put in terms of the right triangle with legs *a* and *b* and the hypotenuse *c*.

Example: Find the length of the hypotenuse of a right triangle with legs 6 inches and 8 inches.

First, draw a right triangle and label its sides. Next, substitute the number values in the Pythagorean theorem and simplify the equation.

STEP 1. Write the Pythagorean theorem. $c^2 = a^2 + b^2$

STEP 2. Substitute the numbers for *a* and *b* $c^2 = 6^2 + 8^2$ (the legs of the triangle).

STEP 3. Square the numbers. $c^2 = 36 + 64$

STEP 4. Add the numbers. $c^2 = 100$

STEP 5. Take the square root. $c = \sqrt{100} = 10$ in

8 in *C* 6 in

SOLVING PYTHAGOREAN THEOREM PROBLEMS

1. Sketch the information in the problem and label the parts.
2. Identify the right angle and then the hypotenuse.
3. Substitute the values into the formula $c^2 = a^2 + b^2$.
4. Square the values.
5. Add if you are looking for the hypotenuse, or subtract if you are looking for a leg.
6. Take the square root.

EXERCISE 5: THE PYTHAGOREAN THEOREM

Directions: Solve each problem.

1. In a right triangle whose legs are *a* and *b* and whose hypotenuse is *c*, find the length of the missing side when $a = 9$ and $b = 12$.

2. The screen on Alberto's TV has the measurements shown at the right. Find the measure of the diagonal for Alberto's TV.

15 in
20 in

3. At summer camp, the swimming course runs the length (*L*) of a small lake. To determine the length of the course, the camp counselors measure the two "dry" legs of a right triangle. What is the length in meters of the swimming course in the figure below?

   (1) 75
   (2) 90
   (3) 100
   (4) 120
   (5) 144

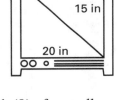

60 m
L 80 m
Blue Lake

4. A ladder that is 13 feet long is placed against a house. The foot of the ladder is 5 feet from the base of the house. How many feet above the ground does the ladder touch the building?

(1) 10   **(4)** 16
(2) 12   **(5)** 20
(3) 15

Plane Figures

Rectangles and squares are used extensively in the construction of buildings. Floor tile, tabletops, windowpanes, doors, books, and picture frames are a few of the items that often are rectangular or square. The GED Mathematics Test will ask you to recognize these shapes and to solve problems based on them.

Types of Figures

A *rectangle* is a closed four-sided figure. The points where the four sides meet are called *vertices*. At each vertex there is a right angle (90°).

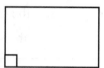

1. The sum of the four angles is 360°.
2. Opposite sides are equal.
3. Opposite sides are parallel.
4. All four angles are equal (90°).

A *parallelogram* is a closed four-sided figure. It has four angles (not necessarily right angles).

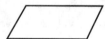

1. The sum of the four angles is 360°.
2. Opposite sides are equal.
3. Opposite sides are parallel.
4. Opposite angles are equal.

A *square* is a four-sided figure with four right angles.

1. All four sides are equal.
2. All four angles are equal; each is 90°.
3. Opposite sides are parallel.

Circles

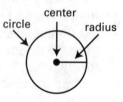

In geometry, we define a *circle* as a set of points all the same distance from a center point. The distance from the center to the circle is called the *radius*. A radius can be drawn from any point on the circle to the center. A *diameter* is a straight line that goes through the center of the circle and has its endpoints on the circle. A diameter is twice as long as a radius.

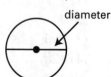

Measurement of Figures
Perimeter

Perimeter is the distance around a figure. Measuring for a fence around a yard or putting a baseboard around a room are some uses of perimeter. You will find formulas for perimeter on the formulas page of the GED Mathematics Test.

▶ **TIP:** Keep in mind that the perimeter of a figure is the distance all the way around the figure, so you can also *add* all the sides of the figure.

The perimeter of a square is $P = 4s$ where P is the perimeter and s is one side. Since all four sides of a square are equal, multiply one side by 4 to get the total distance around the square.

Example 1: Find the perimeter of this square. 7 yd

$P = 4s$
$P = 4 \times 7 = 28$ yd

The perimeter of a rectangle is $P = 2l + 2w$ where P is the perimeter, l is the length, and w is the width. Since opposite sides of a rectangle are equal, double the length and double the width, then add to find the total distance around the rectangle.

Example 2: Find the perimeter of this rectangle.

7 ft   3 ft   3 ft   7 ft

$P = 2l + 2w$
$P = (2 \times 7) + (2 \times 3) = 20$ ft

The perimeter of a triangle is $P = a + b + c$ where P equals the perimeter and a, b, and c are the lengths of the three sides. To find the perimeter, add the lengths of the three sides.

Example 3: Find the perimeter of this triangle.

4 in   7 in   9 in

$P = a + b + c$
$P = 4 + 7 + 9 = 20$ in

The *circumference* of a circle is the perimeter of (or distance around) a circle. The formula is $C = \pi d$ where C is the circumference, pi or $\pi \cong 3.14$, and d is the diameter. The circumference is equal to approximately 3.14 times the diameter. You could also use $\frac{22}{7}$ for π if the diameter or radius is given as a fraction or when the problem would be easier to solve with $\frac{22}{7}$.

Example 4: Find the circumference of this circle.

42 in

$C = \pi d$
$C = \frac{22}{7} \times 42 = 132$ in

EXERCISE 6: PERIMETER

Directions: Solve each problem.

1. A baseball diamond is a square with distances between the bases as shown. How far will the batter run if he hits a home run?

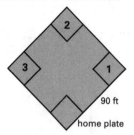

4. Find the perimeter of the figure shown below.

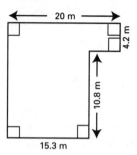

2. How much binding is needed around a triangular sail for the toy sailboat shown below?

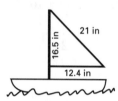

3. A farmer wants to fence a rectangular pasture 400 yards by 224 yards. The cost of fencing is $5.75 per eight-foot section. What will his cost be?

5. How many feet of fencing are needed to fence the yard below?

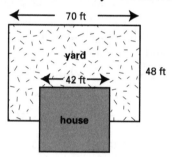

Area

Area is the amount of surface over a certain region. Area is measured in square units such as square inches or square feet. Imagine a square one inch on each side. This is a square inch.

When we are asked to find the area in square inches, we are actually finding the number of squares one inch by one inch that could fit on the surface we are measuring. For example, the rectangle to the right contains 8 square inches of area.

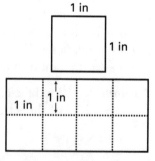

▶ **TIP:** Answers in area problems are given in square units, such as square inches or square meters.

The area of a square is $A = s^2$ where A is the area and s is one side. The area equals the side times the side. Given a square with a side of 7 inches, the area equals 7 in × 7 in = 49 square inches.

The area of a rectangle is $A = lw$ where A is the area, l is the length, and w is the width. The area equals the length times the width.

Example 1: How much surface area is the rectangular top of a desk 3 feet by 5 feet?

Solution: The area is $A = lw = 3 \text{ ft} \times 5 \text{ ft} = 15$ square feet, or 15 ft^2

The area of a triangle is $A = \frac{1}{2}bh$ where A is the area, b is the base, and h is the height. To find the area of a triangle, multiply the base by the height and find $\frac{1}{2}$ of that amount.

Example 2: Find the area of a triangle with a base 6 inches and height of 9 inches.

STEP 1. Multiply the base by the height. $\quad A = \frac{1}{2}bh$

$$A = \frac{1}{2}(6 \times 9) = \frac{1}{2}(54)$$

STEP 2. Divide the product by 2 to find $\frac{1}{2}$. $\quad A = \frac{1}{2}(54) = 27$ square inches, or 27 in^2

The area of a circle is $A = \pi r^2$, where A is the area; π is approximately 3.14, or $\frac{22}{7}$, and r is the radius.

Example 3: Find the area of a circle whose diameter is 12 inches.

STEP 1. Find the radius. $\quad 12 \div 2 = 6$

STEP 2. Substitute numbers in the formula and do the calculation.

$$A = \pi r^2$$
$$A = 3.14(6)^2$$
$$A = 3.14(36)$$
$$A = 113.04 \text{ sq in, or } 113.04 \text{ in}^2$$

EXERCISE 7: AREA

Directions: Solve each problem. *For questions 1 and 2,* find the area of the figures.

1.

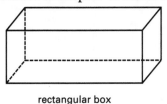

(This shape combines a square and a rectangle.)

2.

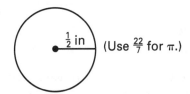

(Use $\frac{22}{7}$ for π.)

3. How many square yards of carpet are needed for a room 30 feet by 15 feet? (1 sq yd = 9 sq ft)

4. How many square feet is the largest circular rug that can be put on the floor of a room 10 feet by 12 feet?

Volume

Volume is the amount of space that a solid, or a three-dimensional figure, contains. Examples of solids are a rectangular box, a cube, and a cylinder.

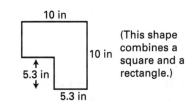

rectangular box

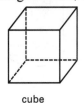

cube

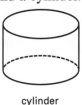

cylinder

Volume is measured in **cubic units** such as cubic feet, cubic inches, or cubic yards. For example, a cubic inch is a cube with edges of 1 inch each.

The formulas page of the GED Mathematics Test gives formulas for the volume of a cube, a rectangular container, and a cylinder. Let's look at each formula.

The volume of a **cube** is $V = s^3$ where V is the volume and s is the edge of the cube. A number cube and a square box are examples of cubes. Each edge of the cube has the same length. Thus, the volume of a cube is equal to the edge cubed, or edge times edge times edge.

Example 1:

Find the volume of the cube at the right.

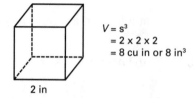

$V = s^3$
$= 2 \times 2 \times 2$
$= 8$ cu in or 8 in³

2 in

The volume of a **rectangular container** is $V = lwh$, where V is the volume, l is the length, w is the width, and h is the height. The volume is equal to the length times the width times the height.

Example 2:

What is the volume of the container at the right?

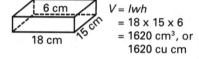

6 cm $V = lwh$
        $= 18 \times 15 \times 6$
15 cm $= 1620$ cm³, or
18 cm   1620 cu cm

The volume of a **cylinder** is $V = \pi r^2 h$, where V is the volume, r is the radius of the circular base, and h is the height of the cylinder. π is approximately 3.14 or $\frac{22}{7}$.

Example 3:

Find the volume of the container at the right.

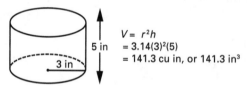

5 in $V = r^2 h$
       $= 3.14(3)^2(5)$
3 in $= 141.3$ cu in, or 141.3 in³

EXERCISE 8: VOLUME

Directions: Solve each problem.

1. How many gallons of water will fill a fish tank that is 18 inches by 12 inches by 48 inches? (There are 231 cubic inches per gallon.) Round your answer to the nearest gallon.

2. How much topsoil is needed to cover a garden 25 feet by 40 feet to a depth of 6 inches?

3. The farmer's silo has the dimensions shown below. What is the volume of the silo? (Use $\frac{22}{7}$ for π).

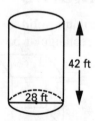

42 ft

28 ft

9
ALGEBRA

The Language of Algebra

Algebra, an extension of arithmetic, is an organized system of rules that helps us solve problems. Algebra uses letters of the alphabet to represent numbers or unknown quantities. These letters are called *variables*. These values are variable because they change from problem to problem. The letters can be capital letters, lowercase letters, or even Greek letters. Some examples are x, t, B, R, and P. *Constants* are fixed numbers. The value of a constant is known and does not change from problem to problem. Some constants are 8, 75, 0, π, and $\sqrt{3}$.

In algebra, we still work with the four operations of addition, subtraction, multiplication, and division. Look at the chart below to see the symbols that are used.

TABLE OF OPERATIONS			
Operation	Symbol	Example	Meaning
Addition	$+$	$5 + x$	5 plus x
Subtraction	$-$	$8 - x$ $y - 8$	8 minus x y minus 8
Multiplication	$\cdot$ (dot) ( ) parentheses no symbol	$5 \cdot 3$ $10(2)$ xy	5 times 3 10 times 2 x times y
Division	$\div$ — (fraction bar)	$x \div y$ $\frac{x}{12}$ $\frac{3}{x}$	x divided by y x divided by 12 3 divided by x

Whenever a number and a variable are multiplied together, the number part is called the *coefficient* of the variable. in the expression $7x$, the coefficient of x is 7. The variable x is multiplied by 7.

▶ TIP: Whenever the variable is written without a number in front of it, the coefficient is understood to be 1. Therefore, y means $1y$, and the coefficient is 1.

Algebraic Expressions

An *algebraic expression* connects variables to variables or variables to constants using the operation signs. For example, $a + 4$, $5 - 3y$, and $\frac{m + n}{4}$ are all algebraic expressions. In the expression $x + 5$, x is the variable that represents the unknown, and 5 is the constant value. The operation is addition.

$$x \qquad\qquad + \qquad\qquad 5$$
$$\uparrow \qquad\qquad \uparrow \qquad\qquad \uparrow$$
$$\text{variable} \qquad \text{operation} \qquad \text{constant}$$

Algebraic expressions contain *terms*. A term can be a number, a variable, or the multiplication or division of numbers with variables. Some examples of terms are

5 (a number) $7y$ (the product of a number and a variable)
y (a variable) $\frac{y}{3}$ (the quotient of a variable and a number)

In an algebraic expression, terms are separated by + and − signs. The sign before the term belongs to the term.

Examples: $\frac{x}{5}$ -2
                        ↑   ↑
                    1st term   2nd term
is an expression that contains two terms: $\frac{x}{5}$ and -2.

              $8x^2$ $-4x$ $+7$
               ↑   ↑   ↑
            1st term   2nd term   3rd term
is an expression that contains three terms: $8x^2$, $-4x$, and $+7$.

▶ **TIP:** Keep the plus or minus sign with the term, as in -2 above.

ANSWERS TO EXERCISES IN THIS CHAPTER BEGIN ON PAGE 440.

EXERCISE 1: TERMS
Directions: Name the terms in the following expressions.

1. $8x + 7y - 5$ **2.** $2x^2 - \frac{3}{x}$ **3.** $8ab + 12$

Equations

An algebraic *equation* sets one expression equal to another expression or a value.

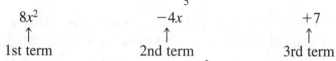

$x + 7$	$=$	10		$x + 3$	$=$	$2x - 9$
↑	↑	↑		↑	↑	↑
expression	equals	value		expression	equals	expression

AN ALGEBRAIC EQUATION ALWAYS HAS THREE PARTS:
1. left-side expression
2. an equal sign (=)
3. right-side expression

The equation $x + 7 = 10$ says that some number (x) added to 7 equals 10. We know that 3 added to 7 equals 10, so 3 is the *solution* of the equation. The solution is the value of the variable that makes the statement true. You *solve* an equation when you find the solution for the variable. On the Mathematics Test, you may have to translate a word problem into an equation. You will also write and interpret your own equations.

Example: $2x + 5 = 17$. This expression means that a number multiplied by 2 and added to 5 equals 17. The number is 6 because $2(6) + 5 = 17$.

EXERCISE 2: EQUATIONS

Directions: Write in words what each expression means. Use the words *a number* for any letter, as shown in the previous example.

1. $5 + 7y = 19$ 2. $a - 5 = 23$ 3. $\frac{10}{y} - 5 = 0$

Solving One-Step Equations

Among the most important uses of algebra are the solution of equations and the use of equations to solve word problems.

Eyeballing the Solution

Solving an equation means finding the value of the variable that makes the equation true. Some equations will be fairly easy to solve because you know your math facts. If you can just look at the equation and see the answer, you are "eyeballing" the equation. For example, $x + 3 = 10$ is an algebraic equation. What value of x will make this true? You would choose $x = 7$ because you know $7 + 3 = 10$.

Algebraic Solutions

Let's look at algebraic methods of solving one-step equations. Before you start solving equations, you must understand mathematical ideas. First of all, an equation is a perfect balance between what is on the left side of the equal sign and what is on the right side of the equal sign.

If you make any changes on the left side, you must make the *same* changes on the right side. For instance, if you add 7 to the left side, you must add 7 to the right side for the 2 sides to remain equal. Then you know the result will be true.

Second, your goal in solving an equation is to get the variable all by itself on one side of an equation. Concentrate on the variable. In the equation $x + 3 = 10$, concentrate on the x. Notice that the x is being added to 3. This will tell you how to solve the equation.

To solve an equation, perform the opposite, or ***inverse***, operation. Addition and subtraction are opposites, and multiplication and division are opposites. In the equation $x + 3 = 10$, you see that x is being added to three. The opposite of "adding three" is "subtracting three." If you subtract three from both sides, you will get x all by itself.

Example 1: $x + 3 = 10$

STEP 1.   Look at x. It is added to 3. $x + 3 = 10$

STEP 2.   Subtract 3 from both sides. $x + \underbrace{3 - 3}_{0} = \underbrace{10 - 3}_{7}$

STEP 3.   Solve the equation. $x = 7$

WHEN SOLVING AN EQUATION, REMEMBER:
1. Keep the equation in balance.
2. Concentrate on the variable.
3. Perform the opposite operation.

Example 2: $7x = 21$

STEP 1. Look at x. It is multiplied by 7. $7x = 21$

STEP 2. Divide by 7 on both sides. The $\frac{\cancel{7}x}{\cancel{7}} = \frac{21}{7}$
7s on the left side "cancel out."

STEP 3. Solve the equation. $x = 3$

Check the answers to each problem by substituting the answer in the original equation. For example, when we solved $7x = 21$, we got $x = 3$. Check that answer by substituting 3 for x in the original problem.

$7x$ $= 21$
$7(3) = 21$ Substitute 3 for x.
21 $= 21$ This is a true statement, so $x = 3$ is the solution for $7x = 21$.

EXERCISE 3: ONE-STEP EQUATIONS
Directions: Solve for x. Check your answers.

1. $3 + x = 7$ **2.** $\frac{x}{3} = 12$ **3.** $x - 8 = 0$ **4.** $5x = 75$

Solving Algebra Word Problems

To use algebra to solve mathematical problems, you have to translate the problem into algebraic language. Let a letter of the alphabet, a variable, represent the unknown quantity. The letters x, y, and z are most often used as variables.

TRANSLATING EXPRESSIONS
1. First assign a variable to the unknown quantity.
2. Use that variable to write an expression for any other unknown quantity.
3. Identify the phrases that indicate the mathematical operation.
4. Use the operation to write the expression.

Translate: "The square of a number decreased by the number."
1. Let x be the number.
2. The square of a number is x^2.
3. *Decreased by* means "subtract."
4. Write $x^2 - x$.

TRANSLATION CHART		
English Phrase	Operation	Algebraic Expression
the *sum* of two numbers	+ (add)	$x + y$
five *more than* a number		$x + 5$
a number *increased by* 4		$x + 4$
a number *added to another* number		$x + y$
nine *plus* a number		$9 + x$
the *difference* between two numbers	− (subtract)	$x - y$
seven *decreased* by a number	(Be sure the number subtracted follows the minus sign.)	$7 - x$
a number *reduced by* 4		$x - 4$
three *less than* a number		$x - 3$
six *subtracted* from a number		$x - 6$
six *minus* a number		$6 - x$
the *product* of two numbers	multiply	xy
six *times* a number	( )	$(6)(x)$
twice a number	or •	$2 \cdot x$
two-thirds *of* a number	or no sign	$(\frac{2}{3})x$ or $\frac{2x}{3}$
double a number		$2x$
one number *multiplied* by another number		xy
the *quotient* of two numbers	divide	$\frac{x}{y}$ $x \div y$
a number *divided* by three	(Be sure the number you are dividing by is below the fraction bar or follows the division symbol.)	$\frac{x}{3}$
seven *divided by* a number		$\frac{7}{x}$
half a number		$\frac{x}{2}$ or $\frac{1}{2}x$
a number *squared*	raise to the second power	x^2
a number *cubed*	raise to the third power	y^3
the *square root* of a number	square root	$\sqrt{x}$

Using the chart as a guide to the examples below, translate the following English phrases into algebraic expressions.

Examples:

$$\underbrace{\text{four}}_{4} \ \underbrace{\text{more than}}_{+} \ \underbrace{\text{a number}}_{x} \qquad = 4 + x$$

$$\underbrace{\text{six}}_{6} \ \underbrace{\text{decreased by}}_{-} \ \underbrace{\text{half a number}}_{\frac{1}{2}x} \qquad = 6 - \frac{1}{2}x \text{ or } 6 - \frac{x}{2}$$

$$\underbrace{\text{twelve}}_{12} \underbrace{\text{divided by}}_{\div} \underbrace{\text{a number squared}}_{x^2} \qquad = \frac{12}{x^2}$$

$$\underbrace{\text{twice}}_{2} \underbrace{\text{the sum of a number and 4}}_{(x+4)} \qquad = 2(x+4)$$

$$\underbrace{\text{the sum of}}_{+} \underbrace{\text{twice a number}}_{2x} \underbrace{\text{and 4}}_{4} \qquad = 2x + 4$$

EXERCISE 4: TRANSLATING ENGLISH TO ALGEBRA

Directions: Translate the English phrases to algebraic expressions using x and y to stand for the unknown numbers.

1. the difference between two numbers, divided by 3
2. the sum of a number squared and another number squared
3. four times the sum of ten and a number
4. seven less than twice a number
5. a number cubed divided by 4
6. five times a number divided by twice the same number

Translating Equations

We can now practice translating an entire sentence into an algebraic equation. Remember, an equation has three parts: left-side expression, equal sign, and right-side expression.

Many key words or phrases indicate "equal." Become familiar with the list below:

equals	is	was
is equal to	are	were
equal to	gives	leaves
the same as	the sum is	makes
the result is	the difference is	yields
the product is	the quotient is	the answer is

TRANSLATING EQUATIONS
1. Assign a variable to the unknown quantity.
2. Write two expressions for the values.
3. Use an equal sign between the expressions.

Example 1:

Three times a number is one more than twice the number.

$$\underbrace{\text{Three times a number}}_{3x} \underbrace{\text{is}}_{=} \underbrace{\text{one}}_{1} \underbrace{\text{more than}}_{+} \underbrace{\text{twice the number.}}_{2x} \text{ or } 3x = 1 + 2x$$

Example 2: Four more than a number equals 15.

$$\underbrace{\text{Four more than a number}}_{x+4} \underbrace{\text{equals}}_{=} \underbrace{15.}_{15} \text{ or } x + 4 = 15$$

▶ TIP: To identify the variable in a word problem, isolate the term or element that you don't know. Then assign a letter to that term.

EXERCISE 5: TRANSLATING SENTENCES TO EQUATIONS

Directions: Translate each sentence to an equivalent algebraic equation as shown above.

1. One-fourth of a number equals 18.
2. Nine increased by half a number gives a result of 13.
3. The difference between two numbers is 8.
4. Twice a number, reduced by 3, is equal to 5 times the same number increased by 9.

In questions 5–7, select the equation that could be used to find the unknown in the problem.

5. Doug had x number of golf balls. After playing eighteen holes of golf, he lost 5 balls and had 19 left. How many balls did he have before he played the eighteen holes of golf?

    (1) $x - 5 = 19$ **(2)** $\frac{x}{5} = 19$ **(3)** $x - 18 = 19$ **(4)** $x + 5 = 19$

6. In a wrestling meet, Mike scored 5 points, which represented one-seventh of his team's final score. What was the final score, x?

    (1) $x + \frac{1}{7} = 5$ **(2)** $x - 5 = \frac{1}{2}$ **(3)** $x - 5 = 7$ **(4)** $\frac{x}{7} = 5$

7. Sue will not tell her age, x. But in six years, her age will be $\frac{7}{6}$ as much as it is now. How can her age be written?

    (1) $x + 6 = \frac{7}{6}x$ **(2)** $x - \frac{7}{6}x = 1$ **(3)** $\frac{x}{6} = \frac{7}{6}x$ **(4)** $\frac{7}{6}x = 6$

Solving One-Step Algebra Word Problems

This next exercise combines practice in translating, setting up, and solving one-step algebra problems. Let's look at an example before you begin the exercise.

Example: Sue has x dollars, and Tom has $\frac{2}{3}$ as much money as Sue. If Tom has $48, how much does Sue have?

STEP 1. Translate and set up.

Tom has $48.

$\frac{2}{3}$ of Sue's money is $48 $\frac{2}{3}x = 48$

STEP 2. Solve the equation. Divide both $\frac{2}{3}x = 48$
sides by $\frac{2}{3}$.

$$\frac{2}{3}x \div \frac{2}{3} = 48 \div \frac{2}{3}$$
$$x = 48 \times \frac{3}{2}$$
$$x = \$72$$

EXERCISE 6: SOLVING ONE-STEP ALGEBRA WORD PROBLEMS

Directions: Solve each problem.

1. Jack saved one-eighth of his allowance. If he saved $2.50, how much is his allowance?
2. Amanda sold her stereo set for $120 less than she paid for it. If she sold the stereo set for $72, what did she originally pay for it?

3. After $5\frac{1}{2}$ feet were cut off a wooden beam, $6\frac{1}{2}$ feet were left. What was the original length of the beam?

4. By purchasing a fleet of cars for its salespeople, Tower Manufacturing gets a discount of $927 on each car purchased. This is 16% of the regular price. Find the regular price.

Solving Multi-Step Problems

Many algebraic expressions contain two or more terms. For instance, $2x - 7$ has two terms, and $3x - 9y + 7z$ has three terms. It is best to write algebraic expressions in the simplest form possible.

Simplifying Algebraic Expressions

To simplify an algebraic expression, combine like terms and remove all symbols of grouping such as parentheses and brackets.

Simplifying by Combining Like Terms.

Like terms are terms that contain the same variables to the same power.
Examples of like terms: $4x$ $7x$ $12x$ $2xy$ xy $17xy$ $9x^2$ $4x^2$ x^2
Examples of unlike terms: $3x$ $4y$ $-$ 2 $2xy$ $3x$ $4y$ $3x^2$ $2x$ -5

We can combine like terms to simplify an expression.

Example 1: $3x + 5x = 8x$ (Just add the coefficients—the numbers.)

Example 2: $7y^2 - 5y^2 = 2y^2$ (You can also subtract coefficients.)

Example 3: $2x - 3y - 5y + 2 + 4x - 6 = 6x - 8y - 4$

     Combine x terms.   Combine y terms.   Combine numbers.
       $2x + 4x = 6x$ $-3y - 5y = -8y$ $-6 + 2 = -4$

▶ TIP: Notice that in Example 3, three of the terms had answers with a minus sign. These are called *negative numbers* and will be discussed on pages 333-336. If the signs of numbers are the same (+ or −), combine the numbers and just attach the sign (+6 and +3 = +9; −6 and −3 = −9). If the signs are different, find the difference between the numbers and attach the sign of the larger number (−6 + 2 = −4).

EXERCISE 7: COMBINING LIKE TERMS
Directions: Simplify the following expressions by combining the like terms.

1. $2x + 3y + 6y + 7x$
2. $7x^2 + 3x + 4x - 2x$
3. $x + 2y - y$

4. $9a^2 + 4a + a + 3a^2$
5. $5xy + 7x - 3y - x + 4xy$

Removing Grouping Symbols

Sometimes algebraic expressions are grouped together. Grouping symbols can be parentheses or brackets. These symbols draw your attention first when you simplify an expression.

Example 1: $3(2x - 4)$

       Multiply 3 by $2x$ and 3 by (-4).
       $3(2x - 4) = 3(2x) - 3(4) = 6x - 12$

If a plus sign or no sign is in front of parentheses, the terms do not change when you remove the parentheses.

Example 2: $6x + (2x - 7) = 6x + 2x - 7 = 8x - 7$

A minus sign in front of a set of parentheses changes the sign inside to the opposite sign. With a minus and a number, you change the signs, multiply the numbers, and combine like terms.

                            changed sign

Example 3: $3x - 2(6x - 4) = 3x - 12x + 8 = -9x + 8$

REMOVING GROUPING SYMBOLS

1. Remove the parentheses or brackets.
2. Distribute the multiplication over every term in the parentheses.

EXERCISE 8: REMOVING GROUPING SYMBOLS

Directions: Simplify the following expressions by removing grouping symbols.

1. $5(3x + 2)$ **4.** $-6(5x - 12)$

2. $6x + 2(12x - 7)$ **5.** $2(x - y)$

3. $3(2x + 4 - 3y)$

Solving Multi-Step Equations

STEP 1.   Simplify expressions on both sides of the equation.
STEP 2.   Get all the variables on the left side of the equation using addition or subtraction from the right side.
STEP 3.   Concentrate on the variable and *undo addition and subtraction using the opposite operation.*
STEP 4.   Concentrate on the variable and *undo multiplication and division using the opposite operation.*

Example: $3(x - 2) + 18 = 6 + 2(x + 6)$

   STEP 1. $3x - 6 + 18 = 6 + 2x + 12$

              $3x + 12 = 2x + 18$

   STEP 2. $3x - 2x + 12 = 2x - 2x + 18$

            x 0

             $x + 12 = 18$

   STEP 3. $x + 12 - 12 = 18 - 12$

                0

               $x = 6$

EXERCISE 9: SOLVING MULTI-STEP EQUATIONS

Directions: Solve the following equations.

1. $2x - 26 = 2$
2. $\frac{x}{3} + 4 = 9$
3. $\frac{4x}{3} - 14 = 14$
4. $2(5x - 11) + 12x = 0$

Translating in Multi-Step Problems

To set up a multi-step problem, we have to translate from English to algebra. Remember to check your answer to see if it satisfies the original problem.

Example: Tony worked 35 hours last week and only a few hours this week. He makes $9 per hour, and his paycheck for the two weeks is $477 before deductions. How many hours did he work this week?

STEP 1. Let x be the number of hours he worked this week.

STEP 2. $x + 35$ is the total number of hour worked during both weeks. $9(x + 35)$ is the amount of money he is paid for working. $x + 35$ hours at $9 per hour.

STEP 3. $9(x + 35) = 477$ (The amount of money he is paid equals $477.)

STEP 4. $9(x + 35) = 477$
$9x + 315 = 477$
$9x + 315 - 315 = 477 - 315$
$$\underbrace{\qquad\qquad}_{0}$$
$9x = 162$
$\frac{9x}{9} = \frac{162}{9}$
$x = 18$ hours this week

EXERCISE 10: SETTING UP AND SOLVING MULTI-STEP EQUATIONS

Directions: Solve each problem.

1. Oscar went on a ski trip for 3 days and 3 nights. His chalet cost him $32 a night, and he paid for a lift ticket each day. His total bill was $123. Find the cost of the daily lift ticket, x. Which equation best describes the problem?
   (1) $x + 96 = 123$ **(2)** $3x + 32 = 123$ **(3)** $x + 32 = 123$
   (4) $3(x + 32) = 123$ **(5)** not enough information is given

2. The perimeter of a triangle is 56 inches. If one side is 24 inches and the other two sides have the same measure, find the length, x, of one of these two sides. Which equation best describes the problem?
   (1) $x + 24 = 56$ **(2)** $2x + 56 = 24$ **(3)** $2x - 24 = 56$
   (4) $2x + 24 = 56$ **(5)** $x - 24 = 56$

3. Nick's age is six years less than twice Tom's age, x. The sum of their two ages is 42. Find Tom's age. Which equation best describes the problem?
   (1) $2x - 6 = 42$ **(2)** $x - 6 = 42$ **(3)** $x + 2x = 42$
   (4) $(2x - 6) + x = 42$ **(5)** not enough information is given

4. Eric purchased a new car for $10,200. He made a $4800 down payment and agreed to pay the balance in 36 equal monthly payments. How much will he pay each month? Which equation best describes the problem? Let x be the amount of the monthly payment.

(1) $36x = 10,200$ **(2)** $36x = 4800$ **(3)** $36x - 4800 = 10,200$
(4) $4800 - 36x = 10,200$ **(5)** $4800 + 36x = 10,200$

5. Twice as many adult tickets for a soccer game were sold as children's tickets. Also, some of the tickets were given free of charge to contest winners. The attendance at the game was 8324 people. How many tickets of each type were sold? Which equation best describes the problem? Let x be the number of children's tickets sold.

(1) $x + 2x = 8324$ **(2)** $x (2x = 8324$ **(3)** $2(x + 2) = 8324$
(4) $2(x - 2) = 8324$ **(5)** not enough information is given

Signed Numbers
Number Line

The ***number line***, shown below, represents all of the real numbers that we use. In algebra, we use zero and the numbers greater than zero, called the ***positive numbers***, but we also use the numbers less than zero, called the ***negative numbers***. Signed numbers include all positive numbers, zero, and all negative numbers.

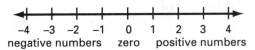

Positive numbers have a plus sign in front of them, like $+7$, or no sign in front of them, like 8. Negative numbers have a minus sign in front of them, like -2 (read as "negative two"). The graph of a signed number is a dot on the number line. On the number line below, we see the graph of $-3.5, -1,$ and 3.

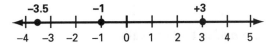

We can use the number line to show the relationship among signed numbers. A number to the right of another number is greater than ($>$) the other number. A number to the left of another number is less than ($<$) the other number.

▶ **TIP:** The symbols $<$ and $>$ always point to the smaller number.

Example 1: $1 > -3$

1 is greater than -3 because it is to the right of -3 on the number line.

Example 2: $-3\frac{1}{2} < -\frac{1}{2}$

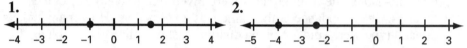

$-3\frac{1}{2}$ is less than $-\frac{1}{2}$ because it is to the left of $-\frac{1}{2}$.

EXERCISE 11: NUMBER LINE

Directions: Identify the relationships between the numbers graphed below.

1.

2.

Absolute Values

The ***absolute value*** is the distance on the number line between zero and the number. Since distance is always a positive value, the absolute value of a number is always positive or zero. The symbol for absolute value is $|\ \ |$.

$|\ 7\ | = 7$ The absolute value of 7 is 7.

$|-2| = 2$ The absolute value of -2 is 2.

▶ **TIP:** The absolute value of a positive number is the same positive number. The absolute value of a negative number is the same number but with a positive sign. The absolute value of zero is zero.

EXERCISE 12: SIGNED NUMBERS

Directions: Solve each problem. *For questions 1 and 2,* represent the quantities with either positive or negative numbers.

1. a three-yard loss on the second down of a football game

2. a stock rise of $4\frac{1}{2}$ points for the week

For questions 3–5, place the correct symbol, $<$ or $>$, between the pairs of numbers.

3. $-9\ \ -4$ **4.** $-3\ \ 1$ **5.** $-\frac{1}{4}\ \ -\frac{1}{2}$

For questions 6 and 7, find the values.

6. $|\ 2\frac{1}{3}\ |$ **7.** $|-3|$

Operations with Signed Numbers

Signed numbers can be added, subtracted, multiplied, and divided.

Combining Signed Numbers

> If the numbers being combined are *all positive* or *all negative*, add the numbers and keep the same sign.

        Both positive   Both negative
        $+8 + 7 = +15$ $-8 - 7 = -15$

> If two numbers being combined are *opposite* in sign, subtract the numbers and use the sign from the number with the larger absolute value.

Opposite signs
$-8 + 7 = -1$

sign of the larger number

Opposite signs
$-7 + 8 = +1$ or 1

sign of the larger number

The next problem contains several numbers. Some of them are positive, and some of them are negative. We'll use both rules to solve.

Example: $-6 + 1 + 14 - 2 - 8 + 6 - 9$
First, combine the positive numbers. $1 + 14 + 6 = 21$
Then, combine the negative numbers. $-6 - 2 - 8 - 9 = -25$
The difference between 21 and -25 is 4.
The absolute value of -25 (the negative number) is larger, so the answer is -4.

EXERCISE 13: COMBINING SIGNED NUMBERS
Directions: Solve each problem.

1. $-9 - 8$	**3.** $-127 + 94$	**5.** $-5 - 7 - 1 - 6$
2. $6 - 8$	**4.** $-12 + 6 + 3$	**6.** $-4.5 - 3.2$

Eliminating Double Signs

Sometimes, we encounter a number that has two signs in front of it. We always want to *eliminate* double signs. There are two rules for doing this:

ELIMINATING DOUBLE SIGNS

1. If the double signs are the same, replace them with +.
   Examples: $+ (+3) = +3$
                              $- (-8) = +8$
             $-4 - (-12) = -4 - (-12) = -4 + 12 = +8$
                                                same

(*Note:* a minus sign [$-$] changes the sign of the negative following number to a positive number [$+$] as in the last two examples above.)

2. If the double signs are opposite, replace them with $-$.
   Examples: $+ (-4) = -4$
                              $- (+2) = -2$
             $5 + (-7) = 5 + (-7) = 5 - 7 = -2$
                                      opposite

EXERCISE 14: ELIMINATING DOUBLE SIGNS
Directions: Solve each problem.

1. $-6 + (-2) - (-9)$
2. A running back on a football team makes the following yardage on six plays: $+23, -4, +8, +3, -6, -2$. What is his total gain or loss?
3. What is the drop in temperature if the thermometer goes from $12°F$ to $-7°F$?
4. At Arlington Park Race Track, Larry had $140 to begin the day. On the first race, he won $56; on the second race, he lost $14; on the third race, he lost $32; on the fourth race, he lost $18; on the fifth race, he won $26. How much money did he have at the end of the 5 races?

Multiplying and Dividing Signed Numbers

1. If the two numbers being multiplied or divided *have the same sign*
   a. Multiply or divide.
   b. Make the answer *positive*.

Both positive	Both negative
$8(7) = 56$	$-8(-7) = 56$
$26 \div 2 = 13$	$-32 \div -16 = 2$

2. If the two numbers being multiplied or divided are *opposite* in sign
   a. Multiply or divide.
   b. Make the answer *negative*.

Opposite in sign	Opposite in sign
$-7(8) = -56$	$8(-7) = -56$
$\frac{-48}{12} = -4$	$\frac{-56}{7} = -8$

MULTIPLYING AND DIVIDING SIGNED NUMBERS

1. When you are multiplying or dividing two numbers with the *same* sign, the answer is *positive*.
2. When you are multiplying or dividing two numbers with *opposite* signs, the answer is *negative*.

When multiplying a string of signed numbers, you may want to count the number of negative signs to determine whether the answer is positive or negative.
   a. Even number of negative signs: answer is positive.
   b. Odd number of negative signs: answer is negative.

Example 1: $(-3)(-2)(-1)(-5) = 30$ (4 negative signs, EVEN: answer is +)
$$\downarrow \quad \downarrow \quad \downarrow \quad \downarrow$$
$$(+6) \quad (+5)$$
$$\downarrow \quad \downarrow$$
$$(+30)$$

EXERCISE 15: MULTIPLYING AND DIVIDING SIGNED NUMBERS

Directions: Solve each problem.

1. $(8)(5)$ **3.** $(-6)(-7)(-2)$ **5.** $\dfrac{-48}{-16}$

2. $12(-12)$ **4.** $-\dfrac{25}{5}$ **6.** $\dfrac{56}{-14}$

7. A-One Sales bought 9 car telephones at a cost of $2476 each. How much does the company owe for the telephones? (Express the answer as a negative number.)

Inequalities

The relationship between two things is not always equal, so we cannot always use an equation to solve a problem. If the relationship is not equal, we can use *inequalities* such as $<$ (is less than) or $>$ (is greater than) to solve the problem. For example, $x + 3 > 10$ is an algebraic inequality. What value of x would make this a true statement? Several values of x would make this statement true. The letter x could be 8 because $8 + 3 > 10$. It could be 25 because $25 + 3 > 10$. In fact, x could be any number larger than 7. Our solution is $x > 7$.

When you solve any inequality, the set of possible solutions is often infinite. You must be aware of the boundary of the solution. In this case, the boundary is 7; x cannot be 7, but it can be any number larger than 7.

Solving Inequalities

The algebraic methods for solving an inequality are much the same as for algebraic equations.

SOLVING INEQUALITIES

1. Keep the inequality in balance. Whatever operation you perform on one side of the inequality, perform on the other.
2. Concentrate on the variable. Your goal is to get the variable on one side of the equation.
3. Perform the opposite operation. First, do addition or subtraction; then, do multiplication or division.

Example: $x + 3 > 10$

Look at x. It is added to 3. Subtract 3 from both sides. $x + 3 > 10$
The inequality is solved (x is all by itself on the left $x + 3 - 3 > 10 - 3$
side of the inequality).

$$0$$
$$x > 7$$

Check: Choose any number greater than 7. Let's $x + 3 > 10$
choose 9. $9 + 3 > 10$
$$12 > 10$$

There is one major rule that you must keep in mind when solving an equality.

> When you multiply or divide both sides of an inequality by a negative number, it changes the direction of the inequality sign.

For example, we know that $8 < 12$.
If we multiply both sides by -2, we get $8(-2)$, which is -16, and $12(-2)$, which is -24. You know that -16 is greater than -24. So the answer is

$$8 < 12$$
$$8(-2) > 12(-2)$$
$$-16 > -24$$

Notice that the arrow changed direction from less than to greater than.

Sometimes, you may see the signs $\leq$ and $\geq$. These mean "less than or equal to" and "more than or equal to," respectively. So, if the answer is $x \geq 3$, this means that the answer is 3 or a number larger than 3.

EXERCISE 16: ONE-STEP INEQUALITIES
Directions: Solve for x. Check your answers.

1. $x - 3 > -5$
2. $-3 + x < -10$
3. $\frac{x}{-3} < 12$
4. $x - 5 \geq -1$
5. $-4x > -16$

Factoring

Some problems require factoring algebraic expressions. To *factor* means to find and separate numbers that have been multiplied. An example from arithmetic helps to explain factoring. There are two ways to multiply to get the number 15: $3 \times 5 = 15$ and $15 \times 1 = 15$. We can say that 3 and 5 are factors of 15 and that 1 and 15 are also factors of 15. The factors are the numbers that were multiplied.

Factoring is the process of looking for the factors in a multiplication problem. This process can be used to solve some types of equations and to simplify some expressions. As with arithmetic, an algebraic expression is the answer to a multiplication problem. We must determine what expressions were multiplied to get that answer.

Multiplying Algebraic Expressions

Algebraic expressions can be multiplied together. An algebraic expression may consist of a number (coefficient), a letter (variable), and an exponent. Remember, an exponent is a small raised number to the right of the variable.

When we multiply variables with exponents, the base must be the same. For example, x^2, x^3, and x^5 all have the same base, x. However, x^2 and y^2 have different bases; they are x and y.

> **MULTIPLYING VARIABLES WITH EXPONENTS**
> 1. Keep the same base.
> 2. Add the exponents.

Examples: $\quad x^2 \cdot x^3 = x^{2+3} = x^5 \qquad x^2 y^3 \cdot x^4 y^5 = x^{2+4} \cdot y^{3+5} = x^6 y^8$

$\qquad\qquad\quad y^4 \cdot y^7 = y^{4+7} = y^{11} \qquad x \cdot x^3 = x^1 \cdot x^3 = x^{1+3} = x^4$

▶ **TIP:** The last example shows that the letter x alone is understood to have an exponent of 1. Although no number is written in front of the variables above, the number 1 is understood to be there. The examples following show what you do when there are coefficients in front of the variables.

ONE TERM TIMES ONE TERM

1. Multiply the coefficients.
2. Multiply the variables—keep the same base and add the exponents.

Examples: $\quad 4x \cdot 7x^2 = 4 \cdot 7 \cdot x^1 \cdot x^2 = 28x^{1+2} = 28x^3$

$\quad\quad\quad -3y^2 \cdot 5xy = -3 \cdot 5 \cdot x^1 \cdot y^2 \cdot y^1 = -15x \cdot y^{2+1} = -15xy^3$

ONE TERM TIMES AN EXPRESSION OF TWO OR MORE TERMS

Distribute the multiplication over the expression by multiplying each term.

Examples: $\quad 5x(2x+3) = 5x \cdot 2x + 5x \cdot 3$

$$= 10x^2 + 15x$$

$$-x(2x^2 + 3x - 7 = -x \cdot 2x^2 - x \cdot 3x - x(-7)$$

$$= -2x^3 - 3x^2 + 7x$$

EXERCISE 17: MULTIPLYING ALGEBRAIC EXPRESSIONS

Directions: Solve each problem.

1. $8x \cdot 3x^2$

2. $7xy(-4x)$

3. $(-6ab^2)(3a^2)$

4. $3y(2y^2 - 4y - 7)$

Finding the Greatest Common Factor

The expression $2x + 10$ has two terms, $2x$ and 10. To factor $2x + 10$, look for the largest number that is a factor of both $2x$ and 10: $2x = 2 \cdot x$ and $10 = 5 \cdot 2$. Therefore, 2 is a common factor of both $2x$ and 10. In factored form, we write $2x + 10 = 2(x + 5)$.

Example 1: Factor $65y^3 - 35y^2 + 15y$

The greatest common factor for the terms of this expression is $5y$.

$$65y^3 - 35y^2 + 15y =$$
$$\boxed{5y} \cdot 13y^2 + \boxed{5y} \cdot -7y + \boxed{5y} \cdot 3 =$$
$$5y(13y^2 - 7y + 3)$$

Example 2: Factor $3x^2 + x$

The greatest common factor for the terms of this expression is x.

$$3x^2 + x =$$
$$3x(x) + 1(x) =$$
$$x(3x + 1)$$

Note that 1 is a factor of x; x means "1 times x." So if you can't factor a variable any other way, show it as 1 times the variable.

EXERCISE 18: THE GREATEST COMMON FACTOR
Directions: Write each expression in factored form.

1. $21x^3 - 14x^2$ **3.** $9x^3y^2 + 36x^2y^3$
2. $121p^5 - 33p^4$ **4.** $5x^4 + 25x^3 - 20x^2$

Factoring by Grouping

In an expression of four or more terms, we can use the method of factoring by grouping to factor the expression. We generally separate the four terms of the expression into pairs of terms. Then we factor out the common factor from each pair. If possible, factor the common factor from the results.

Example: $x^2 + 5x + 2x + 10$

STEP 1.   Separate into pairs of terms. $\boxed{x^2 + 5x} + \boxed{2x + 10}$

STEP 2.   Factor each pair. $x(x + 5) + 2(x + 5)$

STEP 3.   Put the common factor $(x + 5)$ in front. $(x + 5)(x + 2)$

FACTORING BY GROUPING

1. Separate the four terms into pairs that have common factors.
2. Factor out the common factor from each pair of terms.
3. Put the common factor in front of the other factors.

EXERCISE 19: FACTORING BY GROUPING
Directions: Use grouping to factor the following expressions.

1. $x^2 + 4x + 3x + 12$ **2.** $8y^2 + 6yz + 12yz + 9z^2$

Graphing

Graphs can also be used to represent an equation.

Rectangular Coordinates

To understand the graph of an equation, we must first learn how points are plotted on a grid. The grid is called a *rectangular coordinate plane*. A horizontal number line called the *x-axis* and a vertical number line called the *y-axis* intersect at a point called the *origin*.

Each point that is graphed is identified by an *ordered pair* of numbers (x,y). The first number in the ordered pair is called the *x-coordinate*, and the second number is called the *y-coordinate*. The order of the coordinates is very important. The x-coordinate is always given first in the ordered pair, and the y-coordinate is always given second.

**PLOTTING A POINT WITH
THE COORDINATES (x, y)**

1. Start at the origin (0,0).
2. If *x* is positive, move *x* units to the right.
   If *x* is negative, move *x* units to the left.
   If *x* is 0, make no move.
3. If *y* is positive, move *y* units upward.
   If *y* is negative, move *y* units downward.
   If *y* is 0, make no move.
4. Place a point at the location and label it with the
   positive or negative numbers of the ordered pair (*x,y*).

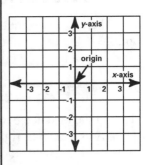

Example 1: Plot the point (3,4).
Start at the origin.
x is 3 → move 3 units right.
y is 4 → move 4 units up.

Example 2: Plot the point (−3,5).
Start at the origin.
x is −3 → move 3 units left.
y is 5 → move 5 units up.

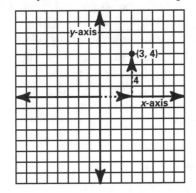

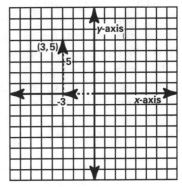

EXERCISE 20: ORDERED PAIRS

Directions: Label the ordered pairs given below.

1. *A* (,)   **4.** *G* (,)
2. *C* (,)   **5.** *H* (,)
3. *F* (,)

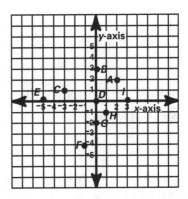

Distance Between Two Points

There are two methods of finding the distance between two points on a graph. If the two points are on the same horizontal line or the same vertical line, we can simply count the units between the two points.

Counting

To find the distance between point C and point A as shown at right, count the units from C to A. The distance is 10 units.

To find the distance between point A and point B as shown at right, count the units from A to B. The distance is 7 units.

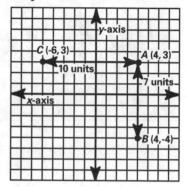

Using a Formula

The second method of finding the distance between two points uses the formula $d = \sqrt{(x_2 - x_1)^2 + (y_2 - y_1)^2}$ for two points. You will not need to memorize this formula; it will be on the formulas page of the Mathematics Test. We can use this formula to find the distance between *any* two points, whether or not they are on the same horizontal or vertical line.

In the formula, x_1 is the x-coordinate of one graphed point and x_2 is the x-coordinate of the other. Similarly, y_1 is the y-coordinate of the first graphed point and y_2 is the y-coordinate of the other.

Example: Find the distance from A to B.

Point A is $(-4,5)$. Let that be (x_1,y_1). So $x_1 = -4$ and $y_1 = 5$.
Point B is $(2,3)$. Let that be (x_2,y_2). So $x_2 = 2$ and $y_2 = 3$.

$$d = \sqrt{(x_2 - x_1)^2 + (y_2 - y_1)^2}$$
$$= \sqrt{(2 - (-4))^2 + (3 - 5)^2}$$
$$= \sqrt{6^2 + (-2)^2}$$
$$= \sqrt{36 + 4}$$
$$d = \sqrt{40}$$

Simplify $\sqrt{40}$ to $\sqrt{4 \cdot 10} = 2\sqrt{10}$

▶ **TIP:** Use the distance formula only if the points are not on a horizontal or vertical line. If the points are on the same horizontal or vertical line, simply count the units between them.

EXERCISE 21: DISTANCE BY COUNTING
Directions: Find the distance between the following points.

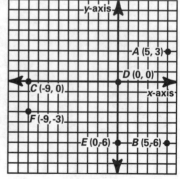

1. A to B _____

2. C to D _____

3. D to E _____

EXERCISE 22: DISTANCE BETWEEN TWO POINTS

Directions: Use the graph to find the distances indicated.

1. *I* to *J* _____
2. *E* to *F* _____
3. *G* to *H* _____

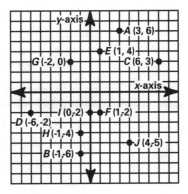

The Slope of a Line

An equation whose graph is a straight line has a special number associated with the line. This number is called the *slope* of the line. The slope is actually the ratio of the change in *y*-values to the change in *x*-values as we go from point to point on the line.

Look at the graph of the line $2x - 3y = 6$.

As we go from $(-3, -4)$ to $(0, -2)$, there is a 2-unit change in the *y* values at the same time there is a 3-unit change in the *x* values.

The slope then is

$$\frac{\text{change in } y}{\text{change in } x} = \frac{2}{3}$$

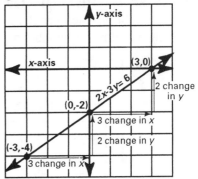

Example 1: Find the slope of the line that contains the points $(-6, -3)$ and $(-2, -1)$.

Change in *y*: $-3 - (-1) = -3 + 1 = -2$

Change in *x*: $-6 - (-2) = -6 + 2 = -4$

Slope $= \dfrac{\text{change in } y}{\text{change in } x} = \dfrac{-2}{-4} = \dfrac{1}{2}$

The slope is $\frac{1}{2}$. The line has a positive slope and slants upward.

Example 2: Find the slope of the line graphed at the right.

Change in $y = 6 - 0 = 6$

Change in $x = 0 - 2 = -2$

Slope $= \dfrac{6}{-2} = -3$

The slope is -3. The line has a negative slope and slants downward.

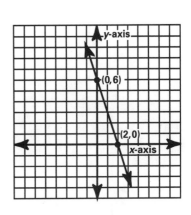

If the slope is a positive number, it represents a line that slants upward from left to right. A line that slants downward is said to have a negative slope. A line that is parallel to the *x*-axis has a slope of zero. A line that is parallel to the *y*-axis has no slope.

> ### FINDING THE SLOPE OF A LINE
> 1. Choose two points on the line.
> 2. Subtract the *y* values to find the change in *y*.
> 3. Subtract the *x* values to find the change in *x*.
> 4. Write the slope as the ratio: $\frac{\text{change in } y}{\text{change in } x}$

▶ **TIP:** The formula for the slope of a line is given on the formulas page. For two general points (x_1, y_1) and (x_2, y_2), the slope is $\frac{y_2 - y_1}{x_2 - x_1}$. This says the slope is the change in *y* values over the change in *x* values.

EXERCISE 23: THE SLOPE OF A LINE
Directions: Solve each problem. *For questions 1 and 2*, find the slope of the line that contains the two given points.

1. (0,0) and (3,4)   **2.** $(-5, -1)$ and (6,0)

For questions 3 and 4, find the slope of the graphed lines.

3.
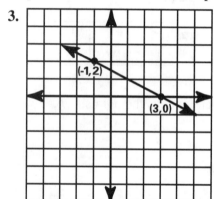

4.
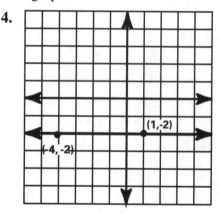

POST-TESTS

GENERAL DIRECTIONS:
Realizing that practice makes perfect, the Post-Tests are final indicators of your readiness for the real GED Test. Evaluation Charts are included to help you judge your performance. We recommend the following approach to the Post-Tests.

1. Take only one Post-Test at a time. Try to finish the test within the allotted time so that you can see how you will do on the actual GED Tests. If you are not done within that time period, mark where you were when the time was up and finish the test. You want to finish the entire Post-Test so that you can make use of the Evaluation Charts.

2. After you have finished each of the Post-Tests, check the answers in the answer key and fill in the Evaluation Charts. Answer keys and Evaluation Charts begin on page 445. Be sure to read the explanations for all of the questions that you missed.

3. If the Evaluation Charts indicate that you still need work in a certain area, refer to the review pages given in the charts.

4. When you have finished all of the tests, checked your answers, and filled out the Evaluation Charts, transfer your test scores from the Evaluation Charts to the GED Readiness Worksheet on page 393. Use the Worksheet to determine whether you are ready for the actual GED Tests.

5. Although the intent of these tests is practice, give them your best effort. If an item seems difficult, mark it and come back later. Always answer every question—even if you have to make an "educated guess." Sometimes you may know more than you give yourself credit for. Also, on the real GED Tests a blank counts as a wrong answer. It's always wise to answer every question as best you can.

Good luck on the Post-Tests and on the GED!

Time Allowed for Each Test

Writing Skills	Part 1	38 minutes
	Part 2	45 minutes
Social Studies		43 minutes
Science		48 minutes
Literature and the Arts		33 minutes
Mathematics		45 minutes

POST-TEST 1: WRITING SKILLS
Part 1: Conventions of English

Directions: This test contains 27 items. The items are based on paragraphs that contain numbered sentences. Some of the sentences may contain errors in sentence structure, usage, or mechanics. A few sentences, however, may be correct as written. Read the paragraph and then answer the items based on it. *For each item, choose the answer that would result in a needed correction to the sentence, the best rewriting of the sentence or sentences, or the most effective combination of sentences.* The best answer must be consistent with the meaning and tone of the rest of the paragraph. If you think the original is the best version, choose option (1).

You should take approximately 38 minutes to complete this test. At the end of 38 minutes, stop and mark your place. Then finish the test so that you can make use of the Evaluation Chart.

POST-TEST 1: WRITING SKILLS ANSWER GRID

1 ① ② ③ ④ ⑤	8 ① ② ③ ④ ⑤	15 ① ② ③ ④ ⑤	22 ① ② ③ ④ ⑤
2 ① ② ③ ④ ⑤	9 ① ② ③ ④ ⑤	16 ① ② ③ ④ ⑤	23 ① ② ③ ④ ⑤
3 ① ② ③ ④ ⑤	10 ① ② ③ ④ ⑤	17 ① ② ③ ④ ⑤	24 ① ② ③ ④ ⑤
4 ① ② ③ ④ ⑤	11 ① ② ③ ④ ⑤	18 ① ② ③ ④ ⑤	25 ① ② ③ ④ ⑤
5 ① ② ③ ④ ⑤	12 ① ② ③ ④ ⑤	19 ① ② ③ ④ ⑤	26 ① ② ③ ④ ⑤
6 ① ② ③ ④ ⑤	13 ① ② ③ ④ ⑤	20 ① ② ③ ④ ⑤	27 ① ② ③ ④ ⑤
7 ① ② ③ ④ ⑤	14 ① ② ③ ④ ⑤	21 ① ② ③ ④ ⑤	

Questions 1–6 refer to the following passage.

(1) One popular way to cope with stress the practice of meditation. (2) Many people spend ten minutes meditating quietly. (3) Meditating lets them get back to their day feeling refreshed and energetic. (4) First, sit comfortably in a chair with your back straight but not stiff. (5) Relax, place your hands in your lap, and your feet flat on the floor. (6) Close your eyes feel your abdomen expand when you breathe in and collapse when you breathe out. (7) If the worries of the day keep intruding, don't fight it off. (8) Just let let them go gently out of your mind. (9) Once you got the hang of it, ten minutes of meditating can leave you feeling as rested as a night's sleep.

1. Sentence 1: **One popular way to cope with stress the practice of meditation.**
   (1) with stress the practice of
   (2) with stress is to practice
   (3) with stress, the practice of
   (4) with stress, practice
   (5) with stress. The practice of

2. Sentences 2 and 3: **Many people spend ten minutes meditating quietly. Meditating lets them get back to their day feeling refreshed and energetic.**
   The most effective combination of sentences 2 and 3 would include which of the following groups of words?
   (1) After meditating quietly for ten minutes,
   (2) Before meditating quietly for ten minutes,
   (3) Meditating quietly for ten minutes, therefore,
   (4) To spend ten minutes meditating quietly,
   (5) While meditating quietly for ten minutes,

3. Sentence 5: **Relax, place your hands in your lap, and your feet flat on the floor.**
   (1) lap, and your feet
   (2) lap, and you're feet
   (3) lap, and put your feet
   (4) lap and your feet,
   (5) lap; and your feet

4. Sentence 6: **Close your eyes feel your abdomen expand when you breathe in and collapse when you breathe out.**
   (1) change *Close* to *Closed*
   (2) insert a semicolon after *eyes*
   (3) insert a comma after *eyes*
   (4) change *expand* to *expands*
   (5) insert a comma after *in*

5. Sentence 7: **If the worries of the day keep intruding, don't fight it off.**
   (1) change *If* to *Because*
   (2) insert a comma after *day*
   (3) change *keep* to *keeps*
   (4) change *don't* to *dont*
   (5) change *it* to *them*

6. Sentence 9: **Once you got the hang of it, ten minutes of meditating can leave you feeling as rested as a night's sleep.**
   (1) change *you* to *you'll*
   (2) change *got* to *get*
   (3) change *it* to *them*
   (4) change *leave* to *left*
   (5) change the spelling of *night's* to *nite's*

Questions 7–14 refer to the following passage.

(1) Americans throwed away almost 1,500 pounds of garbage per person last year. (2) Times are tough it's harder than ever to live within your income. (3) A lot of people are looking for ways to live more cheaply than he or she used to. (4) Even people who used to have money, are trading in their BMWs for sensible, high-mileage compact cars. (5) One of the best ways to save money is to stop buying on credit. (6) The interest is so high. (7) You might also have skipped one meat-based meal each week. (8) Pasta, rice, and to eat other grains are much cheaper than meat. (9) Avoid buying everything from food to CDs on impulse, you'll be surprised at how much you save.

7. Sentence 1: **Americans throwed away almost 1,500 pounds of garbage per person last year.**
   (1) change *Americans* to *americans*
   (2) change *throwed* to *threw*
   (3) change the spelling of *almost* to *allmost*
   (4) change *garbage* to *Garbage*
   (5) no correction is necessary

8. Sentence 2: **Times are tough it's harder than ever to live within your income.**
   (1) are tough it's
   (2) is tough it's
   (3) are tough, it's
   (4) are tough, and it's
   (5) are tough its

9. Sentence 3: **A lot of people are looking for ways to live more cheaply than he or she used to.**
   (1) change the spelling of *people* to *poeple*
   (2) change *are* to *is*
   (3) change *are looking* to *looked*
   (4) change *ways* to *way*
   (5) change *he or she* to *they*

10. Sentence 4: **Even people who used to have money, are trading in their BMWs for sensible, high-mileage compact cars.**
    (1) change *who* to *what*
    (2) change the spelling of *sensible* to *sensable*
    (3) remove the comma after *money*
    (4) change *are* to *is*
    (5) change *their* to *they're*

11. Sentences 5 and 6: **One of the best ways to save money is to stop buying on credit. The interest is so high.**

    The most effective combination of sentences 5 and 6 would include which of the following groups of words?
    (1) credit, even if the interest
    (2) credit because the interest
    (3) credit, although the interest
    (4) credit; however, the interest
    (5) credit, and the interest

12. Sentence 7: **You might also have skipped one meat-based meal each week.**
    (1) You might also have skipped
    (2) One might also have skipped
    (3) You might also, have skipped
    (4) You might also skip
    (5) You might also skips

13. Sentence 8: **Pasta, rice, and to eat other grains are much cheaper than meat.**
    (1) remove the comma after *pasta*
    (2) remove *to eat*
    (3) change *to eat* to *eating*
    (4) change *are* to *is*
    (5) change *than* to *then*

14. Sentence 9: **Avoid buying everything from food to clothes to CDs on impulse, you'll be surprised at how much you save.**
  (1) impulse, you'll be surprised
  (2) impulse you'll be surprised
  (3) impulse. You'll be surprised
  (4) impulse, youll be surprised
  (5) impulse, you'll be surprized

Questions 15–20 refer to the following passage.

(1) The average person catches four colds a year and miss about seven days of work, according to a medical study. (2) The best way to stay healthy is to avoid exposure to cold germs. (3) Colds are usualy passed on by hand-to-hand contact. (4) This could include shaking hands with a sick person which has just rubbed his eyes or even using the phone of a sniffling co-worker. (5) While a cold virus can't penetrate skin, it can penetrate mucous membranes in your mouth, nose, and eyes. (6) All colds are caused by germs. (7) If one is unlucky enough to come down with a cold, your best cures are resting, eating right, and avoiding stress.

15. Sentence 1: **The average person catches four colds a year and miss about seven days of work, according to a medical study.**
  (1) change *catches* to *catch*
  (2) change the spelling of *four* to *for*
  (3) change *miss* to *misses*
  (4) change *days* to *days'*
  (5) no correction is necessary

16. Sentence 3: **Colds are usualy passed on by hand-to-hand contact.**
  (1) change *are* to *is*
  (2) change the spelling of *usualy* to *usually*
  (3) insert a comma after *usualy*
  (4) insert a comma after *on*
  (5) no correction is necessary

17. Sentence 4: **This could include shaking hands with a sick person which has just rubbed his eyes or even using the phone of a sniffling co-worker.**
  (1) person which has just rubbed his eyes
  (2) person, which has just rubbed his eyes
  (3) person who has just rubbed his eyes
  (4) person which will rub his eyes
  (5) person which has just rubbed their eyes

18. Sentence 5: **While a cold virus can't penetrate skin, it can penetrate mucous membranes in your mouth, nose, and eyes.**

If you rewrote sentence 5 beginning with *A cold virus can't penetrate skin*, the next word should be

  (1) since
  (2) therefore
  (3) and
  (4) but
  (5) so

19. Sentence 6: **All colds are caused by germs.**
  (1) change *All* to *Every*
  (2) change *colds* to *Colds*
  (3) insert a comma after *colds*
  (4) change *are* to *were*
  (5) no correction is necessary

20. Sentence 7: **If one is unlucky enough to come down with a cold, your best cures are resting, eating right, and avoiding stress.**
(1) change *If* to *Because*
(2) change *one is* to *you are*
(3) change *your* to *you're*
(4) change *cures* to *cure*
(5) change *avoiding* to *to avoid*

Questions 21–27 refer to the following passage.

(1) Did you know their are people who work as garbologists? (2) They have learned that almost none of the garbage buried in landfills breaks down into useful soil. (3) Garbologists have found 40-year-old hot dogs and old newpapers that are still readable. (4) A year's subscription, to the *New York Times*, takes up as much space as 19,000 crushed aluminum cans. (5) Potato peels take up more room than any other fresh food. (6) Garbologists have found that most people eat both Health Foods and junk foods. (7) When they find the remains of lettuce and high-fiber bread, he knows the Twinkies wrappers aren't far behind. (8) The contents of landfills varies depending on the geographic region and local income level.

21. Sentence 1: **Did you know their are people who work as garbologists?**
(1) change *Did* to *Does*
(2) change *know* to *knew*
(3) change *their* to *there*
(4) change *are* to *were*
(5) change *garbologists* to *Garbologists*

22. Sentence 2: **They have learned that almost none of the garbage buried in landfills breaks down into useful soil.**
(1) They have learned
(2) They will learn
(3) One has learned
(4) They has learned
(5) They will be learning

23. Sentence 3: **Garbologists have found 40-year-old hot dogs and old newpapers that are still readable.**
(1) change *have* to *has*
(2) change the spelling of *newpapers* to *newspapers*
(3) insert a comma after *newpapers*
(4) change *are* to *is*
(5) no correction is necessary

24. Sentence 4: **A year's subscription to the *New York Times*, takes up as much space as 19,000 crushed aluminum cans.**
(1) subscription, to the *New York Times*, takes
(2) subscription, to the *New York Times*, take
(3) subscription, to the *new york times*, takes
(4) subscription to the *New York Times* takes
(5) subscription, to the *New York Times*, took

25. Sentence 6: **Garbologists have found that most people eat both Health Foods and junk foods.**
(1) change *have* to *has*
(2) insert a comma after *found*
(3) change *eat* to *were eating*
(4) change *Health Foods* to *health foods*
(5) change *junk foods* to *Junk Foods*

26. Sentence 7: **When they find the remains of lettuce and high-fiber breads, he knows the Twinkies wrappers aren't far behind.**
(1) change *When* to *Until*
(2) change *they find* to *he finds*
(3) remove the comma after *bread*
(4) change *he knows* to *they know*
(5) change *aren't* to *weren't*

27. Sentence 8: **The contents of landfills varies depending on the geographic region and local income level.**
(1) change *geographic region* to *Geographic Region*
(2) change *varies* to *veries*
(3) change *depending* to *depends*
(4) change *varies* to *vary*
(5) insert a comma before *and*

Answers begin on page 445.

Part 2: The Essay

Directions: This part of the test is designed to find out how well you write. The test has one question that asks you to present an opinion on an issue or explain something. In preparing your answer for this question, you should take the following steps.

1. Read all of the information accompanying the question.

2. Plan your answer carefully before you write.

3. Use scratch paper to make any notes.

4. Write your answer on a separate sheet of paper.

5. Read carefully what you have written and make any changes that will improve your writing.

6. Check your paragraphing, sentence structure, spelling, punctuation, capitalization, and usage and make any necessary corrections.

Take 45 minutes to plan and write on the assigned topic. Write legibly and use a ball-point pen.

Topic

Movies are increasingly available on videocassettes for use on a VCR, and many people have less and less reason to go to the movie theaters. These changes are profoundly affecting the entire motion picture industry.

Write a composition of about 200 words describing the effects of these changes on your life. You may write about the positive and negative aspects of the video revolution, as well as the way you prefer to watch movies and why. Be specific and use examples to support your view.

Information on evaluating your essay is on page 446

POST-TEST 2: SOCIAL STUDIES

Directions: This test contains 32 questions. Some of the questions are based on short reading passages, and some of them require you to interpret a chart, map, graph, or editorial cartoon. Choose the best answer to each question that follows.

You should take approximately 43 minutes to complete this test. At the end of 43 minutes, stop and mark your place. Then finish the test so that you can make use of the Evaluation Chart.

POST-TEST 2: SOCIAL STUDIES ANSWER GRID

1 ① ② ③ ④ ⑤ 9 ① ② ③ ④ ⑤ 17 ① ② ③ ④ ⑤ 25 ① ② ③ ④ ⑤

2 ① ② ③ ④ ⑤ 10 ① ② ③ ④ ⑤ 18 ① ② ③ ④ ⑤ 26 ① ② ③ ④ ⑤

3 ① ② ③ ④ ⑤ 11 ① ② ③ ④ ⑤ 19 ① ② ③ ④ ⑤ 27 ① ② ③ ④ ⑤

4 ① ② ③ ④ ⑤ 12 ① ② ③ ④ ⑤ 20 ① ② ③ ④ ⑤ 28 ① ② ③ ④ ⑤

5 ① ② ③ ④ ⑤ 13 ① ② ③ ④ ⑤ 21 ① ② ③ ④ ⑤ 29 ① ② ③ ④ ⑤

6 ① ② ③ ④ ⑤ 14 ① ② ③ ④ ⑤ 22 ① ② ③ ④ ⑤ 30 ① ② ③ ④ ⑤

7 ① ② ③ ④ ⑤ 15 ① ② ③ ④ ⑤ 23 ① ② ③ ④ ⑤ 31 ① ② ③ ④ ⑤

8 ① ② ③ ④ ⑤ 16 ① ② ③ ④ ⑤ 24 ① ② ③ ④ ⑤ 32 ① ② ③ ④ ⑤

Questions 1 and 2 are based on the pie charts to the left.

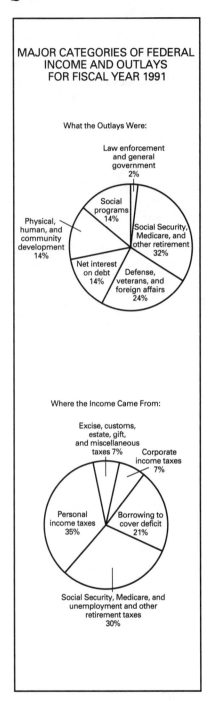

MAJOR CATEGORIES OF FEDERAL
INCOME AND OUTLAYS
FOR FISCAL YEAR 1991

What the Outlays Were:

Law enforcement
and general
government
2%

Social
programs
14%

Physical,
human, and
community
development
14%

Social Security,
Medicare, and
other retirement
32%

Net interest
on debt
14%

Defense,
veterans, and
foreign affairs
24%

Where the Income Came From:

Excise, customs,
estate, gift,
and miscellaneous
taxes 7%

Corporate
income taxes
7%

Personal
income taxes
35%

Borrowing to
cover deficit
21%

Social Security, Medicare, and
unemployment and other
retirement taxes
30%

1. Based on these charts, from
   which of the following sources
   does the federal government
   derive most of its income?
   (1) a variety of taxes on
       individuals
   (2) business taxes
   (3) income tax alone
   (4) taxes on goods
   (5) trade with other countries

2. According to the pie charts,
   which of the following was true
   about federal spending in 1991?
   (1) More was spent on social
       programs than on physical,
       human, and community
       development.
   (2) More was spent on social
       security, Medicare, and other
       retirement benefits than was
       taken in through taxes.
   (3) More was spent on deficit
       interest than was taken in
       through borrowing.
   (4) Seven percent of borrowed
       money was actually spent on
       paying off the deficit.
   (5) Defense spending accounted
       for the largest expenditure.

Question 3 is based on the following passage.

Humans share two methods of learning with the other animals. One is individual situational learning, in which individuals learn from their own experience. For example, both a person and an animal learn that standing out in the rain will make them wet. The second shared method is social situational learning, in which behavior is learned from other members of a social group through observation. Kittens learn to catch mice by imitating their mothers, and children learn to play tag by watching other children. A third method of learning is uniquely human. Cultural learning relies on concepts and values to guide behavior. For example, mothers tell children to share their toys, and people learn that certain behaviors are thought of as right or wrong. No other animal has been observed to learn in this manner.

3. Which of the following is a conclusion that the author draws?
   (1) Cultural learning is uniquely human.
   (2) Cultural learning is based on concepts and values.
   (3) Mothers teach children to share.
   (4) People learn that some behavior is right and some is wrong.
   (5) No other animals learn about concepts and values.

Questions 4 and 5 are based on the following passage.

The Bill of Rights, which most Americans take for granted, was not unanimously accepted by the thirteen original colonies. Federalist delegates to the Constitutional Convention in 1787 didn't think that a Bill of Rights was needed. They argued that most of the states already provided enough protection for citizens. Anti-Federalists believed that a national Bill of Rights was important to protect the people from an overly powerful central government. Ratification of the Bill of Rights (the first ten amendments to the Constitution) was completed in 1791.

4. The Federalists' argument was based on which of the following assumptions?
   (1) A central government might override states' rights.
   (2) The states were powerful enough to protect the rights of their citizens.
   (3) Citizens' rights were unimportant.
   (4) Citizens' rights were too important to be ignored.
   (5) A Bill of Rights would take too long to be ratified.

5. Which of the following conclusions is supported by the information in the passage?
   (1) The Bill of Rights wasn't really necessary.
   (2) The Bill of Rights was never ratified by the original states.
   (3) The Founding Fathers had differing views about the role of the central government.
   (4) Members of the Constitutional Convention all agreed about political issues.
   (5) The federal government is too powerful.

6. Clearing of forest lands for timber and pasture has been blamed for soil erosion. Cattle grazing on newly cleared land tend to leave the earth bare. The small root systems of shrubs and weeds can't anchor the soil, so topsoil is blown or washed away. Which of the following is most likely to result in prevention of soil erosion?

(1) bringing in sheep instead of cattle

(2) letting nature take its course

(3) watering the land intensively

(4) replanting trees and grasses immediately

(5) clearing more forest land

Question 7 is based on the following information.

To sociologists, crowds are groups of people who get together temporarily with a common focus. There are five general types of crowds.

casual crowd—share a brief interest on an unplanned basis

conventional crowd—result from deliberate and formal planning

expressive crowd—informally share an emotional or entertaining experience

acting crowd—commit violent and destructive acts

protest crowd—intentionally promote a political goal

7. A group of people who had gathered to watch a hockey game became upset by a ruling. The people began to throw things into the rink and then started climbing over the barricades and attacking the players. This is an example of

(1) a casual crowd

(2) a conventional crowd

(3) an expressive crowd

(4) an acting crowd

(5) a protest crowd

8. Psychologists believe that social play is an important part of a child's development. One study shows that riddling builds language and logic skills. In addition to telling traditional riddles, a child will often experiment by creating new riddles based on already-learned patterns. This information supports the conclusion that

(1) verbal play is more than simply a way for children to amuse each other

(2) a child who does not create riddles will not develop properly

(3) a child who tells only traditional riddles does not understand the underlying pattern

(4) psychologists are wrong to place importance on social play

(5) language and logic skills cannot be learned from social play

Questions 9 and 10 are based on the following information.

The president of the United States is often advised by members of his cabinet, most of whom are heads or secretaries of one of the executive government departments. The executive departments help regulate and serve many aspects of American life. The general services for which five of the departments are responsible are as follows.

Department of Agriculture— improve farms and farm income and reduce poverty, hunger, and malnutrition

Department of Commerce— encourage international trade and economic growth and prevent unfair trade

Department of the Interior—
conserve public lands and natural
resources, including wildlife and
historic places

Department of State—formulate
and carry out foreign policy and
protect American overseas interests

Department of Transportation—
plan and provide for safety of
highways, mass transit, railroads,
aviation, and waterways

9. An agency helps the establishment
and development of businesses
owned by minorities. Which
cabinet member heads this
agency's department?
   (1) secretary of commerce
   (2) secretary of agriculture
   (3) secretary of the interior
   (4) secretary of state
   (5) secretary of transportation

10. An agency protects and
maintains the nation's system of
national parks and recreation
areas. Which cabinet member
heads this agency's department?
   (1) secretary of commerce
   (2) secretary of agriculture
   (3) secretary of the interior
   (4) secretary of state
   (5) secretary of transportation

11. One factor in the law of supply
and demand is the ratio of sellers
to buyers. The more sellers of a
product, the greater the choices a
buyer has. This principle of
supply and demand has a special
effect on the real estate market.
When there have been more
houses on the market for a long
period than there have been
buyers, which of the following is
likely to happen?
   (1) A buyer will offer more than
the seller's asking price.
   (2) A seller will refuse to
consider an offer lower than
the stated asking price.

(3) A seller will accept an offer
lower than the asking price.
(4) More people will put up their
homes for sale.
(5) Potential buyers will wait
until house prices go down.

12. *Acculturation* refers to the
process by which members of
one culture adopt the customs
and tastes of the culture into
which they have moved. But
firsthand contact between two
cultures can also influence the
dominant culture. Chinese-
Americans have adopted many
American ways. Which of the
following is the best example of
how Americans have adapted to
Chinese culture?
   (1) trade with Hong Kong
   (2) Nixon's diplomatic trip
to China
   (3) the use of Chinese lanterns
at pool parties
   (4) the use of bicycles as
inner-city transportation
   (5) the acceptance of Chinese
cuisine as a popular
American food

*Questions 13 and 14 are based on
the graph on the next page.*

13. According to the graph, which of
the following is true about the
population of the world?
   (1) The populations of both
developed and developing
regions have already reached
their peak.
   (2) The population of developed
regions will drop in the
future while the population
of developing regions will
continue to grow.
   (3) A sharp rise in world population will not begin until the
year 2000.

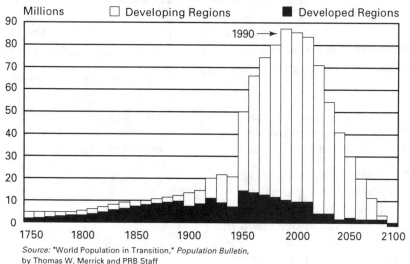

WORLD POPULATION: AVERAGE ANNUAL INCREASE FOR EACH DECADE, 1750–2100 (PROJECTED)

Millions ☐ Developing Regions ■ Developed Regions

1990 →

90
80
70
60
50
40
30
20
10
0

1750　1800　1850　1900　1950　2000　2050　2100

Source: "World Population in Transition," *Population Bulletin*, by Thomas W. Merrick and PRB Staff

(4) The population of developed regions and developing regions grow and decline at about the same rate.

(5) The population of developed regions will continue to grow, while the population of developing regions will drop in the future.

14. Which of the following is the most probable cause of the change in population in developing regions between 1950 and 1990?

(1) Developing regions began using effective forms of birth control.

(2) Residents of developing regions migrated in large numbers to developed regions.

(3) Improved health care and agricultural practices had been adopted by developing regions.

(4) The pregnancy rate in developed regions began to drop.

(5) Women in developed regions realized the economic value of having large families.

Questions 15 and 16 are based on the following passage.

The first post office mail deliveries to the American West went by steamship to Panama, crossed to the Pacific by rail, and then traveled again by ship to San Francisco. The process took at least a month, and letters arrived in huge, unsorted bundles.

Official overland delivery began in 1858, with John Butterfield's stagecoach company bringing the mail over a 2,800-mile route in only twenty-four days. The short-lived Pony Express further reduced the time to ten days. But the effort had its dangers. The ad for riders read, "Wanted: Young, skinny, wiry fellows not over 18. Must be expert riders, willing to risk death daily. Orphans preferred."

The completion of the transcontinental railroad in 1869 changed mail delivery to the West forever. Letters and packages began to arrive in cities and small towns alike, quickly and presorted.

15. California residents requested improved overland mail delivery in 1856. They took this action because they placed a high value on which of the following?

(1) support of the government
(2) communication with friends and family
(3) employment of orphans
(4) the hardships of frontier life
(5) railroad travel

16. The major change in mail service to the West is comparable to which of the following?

(1) the gradual settlement of the Midwestern states
(2) the increase in postal rates between the 1960s and 1990s
(3) the development of small telephone companies because of demonopolization of AT&T
(4) the growing competition among personal computer companies
(5) the improvement of international telephone communication because of the laying of the transatlantic cable

17. In April 1993, the passage of President Clinton's short-term job-stimulus package was prevented by Republicans' filibustering. The rule of unlimited debate allows a senator to keep the floor by filibustering, or talking long enough to force the withdrawal of the bill under discussion. By engaging in a filibuster, the Republicans made it clear that they

(1) could talk longer than the Democrats
(2) objected to the contents of the bill
(3) wanted the bill to pass
(4) wanted to embarrass President Clinton
(5) believed that America had enough jobs

Question 18 is based on the following cartoon.

Situation Room at Rand McNally--1992 Edition

18. Which of the following *best* expresses the artist's opinion about mapmakers?
- **(1)** Making accurate maps today is as complicated as going to war.
- **(2)** Mapmakers depend too much on secondhand reports.
- **(3)** Mapmakers don't try hard enough to keep up with world changes.
- **(4)** Mapmakers should be more concerned about political geography.
- **(5)** Mapmakers take their job too seriously.

Questions 19 and 20 are based on the following information.

Lobbyists work to affect foreign policy and to influence domestic issues. There are five general types of lobbyists:

economic lobby groups—
representatives of American businesses and industries who attempt to influence domestic and international policy in their own favor

ethnic lobby groups—representatives of associations based on common national or cultural background

foreign government lobby groups—
representatives of foreign countries who attempt to influence legislation in favor of their own nation's business and national interests

public-interest lobby groups—
representatives working to protect the welfare of most or all of the American public

single-issue lobby groups—
representatives working to promote legislation that affects only one issue, usually not related to economics

19. A group works to promote laws that protect the environment. This is an example of a(n)
- **(1)** economic lobby
- **(2)** ethnic lobby
- **(3)** foreign government lobby
- **(4)** public-interest lobby
- **(5)** single-issue lobby

20. A group works to promote legislation that outlaws abortions. This is an example of a(n)
- **(1)** economic lobby
- **(2)** ethnic lobby
- **(3)** foreign government lobby
- **(4)** public-interest lobby
- **(5)** single-issue lobby

21. The term *melting pot* was coined by Israel Zangwell in 1907 to express the idea that immigrants from many countries came to America to form one nation. Zangwell had a vision of people sharing their traditions to become one united people. Fifty years later, Jesse Jackson said that the United States was more like a "vegetable soup." Jackson expressed a vision of the American people in which
- **(1)** many types of people live together but do not give up their distinct identities
- **(2)** all Americans look and act alike
- **(3)** Americans would never be able to live together in peace
- **(4)** Americans are more concerned with food than with cultural ideas
- **(5)** people from other cultures are no longer accepted as true Americans

Question 22 is based on the following graph.

PROJECTED FEDERAL DEFICIT
(in billions of dollars)

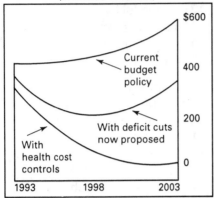

22. According to the graph, health cost controls will result in
    (1) a continued rise in the federal deficit
    (2) a higher federal deficit than would occur with the current budget policy
    (3) the same decrease in the federal deficit as would occur with the deficit cuts now proposed
    (4) a dramatic decrease in the federal deficit
    (5) little or no change in the federal deficit

23. Acid rain is a toxic by-product of coal-and oil-burning industries, power plants, and automobile exhaust. Because of the natural water cycle, acid rain can travel as far as 2,500 miles from its source. This information supports which of the following conclusions?
    (1) Acid rain cannot be considered a localized pollution problem.
    (2) Acid rain is a natural phenomenon.
    (3) The effects of acid rain can easily be contained to industrial areas.
    (4) Acid rain is limited to cities.
    (5) Rural areas are free from the effects of acid rain.

Questions 24 and 25 are based on the following information.

Any new business faces many challenges and obstacles. There are five major barriers to new businesses entering into economic competition:

previous patent on a product— A patent guarantees the right of its owner to be the sole producer of a product for seventeen years. If a patent for a product already exists, even if it has not been put on the market, the inventor of a similar product cannot manufacture the product until the previous patent expires or is purchased from the patent holder.

government licensing—Federal, state, and local governments can restrict the number of similar businesses in an area by issuing a limited number of licenses.

control of raw materials—Others may control access to materials needed to produce a product.

limited market size—A market needs to be large enough to provide enough consumers for the product or service.

large capital outlay—A large amount of money is needed to begin and sustain operation of a business, including equipment, raw materials, and wages.

24. A new restaurant in town wanted to begin serving alcoholic drinks with dinner to attract a broader clientele. But the owners discovered that the city issued only a certain number of liquor permits, and none would be available until an existing business gave up its permit. This situation describes which barrier to competition?
    (1) patent on a product
    (2) government licensing
    (3) control of raw materials
    (4) limited market size
    (5) large capital outlay

25. A couple who had run a video rental store moved to a new neighborhood. They wanted to open a similar store in their area, but they found that two video stores were already operating there. Which barrier to competition is the couple facing?

(1) patent on a product
(2) government licensing
(3) control of raw materials
(4) limited market size
(5) large capital outlay

26. Bill Clinton's first nominee for attorney general, Zoe Baird, was rejected by the Senate because she once had hired undocumented workers as household help without paying taxes on their wages. Congress later approved the appointment of Janet Reno, the first woman to hold this important position. These events support which of the following conclusions about the members of the Senate?

(1) They did not want a woman as attorney general.
(2) They wanted the attorney general to obey the laws.
(3) They did not trust the president's judgment.
(4) They believed that undocumented workers should not be discriminated against.
(5) They preferred Baird to Reno.

27. Post-traumatic stress disorder is a random recurrence of a horrifying event in the mind of the person who experienced it. PTSD victims also suffer from depression, nightmares, memory loss, or delayed feelings of isolation, guilt, and rage. Which of the following might be a cause of this disorder?

(1) watching a violent movie
(2) being in a massive traffic accident
(3) witnessing a fire
(4) hearing that a friend has been murdered
(5) reading about a rape in the newspaper

Questions 28 and 29 are based on the following passage.

Aristotle said it was the reward of an active life lived with sweet reason. Sigmund Freud said it was mostly a matter of work and love. Charles Shultz, the cartoonist-philosopher, claimed it was really a warm puppy. So just what is this thing called happiness? For centuries, people were too busy pursuing it to spend much time analyzing it. Now a pioneering band of researchers has finally bagged the elusive quarry—or at least taken its measure. . . . And their answer to the age-old mystery is that it all depends.

Happiness, that is, depends on what makes you feel happy, which is why psychologists often call it "subjective well-being." But from studies of various age and population groups in the United States and abroad, they have reached some objective conclusions on the makings of happiness. What comes up consistently at the top of the charts is not, as many might expect, success, youth, good looks or any of those enviable assets. The clear winner is relationships. Close ones. Followed by a happy marriage. Next comes religious faith, of almost any kind. "Supportive, intimate connections with other people seem tremendously important," says psychologist David Myers, whose book *The Pursuit of Happiness* is one of the cluster of recent publications in the field.

28. According to the passage, what is the primary cause of happiness?
- **(1)** success
- **(2)** youth
- **(3)** good looks
- **(4)** close relationships
- **(5)** religious faith

29. The information in the passage supports which of the following conclusions about the definition of happiness?
- **(1)** Happiness was best defined by early philosophers.
- **(2)** Happiness is easy to define.
- **(3)** There is no one clear definition of happiness.
- **(4)** There is only one clear definition of happiness.
- **(5)** Psychologists have finally defined happiness.

Questions 30 and 31 are based on the following map.

Allies Reply to Saddam, 1991

After Saddam Hussein violated international agreements by sending Iraqi troops into Kuwait and missiles into other neighboring countries, the Allies responded with military action.

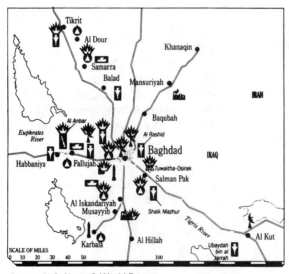

Source: U.S. News & World Report

30. Which part of the allied action is detailed on the map?
  (1) the ground war in the desert
  (2) the air campaign in the Baghdad area
  (3) the battle on the Kuwait-Iraq border
  (4) the Allied bases in Saudi Arabia
  (5) the movement of Allied troops into Iraq

31. The strategy of this attack was based on which of the following assumptions?
  (1) The action would totally destroy Iraq's economy.
  (2) Saddam Hussein would be killed during the attack.
  (3) Saddam Hussein would be forced to renew his offensive.
  (4) Residents of Baghdad would join forces with the Allies.
  (5) Destruction of major military centers would help bring a quick end to the conflict.

32. *La Linea* is the Hispanic name for America's 1,950-mile southern border. It draws thousands of jobless migrants from Mexico's interior. To them, *La Linea* represents much more than a national boundary. The crossing of the muddy waters of the Tijuana River and Rio Grande River by these families is similar to which of the following?
  (1) the crossing of the Atlantic by Columbus
  (2) the crossing of the Atlantic by enslaved Africans
  (3) the ocean crossings by the ancestors of Irish, Polish, and Chinese-Americans
  (4) the crossing of the Delaware River by Washington's troops
  (5) the crossing of the English Channel by American soldiers

Answers begin on page 447.

POST-TEST 3: SCIENCE

Directions: This test contains 33 questions. Some of the questions are based on short reading passages, and some require you to interpret a chart or diagram. Choose the best answer to each question that follows.

You should take approximately 48 minutes to complete this test. At the end of 48 minutes, stop and mark your place. Then finish the test so that you can make use of the Evaluation Chart.

POST-TEST 3: SCIENCE ANSWER GRID

1 ① ② ③ ④ ⑤   10 ① ② ③ ④ ⑤   19 ① ② ③ ④ ⑤   28 ① ② ③ ④ ⑤

2 ① ② ③ ④ ⑤   11 ① ② ③ ④ ⑤   20 ① ② ③ ④ ⑤   29 ① ② ③ ④ ⑤

3 ① ② ③ ④ ⑤   12 ① ② ③ ④ ⑤   21 ① ② ③ ④ ⑤   30 ① ② ③ ④ ⑤

4 ① ② ③ ④ ⑤   13 ① ② ③ ④ ⑤   22 ① ② ③ ④ ⑤   31 ① ② ③ ④ ⑤

5 ① ② ③ ④ ⑤   14 ① ② ③ ④ ⑤   23 ① ② ③ ④ ⑤   32 ① ② ③ ④ ⑤

6 ① ② ③ ④ ⑤   15 ① ② ③ ④ ⑤   24 ① ② ③ ④ ⑤   33 ① ② ③ ④ ⑤

7 ① ② ③ ④ ⑤   16 ① ② ③ ④ ⑤   25 ① ② ③ ④ ⑤

8 ① ② ③ ④ ⑤   17 ① ② ③ ④ ⑤   26 ① ② ③ ④ ⑤

9 ① ② ③ ④ ⑤   18 ① ② ③ ④ ⑤   27 ① ② ③ ④ ⑤

1. Which of the following facts is the *best evidence* that helium gas is lighter than air?
   (1) Helium will not burn when exposed to flame in the presence of oxygen.
   (2) By volume, helium makes up only 0.0005 percent of air.
   (3) Helium atoms do not combine with other air atoms.
   (4) Helium-filled balloons rise in air.
   (5) Helium has the lowest boiling point of all known elements.

2. To fight the effects of acid rain, scientists in many countries dump large quantities of calcium carbonate into polluted lakes. You can infer from this action that calcium carbonate is
   (1) an acid
   (2) a base
   (3) a neutral substance
   (4) a powdered substance
   (5) not harmful to fish

Question 3 refers to the following passage.

When a green plant cell is exposed to sunlight, a chemical reaction called photosynthesis takes place. During photosynthesis, carbon dioxide gas (CO_2) reacts with water (H_2O) to produce three compounds: a type of sugar called glucose ($C_6H_{12}O_6$), oxygen gas (O_2), and water. The chemical equation for photosynthesis is written as follows:

$$6CO_2 + 12H_2O$$
$$\downarrow$$
$$C_6H_{12}O_6 + 6O_2 + 6H_2O$$

3. Which of the following must be present in order for photosynthesis to take place?
   (1) glucose
   (2) oxygen
   (3) nitrogen
   (4) water
   (5) soil

4. Precipitation is the process by which atmospheric water vapor returns to Earth's surface in one form or another. Each of the following is an example of precipitation *except*
   (1) rain
   (2) sleet
   (3) dust
   (4) snow
   (5) hail

Questions 5 and 6 are based on the following passage.

Organisms vary greatly in complexity. Single-celled organisms, such as bacteria, are much less complex than multicellular organisms such as flowers. Here are five of the most common levels of structural organization.

organelle—an organized structure found in a cell's cytoplasm; each organelle takes part in carrying out some cellular function. Example: Plant cells contain chloroplasts that absorb and use light energy to make the cell's food.

cell—the basic structural and functional unit of life; a cell uses energy, moves, grows, responds to changes in its environment, and reproduces. In a multicellular organism, a cell performs a specific function. Example: a human nerve cell

tissue—a group of structurally similar cells that are organized to perform the same activity. Example: In a plant cell, vascular tissue carries water and nutrients to all parts of the cell.

organ—a structural unit composed of several tissues that work together to perform a specific function. Example: the heart

organ system—an association of several organs that work together to perfom one or more functions. Example: the muscular system

5. In a plant, the epidermis is a special layer of cells that covers and helps protect roots, stems, leaves, flowers, and seeds. This layer of specialized cells is best classified as a(n)
   (1) organelle
   (2) cell
   (3) tissue
   (4) organ
   (5) organ system

6. When Derek reached forty-three years of age, his pancreas no longer produced sufficient insulin, a hormone that controls sugar levels in the blood. As a result, Derek was diagnosed as having diabetes, a condition that often can be controlled through proper diet. Because it is made up of several types of specialized tissues, the pancreas is best classified as a(n)
   (1) organelle
   (2) cell
   (3) tissue
   (4) organ
   (5) organ system

7. Which of the following shows that sunlight can be changed to heat energy?
   A. A magnifying glass can focus a beam of sunlight.
   B. You feel warmer in sunlight than in shade.
   C. The surface of a car gets hot when sitting in direct sunlight.
   D. Sunlight reflects off a mirror without noticeably warming the mirror.
   (1) A and B
   (2) A and C
   (3) A and D
   (4) B and C
   (5) B and D

Questions 8 and 9 refer to the following passage.

Celery has long been used in Asian countries to help in the treatment of high blood pressure. Recently, researchers at the University of Chicago have found a possible explanation for this medical benefit of celery. They discovered that celery contains a chemical called 3-n-butyl phthalide. They believe that this phthalide compound causes muscles that line blood vessels to relax, allowing the vessels to widen, lowering blood pressure.

In an experiment with rats, these researchers found that a dose of the phthalide compound equivalent to four stalks of celery for humans lowered blood pressure by 13 percent. The hope is that further studies may lead to the development of a safer, more effective drug treatment of high blood pressure than is now available.

The statements in questions 8 and 9 can be classified into one of the five categories defined below.

experiment—a procedure used to investigate a problem

finding—an experimental result obtained or a conclusion reached as part of the investigation

hypothesis—a reasonable, but not proved, explanation of an observed fact

prediction—an opinion about something that may occur in the future

nonessential fact—a fact that does not help the researcher understand the problem being investigated

8. Researchers believe that eating celery helps lower blood pressure by causing muscles that line blood vessels to relax. This is best classified as a(n)

(**1**) experiment
(**2**) finding
(**3**) hypothesis
(**4**) prediction
(**5**) nonessential fact

9. Researchers discovered that the chemical 3-n-butyl phthalide can lower the blood pressure of rats. You should classify this statement as a(n)

(**1**) experiment
(**2**) finding
(**3**) hypothesis
(**4**) prediction
(**5**) nonessential fact

Questions 10–12 are based on the following passage.

In recent years, scientists have discovered that Earth's temperature is slowly increasing. In fact, scientists believe that today's average temperature is several degrees higher than the average at the beginning of the industrial revolution in the late 1700s. This warming is thought to be caused by a phenomenon known as the greenhouse effect.

In a greenhouse, sunlight passes through a glass roof and provides energy to the plants growing inside. The glass prevents heat in the greenhouse from escaping. Similarly, sunlight passes through our atmosphere and warms Earth's surface. Much of the surface heat is prevented from escaping because it is absorbed by greenhouse gases in the atmosphere. As long as the average level of greenhouse gases does not increase, Earth's average temperature stays constant.

Two main greenhouse gases are carbon dioxide and carbon monoxide. Since the industrial revolution, humans have increased the amount of atmospheric carbon dioxide by burning fossil fuels (wood, coal, and oil) both for the production of electricity and for home heating. By driving cars, humans have increased the amount of atmospheric carbon monoxide, present in car exhaust.

Scientists point out that further increases in Earth's average temperature could result in the melting of the polar ice caps and in the changing of weather patterns worldwide.

10. Which of the following best demonstrates the greenhouse principle?

(**1**) a kettle-type barbecue grill
(**2**) a heated aquarium
(**3**) a car with rolled-up windows parked in the sun
(**4**) a solar battery-powered calculator
(**5**) a microwave oven

11. Which of the following would most likely result from a gradual increase in Earth's average temperature?
  (1) a gradual increase in the length of a day
  (2) a gradual increase in the length of a year
  (3) a lowering of ocean levels
  (4) a gradual increase in the number of active volcanoes
  (5) a gradual rise in ocean levels

12. Scientists predict that if something is not done to stop the increase in atmospheric greenhouse gases, the average temperature of Earth may increase 6°F to 10°F in the next fifty years. Which of the following actions would be *most effective* toward helping solve the greenhouse effect?
  (1) reducing human dependence on all types of fossil fuels
  (2) raising the gas tax on cars
  (3) restricting the use of fireplaces to wintertime only
  (4) developing efficient electric cars to replace gasoline-powered cars
  (5) recording changes in Earth's average temperature during the next fifty years

13. Which of the following can be determined from information given on the table?
  A. the difference in percent of helium and oxygen present in pure dry air
  B. the volume of oxygen present in a one cubic foot sample of pure dry air
  C. the difference in the percent of argon and carbon dioxide present in pure dry air
  D. the volume of water vapor present in 100 percent humid air

  (1) A and B
  (2) A and C
  (3) B and C
  (4) B and D
  (5) C and D

Question 14 refers to the following passage.

Temperature and pressure affect the amount of gas that can be dissolved in a liquid. An increase in temperature decreases the amount of dissolved gas. An increase in pressure increases the amount of dissolved gas.

14. Soda pop has a fizz because of dissolved carbon dioxide gas. If a cold bottle of soda is left open on a kitchen counter, which of the following will occur?
  (1) The amount of dissolved carbon dioxide gas will remain the same.
  (2) The amount of dissolved carbon dioxide gas will increase.
  (3) The amount of dissolved carbon dioxide gas will decrease.
  (4) The temperature of the soda will decrease.
  (5) The pressure that the soda exerts on the bottle will increase.

COMPOSITION OF PURE DRY AIR

Gas	Symbol or Formula	Percent by Volume
Nitrogen	N_2	78.1%
Oxygen	O_2	20.9%
Argon	Ar	0.9%
Carbon dioxide	CO_2	0.03%
Neon	Ne	
Helium	He	
Krypton	Kr	very small amounts
Xenon	Ze	
Hydrogen	H_2	
Nitrous oxide	N_2O	
Methane	CH_4	

Question 15 is based on the following passage.

What does an aluminum rowboat have in common with a helium-filled balloon? Both the rowboat and the balloon exhibit buoyancy—the tendency of an object to float in liquid or to rise in gas.

The rowboat and balloon each have two forces acting on them: a downward gravitational force (which is equal to the object's weight) and an upward buoyancy force. The buoyancy force is equal to the weight of liquid or gas that the object displaces (takes the place of).

- A rowboat floats in water because the upward buoyancy force exactly balances the downward gravitational force. A 500-pound rowboat sinks just to the point where it displaces 500 pounds of water.
- A rock sinks in water because the gravitational force is greater than the buoyancy force.
- A helium-filled balloon rises in air because it displaces a volume of air that weighs more than the weight of the helium gas-filled balloon—in other words, the upward buoyancy force is greater than the downward gravitational force.

15. An iceberg floats with about 11 percent of its ice above the water's surface. From the passage, we know that the weight of the water displaced by the iceberg is
   (1) 11 percent greater than the weight of the iceberg
   (2) 11 percent less than the weight of the iceberg
   (3) equal to the weight of that part of the iceberg rising above the surface
   (4) equal to the weight of that part of the iceberg lying below the surface
   (5) equal to the weight of the iceberg

Question 16 refers to the following drawing.

NORMAL DAYTIME CONDITIONS

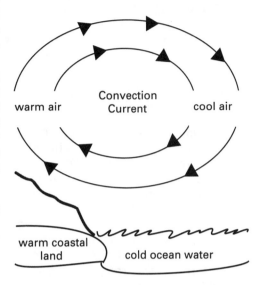

16. The best definition of a convection current is movement of
   (1) air caused by elevation differences
   (2) air caused by differences in distance from the ocean
   (3) air caused by temperature differences
   (4) water caused by the presence of land
   (5) water caused by elevation differences

Question 17 refers to the following passage.

Respiration takes place in the body cells and provides a source of energy. During respiration, oxygen (O_2) reacts with sugar glucose $(C_6H_{12}O_6)$. The products of the reaction are carbon dioxide (CO_2), water (H_2O), and energy. The chemical equation for respiration is written as follows:

$$C_6H_{12}O_6 + 6O_2$$
$$\downarrow$$
$$6CO_2 + 6H_2O + energy$$

17. Which of the following is most likely considered a waste product of cellular respiration?
  (1) glucose
  (2) oxygen
  (3) carbon dioxide
  (4) nitrogen
  (5) energy

Questions 18 and 19 refer to the following information.

An electric circuit can be either a series circuit or a parallel circuit. In a series circuit, there is only one path for the electric current to take. A break anywhere in this circuit stops all of the current flow.

In a parallel circuit, there is more than one electric current path. A break in one part of the circuit does not stop current from flowing in a second (or third) path.

SERIES CIRCUIT

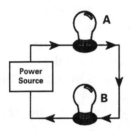

If bulb A burns out, bulb B
also goes out.

PARALLEL CIRCUIT

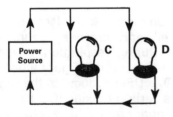

If bulb C burns out, bulb D
stays lit.

18. Four wall sockets are wired in series with an emergency shutoff switch. If the shutoff switch is opened, what happens to the wall sockets?
  (1) Only the socket closest to the switch goes out.
  (2) All four wall sockets go out.
  (3) All four wall sockets stay on.
  (4) Two wall sockets go out, one on each side of the switch.
  (5) Only the socket farthest from the switch goes out.

19. Which statement is true about the circuit drawn below?

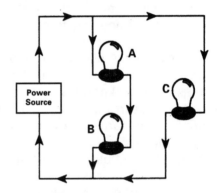

  (1) If bulb B burns out, bulb A and bulb C will stay lit.
  (2) If bulb C burns out, bulb A and bulb B will go off.
  (3) If bulb A burns out, bulb B will go off, but bulb C will stay lit.
  (4) If bulb B burns out, bulb A and bulb C will go off.
  (5) If bulb A burns out, bulb B will stay lit, but bulb C will go off.

20. An increase in the number of reported HIV-positive people is occurring in the United States. This increase is most likely due to each of the following reasons *except*
  (1) an increasing awareness by doctors of the symptoms of AIDS
  (2) an increasing effort to educate U.S. citizens about the AIDS problems
  (3) an increase in the spread of AIDS
  (4) an increase in testing to determine who has the HIV virus
  (5) an influx of HIV-positive people into the United States from foreign countries

21. Two important processes performed for plants by leaves are photosynthesis and transpiration. During photosynthesis, leaves produce glucose, a form of sugar. During transpiration, plants release water by evaporation from the leaf surfaces. What is the most likely reason that a desert plant has few or no leaves?
  (1) to increase photosynthesis
  (2) to decrease photosynthesis
  (3) to keep photosynthesis at a constant level, day and night
  (4) to increase transpiration
  (5) to decrease transpiration

Questions 22 and 23 are based on the following drawing and passage.

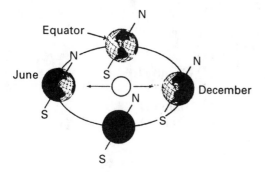

Earth's rotational axis is tilted with respect to the direction of the Sun's rays. This tilt remains constant as Earth rotates on its axis and as it moves around the Sun. The tilt leads to two important consequences for Earth:

• Summer occurs in the hemi sphere that is tilted toward the Sun, while winter occurs in the hemisphere that is tilted away from the Sun.
• The hemisphere that is tilted toward the Sun has longer days and shorter nights than the hemisphere that is tilted away from the Sun.

22. During summer in the northern hemisphere, the North Pole experiences
  (1) twenty-four hours of darkness each day
  (2) twenty-four hours of daylight each day
  (3) twelve hours of daylight each day
  (4) twelve hours of darkness each day
  (5) eighteen hours of daylight each day

23. Which of the following would be true if Earth's rotation axis did not tilt?
  A. Days and nights would be the same length everywhere on Earth.
  B. There would be no hours of darkness on points along the equator.
  C. Earth would have no seasons.
  D. Each part of Earth would have the same daily temperature pattern.
  (1) A
  (2) A and C
  (3) A and D
  (4) B
  (5) B and C

Questions 24 and 25 refer to the following drawing and passage below.

CEREBRUM OF THE HUMAN BRAIN

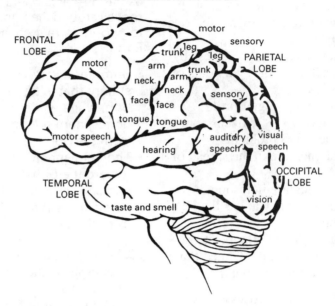

The largest region of the human brain is the cerebrum, or forebrain. The cerebrum consists of two halves, or hemispheres, joined through the center by a bundle of nerve fibers known as the corpus callosum. Each hemisphere is made up of four parts, or lobes, that control specific motor (voluntary movement) and sensory (sensation) functions.

Scientists have long known that the left hemisphere (shown above) controls the right side of the human body and the right hemisphere controls the left side. In recent years, scientists have also discovered that each hemisphere is specialized for specific learning activities. The left hemisphere seems best suited for written language, scientific skills, math, and logical reasoning. The right hemisphere seems more specialized for art, music, insight, and imagination.

24. Which area of the brain controls feeling on the left side of a person's face?
(1) the right occipital lobe
(2) the left parietal lobe
(3) the left temporal lobe
(4) the right frontal lobe
(5) the right parietal lobe

25. Which facts below represent the best evidence that brain size is not the main cause for differences in intelligence?

A. An adult's brain is larger than a baby's brain.
B. A human being's brain is larger than a cat's.
C. All adult human brains are about the same size.
D. An elephant's brain is larger than a human being's.

(1) A and B
(2) A and D
(3) B and C
(4) B and D
(5) C and D

26. Which of the following is the best evidence that light travels at a greater speed than sound?

(1) Humans have separate sense organs for vision and hearing.

(2) Light travels through outer space, but sound doesn't.

(3) Light passes easily through thick glass, but sound doesn't.

(4) You see lightning before you hear thunder.

(5) The frequency of visible light is much greater than that of sound.

Question 27 refers to the graph below.

PERCENT OF CARBOHYDRATES IN SELECTED FOODS

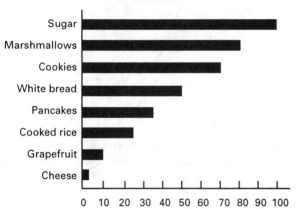

27. Which of the following foods has a carbohydrate content of 50 percent or more?

(1) grapefruit

(2) rice

(3) marshmallows

(4) items 1 and 3 above

(5) items 2 and 3 above

Question 28 is based on the following graph.

MAIN SUBSTANCES IN SEA WATER (by weight)

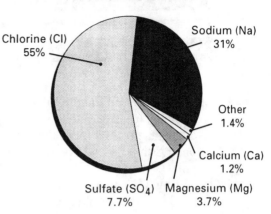

28. From information given on the graph, you can deduce that the main substance dissolved in sea water is

(1) magnesium oxide (MgO)

(2) sulfuric acid (H_2SO_4)

(3) calcium chloride ($CaCl_2$)

(4) potassium chloride (KCl)

(5) sodium chloride ($NaCl$)

Question 29 refers to the following drawing.

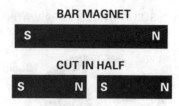

29. You can infer from the drawing above that
   (1) a bar magnet has more than one north pole and one south pole
   (2) cutting a bar magnet in half produces two weaker bar magnets
   (3) cutting a bar magnet in half produces two shorter bar magnets
   (4) cutting a bar magnet in half doubles the magnetic strength available
   (5) to produce two bar magnets, a larger bar magnet must be cut exactly in half

Question 30 is based on the following drawing.

30. You can infer from the drawing above that the density of water
   A. is less than the density of olive oil
   B. is less than the density of mercury
   C. is greater than the density of ice
   D. is greater than the density of olive oil
   (1) A and B
   (2) B
   (3) B and D
   (4) C and D
   (5) D

Question 31 is based on the following drawing.

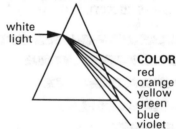

31. What is the *best evidence* that sunlight is a form of white light (light that looks white but consists of many colors)?
   (1) a clear blue sky
   (2) white moonlight
   (3) a color television
   (4) a rainbow
   (5) a color photograph

Question 32 is based on the drawing below.

PROPANE MOLECULE

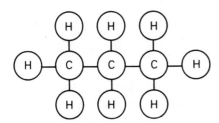

32. The drawing above shows the molecular structure of propane. Each H stands for one hydrogen atom, and each C stands for one carbon atom. The formula for a propane molecule is written as
    (1) 3C8H
    (2) $3C_8H$
    (3) C_3H_8
    (4) C_8H_3
    (5) C_8H_8

Question 33 is based on the drawing below.

SIMPLE REFLEX ARC

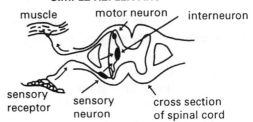

33. A reflex reaction, such as pulling your hand back from a hot stove, does not immediately involve the brain. The nerve impulse that controls the reaction takes place in a simple reflex arc as shown in the drawing. In a simple reflex arc, an interneuron
    (1) starts the nerve impulse at sensory receptor
    (2) transmits the nerve impulse to a motor neuron
    (3) transmits the nerve impulse to the brain
    (4) transmits the nerve impulse to the spinal cord
    (5) transmits the nerve impulse to the muscles that react

Answers begin on page 450.

POST-TEST 4:
LITERATURE AND THE ARTS

Directions: This test contains 23 questions. Most of the questions are based on excerpts from novels, short stories, plays, and speeches; some questions are based on a complete poem, essay, or review. Choose the best answer to each question that follows.

You should take approximately 33 minutes to complete this test. At the end of 33 minutes, stop and mark your place. Then finish the test so that you can make use of the Evaluation Chart.

POST-TEST 4: LITERATURE AND THE ARTS ANSWER GRID

1 ① ② ③ ④ ⑤   7 ① ② ③ ④ ⑤   13 ① ② ③ ④ ⑤   19 ① ② ③ ④ ⑤

2 ① ② ③ ④ ⑤   8 ① ② ③ ④ ⑤   14 ① ② ③ ④ ⑤   20 ① ② ③ ④ ⑤

3 ① ② ③ ④ ⑤   9 ① ② ③ ④ ⑤   15 ① ② ③ ④ ⑤   21 ① ② ③ ④ ⑤

4 ① ② ③ ④ ⑤   10 ① ② ③ ④ ⑤   16 ① ② ③ ④ ⑤   22 ① ② ③ ④ ⑤

5 ① ② ③ ④ ⑤   11 ① ② ③ ④ ⑤   17 ① ② ③ ④ ⑤   23 ① ② ③ ④ ⑤

6 ① ② ③ ④ ⑤   12 ① ② ③ ④ ⑤   18 ① ② ③ ④ ⑤

---

1. Maya Angelou wrote that among the African Americans in the rural South, "Age has more worth than wealth, and religious piety more value than beauty." Imagine that you're taking a poll there. Which of the following individuals would you expect to top the town's Most Admired People list?
   (1) an Oscar-winning actor
   (2) the head of the nation's largest corporation
   (3) a local religious leader
   (4) the wealthiest person in the county
   (5) the winner of a state beauty pageant

Questions 2–5 refer to the following excerpt from an article.

IS HER FUTURE IN BASEBALL?

"I'm going to be the first woman playing in the major leagues." The speaker is my daughter, Casey, age 10. She is
5 convinced of her future as a first baseman for the Red Sox. "Baseperson sounds stupid," she tells me, looking at me evenly. "If a woman has the same
10 athletic skills as a man, why shouldn't she play baseball in the major leagues?" This much has changed in 14 years.
   We sit in the stands, mother
15 and daughter. There have been hundreds of women sportswriters since I was in Boston. I would like to be able to say that Casey and I talk baseball stats
20 but the truth is her father, a scholar of Red Sox history, has infected her with his love of the game. As a 10-year-old girl, she understands the mechanisms.
25 She has a feel for the individual players, a sense of their capabilities and the benighted baseball fate of her beloved team.
30 She has thoughts about the 1993 Red Sox and is filled with judgments on the skills of Ivan Calderon, Roger Clemens and Frank Viola. Baseball cards clog
35 her room. At spring training batting practice, as always, young fans push baseballs at the players, begging for autographs. "Mr. Clemens!" "Mr. Calderon!"
40 "Mr. Dawson, pulleese." I look down at the crowd of kids. Half of them are girls. This is new. During a game against the Minnesota Twins, I noticed that
45 the bat boy was a girl.

—Marie Brenner, excerpted from "Girls of Summer," *New York Times*, April 5, 1993

2. Casey, the ten-year-old girl, would like to become a
   (1) sportswriter
   (2) sports announcer
   (3) baseball historian
   (4) bat girl
   (5) first baseman

3. The excerpt is mainly about how
   (1) females are becoming more and more involved in professional sports
   (2) a father helped his daughter develop an intense interest in sports
   (3) the daughter of a female sportswriter shares her love of sports
   (4) girls make up a large part of the audience for a typical Red Sox game
   (5) major league baseball is making an effort to attract female fans

4. The purpose of the last sentence is to

(1) make the article more interesting by giving specific details

(2) prove that the team does not discriminate against females

(3) give an example of how the Red Sox are preparing for the future

(4) support the idea that females are taking a more active role in sports

(5) convince girls to become participants in major league baseball

5. Which of the following statements would the author of the excerpt be most likely to make?

(1) "A woman's place is at home plate."

(2) "It's a man's world."

(3) "The more things change, the more they stay the same."

(4) "Anything men can do, women can do better."

(5) "Girls don't have the same interests as boys."

Questions 6–8 refer to the following excerpt from a short story.

WHO'S LISTENING?

In the living room the voice-clock sang, *Tick-tock, seven o'clock, time to get up, time to get up, seven o'clock!* as if it
5 were afraid that nobody would. The morning house lay empty. The clock ticked on, repeating and repeating its sounds into the emptiness. *Seven-nine,*
10 *breakfast time, seven-nine!*

In the kitchen the breakfast stove gave a hissing sigh and ejected from its warm interior eight pieces of perfectly
15 browned toast, eight eggs sunnyside up, sixteen slices of bacon, two coffees, and two cool glasses of milk.

"Today is August 4, 2026,"
20 said a second voice from the kitchen ceiling, "in the city of Allendale, California." It repeated the date three times for memory's sake. "Today is Mr.
25 Featherstone's birthday. Today is the anniversary of Tilita's marriage. Insurance is payable, as are the water, gas, and light bills."

30 Somewhere in the walls, relays clicked, memory tapes glided under electric eyes.

Eight-one, tick-tock, eight-one o'clock, off to school, off to
35 *work, run, run, eight-one!* But no doors slammed, no carpets took the soft tread of rubber heels. It was raining outside. The weather box on the front door sang
40 quietly: "Rain, rain, go away; rubbers, raincoats for today. . . ." And the rain tapped on the empty house, echoing.

Outside, the garage chimed
45 and lifted its door to reveal the waiting car. After a long wait the door swung down again.

At eight-thirty the eggs were shriveled and the toast was like
50 stone. An aluminum wedge scraped them into the sink, where hot water whirled them down a metal throat which digested and flushed them away
55 to the distant sea. The dirty dishes were dropped into a hot washer and emerged twinkling dry.

—Ray Bradbury, excerpted from "There Will Come Soft Rains," 1950

6. How are the details in the excerpt organized?
   (1) order of importance (least significant details presented first)
   (2) flashback (past events interspersed with events currently happening)
   (3) general to specific (a general statement followed by specific details)
   (4) time order (events presented in the order in which they might actually happen)
   (5) main idea and example (a major point followed by specific instances)

7. Given the details in the excerpt, you can tell that the family
   (1) liked doing housework
   (2) enjoyed cooking breakfast together
   (3) thought it was important to be well organized
   (4) hated to be told what to do
   (5) was unemployed and out of money

8. Which of the following TV programs would be most likely to include an episode based on the excerpt?
   (1) "Science Fiction Stories," which features dramas showing the interaction of people and technology of the future
   (2) "The Model Home," which takes prospective home buyers on tours of houses that have the latest home gadgets
   (3) "Tomorrow Is Here," which presents documentaries on scientific innovations that are sweeping the United States
   (4) "Comedy Showcase," which specializes in funny skits on subjects that are currently in the news
   (5) "Tell Me How," which takes new inventions and explains to children how they work and who developed them

Questions 9–11 refer to the following excerpt from a short story.

IS HE HIS MOTHER'S FAVORITE?

Life was very hard for the Whipples. It was hard to feed all the hungry mouths, it was hard to keep the children in flannels
5 during the winter, short as it was: "God knows what would become of us if we lived north," they would say: keeping them decently clean was hard. "It
10 looks like our luck won't never let up on us," said Mr. Whipple, but Mrs. Whipple was all for taking what was sent and calling it good, anyhow when the neigh-
15 bors were in earshot. "Don't ever let a soul hear us complain," she kept saying to her husband. She couldn't stand to be pitied. "No, not if it comes
20 to it that we have to live in a wagon and pick cotton around

the country," she said, "nobody's going to get a chance to look down on us."

25 Mrs. Whipple loved her second son, the simple-minded one, better than she loved the other two children put together. She was forever saying so, and
30 when she talked with certain neighbors, she would even throw in her husband and her mother for good measure.

"You needn't keep on saying
35 it around," said Mr. Whipple, "you'll make people think nobody else has feelings about Him but you."

"It's natural for a mother,"
40 Mrs. Whipple would remind him. "You know yourself it's more natural for a mother to be that way. People don't expect so much of their fathers, some
45 way."

This didn't keep the neighbors from talking plainly among themselves. "A Lord's pure mercy if He should die," they
50 said. "It's the sins of the fathers," they agreed among themselves. "There's bad blood and bad doings somewhere, you can bet on that." This behind the
55 Whipples' backs. To their faces everybody said, "He's not so bad off. He'll be all right yet. Look how He grows!"

Mrs. Whipple hated to talk
60 about it, she tried to keep her mind off it, but every time anybody set foot in the house, the subject always came up, and she had to talk about Him first,
65 before she could get on to anything else. It seemed to ease her mind. "I wouldn't have any thing happen to Him for all the world, but it just looks like I can't keep
70 Him out of mischief. He's strong and active, He's always into everything; He was like that since He could walk. It's actually funny sometimes, the way He
75 can do anything; it's laughable to see Him up to His tricks."

—Katherine Anne Porter
excerpted from "He," 1935

9. Which of the following phrases best describes the Whipple family?
(1) poor and struggling
(2) isolated and feared
(3) popular and admired
(4) arrogant and conceited
(5) open and honest

10. Mrs. Whipple fears that
(1) she will have to become a migrant farm worker to earn a living
(2) the second son's problems are God's punishment for being sinful
(3) her husband and children think she doesn't love them
(4) her family is angry with her for complaining too much
(5) the neighbors might look down on her and the rest of the family

11. Imagine that you are planning to make a film version of the excerpt. Which of the following places would make the best setting for the story?
(1) an urban neighborhood of high-rise apartments
(2) a wealthy resort community in the mountains
(3) a white-collar suburb of a large eastern city
(4) an oceanside retirement village on the west coast
(5) a small town in the rural South

Questions 12–14 refer to the following poem.

DID THESE FORMER CLASSMATES ENJOY THEIR REUNION?

25th High School Reunion

We come to hear the endings
of all the stories
in our anthology
of false starts:
5   how the girl who seemed
as hard as nails
was hammered into shape;
how the athletes ran
out of races;
10 how under the skin
our skulls rise
to the surface
like rocks in the bed
of a drying stream.
15 Look! We have all
turned into
ourselves.

—Linda Pastan, 1978

12. According to the speaker in the poem, the former classmates attend their twenty-fifth high school reunion to
  (1) see what kind of physical shape everyone is in
  (2) find out how people's lives have turned out
  (3) reminisce about their school experiences
  (4) cheer on the school's former athletic stars
  (5) compare how much they all have aged

13. What is the meaning of the following comparison "under the skin / our skulls rise / to the surface / like rocks in the bed / of a drying stream" (lines 10–14)?
  (1) The former students' facial features are as sharp and pointed as the rocks a person might find in a stream.
  (2) Rocks that are located beneath the surface of a stream become visible when the water dries up.
  (3) Just as rocks become prominent when a stream begins to dry up, so the skulls of the ex-classmates have become more prominent with age.
  (4) The once-young students are now as old and shriveled as a stream that is losing its water supply.
  (5) The manner in which the sun has dried out the skin of the former classmates is similar to the manner in which the sun dries out rocks in a stream.

14. The language used in the poem might best be described as
  (1) flowery and poetic
  (2) complex and hard to understand
  (3) formal and scholarly
  (4) unusual and original
  (5) simple and conversational

Questions *15–17* refer to the following excerpt from a play.

DO THIS MOTHER AND SON SHARE IN THE AMERICAN DREAM?

DOLORES: I'll never be okay until I go home again

JAVIER: [*Crossing to chair*]: Oh Mom . . .

5 DOLORES: What's wrong with you? The first sky you saw was a Puerto Rican sky. Your first drink of water was Puerto Rican water. But you don't remember. You
10 were just a baby! But I remember. Son, I want to see chickens run across my yard, all year round. I want to hear my language spoken by everyone I
15 meet, even little children. Spanish is so beautiful when children speak it. I left everything I cared about when I left Puerto Rico.

20 JAVIER: Hasn't this ever been home?

DOLORES: Never. This place has never been any good to any of us—

25 JAVIER: It's been good to me. I think I can go far here. [*He crosses to Dolores and takes her hand.*]

DOLORES: I don't doubt that for
30 a moment. But Ramon is not you.

JAVIER: Is that why you can't accept this as your home?

DOLORES: [*Crosses to her altar*]:
35 This "home" took away my little girl . . .

JAVIER: Mom, you've got to let her go. You've got to bury her. You can't blame this house for—

40 DOLORES: Yes I can!

JAVIER: It would have happened down there. She would have died down there—

DOLORES: For six days she lived
45 here! This cold house killed her!

JAVIER: She was born sickly, Mom; anything could've—

DOLORES: She was strong. I could feel how strong she was.
50 I could feel it in her hands. I could see it in her busy, red face. I heard it when she cried. [*Trying not to cry*] I came to her. I warmed her. I held her against
55 me, keeping her from the cold air in this dying house. For six days Ramon worked on the furnace, trying to make it start, but it wouldn't start. One day, as I
60 was making the coffee, while Ramon was at work, she died. I . . . stood by that window for a whole day, facing Puerto Rico. And poor Ramon. He almost
65 went crazy. [*She starts to cry openly.*]

JAVIER: Oh Mom, don't do that.

—Jose Rivera, excerpted from *The House of Ramon Iglesia*, 1983

15. In the excerpt, Dolores is experiencing an inner conflict, or psychological struggle, over the

  (1) negative attitude her son has developed toward his new home
  (2) difficulty of speaking Spanish in an English-speaking community
  (3) difference between life in Puerto Rico and life in the United States
  (4) inability of her husband, Ramon, to find a job with a future
  (5) family's move to a chicken farm in a Hispanic community

16. Read the stage directions for the character of Javier in line 3 and lines 26–28. The character's actions and his conversation with Dolores reveal him to be

  (1) nervous
  (2) explosive
  (3) rigid
  (4) shy
  (5) caring

17. How does Javier feel about his future?

  (1) confident
  (2) worried
  (3) depressed
  (4) angry
  (5) confused

Questions 18–20 refer to the following excerpt from a review of a play.

WHAT IS THE PLAY ABOUT?

Fifty years ago, a struggle erupted in Munich that sadly seems timely today also: Five brave university students pub-
5 lished and distributed through-out Germany and Austria anony-mous anti-Nazi leaflets entitled "The White Rose." Their propa-ganda was a rare public act of
10 defiance against the vicious Third Reich. Arrested by the Gestapo on February 22, 1943, the freedom fighters of the White Rose were quickly put on
15 trial for high treason and denied the defense of a jury, press cov-erage or the opportunity to appeal. The punishment was grimly predictable.
20 Honoring these young ideal-ists and chronicling the moral struggle of the security officer who must decide their fate, "The White Rose," . . . written by
25 Lillian Garrett-Groag, . . . is inspired in part by the experi-ence of the playwright's father, an Austrian who fled Vienna in 1938 to avoid the Nazis'
30 takeover.

—Lawrence Bommer,
"'White Rose' Celebrates
Anti-Nazi Heroes,"
Chicago Tribune
March 5, 1993

18. According to the excerpt, the playwright was inspired to write *The White Rose* as a result of her
(1) arrest by the Gestapo in Nazi Germany
(2) experiences as a World War II journalist in Munich
(3) father's escape from the Nazis in Vienna
(4) friendship with anti-Nazi artists in Berlin
(5) participation in the trial of freedom fighters in Austria

19. The central situation of the play is similar to which of the following more recent world events?
(1) The Chinese government's execution of young people who protested in Tiananmen Square for government reform
(2) The disbanding of the Union of Soviet Socialist Republics (U.S.S.R.) after the collapse of the communist government
(3) The United Nations relief mission into Somalia to maintain order and distribute food and medical supplies
(4) The conflict between people of different ethnic groups in the formerly communist state of Yugoslavia
(5) The trial and acquittal in Israel of "Ivan the Terrible," a retired autoworker accused of murdering prisoners in a Nazi death camp

20. The reviewer's writing style is characterized by the
(1) reliance on slang and other informal language
(2) lack of description and other vivid words
(3) development of a bitter, negative tone
(4) use of long, flowing sentences
(5) large number of witty puns

Questions 21–23 refer to the following excerpt from a book review.

WHAT IS THE BOOK *IN MY PLACE* ABOUT?

[Charlayne] Hunter-Gault, now a well-known television correspondent, was one of the two black students whose entrance to the University of
5 Georgia in 1961 desegregated that institution—with much national attention and local uproar. Her graceful and unpretentious memoir, how-ever, is
10 concerned less with that civil-rights triumph than with what it was like to grow up as the daughter of a distinguished dynasty of preachers in a gener-
15 ally self-sufficient minority community.
    The Hunters were not poor—her father was an Army chaplain—and unpleasant colli-
20 sions with neighboring whites were either unknown or have been omitted. The brick-throwing that greeted the author at the university is described without
25 rancor, as her commitment to the cause of civil rights is described without heat. One learns about segregated schools (poor equipment, dedicated
30 teachers), visits to farming rela-

tives with lavish tables, prom dresses, and Ms. Hunter-Gault's early addiction to journalism by way of the *Brenda Starr* comic
35 strip. Most of these amiable recollections—including the compulsory home-economics class in which she learned "how to make white sauce"—parallel
40 white ex-perience. Perhaps the implication of similarity was precisely Ms. Hunter-Gault's intention. It is only in the book's final chapter, containing her address
45 to the graduating class of 1988 at the University of Georgia, that she speaks bluntly of the need for "acknowledging the guiding principles of fundamental
50 human decency and then living by them" in "a waiting and needful world."
　　—Review of *In My Place*,
　　The Atlantic, December 1992

21. Hunter-Gault might describe her childhood as
　(**1**) happy
　(**2**) violent
　(**3**) insecure
　(**4**) tragic
　(**5**) lonely

22. Most of the review focuses on
　(**1**) persuading readers that Hunter-Gault's book is badly written
　(**2**) making suggestions on how the book might be improved
　(**3**) pointing out and correcting factual errors in the book
　(**4**) giving an overview of the contents of the book
　(**5**) providing background information on Hunter-Gault's TV career

23. According to the review, Hunter-Gault's book consists mainly of
　(**1**) her impressions of what it was like to grow up in her family and community
　(**2**) an explanation of how the civil rights movement developed in the United States
　(**3**) her recollections of racist acts committed by whites in her neighborhood
　(**4**) an account of the profound difference between black and white life experiences
　(**5**) her descriptions of life as the first African-American TV anchor

Answers begin on page 452.

POST-TEST 5: MATHEMATICS

Directions: The test contains 28 questions and should take approximately 45 minutes to complete. At the end of 45 minutes, stop and mark your place. Then finish the test so that you can make use of the Evaluation Chart.

You may find the formulas on page 26 useful for some of the problems.

POST-TEST 5: MATHEMATICS ANSWER GRID

1 ① ② ③ ④ ⑤   8 ① ② ③ ④ ⑤   15 ① ② ③ ④ ⑤   22 ① ② ③ ④ ⑤

2 ① ② ③ ④ ⑤   9 ① ② ③ ④ ⑤   16 ① ② ③ ④ ⑤   23 ① ② ③ ④ ⑤

3 ① ② ③ ④ ⑤   10 ① ② ③ ④ ⑤   17 ① ② ③ ④ ⑤   24 ① ② ③ ④ ⑤

4 ① ② ③ ④ ⑤   11 ① ② ③ ④ ⑤   18 ① ② ③ ④ ⑤   25 ① ② ③ ④ ⑤

5 ① ② ③ ④ ⑤   12 ① ② ③ ④ ⑤   19 ① ② ③ ④ ⑤   26 ① ② ③ ④ ⑤

6 ① ② ③ ④ ⑤   13 ① ② ③ ④ ⑤   20 ① ② ③ ④ ⑤   27 ① ② ③ ④ ⑤

7 ① ② ③ ④ ⑤   14 ① ② ③ ④ ⑤   21 ① ② ③ ④ ⑤   28 ① ② ③ ④ ⑤

---

1. Assuming no waste, how many boards each $1\frac{1}{2}$ feet long can be cut from a board that is 12 feet long?

    (1) 6
    (2) 8
    (3) 9
    (4) 15
    (5) 18

2. Each of the four members of the Rodriguez family bought a ticket for a music festival. A total of 360 tickets was sold. If one ticket holder will win the grand prize, what is the probability that the winner will be someone in the Rodriguez family?

    (1) $\frac{1}{200}$
    (2) $\frac{1}{100}$
    (3) $\frac{1}{90}$
    (4) $\frac{1}{36}$
    (5) $\frac{1}{4}$

3. If $3m + 6 = 30$, what is the value of m?

    (1) 4
    (2) 6
    (3) 8
    (4) 10
    (5) 12

Question 4 is based on the following information.

A man's shirt is listed in a catalog for $30. Below is a list of prices for the same shirt at several stores.

Clyde's Clothes	$24
Sam's Supply	$32
Florence's Fashion	$33
Dave's Duds	$27
Alma's Apparel	$35

4. For which store is the price of the shirt *10% less* than the catalog price?

    (1) Clyde's Clothes
    (2) Sam's Supply
    (3) Florence's Fashion
    (4) Dave's Duds
    (5) Alma's Apparel

5. What is the value of $20^2 + 2^3$?

    (1) 46
    (2) 48
    (3) 392
    (4) 408
    (5) 484

6. What is the ratio of the width to the height of the door illustrated below?

    27 in

    81 in

    (1) 2:3
    (2) 1:2
    (3) 1:3
    (4) 2:7
    (5) 1:8

Question 7 is based on the graph below, which shows the percent of the U.S. population living in each of the four major areas in the continental United States.

DISTRIBUTION OF U.S. POPULATION

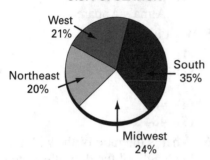

7. What fraction of the population lives in the South?

(1) $\frac{1}{5}$

(2) $\frac{1}{4}$

(3) $\frac{1}{3}$

(4) $\frac{7}{20}$

(5) $\frac{13}{20}$

8. Arrange the packages pictured below in order from lightest to heaviest.

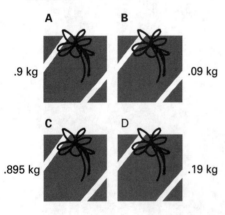

(1) A, D, C, B
(2) D, B, C, A
(3) B, D, C, A
(4) A, B, D, C
(5) B, A, C, D

Question 9 is based on the figure below.

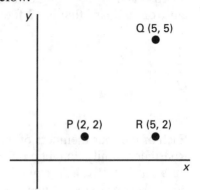

9. What is the distance between *P* and *Q*?

(1) 3

(2) $\sqrt{3^2 + 3^2}$

(3) 5

(4) 3^2

(5) 5^2

10. The figure below shows the plan of a pool. Which of the following is closest in feet to the distance around the pool?

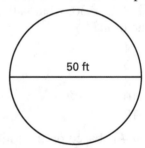

(1) 1.57
(2) 15.7
(3) 157
(4) 314
(5) 1963

Question 11 is based on the following information.

The Martins bought a house that cost $80,000. They made a down payment of $12,000. The will have to pay $420 a month in mortgage payments and $700 a year in real estate taxes.

11. The down payment was what percent of the total cost of the house?

   (1) 9
   (2) 10
   (3) 12
   (4) 15
   (5) 20

12. A team can assemble 15 machine parts in two hours. How many parts can it assemble in a 40-hour workweek?

   (1)   180
   (2)   200
   (3)   240
   (4)   300
   (5)   360

13. What is the diagonal *JL* for the rectangle pictured below?

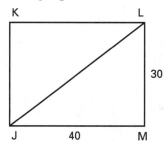

   (1)   30
   (2)   40
   (3)   50
   (4)   60
   (5)   70

14. Which of the following represents the volume in cubic inches of the rectangular box pictured below?

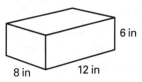

   (1) 12×8
   (2) $12 + 8$
   (3) $12 \times 8 \times 6$
   (4) $2(12 + 8)$
   (5) $6(8 + 12)$

15. If $12a - 5 = 4a + 11$, then $a =$

   (1)   2
   (2)   3
   (3)   5
   (4)   8
   (5)   12

16. The expression $3a - 12$ is the same as which of the following?

   (1) $3(a - 4)$
   (2) $3(a - 12)$
   (3) $12(a - 3)$
   (4) $3(4a)$
   (5) $3a(12)$

17. Find the number of degrees in $\angle C$ of the triangle pictured below.

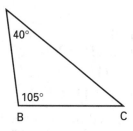

   (1)   25
   (2)   35
   (3)   60
   (4)   70
   (5)   90

Question 18 is based on the number line below.

18. How many units apart are points *A* and *B*?
    (1) 2
    (2) 5
    (3) 7
    (4) 12
    (5) 35

19. Which of the following equals $(1.5)^2$?
    (1) .75
    (2) 2.25
    (3) 3
    (4) 4.5
    (5) 15

20. Which of the following represents the area of the figure below?

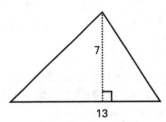

    (1) $2 \times 13 \times 7$
    (2) 13×7
    (3) $2(13) + 2(7)$
    (4) $\frac{1}{2}(13 + 7)$
    (5) $\frac{1}{2} \times 13 \times 7$

21. Giorgos drove for three hours at an average speed of 55 mph and then for another two hours at 40 mph. Which of the following represents the total distance that he drove?
    (1) 5×45
    (2) 5×95
    (3) $55 \times 3 + 2$
    (4) $55 \times 3 + 40 \times 2$
    (5) $\frac{55 + 40}{5}$

22. For the figure below, $QR = 120$. What is the length of PQ?

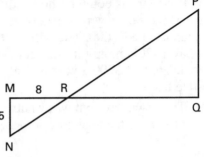

    (1) 15
    (2) 24
    (3) 64
    (4) 75
    (5) 100

23. Find the slope of the line that passes through the two points indicated on the graph below.

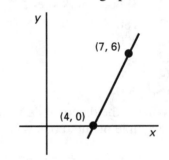

    (1) 2
    (2) 3
    (3) 4
    (4) 6
    (5) 7

Question 24 is based on the illustration below.

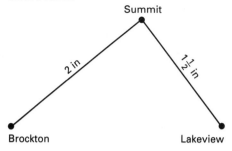

Summit

2 in

$1\frac{1}{2}$ in

Brockton

Lakeview

Scale: 1 in = 12 mi

24. What is the distance in miles from Brockton to Lakeview by way of Summit?

(1) 18
(2) 24
(3) 30
(4) 36
(5) 42

25. Maxine is 20 years older than her daughter, Pilar. Let y stand for Maxine's age. Which equation expresses the sum of Maxine's and her daughter's age if the sum of their ages equals 58?

(1) $y + 20 = 58$
(2) $y - 20 = 58$
(3) $2y - 20 = 58$
(4) $20y = 58$
(5) $\frac{y}{20} = 58$

Question 26 is based on the graph below.

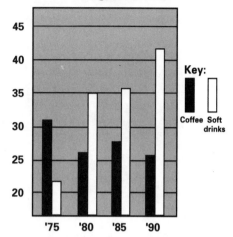

PER-CAPITA CONSUMPTION OF COFFEE AND SOFT DRINKS (in gallons)

Key:

Coffee Soft drinks

'75 '80 '85 '90

26. By approximately how many gallons did the yearly consumption of soft drinks increase from 1975 to 1990?

(1) 5
(2) 10
(3) 15
(4) 20
(5) 25

27. In a recent year, the U.S. government received $98,000,000,000 in corporate income tax. Which of the following expresses that number in scientific notation?

(1) 98×10^6
(2) 9.8×10^6
(3) 9.8×10^8
(4) 9.8×10^{10}
(5) 9.8×10^{12}

28. At a cost of $.90 per linear foot, what is the price of a board that is 78 inches long?

(1) $4.95
(2) $5.40
(3) $5.85
(4) $7.02
(5) $7.20

GED READINESS WORKSHEET

Congratulations! You have finished the five Post-Tests, checked your answers, and filled out the Evaluation Charts at the end of each test. At this point, it's important to know if you are ready to take the actual GED Tests. Use the chart and the directions below to help you make that decision.

You will use the number of correct answers to estimate what is called your standard score. Every GED examinee's results are reported as a standard score, so it is important to see how your numbers relate to the standard scores.

Test	Number Correct	Standard Scores									Standard Score	Required Score
		25	30	35	40	45	50	55	60	65		
Writing Skills	←	See page 398 for evaluation, and then refer to the Important Note on page 396 for final scoring. →										
Social Studies		6	8	10	14	18	22	25	28	29		__ / __
Science		7	8	10	14	18	22	25	27	29		__ / __
Literature and the Arts		4	5	8	10	13	16	18	19	20		__ / __
Mathematics		6	7	9	12	16	20	22	24	25		__ / __
										Average		

1. **Fill in the number of answers that you got correct** in the column labeled **Number Correct**. Do this for all of the tests except Writing Skills. (Because evaluation of the writing samples makes this test more complicated, consult pages 396 and 398 to determine your readiness for the Writing Skills Test.)

2. **Figure your approximate standard score for each test.** Look across each row and find the number that is closest to your number of correct answers. The number in bold type at the top of that column will be your **Standard Score**.

For example, Henry got 9 questions right on the Social Studies Test. This is closest to the given number of 10 correct answers. Now look at the top of the column that 10 falls in. This represents a standard score of 35. Henry would fill in 35 as his standard score in Social Studies. On Science, Henry got 19 right. This is closest to the given number of 18, which corresponds to the standard score of 45, so Henry would fill in 45 as his standard score for Science. As this example shows, you may estimate up or down, depending on which given number of correct answers you are closest to.

Following this example, estimate your standard scores for Tests 2–5.

3. **Compare your standard scores to those required by your state, province, or territory.** Look at the *minimum score per test* and the *minimum average score*. To find out the scores required in your area, consult the listing on the following page. Write the minimum and minimum average numbers for your area in the column titled **Required Score**.

Are You Ready?

Here are some guidelines to help you decide whether or not you are ready to take any or all of the GED Tests.

If any of your standard scores are at or below the first minimum score that is given on page 395, you need more review before you take the GED Tests. (In most cases, the minimum score is a 35 or 40.) Any score below the minimum will keep you from passing that test and from getting the average score needed for all of the five tests.

If this is the case, use the Evaluation Charts following each Post-Test Answer Key to determine which areas of the book you need to study more.

If all of your scores exceed the first minimum score that is given and are around the second score (in most cases, 45), you are probably ready to take the GED Tests. Some scores can be a little higher and some can be a little lower because the second score given is really an average.

Be sure to consult your evaluation of the Writing Skills Post-Test before making any final decisions.

Remember, if you try the GED Tests and do not pass the first time, you will have the opportunity to study some more and retake all or some of the tests. (See page xvii for advice on this.)

Minimum Score Requirements for Award of the GED Credential[1]

The following are the minimum score requirements for the award of the GED credential in the United States, the territories, and the Canadian Provinces. When two numbers are given, the **first** is the **minimum score required on each test**, and the **second** is the **minimum average score for all five GED Tests**.

United States	Minimum Scores		Minimum Scores		Minimum Scores
Alabama	35 and 45	Kentucky	40 and 45	North Dakota	40 and 45
Alaska	35 and 45	Louisiana	40 or 45	Ohio	35 and 45
Arizona	35 and 45	Maine	35 or 45	Oklahoma	40 and 45
Arkansas	40 and 45	Maryland	40 and 45	Oregon	40 and 45
California	40 and 45	Massachusetts	35 and 45	Pennsylvania	35 and 45
Colorado	40 and 45	Michigan	35 and 45	Rhode Island	35 and 45
Connecticut	35 and 45	Minnesota	35 and 45	South Carolina	35 and 45
Delaware	40 and 45	Mississippi	40 or 45	South Dakota	40 and 45
D.C.	40 and 45	Missouri	40 and 45	Tennessee	35 and 45
Florida	40 and 45	Montana	35 and 45	Texas	40 or 45
Georgia	35 and 45	Nebraska	40 or 45	Utah	40 and 45
Hawaii	35 and 45	Nevada	35 and 45	Vermont	35 and 45
Idaho	40 and 45	New Hampshire	35 and 45	Virginia	35 and 45
Illinois	35 and 45	New Jersey	See note 2	Washington	40 and 45
Indiana	35 and 45	New Mexico	40 or 50	West Virginia	40 and 45
Iowa	35 and 45	New York	40 and 45	Wisconsin	40 and 45
Kansas	35 and 45	North Carolina	35 and 45	Wyoming	35 and 45

U.S. Territories	Minimum Scores	Canada	Minimum Scores
American Samoa	40 each test	Alberta	45 each test
Panama Canal Area	40 and 45	British Columbia	45 each test
Guam	35 and 45	Manitoba	45 each test
Kwajalein	35 and 45	New Brunswick	45 each test
Northern Mariana Is.	40 or 45	Newfoundland	40 and 45
Marshall Islands	40 or 45	Northwest Territories	45 each test
Micronesia[3]	40 or 45	Nova Scotia	45 each test
Republic of Palau	40 and 45	Ontario	45 each test
Puerto Rico	35 and 45	Prince Edward Island	45 each test
Virgin Islands	35 and 45	Saskatchewan	45 each test
		Yukon Territory	45 each test

[1] As of January 1, 1997, the minimum score on each test will be 40 with a minimum average of 45. States, terriories, and the Canadian Provinces may require scores higher than these minimums. It is important to verify the score requirements in your area by contacting your local GED Testing Center.

[2] Minimum scores in New Jersey are 42 on Test 1, 40 on Tests 2–4, and 45 on Test 5, with a total score of 225.

[3] Micronesia is an independent country.

Important Note

On the GED Writing Skills Test, you will be given one composite score from Part 1 and Part 2 (the essay) in a proportion determined by the GED Testing Service. Each of two readers will rate the essay holistically (overall) from 2 (lowest) to 6 (highest). Thus, from 1 to 12 points could be factored into your score on Part 1. Generally, every point you earn on the essay results in a composite score that is 2 or 3 points (or from 2% to 4%) higher.

For example, a score of 18 on the Post-Test with an essay scored a "2" by two different readers (equal to 4 points) would result in an overall GED score of 41. The same score of 18 with an essay scored a "4" (equal to 8 points) would result in a composite GED score of 49!

The following will give you a general idea of your readiness based on your performance on Part 1 of the Post-Test

0–10 items correct: You are probably not ready to take the GED Writing Skills Test. You would have to write an essay scored a "6" or a "5" (equal to 12 to 10 points) in order to have a passing composite score. Use this book or others by Contemporary Books for further study.

11–16 items correct: With an essay score from a "5" to "3" (equal to 10 to 6 points), you are probably ready to take the GED Writing Skills Test. Use the evaluation chart on page 397 and determine areas for further study.

17–27 items correct: You are probably ready to take the GED Writing Skills Test if your essay is scored at least from "3" to "1" (equal to 6 to 2 points). Good luck!

ANSWER KEY
PRE-TEST 1: WRITING SKILLS
Part 1: Conventions of English

1. **(1)** The plural of *death* is *deaths*. No possession (*death's*) is shown.
2. **(4)** The subject is *detectors*, so the verb must agree with the plural subject.
3. **(1)** The new sentence would read, "In most cases everyone should evacuate a home when a fire has started or the smoke alarm sounds, and someone outside the home should call the fire department."
4. **(3)** The pronoun *them* incorrectly refers to the singular noun *extinguisher*. The pronoun *it* is singular.
5. **(4)** The indefinite pronoun *each* is always singular, so the verb must agree with a singular subject.
6. **(2)** The original sentence has an incorrect verb form (*coming*). Only choice (2) has the correct verb.
7. **(5)** No correction is necessary.
8. **(2)** This choice eliminates the incorrect pronoun *you*, which does not fit in the passage.
9. **(1)** This sentence contains a series of three items that should be separated by commas.

10. **(1)** The word *European* is derived from the name of a continent, *Europe*, so it should always be capitalized.
11. **(5)** The possessive pronoun *their* should be used here to show that the homes belong to the hosts.
12. **(5)** The phrase *Saying that they feel safer and like being treated as guests* describes the travelers, not the hosts. Choice (5) puts the phrase next to *travelers*.
13. **(3)** This sentence, as well as the passage as a whole, is written in present tense: travelers *can stay*.
14. **(2)** Each of the parts of the series, *can stay at home, make money,* and *meet a variety of people,* must be parallel in wording.
15. **(1)** The original sentence is a fragment because it lacks a verb. Change the preposition *with* to the verb *have* to make it a complete sentence.

Use the answer key to check your answers to the Pre-Test. Then find the item number of each question you missed and circle it on the chart below to determine the writing content areas in which you need more practice.

PRE-TEST 1: WRITING SKILLS EVALUATION CHART

Content Area	Item Number
Nouns, Pronouns	1
Verbs	6
Subject-Verb Agreement	2, 5
Pronoun Reference	4, 8
Sentence Fragments	15
Sentence Combining	3
Sequence of Tenses	13
Misplaced/Dangling Modifiers	12
Parallel Structure	14
Capitalization	10
Punctuation	9
Spelling	11
No Error	7

Part 2: The Essay

If possible, give your essay to an instructor to evaluate. That person's opinion of your writing will be useful in deciding what further work you need to write a good essay.

If, however, you are unable to show your work to someone else, you can try to evaluate your own essay. If you can answer *yes* to the five questions in the Essay Evaluation Checklist below, your essay would probably earn an upper half score (4, 5, or 6) on Part 2 of the Writing Skills Test. If you receive any *no* answers on your evaluation checklist, you should read your essay carefully to see how it could be improved and review Chapter 4 of the Writing Skills section.

Essay Evaluation Checklist

YES   NO

_____ _____ 1. Does the essay answer the question asked?

_____ _____ 2. Does the main point of the essay stand out clearly?

_____ _____ 3. Does each paragraph contain specific examples and details that help prove the main point?

_____ _____ 4. Have the ideas in the essay been arranged and linked in easy-to-follow sentences and paragraphs?

_____ _____ 5. Is the use of grammar and usage effective enough so that the essay is read easily and smoothly?

ANSWER KEY
PRE-TEST 2: SOCIAL STUDIES

1. **(3)** According to the principle of supply and demand, when prices go down, demand goes up. Therefore, the price of computers will be reduced to encourage people to buy them.

2. **(2)** Terrorist acts get wide publicity. For this reason, terrorists are perceived as using the media to promote their causes.

3. **(2)** The graph shows that the average number of months served by criminals convicted by a jury is greater than the sentence imposed by a judge at a bench trial. Therefore, you can conclude that accused criminals are better off pleading guilty and accepting a bench trial instead of a jury trial.

4. **(4)** The longer sentences imposed by juries suggest that they value the community's safety over mercy for the criminal.

5. **(5)** Like the Monroe Doctrine, the Roosevelt Corollary applied only to the countries in the Americas; Panama and Colombia are located in Central and South America, respectively.

6. **(5)** West Virginia was different from eastern Virginia in culture, religion, and economy. Therefore, it is most reasonable to conclude that West Virginia seceded from the rest of the state because of political differences.

7. **(3)** Choices (1), (2), (4), and (5) are all plausible reasons for married women joining in the work force. Choice (3) is least likely to be a reasonable explanation for married women entering the work force.

8. **(4)** Between 1970 and 1980, the percentage of married women who work increased by 15.4 percent— from 38.7 to 54.1 percent.

9. **(1)** Quick marriages after soldiers returned from war is the most reasonable explanation for the surge in births. Choices (2), (3), and (4) did not contribute directly to the baby boom. Choice (5) is not a reasonable explanation.

10. **(1)** When consumers spend more money, businesses capitalize on the increased spending by producing more goods to sell.

11. **(5)** The social security program would be the most affected because it provides payments to the retired and the elderly.

12. **(2)** The passage states that almost half of Australia's exports already go to Asia. Further relations with Asia would probably improve the economy.

13. **(5)** Both Australia and the thirteen original American colonies had a British monarch as head of state. Although the British queen is not much more than a symbolic ruler today, doing away with this tie to Great Britain would be more similar to America's decision to become independent then to any of the other choices, which involve incorporation of one political unit into another.

14. **(5)** The areas of the country with the greatest number of people per square mile are represented in black. The northeastern part of the country has more black areas than any other.

15. **(2)** Johnson's demand that the states ratify an amendment abolishing slavery was not a pro-South action, while all of the other choices could be interpreted as being pro-South.

Use the answer key to check your answers to the Pre-Test. Then find the item number of each question you missed and circle it on the chart below to determine the reading skill and content areas of the questions. The reading skills are covered beginning on page 31. The page numbers for the content areas are listed below on the chart. Knowledge of reading-skill and content-area-based questions is absolutely essential for success on the GED Social Studies Test. The numbers in **boldface** are questions based on graphics.

PRE-TEST 2: SOCIAL STUDIES EVALUATION CHART

Skill Area/ Content Area	Comprehension	Application	Analysis	Evaluation
Behavioral Sciences (pages 93–100)		**11**	9	7
U.S. History (pages 101–113)		5	6	15
Political Science (pages 114–125)	**3**		2	**4**
Economics (pages 126–132)	**8**	10	1	
Geography (pages 133–138)	**14**	13		12

ANSWER KEY
PRE-TEST 3: SCIENCE

1. **(5)** The passage says that white blood cells fight infections and that platelets are important in the clotting of blood. Fighting infections and blood clotting are two processes needed to repair a wound.

2. **(5)** According to the passage, the only opening in the leaf is the stomata. This must be the "mouth" through which a plant breathes.

3. **(5)** Running consumes the most calories per hour, so it is the most efficient weight-loss activity among those listed.

4. **(2)** Like charges repel; unlike charges attract. The north poles of each magnet are alike, so they will repel each other.

5. **(5)** According to the passage, the light-colored moth was preyed upon by birds when it was no longer able to blend in with the soot-darkened tree trunks on which it lived.

6. **(2)** The industrial pollution in Manchester that darkened the tree trunks was caused by humans.

7. **(3)** Since aspirin retards clotting, it is used to reduce the possibility of a stroke, which is caused by the arteries in the brain being blocked by clotted blood.

8. **(3)** The passage says that the early geological periods can be studied with ease and precision.

9. **(1)** The passage describes the relationship between old age and youth; the low mountains are the oldest, and the high mountains are the youngest.

10. **(3)** The metals silver, copper, aluminum, and iron have the highest heat conduction coefficients; therefore, they are the best conductors among the materials listed.

11. **(4)** All the other countries listed are either in the equatorial tropics and/or do not have semiarid regions bordering a desert.

12. **(2)** Sound waves must travel at a constant speed through the sea in order for the principle under which a Fathometer works to be valid.

13. **(1)** The passage shows how organic acids can be both beneficial and harmful. Diluted formic acid has germicidal properties, but concentrated formic acid is corrosive and burns. Acetic acid is beneficial because it is used to make pickles but is harmful because its sharp odors can irritate the nostrils.

14. **(3)** The passage demonstrates how organic acids are beneficial to humans. Examples of beneficial organic acids are formic acid, which can be used as a germicide, and acetic acid, which is used in the processing of cucumbers to make pickles.

15. **(1)** Since people with blood type O can donate blood to people of all blood types, a person with blood type O is known as a universal donor.

Use the answer key to check your answers to the Pre-Test. Then find the item number of each question you missed and circle it on the chart below to determine the reading skill and content of the questions. The reading skills are covered beginning on page 31. The page numbers for the content areas are listed below on the chart. Knowledge of reading-skill and content-area-based questions is absolutely essential for success on the GED Science Test. The numbers in **boldface** are questions based on graphics.

PRE-TEST 3: SCIENCE EVALUATION CHART

Skill Area/ Content Area	Comprehension	Application	Analysis	Evaluation
Biology (pages 141–155)	1	5, 6	**15**	**3**
Earth Science (pages 156–171)	8	9	11	
Chemistry (pages 172–185)	13	2	7	14
Physics (pages 186–198)	**10**	**4**		12

ANSWER KEY
PRE-TEST 4: LITERATURE AND THE ARTS

1. (2) The word *King* implies admiration. The entire passage discusses Presley's early career, and the attitude throughout is one of admiration.

2. (5) Although hard work is important, being in the right place at the right time also contributes to success. Presley's move to Memphis and his recognition by the record company president were circumstances that were crucial to his success.

3. (4) "Humble beginnings" suggests a lack of wealth and influence. Abraham Lincoln, who was born in a log cabin and became president, is the only choice listed who rose from humble beginnings. All the other men were born into wealthy families.

4. (4) The passage states that he "hadn't had the spirit or energy or presence of mind to do it [shop] earlier or thoughtfully." In other words, the son doesn't care what he buys.

5. (3) The excerpt is based almost entirely on the private thoughts of the character; none of the other methods is used.

6. (3) The title and the reference to the other characters implies that Tom, a dead man, is speaking as "I."

7. (4) The poem is written in free verse; there is no rhyme or regular rhythmic pattern.

8. (4) Higgins refers to "the moment I let a woman make friends with me" and "the moment I let myself make friends with a woman," so we know he has had some experience.

9. (3) The reference to directions implies that couples settle for a new direction neither one wants.

10. (1) The first sentence states that Hispanics are "the fastest-growing minority in the USA."

11. (5) In the passage, Sanchez complains that, as a Cuban-American, he was offered only stereotypical roles. He then goes on to explain that his mother suggested that he change his name. The implication is that Sanchez's Hispanic name was keeping him from being offered a wide variety of roles.

12. (2) Sanchez says, "I can't tell you how frustrating it was to go to auditions and know I'd be considered for one of four roles: the drug dealer, the gang member, the lover, or the streetwise youth with a heart of gold." Sanchez would probably welcome the opportunity to play against these stereotypes in a Shakespearean comedy.

Use the answer key to check your answers to the Pre-Test. Then find the item number of each question you missed and circle it on the chart below to determine the reading skill and content areas of the questions. The reading skills are covered beginning on page 31. The page numbers for the content areas are listed below on the chart. Knowledge of reading-skill and content-area-based questions is absolutely essential for success on the GED Literature and the Arts Test.

PRE-TEST 4: LITERATURE AND THE ARTS EVALUATION CHART

Skill Area/ Content Area	Comprehension	Application	Analysis
Prose Fiction (pages 201–212)	4		5
Poetry (pages 213–223)	6		7
Drama (pages 224–232)	8		9
Nonfiction Prose (pages 233–241)	2	3	1
Commentaries (pages 242–247)	10	12	11

ANSWER KEY
PRE-TEST 5: MATHEMATICS

1. 590

$$
\begin{array}{r}
590 \\
9\overline{)5310} \\
-45 \\
\hline
81 \\
81 \\
\hline
00
\end{array}
$$

2. .95

$$
\begin{array}{r}
.95 \\
.4.\overline{).3.80} \\
36 \\
\hline
20 \\
20 \\
\hline
0
\end{array}
$$

3. $53
First, find the total in checks:
$16.75 × 4 = $67
Then, find the difference:
$120 − $67 = $53

4. $\frac{1}{2}$

$$
\begin{array}{ccc}
1\frac{1}{4} & = & \frac{5}{4} \\
-\frac{3}{4} & & \frac{3}{4} \\
\hline
& & \frac{2}{4} = \frac{1}{2}
\end{array}
$$

5. $2\frac{1}{10}$

$4\frac{1}{5} × \frac{1}{2}$

$\frac{21}{5} × \frac{1}{2} = \frac{21}{10} = 2\frac{1}{10}$

6. $3 million
From 1991 to 1995:
$\frac{904{,}400}{323{,}000}$ = approximately 3 times increase in sales
From 1995 to 1999:
904,400 × 3 = 2,713,200 to the nearest million is $3,000,000

7. 416 miles

$\frac{312 \text{ miles}}{6 \text{ hours}} = \frac{x}{8 \text{ hours}}$

$= \frac{312 × 8}{6} = 416$

8. $252

$\frac{x}{\$350} = \frac{72}{100}$

$= \frac{\$350 × 72}{100} = \frac{\$25{,}200}{100} = \$252$

or

350 × .72 = 252

9. 13 feet

$c^2 = a^2 + b^2$
$c^2 = 12^2 + 5^2$
$c^2 = 144 + 25$
$c^2 = 169$
$c = \sqrt{169} = 13$

10. $367.50
Find Nick's hours, including overtime:
40 hours regular; 3 hours overtime
Find Nick's total pay:

$$
\begin{array}{ll}
40 × \$8.40 & = \$336.00 \\
+ 3 × \$12.60 & = \underline{\$37.80} \\
& \$373.80
\end{array}
$$

11. (2) (3.14)(6)
The formula for circumference is
$C = \pi d$; d = twice the radius or
$2 \cdot 3 = 6$
$C = \pi d$
$C = (3.14)(6)$

12. $2.73 × 10^5$

13. 218 million gallons
Smallest increase:
85 million − 80 million = 5 million
Largest increase:
790 − 567 = 223 million
Find the difference:
223 − 5 = 218 million

14. 78.5 sq yd

$A = \pi r^2$
$A = \pi(15)^2$
$A = 3.14 \cdot 225$
$A = 706.5$ sq ft
$A = 706.5 ÷ 9 = 78.5$ sq yd

15. 102° 180° − 78° = 102°

16. 105° The angle above the station is 75°, the same as the angle above Main Street. To find its supplement:
180° − 75° = 105°

17. $x = 70$

$14 = \frac{x}{5}$
$14 \cdot 5 = x$
$70 = x$

18. $x = 4$ $4x - 9 = 7$

$$4x = 7 + 9$$
$$4x = 16$$
$$x = \frac{16}{4} = 4$$

19. $x = 7$

$$3(x - 2) - 3 = x + 5$$
$$3x - 6 - 3 = x + 5$$
$$3x - 9 = x + 5$$
$$3x - x - 9 + 9 = x - x + 5 + 9$$
$$2x = 14$$
$$x = 7$$

20. -5 $-4 + (-3) - (-2)$

$$-4 - 3 + 2$$
$$-7 + 2 = -5$$

21. 13 $5y - 3x^2$

$$5(5) - 3(-2)^2$$
$$25 - 3(4)$$
$$25 - 12 = 13$$

22. 3 quarters, 4 dimes, 7 nickels

Let x = quarters

$$x + 1 = \text{dimes}$$
$$x + 1 + 3 = \text{nickels}$$
$$x + x + 1 + x + 1 + 3 = 14$$
$$3x + 5 = 14$$
$$3x = 14 - 5$$
$$3x = 9$$
$$x = \frac{9}{3} = 3$$

$$x = \quad 3 \text{ quarters}$$
$$x + 1 = \quad 4 \text{ dimes}$$
$$x + 4 = \quad 7 \text{ nickels}$$

23. 30° $\angle C = 180° - 110° = 70°$

$$\angle B = 180° - 100° = 80°$$
$$\angle A = 180° - (80° + 70°)$$
$$= 30°$$

24. more

$$\frac{1 \text{ kg}}{2.2 \text{ lb}} = \frac{3 \text{ kg}}{x \text{ lb}}$$
$$= \frac{3 \times 2.2}{1} = 6.6 \text{ lb}$$

Therefore, the 3-kg roast weighs more than the 6-lb roast.

25. $16\frac{1}{2}$ **feet** $\frac{3}{4} = \frac{x}{22}$

$$= \frac{22 \times 3}{4} = \frac{66}{4} = 16\frac{1}{2}$$

26. $2\sqrt{5}$ $d = \sqrt{(x_2 - x_1)^2 + (y_2 - y_1)^2}$

$$= \sqrt{(5 - 1)^2 + (4 - 2)^2}$$
$$= \sqrt{4^2 + 2^2}$$
$$= \sqrt{16 + 4}$$
$$= \sqrt{20} = \sqrt{4 \cdot 5} = 2\sqrt{5}$$

27. $\frac{1}{2}$ $\frac{y_2 - y_1}{x_2 - x_1}$

$$\frac{4 - 2}{5 - 1} = \frac{2}{4} = \frac{1}{2}$$

28. 70°

First, find $\angle c$:

The measure of angle c is 55° since both side ab and side bc are 6 inches.

Then, find $\angle b$:

$$180° - 2(55°) =$$
$$180° - 110° = 70°$$

29. $\frac{1}{13}$ $\frac{4 \text{ aces}}{52 \text{ cards}} = \frac{1}{13}$

30. 139 $\sqrt{25} + (4 \times 3)^2 - (5 \times 2)$

$$5 + 12^2 - 10$$
$$5 + 144 - 10 = 149 - 10$$
$$= 139$$

Use the answer key on pages 405–406 to check your answers to the Pre-Test. Then find the item number of each question you missed and circle it on the chart below to determine the mathematics content areas of the questions. The page numbers for the content areas are listed below on the chart. The numbers in **bold type** are questions based on graphics.

PRE-TEST 5: MATHEMATICS EVALUATION CHART

Skill Area/ Content Area	Item Number	Review Pages
Whole Numbers & Decimals	1, 2, 3	251–260
Fractions	4, 5	261–274
Ratio & Proportion	**6,** 7	275–278
Percent	8	279–286
Measurement	**10,** 24	287–296
Graphs, Statistics, & Probability	**13,** 29	297–304
Numeration	12, 30	305–310
Geometry	9, 11, **14, 15, 16, 23, 25, 28**	311–322
Algebra	17, 18, 19, 20, 21, 22, **26, 27**	323–344

ANSWER KEY
TEST 1: WRITING SKILLS

CHAPTER 1: BASIC ENGLISH USAGE

Exercise 1: Plural Nouns
page 47

1. countries (4)
2. homes (1)
3. businesses (2)
4. alloys (3)
5. cars (1)
6. factories (4)
7. races (1)
8. lives (5)
9. women (7)
10. dishes (2)

Exercise 2: Possessive Nouns
page 48

1. Over the past two years, the **Wagners'** house has become worn around the doors and windows.
2. **Children's** pants and **toddlers'** playsuits are marked down at **Emily's** favorite shop.

Exercise 3: The Simple Tenses
page 50

Verb	Time Clue
1. will walk	Next week
2. appears	Right now
3. planted	In March of 1994

Exercise 4: The Continuing Tenses
page 50

Verb	Time Clue
1. is barking	Now
2. will be cooking	By next month
3. was sleeping	On yesterday's show

Exercise 5: The Perfect Tenses
page 51

Verb	Time Clue
1. has attended	so far
2. had worked	Before going into the army
3. will have mailed	By next October

Exercise 6: Verbs
page 53

The first sentence in this paragraph is correct, and it is in the present tense. So the passage as a whole must be in the present tense. Sentences 1–3 should be in the simple present, and Sentence 4 should be in the present continuing.

1. (3) 2. (2) 3. (5)

Exercise 7: Subject-Verb Agreement
page 55

Subject	Verb
1. racers	run
2. neither	visits
3. A sandwich and a glass of juice	are
4. crowd	was
5. Clara	is

Exercise 8: Possessive Pronouns and Contractions
page 57

1. **You're** not ready to move out of the house at age twelve.
2. **There's** no one here by that name, Officer.
3. **Whose** coat is lying in the back corner of the bar?

Exercise 9: Identifying Antecedents
page 57

Pronoun	Antecedent
1. their	Murray and Dee
2. her	Marissa
3. they	Murray and Dee
4. who	eager friends

Exercise 10: Relative Pronouns
page 58

1. woman who
2. door that
3. Time, which

Exercise 11: Agreement in Number
page 59

Corrections are in **bold** type.

Over the last twenty years, Knoxville's population center, once clustered around **its** small downtown area, has shifted westward. However, **its** downtown area may become more important again in future years. Many of the city's older buildings are being restored, and its newer downtown buildings are lovely, too.

Exercise 12: Clarifying Antecedents
page 59

The following sentences are *possible* revisions. The words in **bold** type replace the confusing pronoun or pronouns. Remember that your sentences can be different and still be correct. Be sure that you have replaced all vague pronouns.

1. C
2. Dion asked Tony if **Tony** thought **Dion** would win the contest.
3. When the quarterback made the touchdown in the final seconds of the game, **the crowd** went wild in the stands.
4. C

Exercise 13: Agreement in Person
page 60

All instances of **you** should be changed to **we**.

CHAPTER 2: SENTENCE STRUCTURE

Exercise 1: Rewriting Fragments
page 61

Corrected sentences are in **bold** type. Remember, your revised sentences can be different and still be correct.

When President John F. Kennedy was inaugurated in 1960, he stated, "Ask not what your country can do for you; ask what you can do for your country." His philosophy did much for U.S. citizens and underdeveloped areas of the world. **For example, the Peace Corps sent volunteers into underdeveloped areas of the world.** These volunteers educated the citizens of those countries in basic survival skills. The main goal was for the countries to become more self-sufficient. **A second goal was to improve relations between the U.S. and these countries.**

Exercise 2: Conjunctions
page 62

The correct conjunction and punctuation are in **bold** type. More than one conjunction may be correct in some sentences.

1. We are planning a Fourth of July picnic, **and** we hope all of you can attend.
2. He did not study for his driver's test, **but** he passed it.
3. Al has always wanted his own business, **so** he opened a restaurant.

Exercise 3: Using Commas Correctly
page 62

Remember, a comma is needed only when two complete thoughts are joined by a coordinating conjunction such as *and* or *but*. If you use a comma, make sure the ideas you join have both a subject and a predicate.

1. She took off her coat and hung it in the closet.
2. She took off her coat, and she hung it in the closet.
3. Our son has a learning disability but is doing well in school.
4. Our son has a learning disability, but he is doing well in school.

Exercise 4: Run-ons and Comma Splices
page 63

1. Kyle broke his leg, so he was taken to the emergency room.
   OR:
   Kyle broke his leg. He was taken to the emergency room.
2. C
3. I'd rather have hay fever than food allergies. At least I can eat!

Exercise 5: Sentence Structure Practice
page 63

1. order. Their
2. children, so
3. child, and they

Exercise 6: Conjunctive Adverbs
page 64

The conjunctive adverb is in bold type.

1. (a) He was qualified for the job; **therefore**, he got it.
2. (b) The steak is very good; **on the other hand**, you might prefer the chicken.
3. (c) The company is in financial trouble; **as a result**, workers may be laid off.

Exercise 7: Combining Sentences
page 65

The following are *possible* combinations of these sentences. Remember, your answers can be different and still be correct. Be sure that your punctuation is correct and that your conjunction is logical.

1. (a) The salesperson was very polite, so she listened to my complaints.
   (b) The salesperson was very polite; therefore, she listened to my complaints.
2. (a) My friends give me advice, but I do not always listen to them.
   (b) My friends give me advice; however, I do not always listen to them.
3. (a) I could drive you to work in the morning, or you could take the subway.
   (b) I could drive you to work in the morning; otherwise, you could take the subway.

Exercise 8: Dependent Clauses
page 66

Remember, your answers can be different from those in **bold type** and still be correct.

Part A

1. **Even though** Ray was afraid of water, he took swimming lessons.
2. I'm not going to the class reunion **because** my closest friends won't be there.
3. Celia stayed with her mother **until** the nurse returned.

Part B

The subordinating conjunction in each sentence is in bold type.

1. **Because** we arrived at the church late, we missed their wedding ceremony.
2. **Since** Rose was angry with her babysitter, she said she would not hire the young girl again.
3. **When** we drove into the parking lot, we noticed that the store was closed.

Exercise 9: Structure and Usage
pages 66–67

1. (4) When combining two independent clauses with a conjunctive adverb, a semicolon should be placed before the conjunctive adverb and a comma placed after it. Also, be sure to choose the most logical conjunctive adverb. *Therefore* is correct because it links a cause to an effect.
2. (1) no correction is necessary
3. (3) When combining two independent clauses with a conjunctive adverb, a semicolon should be placed before the conjunctive adverb and a comma placed after it.
4. (2) When a dependent clause comes first in a sentence, a comma must separate the two clauses.
5. (2) The passage as a whole refers to a group of people—stockholders. The plural subject pronoun *they* is correct.

Exercise 10: Correct Verb Sequence
page 68

1. should have taken
2. will call
3. had slept
4. could have moved

Exercise 11: Dangling and Misplaced Modifiers
page 68

The modifying phrase in each of the following sentences is in **bold type** and is in its correct place—nearest to the word it modifies.

1. Rich saw the "No Smoking" sign **nailed to the wall.**
2. **While I was taking a shower**, the telephone rang.
3. **When I was traveling through Colorado**, my luggage was lost on the train.
4. We heard the dog **whining for food** under the table.

Exercise 12: Parallelism
page 69

1. (b)
2. (a)
3. (b)

Exercise 13: Structure and Usage
pages 69–70

1. (3) The modifier *ages five and six* should be placed next to *children*, the word it modifies.
2. (4) The dangling modifier in this sentence incorrectly implies that *new questions* were feeling sorry for the children.
3. (5) *Frustrating* is correct because it is parallel to *interesting* and *challenging*.
4. (1) The conjunction *and* joins two related ideas.

CHAPTER 3: MECHANICS

Exercise 1: Capitalization Rules
page 72

1. The mayor of Chestertown requested assistance from Governor Kelly.
2. We will meet on Wednesday, August 9, at Lincoln Center in Memphis, Tennessee.
3. Drive north to Baker Avenue, then turn left at Kennedy Highway.
4. The Ohio River is a beautiful river.

Exercise 2: Using Commas
page 73

Dear Mom,

Because I do not have enough money, I will not be coming home for spring vacation. Unfortunately, I need to stay here in Des Moines and work. I did not, of course, waste my money; but I did not allow enough in my budget for an airline ticket. You will understand that I can't come, I know. I'd really love to be home in March, but I can't afford a ticket until June. Please call Sue, Pam, and Linda for me and relay the message.

Love always,
Dawn

Exercise 3: Punctuation Review
page 74

1. Delete the unneeded comma after *need*.
2. Delete the unneeded comma after *store*.
3. Change the comma before *as a result* to a semicolon.
4. Add a comma after *however*.
5. An apostrophe is needed in the contraction *isn't*.

CHAPTER 4: PREPARING FOR THE GED WRITING SAMPLE

Exercise 1: Warming Up
page 76

Your responses will vary, but take some time to carefully check your spelling, punctuation, sentence structure, and grammar and usage.

Exercise 2: Topic, Audience, and Purpose
page 76

1. writer: a parent
2. topic: a child's absence from class
3. purpose: to ask that Erik be excused from class next Friday
4. audience: a teacher

Exercises 3–9
pages 77–81

Answers for these writing exercises will vary. Make sure your responses have followed the directions precisely.

Exercise 10: Cause and Effect
page 82

The six *effects* of the Wilsons' divorce are

1. The family home will be sold.
2. A property settlement must be decided.
3. Mrs. Wilson may seek full-time employment.
4. Mr. Wilson has moved into an apartment.
5. Mrs. Wilson and the children are living with her sister.
6. The Wilsons' lives have changed.

Exercises 11–14
pages 82–87

Answers will vary.

ANSWER KEY
TEST 2: SOCIAL STUDIES

CHAPTER 1: BEHAVIORAL SCIENCES

Exercise 1: Physical and Cultural Anthropology
page 94
Application
1. **P** Fossils of bones represent the physical aspect of human beings.
2. **C** Hieroglyphics (writings) on walls represent the cultural aspect.
3. **C** Eating habits represent the cultural aspect.

Exercise 2: Primary and Secondary Groups
page 95
Application
1. **S** The math class is a secondary group because the interaction is brief and general.
2. **P** Your family is the most primary of all groups.
3. **S** You may know all of the townspeople, but you do not have a close relationship with each of them.

Exercise 3: Nuclear and Extended Families
page 96
Application
1. **E** Three generations indicate that the parents, children, and grandparents live together; this describes an extended family.
2. **N** Two generations entail the parents and their children living together; this describes a nuclear family.
3. **E** According to the passage, an extended family includes relatives other than the husband, wife, and children, all of whom live together.

Exercise 4: Social Stratification
page 97
Application
1. **CL** A class system encourages self-improvement and achievement.
2. **CA** A caste system is strict and rigid.
3. **CL** Job choices are open in a class system.

Exercise 5: Types of Learning
pages 97–98
Application
1. **(1)** The baby learns to respond (stop crying) when it associates the light (stimulus) with being picked up and comforted (reward).
2. **(4)** The child makes a logical thought process and adapts information to distinguish between the bird and the airplane.

Exercise 6: Defense Mechanisms
page 100
Application
1. **(4)** The fox makes an excuse (the grapes were sour anyway) for his failure to reach them. This is an example of rationalization.
2. **(3)** Michael directs his anger at his dog instead of directing it at the real cause—his team's loss. This demonstrates displacement.

CHAPTER 2: U.S. HISTORY

Exercise 1: The Revolutionary War
page 102
Analysis
1. (c) 2. (a) 3. (b)

Exercise 2: The Beginning of American Government
page 103
Comprehension
1. T 2. T 3. F

Exercise 3: Disputes and Compromises
page 103
Analysis
1. **(2)** Counting slaves as only three-fifths of the population was favorable to the northern states because it meant the South would have fewer representatives in the House of Representatives.

Application
2. **(1)** According to the passage, Anti-Federalists feared authoritative control by a central government. Similarly, today's conservatives of both parties favor state sovereignty over federal sovereignty.

Exercise 4: The War of 1812
page 105
Comprehension
(4) According to the passage, the events that contributed to the United States' sense of nationalism after the War of 1812 were westward expansion (Manifest Destiny) and the increased need to manufacture its own goods because of the British naval blockade.

Exercise 5: A Divided Nation
page 106
Application
1. (3) Popular sovereignty permitted the people to approve or disapprove of legislative action; therefore, of the choices given, popular sovereignty is the most similar to a referendum.

Evaluation
2. (5) When the Supreme Court ruled that Dred Scott could be returned to his master, it was upholding the practice of treating slaves as personal property.

Exercise 6: The Vote on Secession
pages 106–107
Comprehension
1. (b) Virginia split in two over the issue of secession, with the western part (now known as West Virginia) loyal to the Union.
2. (c) Texas seceded from the Union despite the fact that only the eastern part of the state voted to do so.
3. (a) Kentucky was a border state that remained with the Union despite being a slave state.

Exercise 7: Growth of Big Business
page 108
Application
(2) and (3) are the situations that represent economic activity without government intervention. Choice (1) represents a government agency directing a business to do something.

Exercise 8: America Becomes Urbanized
page 108
Comprehension
1. (a) the 1920s
   (b) 70 million

Evaluation
2. (5) In 1930, the height of the bar for America's rural population is at about 52 million people; the bar for the urban population is at about 68 million people. The total population (rural and urban) was about 120 million, which is about half of the current population of 248 million.

Exercise 9: The United States Becomes a World Power
page 110
Analysis
1. (3) The Philippines were ceded to the United States under the terms of the treaty that ended the Spanish-American War; therefore, the U.S. establishment of military bases there is a result of a policy of expanding American control over other areas.
2. (4) The most likely explanation for America's isolationist position from the end of the Civil War until the Spanish-American War is that the country was preoccupied with healing its wounds and rebuilding the South after the Civil War.

Exercise 10: World War I
page 110
Comprehension
(1) Allies
(2) Treaty of Versailles
(3) League of Nations
(4) isolationism

Exercise 11: The New Deal
page 110
Application
1. (a)   2. (c)   3. (b)

Exercise 12: World War II
page 112
Comprehension
1. T   2. T   3. F

Exercise 13: Recent Decades
page 113
1. (d)   2. (f)   3. (a)   4. (c)   5. (e)   6. (b)

CHAPTER 3: POLITICAL SCIENCE

Exercise 1: Methods of Obtaining Power
page 115
Application
1. (4) France's overthrow of the monarchy in favor of a republican form of government is an example of a revolution.
2. (3) Because Hitler overpowered Chechoslovakia militarily, the method used to gain power is conquest.

Exercise 2: Legislative Representation
page 116
Application
1. (3) Alaska has the smallest population among those represented; therefore, it is likely to have the fewest representatives in the House.

Analysis
2. (5) Since the number of representatives a state has is based on its population, you can infer that New Jersey, in spite of its small size, is urban, industrialized, and densely populated. Dense populations are characteristic of urban, industrialized states.

Exercise 3: The Legislative Branch
page 117
Application
1. E The power to impose economic sanctions is not stated in the Constitution; therefore, the elastic clause applies.
2. C The power to pass tax laws is stated in the Constitution.
3. C The power to introduce legislation is stated in the Constitution.

Exercise 4: The Executive Branch
page 118
Application
1. (5) The passage states that strong presidents frequently use their veto power and attempt to dominate the legislature. The actions of Andrew Jackson best fit that description.

Analysis
2. (5) The vice president carries out many functions for the executive branch as a whole. Therefore, if the president and vice president are from different political parties, the president's effectiveness and ability to govern can suffer.

Exercise 5: The Judicial Branch
page 119
Comprehension
(4) The practice of deciding on the constitutionality of a law (which the Supreme Court does) is called the power of judicial review.

Exercise 6: States' vs. Individuals' Rights
page 119
Application
1. (No)
2. I In prohibiting states from outlawing abortions under certain conditions, the Supreme Court upheld the rights of the individual.
3. I In ruling that an accused must be informed of his or her rights, the Supreme Court supported the rights of the individual.

Exercise 7: The Enactment of a Law
page 120
Evaluation
(2) Choice (2) is supported by the part of the chart that shows that a bill must go to a conference committee for compromise. The chart does not indicate that a bill may be introduced directly to the president. A filibuster is an acceptable means by which a vote on a bill may be delayed. Bills introduced by *either* house may be amended as shown in the illustration. The chart shows that bills may become law without the president's signature if approved by two-thirds of both houses.

Exercise 8: System of Checks and Balances
page 120
Comprehension
1. (a) executive   (b) judicial
2. (a) legislative (b) executive
3. (a) judicial   (b) legislative

Exercise 9: Powers of State Government
page 121
Application
1. B   2. F   3. S

Exercise 10: The Political Spectrum
pages 122–123
Application
1. (2) Because the speaker advocates social improvement (improved bilingual programs) through governmental action, the speaker may be classified as a liberal.
2. (4) Because the speaker advocates maintaining the existing social order, the speaker may be classified as a conservative.
3. (1) Because the speaker advocates swift, sweeping changes in laws, the speaker may be classified as a radical.

Exercise 11: Political Parties
page 124
Application
1. R Republicans generally favor stronger state and local authority.
2. D Democrats generally endorse the efforts of labor unions.
3. D Democrats support government expenditures for the disadvantaged and minorities.

Exercise 12: Electing a President
page 125
Comprehension
1. (c) 2. (a) 3. (b)

Exercise 13: The Electoral Process
page 125
Evaluation
(2) Because the purpose of a closed primary is to give members of a party an opportunity to express their preferences for a candidate to run in a general election, it follows that voters must declare their party affiliation; otherwise, the purpose of a primary election is defeated.

CHAPTER 4: ECONOMICS
Exercise 1: Factors of Production
page 126
Application
1. C A plumber's tools are equipment used to provide a service.
2. N Diamonds are a raw material found in nature.
3. L Farmers who plant crops are laborers.

Exercise 2: Economic Systems and Governments
pages 127–128
Comprehension
1. (a) The quote reflects the capitalist feature of government's non-interference in business.
2. (4) Because capitalism and communism occupy the extremes of the continuum, you can conclude that they are opposites.

Exercise 3: Supply, Demand, and Equilibrium
pages 129–130
Comprehension
1. (4) The point where the lines intersect is at about $250.
Analysis
2. (3) As the price decreases, the demand increases.

Exercise 4: Money and Monetary Policy
page 132
Comprehension
1. T
2. T
3. F The **discount rate** is the interest rate the FED charges member banks to borrow; the **prime rate**, not mentioned in the passage, is the rate banks charge to their best customers.

Exercise 5: Fiscal and Monetary Policy
page 132
Comprehension
1. **decrease; lowering** Both actions put more money into the hands of consumers.
2. **decrease; raising; increasing** Inflation is an increase in the amount of money in circulation. To reduce inflation, the Fed reduces the amount of money in circulation by raising the discount rate. This makes it more costly for banks to borrow from the Fed. By increasing the reserve ratio, the Fed reduces the amount of money a bank can lend.

CHAPTER 5: GEOGRAPHY

Exercise 1: Measuring Distance
page 134
Comprehension

1. 900 miles
2. 1,050 miles

Exercise 2: Time Zones
page 136
Application

1. (2) Los Angeles falls within the Pacific time zone, which is three hours earlier than the Eastern time zone, in which Philadelphia falls.

Analysis

2. (5) Northwest Indiana is economically tied to the Chicago metropolitan area; therefore, for economic reasons it falls within the Central time zone.

Exercise 3: U.S. Topography
page 137
Analysis

1. (3) Denver (whose nickname is the "Mile High City") is located in the high plains at the eastern edge of the Rocky Mountains. None of the other cities listed is located close to a mountainous region.

2. (3) New Orleans is the only city represented that lies below sea level and experiences flooding because of its proximity to the Mississippi River. Las Vegas is located in a desert; Phoenix is located in a dry region of the country. Neither New York nor Atlanta lies below sea level.

Exercise 4: The Indian Subcontinent
page 138
Comprehension

1. (4) Mt. Everest, the highest mountain in the world, is also the highest point in the Himalayas at 29,028 feet above sea level.

2. (5) A glance at the map of the Indian subcontinent shows that the largest part of the land is between sea level and 1,000 feet. In the key, white indicates this level of elevation.

ANSWER KEY
TEST 3: SCIENCE

CHAPTER 1: BIOLOGY
Exercise 1: Cell Structure
page 142
Comprehension
1. (c) 2. (a) 3. (b) 4. (d)

Exercise 2: Cells
page 143
Comprehension
1. (4) Choices (1), (2), (3), and (5) are not the main idea. They are details that support the key idea that the cell is a highly organized, complex structure.

Analysis
2. (5) Chloroplasts are important in the food-making process for plants. Since animal cells have no chloroplasts, you can infer that animals must obtain their own food.

Application
3. (5) The organelle present in plants but not in animals that produces energy for important life processes is the chloroplast.

Exercise 3: Cells and Active Transport
page 144
Comprehension
1. high/low
2. low/high

Exercise 4: Diffusion and Osmosis
page 144
Analysis
1. (3) According to the passage, diffusion is the passage of molecules from an area of high concentration to an area of low concentration. This process allows for an even distribution of substances throughout all the cells of the body.
2. (5) In osmosis, water moves from a *lower* concentration to a *higher* one. The salt solution in the blood plasma is higher; therefore, the cell will lose water. If it loses water, it will shrink.

Exercise 5: Mitosis
page 146
Comprehension
1. (a) 2. (b) 3. (d) 4. (c)

Exercise 6: Meiosis
page 147
Comprehension
4, 1, 3, 2

Exercise 7: Cell Division
page 147
Comprehension
1. (3) Because of the exchange and recombination of chromosomal material, the method of reproduction that allows for the most variety is sexual reproduction.

Analysis
2. (3) Because cancerous cells spread to invade healthy cells, you can conclude that cancer cells divide more unpredictably than normal cells.

Exercise 8: Genetics and Heredity
page 148
Comprehension
1. (4) The diagram shows only one child out of four that does not have a dominant green eye gene or a dominant brown eye gene. This is the only child that will have blue eyes; therefore, the chances are that 25 percent of the children will have blue eyes.

Analysis
2. (3) The "Y" chromosome that determines a child's sex is carried by the father.

Exercise 9: The Nitrogen Cycle
page 149
Analysis
1. (1) The only case that shows a mutually beneficial relationship between two different organisms is that of bacteria that live in the stomachs of hoofed animals and at the same time help the animals digest food.

Application
2. (4) Soybeans are legumes and are important in the nitrogen-fixing process. The introduction of soybeans into the crop rotation process improves the possibility of replenishing the supply of nitrogen.

Exercise 10: Photosynthesis
page 150
Analysis

1. (5) Plants that do not possess chlorophyll must use a process other than photosynthesis to obtain the energy they need. One such process is parasitism, in which one organism feeds off another.

2. (1) Green pigment indicates the presence of chlorophyll. The areas of the coleus leaf that were green originally contained starch, which is produced through photosynthesis. Therefore, the starch turns brown when iodine is applied.

Exercise 11: Cellular Respiration
page 151
Analysis

1. (1) Glucose molecules must be present for cellular respiration to occur. Since glucose molecules are the end product of photosynthesis in plants, you can infer that photosynthesis must precede cellular respiration.

Application

2. (4) The more active a person is, the more energy he or she expends and the more carbon dioxide he or she exhales. Athletes are more active than most people; therefore, they would have higher rates of cellular respiration.

Evaluation

3. (4) The rate of cellular respiration is affected by whether or not a person is at rest or is physically active. Choices (3), (4), and (5) include both criteria; however, in choice (4) the greater number of students tested provides more reliable data.

Exercise 12: Classification of Organisms
pages 152–153
Application

1. (1) Streptococcus is a single-celled organism of the bacteria family and fits in the kingdom monera.

2. (3) Mold lacks chlorophyll and obtains food from another organism. It is classified in the kingdom fungi.

Exercise 13: Evolution and Natural Selection
page 154
Application

1. (3) According to the passage, certain forms of life adapted to meet the demands of the environment. The fact that the duckbill platypus is found only in and around Australia supports the hypothesis that the platypus developed independently in a closed environment during the early history of mammals.

Analysis

2. (1) Choice (1) is the best answer because choices (3), (4), and (5) are not true. Choice (2) is not true because the highest forms of animal life are placental mammals.

Evaluation

3. (4) Of the choices listed, the seal is the only mammal listed whose body is adapted for living in water—an environment that is not typically one in which mammals live.

Exercise 14: Ecology and Ecosystems
page 155
Application

1. grass
2. cattle and deer
3. mountain lion

Analysis

4. The destruction of the **mountain lion** led to the increase of grazing by **deer** and **cattle**, which led to **denuding** of the land and its eventual **erosion** by heavy rains.

CHAPTER 2: EARTH SCIENCE
Exercise 1: Stars and Galaxies
page 157
Comprehension
3, 4, 1, 2

Exercise 2: The Solar System
page 158
Application

(4) According to the story of Goldilocks and the Three Bears, Goldilocks tried one bowl of porridge that was too cold, another that was too hot, and a third that was just right. This corresponds to Mars being too cold, Venus too hot, and Earth just right to support life.

Exercise 3: The Planets
pages 158–159
Comprehension
1. Earth, Mars
2. Mercury
3. Venus

Exercise 4: Plate Tectonics
page 160
Comprehension
(5) In the passage, the occurrences of earth quakes, volcanoes, and mountains and the theory of continental drift are explained by the theory of plate tectonics.

Exercise 5: Earthquakes
pages 160–161
Evaluation
(3) The map shows the potential for most moderate and major earthquake damage occurring on the West Coast. Choices (1), (2), and (4) are directly contradicted by the map. Choice (5) is an opinion, not a fact.

Exercise 6: Continental Drift
page 161
Analysis
(3) This choice reflects an understanding of continental drift. Choice (1) is untrue, and choice (2) is not a good explanation.

Exercise 7: Measuring Geologic Time
page 162
Comprehension
1. (5) The text states that sedimentary rocks are deposited near Earth's surface and that metamorphic rock is located just below igneous rock.
Analysis
2. (5) The trilobite rocks are likely to be older than the coral because the greater depth at which a fossil is found, the older it is likely to be.

Exercise 8: Minerals and Rocks
page 163
Analysis
1. (3) Potassium, which makes up 1.85 percent of Earth's crust, is the only element that occupies more than three times as much space as does silicon.
2. (5) The fact that oxygen combines with most of Earth's elements explains why it constitutes such a great part of Earth's crust. Choices (1), (2), and (3) are not true. Choice (4) has no relation to the issue of the composition of Earth's crust.

Exercise 9: The Changing Earth
page 164
Application
(5) Choice (5) is a procedure most farmers follow to increase their chances of a bountiful harvest and has nothing to do with preventing erosion.

Exercise 10: Change in Sea Level
page 165
Comprehension
(5) According to the graph, nearly 18,000 years ago the depth of the oceans was at almost 400 feet below today's sea level.

Exercise 11: The Oceans' Beginning
pages 165–166
Comprehension
1. (4) At 0.001 percent, water vapor in the atmosphere yields the lowest amount of water on Earth.
Analysis
2. (4) According to the text, many scientists believe that oceans were formed by the release of water bound up in Earth's interior.

Exercise 12: The Oceans' Tides
pages 166–167
Analysis
1. (5) According to the illustration, the Moon is in a direct line with the Sun and receives the Sun's greatest attractive force. The periods when this occurs are at full moon and new moon.
Application
2. (2) The opposite condition of syzygy results in unusually low tides because the gravitational pull of the Moon and the Sun on Earth is at its weakest.

Exercise 13: Layers of Earth's Atmosphere
page 168
Comprehension
1. (4) The ionosphere extends from 30 miles to 300 miles in Earth's atmosphere. Noctilucent clouds are found at heights above 40 miles.
2. (3) "D" radio waves are found at the same level as noctilucent clouds— in the lower ionosphere.
3. (5) Clouds (located in the troposphere) shown at the same level as Mt. Everest's peak suggest that the peak may be hidden by clouds.

Exercise 14: Ozone in the Atmosphere
page 169
Analysis
(2) Smog is visible and, therefore, lies in the troposphere, the level of the atmosphere closest to Earth.

Exercise 15: The Water Cycle
pages 169–170
Comprehension
5, 3, 1, 4, 2

Exercise 16: Humidity
page 170
Analysis
1. (4) According to the passage, warm air holds more moisture than cold air; therefore, when the temperature drops, the colder air cannot hold the amount of moisture that the warmer air held. As a result, the saturation point is reached and excess humidity is released. At 45 degrees, the precipitation will most likely be rain.

2. (3) At a given time, water vapor in the air is constant. Cold air can hold less moisture than warm air. When air is heated, it has the capacity to hold more water. If moisture is not added to the air, the humidity level goes down.

Exercise 17: Air Masses, Fronts, and Weather
page 171
Comprehension
1. (2) According to the passage, warm fronts bring low-lying clouds, steady winds, and drizzling rain.

Evaluation
2. (5) The passage discusses all of the properties affecting fronts except the direction in which the air mass moves.

CHAPTER 3: CHEMISTRY
Exercise 1: Atomic Structure
page 173
Understanding Ideas
1. (d) 2. (e) 3. (f) 4. (b) 5. (c) 6. (a)

Exercise 2: Nuclear Energy
page 174
Application
1. (4) The passage states that fusion involves the uniting of two nuclei of a chemical element at high temperatures and pressures to form a new element. Hydrogen, the lightest element, is the only one listed whose nuclei when fused can form the second lightest element—helium.

2. (1) The passage states that fission involves the splitting of the nucleus of a heavy element. Plutonium is not a gas and, therefore, is the only heavy element shown.

Exercise 3: Isotopic Elements
pages 174–175
Application
1. (3) According to the chart, lithium's atomic mass is 6.94. Of all the elements shown, it would be the most likely to have an isotope of 6. If two lithium isotopes are fused, the atomic mass of the new element would be 12—the atomic mass of carbon 12.

2. (1) According to the passage, an isotope is a form of an element that varies in the number of neutrons in its nucleus. The only element represented that is capable of doubling or tripling its mass to achieve a final mass of 2 or 3 would be hydrogen, with an atomic mass of 1.01.

Exercise 4: Elements and Periodicity
page 177
Application
1. (4) The passage states that as the atomic number increases for elements in a column, similar chemical properties occur regularly and to a greater degree. The only *physical* property that gold would have a higher degree of would be malleability because it is a soft and workable metal. Choices (1), (2), and (5) are not physical properties. Choice (3) is not true of gold or the other metals.

Evaluation
2. (4) The fact that radon is found in the ground, choice (1), suggests that it is denser and weighs more than the others. Also, the fact that it has a higher atomic number, choice (2), indicates that its properties, including weight and density, are greater than those of other elements in its family.

Exercise 5: Balanced Equations
page 178
Comprehension
1. **B** The reaction begins and ends with two atoms of nitrogen (N) and two atoms of oxygen (O).
2. **U** The reaction begins with one atom of iron (Fe), one atom of hydrogen (H), and one atom of chlorine (Cl). However, it ends with one atom of iron, two atoms of hydrogen, and three atoms of chlorine. Therefore, it is not balanced.
3. **B** The reaction begins and ends with two atoms of hydrogen (H) and one atom of oxygen (O).

Exercise 6: Chemical Reactions
pages 178–179
Analysis
1. **(2)** None of the others are balanced equations indicating one molecule of carbon dioxide (CO_2) and one molecule of water (H_2O). Choice (4) starts with carbon dioxide and water but does not result in a balanced equation.

Comprehension
2. **(2)** According to the passage, a chemical equation is balanced when it follows the law of conservation of matter, which states that matter can neither be created nor destroyed.

Evaluation
3. **(4)** The fact that there is a copper coating on the aluminum is the only evidence cited that can prove that a chemical change has taken place.

Exercise 7: Types of Substances
page 180
Application
1. **(1)** Salt is a compound composed of the elements sodium and chlorine and has properties different from each.
2. **(2)** Air is a mixture composed of at least four gases. Each gas retains its own distinct properties.

Exercise 8: Compounds and Chemical Bonding
page 181
Comprehension
1. **(2)** The passage says that ionic bonding is achieved by the transfer of electrons.
2. **(1)** The passage says that a covalent bond is one in which atoms are held together by sharing electrons.

Exercise 9: Acids, Bases, and Salts
pages 182–183
Analysis
1. **(4)** Acetic acid, a mild acid contained in vinegar, would be found at the acidic end of the pH scale closest to neutrality—between the values 4 and 5. Choices (1) and (5) represent alkalinity, not acidity, and choices (2) and (3) represent high acidity.
2. **(3)** Water is neither acidic nor alkaline; therefore, it would neutral on the pH scale.

Evaluation
3. **(5)** A substance is an acid if it tastes sour (2) or neutralizes a base (3). An acid has a pH reading under 7, so (1) is eliminated.

Exercise 10: A Car Battery
pages 183–184
Application
1. **(2)** In the example, sulfuric acid, a conductor of electricity, is dissolved in water.
2. **(1)** The passage says that the lead loses two electrons when it reacts with sulfuric acid; therefore, lead is oxidized.
3. **(2)** Sulfuric acid is an oxidizing agent because it causes the lead in the battery to lose electrons. The lead dioxide is a reducing agent because it causes the sulfuric acid to gain electrons.

Analysis
4. **(4)** A battery is completely discharged when the sulfuric acid is no longer capable of oxidizing lead, and the lead dioxide is no longer able to reduce the sulfuric acid; thus, the oxidation-reduction process that causes an electric current to flow cannot occur.

Exercise 11: Reaction Rate, Catalysts, and Equilibrium
page 185
Analysis
1. **(3)** A catalyst is an agent that speeds up a chemical reaction but that is not affected by the reaction itself. Lipase speeds up the rate at which fats are changed into fatty acids. Because lipase is found in the body, it may be described as a biological catalyst. A negative catalyst (2) inhibits, or slows down, a chemical reaction.

Application

2. (5) According to the passage, chemical equilibrium occurs when the rate of forward reaction balances the rate of reverse reaction. In photosynthesis (2), plants take in water and carbon dioxide from the air to make starch with the Sun's help. The by-product oxygen is released. The reverse of this process is respiration (3), the taking in of oxygen by animals and the combining of oxygen with starch to form carbon dioxide and water, which the plants use for photosynthesis. Thus, the forward reaction of photosynthesis is balanced by the reverse reaction of respiration, resulting in chemical equilibrium.

CHAPTER 4: PHYSICS

Exercise 1: Laws of Force and Motion
page 187
Application
1. AF   2. AR   3. G   4. I

Exercise 2: The Force of Gravity
page 187
Comprehension

(1) Weight is a function of the attractive force of one object on another. According to the passage, the strength of the force depends on the masses of the objects. Since Jupiter is larger than Earth, the attractive force must be greater. This would result in an increase in the astronaut's weight relative to his weight on Earth.

Exercise 3: Forms of Energy
page 188
Application
1. K   2. P

Exercise 4: Types of Energy
pages 188–189
Application
1. (1) Nuclear energy results from the splitting of an atom of a heavy chemical element such as U-235.
2. (2) Gas and air are mixtures. When they are ignited, combustion, a chemical process, occurs.

Exercise 5: Simple Machines
page 189
Analysis

(3) According to the passage, the greater distance between the fulcrum and the applied force, the less force required to perform the work. If the distance is increased to 20 feet, then the effort would be halved:
$100 \div 2 = 50$ pounds of applied force.

Exercise 6: Kinetic Theory of Matter
page 191
Comprehension
1. T   2. F   3. T

Exercise 7: Heat and Temperature
page 191
Analysis

(4) Reinforced concrete could not maintain its durability if the two materials, concrete and steel, expanded and contracted at different temperatures—so (1) is correct. Also, because reinforced concrete does not buckle as asphalt does, you can infer that reinforced concrete must expand at a higher temperature than asphalt—so (2) is correct. Choice (3) is not true since reinforced concrete is known to expand and contract.

Exercise 8: Wave Types
page 192
Application
1. T   2. L   3. T

Exercise 9: Properties of Waves
page 193
Comprehension

(3) The passage states that wavelength is the distance between two successive wave crests or troughs. Points Z and Y are two successive wave crests.

Exercise 10: The Photoelectric Principle
page 194
Evaluation

(5) The passage states that an active substance emits electrons when light falls on it. Light intensity determines the strength of the current generated by the emission of electrons. This suggests that light energy is transmitted in packets or bundles and disputes the belief that light exists only as a continuous wave.

Exercise 11: Properties of Light Waves
page 195
Application

1. (2) Refraction is the bending of light waves as they pass from one medium to another—in this case, from water to air.

2. (1) Reflection is the return of a light wave when it strikes a shiny surface.

Exercise 12: Electricity and Magnetism
page 197
Analysis

1. (1) According to the information in the text, the strong magnetic attraction coming from Earth's core tends to align the compass's needle in a northerly-southerly direction.

Comprehension

2. (4) A magnetized object will attract either end of an unmagnetized object made of iron, steel, nickel, or cobalt, but will attract only the opposite pole of another magnetized object. Aluminum, brass, and tin cannot be attracted.

Exercise 13: Conductors and Insulators
page 198
Application

1. I 2. C 3. I 4. C 5. I

Exercise 14: Electromagnets
page 198
Analysis

(3) The only plausible reason listed for a radio's not being placed near navigational instruments is that the radio's electromagnet would exert an attractive force on the compass of a ship or plane, thus throwing it off course. Choices (1) and (2) have nothing to do with navigational instruments. Choices (4) and (5) are neither plausible nor true.

ANSWER KEY
TEST 4: LITERATURE AND THE ARTS

CHAPTER 1: INTERPRETING PROSE FICTION

Exercise 1: Atmosphere as Part of Setting
page 203
Inferential

The words that indicate fear are *crouching, running, dodging, hide,* and *stiffened.*

Exercise 2: Determining Point of View
page 206
Application

The words you should have underlined are in *italic* type, and the words you should have circled appear in **bold** type.

Macomber stepped out of the curved opening at the side of the front seat, onto the step and down onto the ground. The **lion** still stood looking majestically and coolly toward this object that **his** eyes only showed in silhouette, bulking like some super-rhino. There was no *man* smell carried toward **him** and **he** watched the object [jeep], moving **his** great head a little from side to side. Then watching the object, not afraid, but hesitating before going down the bank to drink with such a thing opposite **him, he** saw a *man figure* detach *itself* from it and **he** turned **his** heavy head and swung away toward the cover of the trees as **he** heard a cracking crash and felt the slam of a .30–06 220-grain solid bullet that bit **his** flank and ripped in sudden hot scalding nausea through **his** stomach. **He** trotted, heavy, big-footed, swinging wounded full-bellied, through the trees toward the tall grass and cover, and the crash came again to go past **him** ripping the air apart. Then it crashed again and **he** felt the blow as it hit **his** lower ribs and ripped on through, blood sudden hot and frothy in **his** mouth, and **he** galloped toward the high grass where **he** could crouch and not be seen and make *them* bring the crashing thing close enough so **he** could make a rush and get the *man* that held it.

Exercise 3: Inferring Theme
pages 206–207
Inferential

1. (5) The excerpt concerns Miss Strangeworth's fighting "possible evil lurking nearby."

2. (3) While Miss Strangeworth's motives may have seemed good for her, her actions hurt innocent people.

Exercise 4: Tone and Characterization
page 208
Analysis

1. (4) The last two sentences point to a funny and sarcastic tone of voice.

2. (3) The author seems to feel that people like Julian's mother require tolerance and sympathy.

Exercise 5: Identifying an Author's Style
pages 209–210
Analysis

The descriptions and images that appeal to the senses appear in *italic* type.

The soprano screak of carriage wheels punished my ear. Sun, *seeping through the blinds, filled the bedroom* with a *sulphurous light.* I didn't know how long I had slept, but I *felt one big twitch of exhaustion.*

The twin bed next to mine was empty and unmade.

At seven I had *heard my mother get up, slip into her clothes* and *tiptoe out of the room.* Then the *buzz of the orange squeezer sounded* from downstairs, and the *smell of coffee* and *bacon filtered under my door.* Then the *sink water ran from the tap and dishes clinked* as my mother dried them and put them back in the cupboard.

Then the *front door opened and shut.* Then the *car door opened and shut,* and the *motor went broom-broom* and, edging off with a *crunch of gravel, faded into the distance.*

Exercise 6: Commentary About Fiction
pages 211–212
Literal

1. (2) The review states that "one wants to follow Putus's life as a young woman instead of returning to her decades later. . . ."

Inferential

2. (1) The last sentence of the review makes it clear that the reviewer admires the writer's story-telling abilities.

Application

3. (4) The review of the book indicates that it fits only the real-life drama category.

CHAPTER 2: INTERPRETING POETRY

Exercise 1: Interpreting Two Poems
pages 213–214
Inferential

1. (4) Romantic love is mentioned in both poems; it is referred to repeatedly in Sonnet 43.

Analysis

2. (3) Both poems include rhyme. Rhyming words in "Oh, When I Was in Love with You" include *you* and *grew*, *brave* and *behave*, and *remain* and *again*; rhyming words in Sonnet 43 include *height* and *sight*.

Exercise 2: The Shape of Poetry
pages 215–216
Literal

1. There are three sentences; a period ends each sentence.

Inferential

2. At the end of the second stanza, Grandma smiles. *Smiled* is the clue word that indicates the mood of contentment.

3. The narrator is the grandchild of a Hispanic migrant farm worker.

Exercise 3: The Sound of Poetry
pages 216–217
Analysis

1. Some examples of alliteration are
   (1) "maggie and milly and molly and may"
   (2) "a shell that sang / so sweetly she . . ."
   (3) "blowing bubbles"
   (4) "smooth round stone / as small . . ."
   (You may have found others.)

2. Lines 3 and 4 and 7 and 8 do not rhyme at all.

Inferential

3. (4) The author says that when we "lose" ourselves, the sea can give us a new view on life.

Exercise 4: Words that Stand for Sounds
pages 217–218
Analysis

1. (5) *batter* and *banjos*; alliteration is a repetition of a beginning consonant sound.

2. (3) The word *like* makes a comparison between two things—moan and autumn wind. The sound of the autumn wind is given a human quality.

Exercise 5: Inferring Meaning
page 219
Inferential

1. Inference: The man is a father.
   Lines: 2–3
   Key words: *once balanced our young sons*

2. Inference: The man was athletic.
   Line: 6
   Key words: *once pitched no-hitters*

3. Inference: The man is now elderly.
   Lines 11–12
   Key words: *now crudely arches to grasp a bamboo cane.*
   Line: 14
   Key words: *bow your feeble body in prayer*

Exercise 6: The Language of Poetry
page 221
Analysis

Line 1: imagery
Line 2: personification
Line 3: personification

Exercise 7: More Practice in Interpreting a Poem
page 222
Literal

1. b, c, a, e, d

Analysis

2. (3) Death and Immortality are characters who ride in the carriage with the narrator.

Inferential

3. (5) From the last stanza, we can infer that the poet believes that the narrator was taken from earth but lives on.

Exercise 8: Commentary on Poetry
page 223
Inferential

1. (2) The reviewer (quoting Shakespeare's *Hamlet*) states "that 'the slings and arrows of outrageous fortune' are often gifts which make us stronger."

2. (1) This is a simpler rewording of the cliché.

CHAPTER 3: INTERPRETING DRAMA

Exercise 1: Dialogue and Punctuation
page 225
Literal

1. **Edward and Victoria** The ellipses indicate that Catherine interrupts Edward's speech.
2. **Edward** Edward is bothered by Catherine's interruption.
3. **Edward** Victoria's tone and responses to Edward indicate that she is upset with him.

Exercise 2: Inferring Mood from Dialogue
page 225
Analysis

(1) The rudeness of Edward toward Catherine, Victoria's responses to Edward, and Catherine's abrupt departure all indicate that the mood of the scene is tense.

Exercise 3: Understanding Character
pages 227–228
Inferential

1. (3) In the scene, Jessie's mother asks her a series of questions, including where Jessie put her glasses. Mama's initial statement, "I want to know why," and Jessie's response, "You have no earthly idea of how I feel," suggest that a lack of communication exists between mother and daughter. None of the other choices is supported by the dialogue in the scene.
2. (4) The scene contains several lines of dialogue in which Mama criticizes Jessie for being ungrateful and distant. Also, Mama blames Jessie for Cecil's leaving.

Analysis

3. (4) The angry, accusing tone shown by Jessie's mother and Jessie's responses to her mother suggest a mood of tension.

Exercise 4: Supporting Facts and Inferences
page 229
Inferential

1. Support for the inference that Jessie is separated from Cecil are the following lines: "Why did Cecil leave you?" "Cecil left me because he made me choose between him and smoking." "Cecil left for pretty much the same reason."

2. The inference that Jessie is confused about what her mother wants to know is supported by the lines of dialogue: "Back where?" "What are you talking about?"

3. Support for the inference that Mama doesn't believe Jessie's story about the accident is the line of dialogue, "How did you fall off the horse, really?"

Exercise 5: Interpreting a Scene from a Play
pages 229–230
Inferential

1. (3) Alice's second line of dialogue, in which she suggests finding a home for her father (like her husband Sidney did for his parents) and the discussion about powers of attorney imply that she and Gene are sister and brother. Another clue to their relationship comes later in the scene: "He broke Mother's heart over that for years."

Application

2. (5) Alice's first line of dialogue, in which she says "I'm doing a lot for my kids. I don't expect them to pay me back at the other end," suggests that she believes elderly parents should not expect their children to take care of them.

Inferential

3. (2) Based on Gene's dialogue, he is not relieved; he is ashamed that he can't ask his father to live with him.

Literal

4. (4) Gene's line, "I can't tell you how ashamed I feel . . . not to say with open arms, 'Poppa, come live with me. . . . I love you, Poppa, and I want to take care of you,'" indicates that he feels guilty for not loving his father.

Exercise 6: Interpreting a Film Review
pages 231–232
Analysis
1. (2) The fact that the novel *The Last Tycoon* was unfinished and that Pinter and Kazan nevertheless were able to turn the book into a "fascinating low-key film" implies an attitude of admiration.

Literal
2. (1) The passage states directly that "Stahr himself is a flawed human being."

Inferential
3. (5) Because "Hollywood Boosters" are supporters of Hollywood, and these supporters are likely to be movie producers, the implication is that the film will offend the producers of Hollywood films.

CHAPTER 4: INTERPRETING NONFICTION

Exercise 1: Biography
pages 233–234
Analysis
1. (5) The significance of Thoreau's move to Walden Pond on July 4 is that the date is the anniversary of the nation's independence. On that date, Thoreau was declaring his own independence.

Application
2. (4) While secluded in the woods, Thoreau reflected on the meaning and beauty of life. The other choices have nothing to do with considering the meaning of life.

Literal
3. (1) The passage states that the essay "On the Duty of Civil Disobedience" influenced the works of Gandhi and Martin Luther King, Jr.

Inferential
4. (2) The passage states that Thoreau was imprisoned for refusing to pay a poll tax that supported the Mexican War. Thoreau's action is an example of nonviolent resistance to an unjust law.

Exercise 2: Oral History
page 235
Literal
1. F The passage relates sadness and hope and Chavez's belief that "you don't let [things] get you down."
2. T The passage says that when you're small, you don't question things; you continue to move.

3. T The passage states that "'Following the crops,' we missed much school."
4. F The entire passage describes the effect the Depression had on Chavez's family.

Exercise 3: Autobiography
pages 236–237
Inferential
1. (5) The passage describes the teacher as being unaware, insensitive, and uninterested in the author. She is not described as being understanding.

Analysis
2. (4) The only similarity between Chavez's childhood and Gregory's is that both made successful lives despite their childhood poverty. Choices (1), (2), (3), and (5) are not true of *both* men's childhoods.
3. (5) The title suggests that people do not always think of themselves the way others might think of them. The other choices are not supported by the passage.

Exercise 4: Journal Entries
page 237
Inferential
1. (5) The quote refers to experimenting with life. Experimenting involves taking a risk. The other choices are not supported by the advice in the quote.

Application
2. (3) An astronaut's occupation involves a greater degree of physical risk than the other choices provided.

Exercise 5: The Formal Essay
pages 238–239
Inferential
1. (4) The word *duty* implies an obligation; therefore, the title suggests that a person is obligated to break an unjust law.
2. (3) The government represents the people and is the means by which a people carry out their desires. The other choices do not help to define government in this sense.
3. (1) According to the essay, "The government . . . is only the mode which the people have chosen to execute their will."

Exercise 6: Comparing and Contrasting Styles
pages 239–241
Analysis
1. (3) The short essay is characterized by all of the choices given except long, explanatory paragraphs.

Inferential
2. (4) The statement and the entire thrust of the passage show the agent's total dependence on the computer.

Analysis
3. (4) Passage 2 lacks the humor of Passage 1.

Inferential
4. (3) Throughout the excerpt, the author talks about psychological problems caused by electronic offices—for example, "a rise in loneliness and disconnection" and "fragmentation of self."

Application
5. (4) Both passages illustrate our dependence on and trust in computers. Both writers feel we should retain control over computers.

Exercise 7: Practice Interpreting A Speech
pages 241–242
Analysis
1. (4) As the first speech of his presidency, Kennedy wants to inspire listeners.
2. (3) The most persuasive call to serve the public is in the second to the last paragraph: "ask not what your country can do for you; ask what you can do for your country."
3. (1) The speech does not rhyme or display a standardized rhythmic pattern.

Exercise 8: Interpreting a Book Review
pages 243–244
Analysis
1. +   2. –   3. F

Exercise 9: Interpreting a Review of a Novel
page 244
Analysis
1. (5) The only choice that reflects on the author's skillfulness in creating characters are the words *memorable* and *unique*.

Application
2. (2) The statements "A producer's lunch at Sardi's is preposterous" and "tritely portrayed show-biz worlds of New York or Hollywood" reflect the critic's view that the New York scenes are flawed.

Exercise 10: Interpreting Musical Commentary
pages 244–245
Inferential
1. (2) The reviewer describes Marsalis as belonging to an elite—a superior group. This statement indicates admiration for the musician.

Application
2. (2) To *nurture* means "to further one's development." This suggests that the critic supports Marsalis's improvement of the tradition.

Exercise 11: Interpreting a Painting
pages 245–246
Literal
1. (5) The only topic not discussed in the review is the cost of Wyeth's paintings.

Inferential
2. (3) The passage refers to Wyeth's simplicity twice—"a thoughtful simplicity" and "The simplicity of Wyeth's work discourages complexity of thought. . . ."

Exercise 12: Interpreting a Television Review
page 247
Inferential
1. (5) The reviewer says of "the classic" "M★A★S★H" it "made us laugh till we cried."

Application
2. (2) The reviewer states, "Like all great sitcoms ["M★A★S★H"] succeeded mainly by exploring, indeed celebrating, the chemistry between the characters."

Analysis
3. (1) The reviewer showed his admiration for all the sitcoms discussed.

TEST 5: MATHEMATICS ANSWER KEY

CHAPTER 1: DECIMALS

Exercise 1: Reading Decimals
page 252
1. .05
2. 100.002
3. (a) .7   (c) 305.056
   (b) 2000.08   (d) .0065

Exercise 2: Comparing Decimals
page 253
1. (a) .05   (c) .7
   (b) 4.10   (d) .51
   (e) 1.033
2. 4.67; 4.067; 4.0067

Exercise 3: Rounding Decimals
page 254
1. .375 rounds to **.38**
2. 8.275 rounds to **8.3**
3. 101.68 rounds to **102**

Exercise 4: Adding and Subtracting Decimals
page 255

1. **17.91**
$$\begin{array}{r} 5.9 \\ 2.46 \\ 6 \\ 3.07 \\ + \ .48 \\ \hline 17.91 \end{array}$$

2. **37.8**
$$\begin{array}{r} 43.0 \\ - \ 5.2 \\ \hline 37.8 \end{array}$$

3. **968.749 meters**
$$\begin{array}{r} 237.42 \\ 150.045 \\ 186.21 \\ 298.674 \\ + \ 96.4 \\ \hline 968.749 \text{ meters} \end{array}$$

4. **$357.56**

STEP 1
$$\begin{array}{r} \$42.87 \\ 5.93 \\ 10.00 \\ 17.48 \\ + \ 38.40 \\ \hline \$114.68 \end{array}$$

STEP 2
$$\begin{array}{r} \$472.24 \\ - \ 114.68 \\ \hline \$357.56 \end{array}$$

5. **$265.27**

STEP 1
Add up parts:
$$\begin{array}{r} \$17.50 \\ 4.95 \\ 6.00 \\ 13.44 \\ + \ 60.75 \\ \hline \$102.64 \end{array}$$

STEP 2
Add:
Parts	$102.64
Labor	160.00
Tax	+ 2.63
	265.27

Exercise 5: Multiplying and Dividing Decimals
page 259

1. **.513**
$$\begin{array}{r} .342 \\ \times \ 1.5 \\ \hline 1710 \\ 342 \\ \hline .5130 = .513 \end{array}$$

2. **$22.75**
$$\begin{array}{r} \$6.50 \\ \times \ \ 3.5 \\ \hline 3\,250 \\ 19\,50 \\ \hline \$22.750 = \$22.75 \end{array}$$

3. **120.1**
$$\begin{array}{r} 120.1 \\ .05\overline{)6.005} \\ 5 \\ \hline 1\,0 \\ 1\,0 \\ \hline 0 \\ 0 \\ \hline 05 \\ 5 \\ \hline 0 \end{array}$$

4. **.004**
$$\begin{array}{r} .004 \\ 3\overline{).012} \\ 0 \\ \hline 01 \\ 0 \\ \hline 12 \\ 12 \\ \hline 0 \end{array}$$

5. $472 \times 10{,}000 =$ **4,720,000**
6. $456.12 \div 100 =$ **4.5612**
7. **(3)** $(3.5 \times 1.19) + 2 \times 2.30)$

Exercise 6: Estimating
page 259

1. *estimate:* $9 \times 10 =$ **$90**
2. *estimate:* $36 \div 2 =$ **18**

Exercise 7: Decimal Word Problems
pages 259–260

1. **(2) 3**
$$\begin{array}{r} 3.75 \\ 3.2\overline{)12.0\,00} \\ 9\,6 \\ \hline 2\,4\,0 \\ 2\,2\,4 \\ \hline 1\,6\,0 \\ 1\,6\,0 \\ \hline 0 \end{array}$$

3.75 shelves can be cut, but only 3 *complete* shelves can be cut.

2. (3) 8.6408

$$\begin{array}{r} 3.086 \\ \times\ \ 2.8 \\ \hline 2\,4\,688 \\ 6\,1\,72\ \ \\ \hline 8.6\,408 \end{array}$$

3. (2) $320.54

Gross Earnings:	Total Deductions:	Net Pay:
$265.72	$27.03	$434.47
+ 168.75	+ 86.90	− 113.93
$434.47	$113.93	$320.54

4. (2) 16.1

Miles Traveled:
$$\begin{array}{r} 8747.6 \\ -\ 7353.2 \\ \hline 1394.4 \end{array}$$

Miles per Gallon: 16.13 rounds to 16.1

$$\begin{array}{r} 86.4\,)\overline{1394.4\,00} \\ 864\ \ \ \ \ \\ \hline 530\,4\ \ \ \\ 518\,4\ \ \ \\ \hline 12\,0\,0\ \\ 8\,6\,4\ \\ \hline 3\,3\,60 \\ 2\,5\,92 \\ \hline 7\,68 \end{array}$$

CHAPTER 2: FRACTIONS

Exercise 1: Types of Fractions
page 261

1. like fractions and improper fractions
2. mixed numbers
3. proper fractions and unlike fractions

Exercise 2: Raising and Reducing Fractions
page 262

1. (a) $\frac{9}{24}$
   (b) $\frac{6}{7}\frac{(\times 4)}{(\times 4)} = \frac{24}{28}$
2. (a) $\frac{3}{4}$
   (b) $\frac{30}{42}\frac{(\div 6)}{(\div 6)} = \frac{5}{7}$
3. (a) $\frac{6}{8}\frac{(\div 2)}{(\div 2)} = \frac{3}{4}$
   (b) $\frac{25}{30}\frac{(\div 5)}{(\div 5)} = \frac{5}{6}$

Exercise 3: Changing Fractions to Decimals
page 000

1. (a) $\frac{7}{100}$
   (b) $.32 = \frac{32}{100}\frac{(\div 4)}{(\div 4)} = \frac{8}{25}$
   (c) $3.1 = 3\frac{1}{10}$

2. (a) $.37 = .37\frac{4}{8} = .37\frac{1}{2}$

$$\begin{array}{r} .37 \\ 8\,)\overline{3.00} \\ 2\,4\ \\ \hline 60 \\ 56 \\ \hline 4 \end{array}$$

   (b) $1.33 = 1.33\frac{1}{3}$

$$\begin{array}{r} 1.33 \\ 3\,)\overline{4.00} \\ 3\ \ \\ \hline 1\,0 \\ 9 \\ \hline 10 \\ 9 \\ \hline 1 \end{array}$$

   (c) $.83 = .83\frac{2}{6} = .83\frac{1}{3}$

$$\begin{array}{r} .83 \\ 6\,)\overline{5.00} \\ 4\,8 \\ \hline 20 \\ 18 \\ \hline 2 \end{array}$$

Exercise 4: Changing Improper Fractions and Mixed Numbers
page 265

1. (a) $12\frac{1}{4} = \frac{(12\times 4)+1}{4} = \frac{48+1}{4} = \frac{49}{4}$
   (b) $6\frac{2}{3} = \frac{(6\times 3)+2}{3} = \frac{18+2}{3} = \frac{20}{3}$

2. (a) $\frac{9}{9} = $

$$\begin{array}{r} 1 = 1 \\ 9\,)\overline{9} \\ 9 \\ \hline 0 \end{array}$$

   (b) $\frac{17}{5} = $

$$\begin{array}{r} 3 = 3\frac{2}{5} \\ 5\,)\overline{17} \\ 15 \\ \hline 2 \end{array}$$

Exercise 5: Comparing Numbers
page 268

1. (a) $\frac{7}{8} > \frac{3}{5}$ $\frac{7}{8}\frac{(\times 5)}{(\times 5)} = \frac{35}{40}$
   $\frac{3}{5}\frac{(\times 8)}{(\times 8)} = \frac{24}{40}$
   (b) $\frac{2}{3} > \frac{4}{9}$ $\frac{2}{3}\frac{(\times 3)}{(\times 3)} = \frac{6}{9}$
   $\frac{4}{9} = \frac{4}{9}$

2. **(a)** $3 < 8$

(b) $\frac{3}{4} = \frac{9}{12}$

$\frac{2}{3} = \frac{8}{12}$

$\frac{3}{4} > \frac{2}{3}$

(c) $2\frac{3}{8} = \frac{19}{8}$

$\frac{5}{2} = \frac{20}{8}$

$2\frac{3}{8} < \frac{5}{2}$

(d) $\frac{9}{9} = 1$

$\frac{2}{2} = 1$

$\frac{9}{9} = \frac{2}{2}$

(e) $.07 = .0700$

$.0873 = .0873$

$.07 < .0873$

Exercise 6: Adding and Subtracting Fractions
page 270

1. $\frac{11}{12}$ $\begin{array}{r} \frac{2}{3} = \frac{8}{12} \\ + \frac{1}{4} = \frac{3}{12} \\ \hline \frac{11}{12} \end{array}$

2. $10\frac{1}{24}$ $\begin{array}{r} 3\frac{7}{8} = 3\frac{21}{24} \\ 2\frac{5}{6} = 2\frac{20}{24} \\ + 3\frac{1}{3} = 3\frac{8}{24} \\ \hline 8\frac{49}{24} = 8 + 2\frac{1}{24} = 10\frac{1}{24} \end{array}$

3. $\frac{3}{5}$ $\begin{array}{r} \frac{9}{10} \\ - \frac{3}{10} \\ \hline \frac{6}{10} = \frac{3}{5} \end{array}$

4. $\frac{3}{10}$ $\begin{array}{r} \frac{4}{5} = \frac{8}{10} \\ - \frac{1}{2} = \frac{5}{10} \\ \hline \frac{3}{10} \end{array}$

5. $13\frac{2}{3}$ $\begin{array}{r} 25\frac{1}{6} = 25\frac{1}{6} = 24\frac{7}{6} \\ - 11\frac{1}{2} = 11\frac{3}{6} = 11\frac{3}{6} \\ \hline 13\frac{4}{6} = 13\frac{2}{3} \end{array}$

6. $6\frac{15}{17}$ $\begin{array}{r} 10 \ = 9\frac{17}{17} \\ - 3\frac{2}{17} = 3\frac{2}{17} \\ \hline 6\frac{15}{17} \end{array}$

Exercise 7: Multiplying Fractions
page 272

1. $\frac{3}{8} \times \frac{2}{15} \times \frac{6}{7} = \frac{6}{140} = \frac{3}{70}$

2. $8\frac{1}{6} \times 4 = \frac{49}{6} \times \frac{4}{1} = \frac{98}{3} = \mathbf{32\frac{2}{3}}$

3. $2\frac{1}{2} \times 2\frac{1}{3} - \frac{5}{2} \times \frac{7}{3} = \frac{35}{6} = \mathbf{5\frac{5}{6}}$

4. $2\frac{3}{4} \times \frac{6}{7} = \frac{11}{4} \times \frac{6}{7} = \frac{33}{14} = \mathbf{2\frac{5}{14}}$

Exercise 8: Dividing Fractions
page 273

1. $\frac{2}{5} \div 4 = \frac{2}{5} \times \frac{1}{4} = \frac{1}{10}$

2. $\frac{3}{7} \div \frac{6}{35} = \frac{3}{7} \times \frac{35}{6} = \frac{5}{2} = \mathbf{2\frac{1}{2}}$

3. $9 \div 2\frac{1}{2} = \frac{9}{1} \times \frac{2}{5} = \frac{18}{5} = \mathbf{3\frac{3}{5}}$

Exercise 9: Item Sets
page 274

1. **(3)** $\frac{19}{40}$ **mile**

Information: $\frac{7}{8}$ mile; $\frac{2}{5}$ mile (from map)

Length of Pine Way:

$\frac{7}{8} - \frac{2}{5} = \frac{35}{40} - \frac{16}{40} = \frac{19}{40}$ mile

2. **(4)** $1\frac{1}{8}$ **miles**

Information: $\frac{19}{20}$ and $\frac{3}{10}$ for Birch Trail (from map); $\frac{19}{40}$ for Pine Way (from question 1)

Length of Birch Trail:

$\frac{19}{20} - \frac{3}{10} = \frac{19}{20} - \frac{6}{20} = \frac{13}{20}$

Total of both roads: $\frac{13}{20} + \frac{19}{40} =$

$\frac{26}{40} + \frac{19}{40} = \frac{45}{40} = 1\frac{5}{40} = 1\frac{1}{8}$ miles

3. **(5) not enough information is given**

You need to know the width of Camping Area A, but this is not given.

CHAPTER 3: RATIO AND PROPORTION

Exercise 1: Ratio
page 275

1. First, change 1 hour to 60 minutes to make a comparison of like units.

$\frac{30 \text{ minutes}}{1 \text{ hour}} = \frac{30 \text{ minutes}}{60 \text{ minutes}} = \frac{1}{2}$

2. $\frac{3 \text{ pounds}}{4 \text{ people}} = \frac{3}{4}$

3. $\frac{88 \text{ feet}}{8 \text{ seconds}} = \frac{11}{1}$

4. $\frac{\$80}{12 \text{ boards}} = \frac{20}{3}$

Exercise 2: Application of Ratios
page 276

1. $\dfrac{\text{cost of supplies}}{\text{total expenses}} = \dfrac{\$120}{\$200} \div \dfrac{40}{40} = \dfrac{3}{5}$

2. $\dfrac{\text{total}}{\text{transportation}} = \dfrac{\$200}{\$40} \div \dfrac{40}{40} = \dfrac{5}{1}$

3. $\dfrac{\text{dividend}}{\text{shares}} = \dfrac{\$729}{300} = \$2.43 \text{ per share}$

Exercise 3: Solving Proportions
page 277

1. $m = 4$ 　　　$\dfrac{2}{5} = \dfrac{m}{10}$

　　　　　　　$\dfrac{2 \times 10}{5} = 4$

2. $x = 1$ 　　　$\dfrac{x}{7} = \dfrac{3}{21}$

　　　　　　　$\dfrac{7 \times 3}{21} = \dfrac{21}{21} = 1$

3. $y = 6\frac{2}{3}$ 　　　$\dfrac{5}{y} = \dfrac{15}{20}$

　　　　　　　$\dfrac{20 \times 5}{15} = \dfrac{100}{15} = 6\frac{2}{3}$

Exercise 4: Application of Proportion
page 278

1. $11\frac{1}{5}$ **inches tall**

$\dfrac{5 \text{ inches wide}}{7 \text{ inches tall}} = \dfrac{8 \text{ inches wide}}{i \text{ (inches tall)}}$

$\dfrac{7 \times 8}{5} = \dfrac{56}{5} = 11\frac{1}{5}$ inches tall

2. **40 managers**

$\dfrac{2 \text{ managers}}{9 \text{ salespeople}} = \dfrac{m \text{ (managers)}}{180 \text{ salespeople}}$

$\dfrac{180 \times 2}{9} = \dfrac{360}{9} = 40$ managers

3. **420 calories**

$\dfrac{2 \text{ pancakes}}{120 \text{ calories}} = \dfrac{7 \text{ pancakes}}{c \text{ (calories)}}$

$\dfrac{120 \times 7}{2} = \dfrac{840}{2} = 420$ calories

CHAPTER 4: PERCENTS

Exercise 1: Changing to Fractions and Decimals
page 281

1. $\dfrac{87}{100}$ 　$87 \times \dfrac{1}{100} = \dfrac{87}{1} \times \dfrac{1}{100} = \dfrac{87}{100}$

   $.87$ 　$87 \times .01 = .87$

2. $\dfrac{2}{3}$ 　$66\frac{2}{3} \times \dfrac{1}{100} = \dfrac{200}{3} \times \dfrac{1}{100} = \dfrac{2}{3}$

   $.66\frac{2}{3}$ 　$66\frac{2}{3} \times .01 = .66\frac{2}{3}$

3. $\dfrac{1}{8}$ 　$12.5 \times \dfrac{1}{100} = 12\frac{1}{2} \times \dfrac{1}{100} =$

   　　$\dfrac{25}{2} \times \dfrac{1}{100} = \dfrac{1}{8}$

   $.125$ 　$12.5 \times .01 = .125$

4. $\dfrac{9}{50}$ 　$18 \times \dfrac{1}{100} = \dfrac{18}{1} \times \dfrac{1}{100} = \dfrac{9}{50}$

   $.18$ 　$18 \times .01 = .18$

5. $\dfrac{1}{200}$ 　$\dfrac{1}{2} \times \dfrac{1}{100} = \dfrac{1}{200}$

   $.005$ 　$\dfrac{1}{2} \times .01 = .5 \times .01 = .005$

Exercise 2: Changing to Percents
page 281

1. $\dfrac{3}{8} \times \dfrac{100}{1} = \dfrac{300}{8} = 37\frac{1}{2}\%$

2. $4.5 \times 100 = 450\%$

3. $.625 \times 100 = 62.5\%$

4. $2\frac{1}{4} \times 100 = \dfrac{9}{4} \times \dfrac{100}{1} = \dfrac{900}{4} = 225\%$

Exercise 3: Percent Problems
page 283

1. **1.2** You are looking for the part:

   $\dfrac{n}{30} = \dfrac{4}{100}$

   Cross multiply: $30 \times 4 = 120$

   Divide: $120 \div 100 = 1.2$

2. **400** You are looking for the whole:

   $\dfrac{10}{n} = \dfrac{2.5}{100}$

   Cross multiply:

   $10 \times 100 = 1000$

   Divide: $1000 \div 2.5 = 400$

3. **9%** You are looking for the percent:

   $\dfrac{30.60}{340} = \dfrac{n}{100}$

   Cross multiply:

   $30.60 \times 100 = 3060$

   Divide: $3060 \div 340 = 9$

4. **.31** You are looking for the part:

   $\dfrac{n}{62} = \dfrac{\frac{1}{2}}{100}$

   Cross multiply: $62 \times \dfrac{1}{2} = 31$

   Divide: $31 \div 100 = .31$

Exercise 4: Percent Word Problems
page 284

1. **$252**

   You are looking for the part Jesse saves each month

   $\dfrac{n}{2100} = \dfrac{12}{100}$

   Cross multiply: $2100 \times 12 = 25{,}200$

   Divide: $25{,}200 \div 100 = \$252$

2. $12,000

You are looking for the whole cost of the car.

$$\frac{1800}{n} = \frac{15}{100}$$

Cross multiply:

$1800 \times 100 = 180,000$
Divide: $180,000 \div 15 = \$12,000$

3. 36% undecided

First, find the total number of voters:
$200 + 120 + 180 = 500$
Then, find the percent undecided:

$$\frac{180}{500} = \frac{n}{100}$$

Cross multiply:

$180 \times 100 = 18,000$
Divide: $18,000 \div 500 = 36\%$
undecided

4. $17.98

First, find the total cost of the cassettes:
$\$7.49 \times 3 = \$22.47$
Then, find Hosea's discount:

$$\frac{n}{22.47} = \frac{20}{100}$$

Cross multiply:

$22.47 \times 20 = 449.40$
Divide: $449.40 \div 100 = \$4.49$
Find Hosea's final cost.
$\$22.47 - \$4.49 = \$17.98$

Exercise 5: Interest Problems
page 286

1. (3) $31,968.75

First, find the interest on the loan for 1 year:

$$\frac{n}{31,000} = \frac{12.5}{100}$$

Cross multiply:

$31,000 \times 12.5 = 387,500$
Divide:
$387,500 \div 100 = \$3875$ for 1 year
Then, find the interest for 90 days:
$\frac{90}{360} = \frac{1}{4}$ year
$\$3875 \times \frac{1}{4} = \$968.75$ for 90 days
Finally, find the total amount to be repaid:
$\$31,000 + 968.75 = \$31,968.75$

2. (1) $\dfrac{1500 \times 8\frac{1}{2}}{100}$

This represents how to solve the proportion:

$$\frac{n}{1500} = \frac{8\frac{1}{2}}{100}$$

Cross multiply: $1500 \times 8\frac{1}{2}$
Divide: $(1500 \times 8\frac{1}{2}) \div 100$ or

$$\frac{1500 \times 8\frac{1}{2}}{100}$$

3. (4) $4,500

Find the whole to find how much he borrowed:

$$\frac{360}{n} = \frac{8}{100}$$

Cross multiply: $360 \times 100 = 36,000$
Divide: $36,000 \div 8 = \$4500$

CHAPTER 5: MEASUREMENT

Exercise 1: Conversions
page 288

1. Convert from a small unit (hours) to a larger unit (days). Divide 96 by the number of hours in a day (24 hr = 1 day):
$96 \div 24 = \textbf{4 days}$

2. Convert from a small unit (quarts) to a larger unit (gallons). Divide 20 by the number of quarts in a gallon (4 qt = 1 gal):
$20 \div 4 = \textbf{5 gallons}$

3. Convert from a large unit (days) to a smaller unit (minutes). First, find the number of minutes in one day (1 day = 24 hr, and 1 hr = 60 min):
$24 \times 60 = 1440$
Then, multiply that total by 2 for 2 days:
$1440 \times 2 = \textbf{2880 minutes}$

4. Convert a small unit (feet) to a larger unit (miles). Divide 14,110 by the number of feet in a mile (5280 ft = 1 mi):
$14,110 \div 5280 = 2.67 = \textbf{2.7 miles}$
(to the nearest tenth)

Exercise 2: Basic Operations with Measurement
page 289

1. 7 ft 6 in

$$
\begin{array}{r}
7\text{ ft.}\ \ 6\text{ in} \\
\hline
3)22\text{ ft}\ \ \ 6\text{ in} \\
\underline{21\text{ ft}} \\
1 = \ \ +12\text{ in} \\
\hline
18\text{ in} \\
\underline{18\text{ in}} \\
0
\end{array}
$$

2. 40 min

$$
\begin{array}{r}
0\text{ hr}\qquad\ 40\text{ min} \\
\hline
8)5\text{ hr}\qquad 20\text{ min} \\
\underline{0} \\
5\text{ hr} = \ +\ 300\text{ min} \\
\hline
320 \\
\underline{320} \\
0
\end{array}
$$

3. 7 oz.

$$
\begin{array}{r}
1\text{ lb}\ \ 4\text{ oz}\qquad 20\text{ oz} \\
-\qquad 13\text{ oz} = \ -\ 13\text{ oz} \\
\hline
7\text{ oz}
\end{array}
$$

4. (4) 19($415)

1 lb 3 oz = 16 oz + 3 oz = 19 oz

5. (5) $107.50

First, find the total number of hours:

$$
\begin{array}{r}
2\text{ hr }30\text{ min} \\
3\text{ hr} \\
4\text{ hr }45\text{ min} \\
7\text{ hr }15\text{ min} \\
+\ 4\text{ hr} \\
\hline
20\text{ hr }90\text{ min} = 21\text{ hr }30\text{ min} =
\end{array}
$$

$21\frac{1}{2}$ hr

Then, find the total pay:

$21\frac{1}{2}$ hr $\times$ $5 = \frac{43}{2} \times \frac{5}{1}$ = $107.50

Exercise 3: Metric Measurement
pages 291–292

This chart will help you follow the solutions below:

kilo	hecto	deca	unit	deci	centi	milli

1. First, add

400 cm + 15 cm + 1285 cm + 15 cm = 1715 cm

Second, 1715 centimeters to meters: Move the decimal point 2 places left.

1715 cm = **17.15 m**

2. First, one week = 7 days

857 mg $\times$ 7 = 5999 mg

Second, 5999 milligrams to grams: Move the decimal point 3 places left.

5999 mg = **5.999 g**

3. $\frac{1\text{ km}}{.621\text{ mi}} = \frac{80\text{ km}}{n}$

$\frac{.621 \times 80}{1}$ = 49.68 mph in Canada.

The U.S. allows 55 mph, and Canada allows 49.68 mph.

The U.S. allows a faster speed.

4. 1000 meters to kilometers: Move the decimal point 3 places left.

1000 m = 1.000 = **1 km**

5. (2) .75 $\times$ $6.40

Exercise 4: Money Problems
pages 292–293

1. (3) $200

First, find the number of pounds in two tons:

$\frac{1\text{ T}}{2000\text{ lb}} = \frac{2\text{ T}}{n\text{ lb}}$

$\frac{2000 \times 2}{1}$ = 4000 lb

Then, find the total number of bags:

4000 lb ÷ 50 lb = 80 bags

Then, find the profit:

$5.95 $\times$ 80 = $476 income

2 $\times$ $138 = $276 expenses

$476 − $276 = $200 profit

2. (2) $15.68

First, find the number of yards in 48 feet:

$\frac{1\text{ yd}}{3\text{ ft}} = \frac{n\text{ yd}}{48\text{ ft}}$

$\frac{1 \times 48}{3} = \frac{48}{3}$ = 16 yd

Then, find the total cost:

16 $\times$ $.98 = $15.68

3. (2) 12¢

$\frac{\$6.48}{36}$ = $.18 per capsule

$.18 $\times$ 2 = $.36 per dose

$\frac{\$4.32}{36}$ = $.12 per capsule

$.12 $\times$ 2 − $.24 per dose

$.36 − $.24 = $.12

Exercise 5: Time Problems
page 294

1. (3) $4\frac{1}{2} \times 8 \times 5 \times 4$

   First:

10 a.m. to noon =	2 hr
noon to 2:30 p.m. =	$+2\frac{1}{2}$ hr
	$4\frac{1}{2}$ hr each day

   Second: Multiply $4\frac{1}{2}$ hours per day by \$8 per hour by 5 days per week by 4 weeks.

2. (5) $4\frac{3}{4}$

5/20	8 hr
5/21	$9\frac{1}{2}$ hr
5/22	$10\frac{3}{4}$ hr
5/23	8 hr
5/24	$+ 8\frac{1}{2}$ hr
Total	$44\frac{3}{4}$ hr

   $44\frac{3}{4} - 40 = 4\frac{3}{4}$ hr overtime

3. (4) **\$371**

$40 \times \$7.85 =$	\$314
$4\frac{3}{4} \times \$12\ =$	$+\ \ 57$
Total	\$371

4. (4) **\$248.57**

   $1\% + 25\% + 7\% = 33\%$

   $33\% \times \$371 = \$122.43$ deductions

   $\$371 - \$122.43 =$ \$248.57 take-home pay

5. (2) $960 \times \frac{1}{3}$

   $$d = rt$$

   $(20\ \text{min} = \frac{1}{3}\ \text{hr})$

   $= 960(\frac{1}{3})$ or $960 \times \frac{1}{3}$

Exercise 6: Scales and Meters
page 296

1. (3) **1 in = 200 mi**

   $\frac{2000\ \text{mi}}{10\ \text{in}} = \frac{n\ \text{mi}}{1\ \text{in}}$

   $\frac{2000 \times 1}{10} = 200$ miles

2. (1) **\$113.63**

New reading	4752 kwh
Old reading	$-$ 3843 kwh
difference	909 kwh

   $\frac{\$.125}{1\text{kwh}} = \frac{n\ \text{dollars}}{909\ \text{kwh}}$

   $\frac{\$.125 \times 909}{1} = \$113.625$ or \$113.63

CHAPTER 6: GRAPHS, STATISTICS AND PROBABILITY

Exercise 1: Mean and Median
page 298

1. **44 points**

   $37 + 63 + 42 + 24 + 44 + 51 = 261$

   $261 \div 6 = 43.5 = 44$ points

2. **61 points**

   Find the middle numbers:

   45   48 $\boxed{53\ \ \ 68}$ 72   74

   Find the average: $53 + 68 = 121$

   $121 \div 2 = 60.5$, or 61 points

3. **\$44.80**

   Arrange from smallest to largest and find the middle number:

   \$39.95 \$42.88 $\boxed{\$44.80}$ \$48.95 \$52.25

Exercise 2: Circle Graphs
page 299

1. **\$666.67**

   First, find the yearly expenses for rent:

   $\frac{n}{32,000} \times \frac{25}{100} = \frac{32,000 \times 25}{100} = \$8000$

   Then, find the monthly expenses for rent:

   $\$8000 \div 12 = \$666.67$

2. (5) **not enough information is given**

   Nothing is said about clothing on the graph.

3. (1) **1 to 10**

   $\frac{\text{savings}}{\text{total}} = \frac{10\%}{100\%} = \frac{10}{100} = \frac{1}{10}$

Exercise 3: Bar Graphs
page 299

1. **\$19,750**

   First, find the total:

   $13,000 + 20,000 + 21,000 + 25,000 = \$79,000$

   Then, find the average:

   $\$79,000 \div 4 = \$19,750$

2. (2) **\$2,000**

   $\$23,000 - \$21,000 = \$2,000$

Exercise 4: Line Graphs
pages 300–301

1. sales; 1992; 1995
2. ten thousands of dollars
3. \$60,000
4. higher

Exercise 5: Mixed Graph Practice
pages 301–302

1. $1750

$$\frac{n}{25{,}000} = \frac{7}{100} \quad \frac{25{,}000 \times 7}{100} = \$1750$$

2. $33,333.33

$$\frac{20{,}000}{n} = \frac{60}{100} \quad \frac{20{,}000 \times 100}{60} = \$33{,}333.33$$

3. $15,120

First, find the total deductions:

$27\% + 7\% + 3\% = 37\%$

$$\frac{n}{24{,}000} = \frac{37}{100} \quad \frac{24{,}000 \times 37}{100} = \$8880$$

Now, subtract to find Mike's take-home pay:

$\$24{,}000 - 8880 = \$15{,}120$

4. 200 ft $1450 - 1250 = 200$ ft

5. 2.45 times as tall

$$\frac{\text{World Trade Center}}{\text{Washington Monument}} = \frac{1350}{550} = 2.45$$

6. 1125 ft

$1000 + 1250 = 2250$

$2250 \div 2 = 1125$ ft

7. April and July

8. $69,750

Youth: 4000 at $5.75 $= \$23{,}000$

Adults: 5500 at $8.50 $= \underline{\$46{,}750}$

$\qquad\qquad\qquad\qquad\quad \$69{,}750$

Exercise 6: Probability
page 303

1. $\frac{1}{52}$ $\quad \frac{1 \text{ ace of spades}}{52 \text{ cards}} = \frac{1}{52}$

2. 25% $\frac{13 \text{ hearts}}{52 \text{ cards}} = \frac{1}{4} = 25\%$

3. (1) $\frac{1}{6}$ $\quad \frac{1 \text{ possibility}}{6 \text{ aces}} = \frac{1}{6}$

4. (5) 50% $\quad \frac{3 \text{ possibilities}}{6 \text{ faces}} = \frac{3}{6} = 50\%$

5. (1) **0** This is not possible.

6. (3) $\frac{1}{2}$ $\quad \frac{1 \text{ head}}{2 \text{ possibilities}} = \frac{1}{2}$

Exercise 7: Dependent Probability
page 304

1. $\frac{1}{17}$ $\quad \frac{3 \text{ aces}}{51 \text{ cards}} = \frac{1}{17}$

2. $\frac{4}{51}$ $\quad \frac{4 \text{ aces}}{51 \text{ cards}} = \frac{4}{51}$

3. $\frac{2}{9}$ $\quad \frac{2 \text{ quarters}}{9 \text{ coins}} = \frac{2}{9}$

4. $\frac{1}{4}$ $\quad \frac{2 \text{ quarters}}{8 \text{ coins}} = \frac{1}{4}$

CHAPTER 7: NUMERATION

Exercise 1: Powers
page 305

1. 25 $5 \times 5 = 25$

2. 729 $9 \times 9 \times 9 = 729$

3. $\frac{27}{64}$ $\quad \frac{3}{4} \times \frac{3}{4} \times \frac{3}{4} = \frac{27}{64}$

4. 1 1 to any power is 1.

5. 1 Any number to the 0 power is 1.

6. .008 $(.2)(.2)(.2) = .008$

7. 0 $0 \times 0 = 0$

Exercise 2: Simplifying Square Roots
page 306

1. $4\sqrt{3}$ $\quad \sqrt{48} = \sqrt{16 \cdot 3} = 4\sqrt{3}$

2. $2\sqrt{2}$ $\quad \sqrt{8} \ = \sqrt{4 \cdot 2} = 2\sqrt{2}$

3. $3\sqrt{3}$ $\quad \sqrt{27} = \sqrt{9 \cdot 3} \ = 3\sqrt{3}$

Exercise 3: Square Roots
page 306

1. 9

2. 1

3. 5.3 (approx.); $\sqrt{4 \cdot 7} = 2\sqrt{7}$ (simplified)

4. 7.2 (approx.); $\sqrt{4 \cdot 13} = 2\sqrt{13}$ (simplified)

5. 3.2 (approx.)

6. 4

7. 15

Exercise 4: Order of Operations
page 307

1. 0 $\quad 7 - 5 + 3 - 5$

$\qquad\qquad 2 \ + 3 - 5 = 0$

2. 23 $\quad 8 + 3 \times 5$

$\qquad\qquad 8 + \ 15 \ = 23$

3. 8 $\quad 6 + 21 \div 3 - 5$

$\qquad\quad 6 + \ \ 7 - 5 = 8$

4. 33 $\quad 4 + 3^3 + 3 \times 2 - 2^2$

$\qquad\quad 4 + 27 + 3 \times 2 - 4$

$\qquad\quad 4 + 27 + \ \ 6 - 4 = 33$

Exercise 5: Evaluating Formulas
page 309

1. 125 cu in $\quad V = s^3$

$\qquad\qquad\qquad V = 5^3 = 125$

2. $288 $\qquad i = prt$

$\qquad\quad i = (800)(.12)(3) = \$288$

3. 28.26 sq in $A = \pi r^2$

$\qquad\qquad\qquad A = (3.14)(3^2)$

$\qquad\qquad\qquad A = (3.14)(9) = 28.26$

4. 40 ft $\quad P = 2l + 2w$

Change 2 yards to 6 feet:

$P = 2(14) + 2(6)$

$P = 28 + 12 = 40$

Exercise 6: Scientific Notation
page 310

1. 8.2×10^{-3}　　2. 3.82×10^4
3. $1.624 \times 1000 = \mathbf{1624}$
4. $3.12 \times .10 = \mathbf{.312}$

CHAPTER 8: GEOMETRY

Exercise 1: Pairs of Angles
page 312

1. **38°** because $\angle DBC$ and $\angle ABD$ are supplementary angles.
$180° - 142° = 38°$
2. **38°** because $\angle ABE$ and $\angle DBC$ are vertical angles.
3. **142°** because $\angle EBC$ and $\angle ABD$ are vertical angles.
4. **38°** $90° - 52° = 38°$

Exercise 2: Angles in Triangles
page 313

1. $\angle B = \mathbf{70°}$
Add the two known angles:
$70° + 40° = 110°$
Subtract that sum from 180°:
$180° - 110° = 70°$
2. $\angle Q = \mathbf{125°}$
Add the two known angles:
$30° + 25° = 55°$
Subtract that sum from 180°:
$180° - 55° = 125°$
3. $\angle X = \mathbf{90°}$
Add the two known angles:
$30° + 60° = 90°$
Subtract that sum from 180°:
$180° - 90° = 90°$
4. $\angle E = \mathbf{60°}$
Add the two known angles:
$60° + 60° = 120°$
Subtract that sum from 180°:
$180° - 120° = 60°$

Exercise 3: Types of Triangles
page 314

1. (a) **Scalene triangle**—because all three sides have different lengths
(b) **Isosceles triangle**—because two sides and two angles of the triangle are equal
(c) **Equilateral triangle**—because all three sides of the triangle are equal

(d) **Right triangle**—because $\angle C$ is a right angle
2. **76°**
Find the total of the base angles:
$52° \times 2 = 104°$
Subtract from the total degrees in a triangle: $180° - 104° = 76°$
3. **30°**
Find the total of the known angles —you are told that this is a right triangle (one angle of 90°) and that there is a 60° angle.
$90° + 60° = 150°$
Subtract from the total degrees in a triangle:
$180° - 150° = 30°$

Exercise 4: Similar Triangles
page 316

1. **9 in** $\frac{DF}{AC} = \frac{DE}{AB}$
$\frac{DF}{15} = \frac{6}{10}$
$\frac{15 \times 6}{10} = \frac{90}{10} = 9$ in
2. **12 ft** $\frac{t}{8} = \frac{18}{12}$
$t = \frac{18 \times 8}{12} = \frac{144}{12} = 12$ ft
3. (a) First recognize two similar triangles and draw them. Set up a proportion:
$\frac{d}{b} = \frac{c}{a}$
(b) **150 ft**
$\frac{d}{6} = \frac{50}{2}$
$d = \frac{50 \times 6}{2} = \frac{300}{2} = 150$ ft

Exercise 5: The Pythagorean Theorem
pages 317–318

1. $c = \mathbf{15}$　$c^2 = a^2 + b^2$
$c^2 = 9^2 + 12^2$
$c^2 = 81 + 144$
$c^2 = 225$
$c = \sqrt{225} = 15$
2. $c = \mathbf{25}$ **in.**　$c^2 = a^2 + b^2$
$c^2 = 15^2 + 20^2$
$c^2 = 225 + 400 = 625$
$c = \sqrt{625} = 25$
3. **(3) 100**　$c^2 = a^2 + b^2$
$c^2 = 60^2 + 80^2$
$c^2 = 3600 + 6400 = 10,000$
$c = \sqrt{10,000} = 100$ meters

4. (2)   12

First, draw a sketch of the problem

$c^2 = a^2 + b^2$

$13^2 = a^2 + 5^2$

$169 = a^2 + 25$

$169 - 25 = a^2$

$144 = a^2$

$\sqrt{144} = a$

$12 = a$

Exercise 6: Perimeter
pages 320–321

1. 360 ft $P = 4s$

$P = 4 \times 90 = 360$ ft

2. 49.9 in $P = a + b + c$

$P = 16.5 + 12.4 + 21 = 49.9$

3. $2961

First, find the total perimeter:

$P = 2l + 2w$

$= 2(400) + 2(224)$

$= 800 + 448 = 1248$ yd

Then, convert to feet:

$1248 \times 3 = 3744$ ft

Then, find the number of 8-foot sections:

$3744 \div 8 = 468$ sections

Finally, find the total cost:

$468 \times 5\frac{3}{4} = \frac{468}{1} \times \frac{23}{4} = 117 \times 23 =$ $2691

4. 70 m

First, find the lengths of the sides that are not labeled:

$20 - 15.3 = 4.7$

$10.8 + 4.2 = 15.0$

Then, add all of the sides together:

$20 + 4.2 + 4.7 + 10.8 + 15.3 + 15 = 70$ m

5. 194 ft

Find the perimeter:

$P = 2l + 2w$

$= 2(70) + 2(48) = 236$

Subtract the length of the house:

$236 - 42 = 194$ feet

Exercise 7: Area
page 321

1. 75.09 sq in

This figure consists of two shapes.

Square:

$A = s^2$

$= 4.7 \times 4.7$

$= 22.09$ sq in

Rectangle: $A = lw$

$= 5.3 \times 10$

$= 53$ sq in

Add together for total area:

$53 + 22.09 = 75.09$ sq in

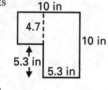

2. $\frac{11}{14}$ sq in. $A = \pi r^2$

$= \frac{22}{7} \times (\frac{1}{2})^2$

$= \frac{22}{7} \times \frac{1}{4}$

$= \frac{11}{7} \times \frac{1}{2} = \frac{11}{14}$ sq in

3. 50 sq yd

First, find the area of the room:

$30 \times 15 = 450$ sq ft

Then, divide by 9 yards to get the number of square yards:

$450 \div 9 = 50$ sq yd

4. 78.5 sq ft

The largest possible diameter for this rug is 10 feet, so the radius is 5 feet. The area is: $A = \pi r^2$

$= 3.14 \, (5^2)$

$= 78.5$ sq ft

Exercise 8: Volume
page 322

1. 45 gallons

Find the volume of the fish tank:

$V = (18)(12)(48)$

$= 10,368$ cu in.

Find how many gallons will fit in this tank:

$10,368 \div 231 = 44.9 = 45$ gallons

2. 500 cu ft

Convert 6 inches to $\frac{1}{2}$ foot:

$V = (25)(40)(\frac{1}{2})$

$= 500$ cu ft

3. 25,872 cu ft

$V = \pi r^2 h$

$= \frac{22}{7}(14^2)(42)$

$= 22(196)(6) = 25,872$ cu ft

CHAPTER 9: ALGEBRA

Exercise 1: Terms
page 324

1. $8x$ and $+7y$ and -5

2. $2x^2$ and $-\frac{3}{x}$

3. $8ab$ and $+12$

Exercise 2: Equations
page 325

1. 5 added to 7 times a number (y) equals 19.

2. A number (a) minus 5 equals 23.

3. 10 divided by a number (y) minus 5 equals 0.

Exercise 3: One-Step Equations
page 326

1. $x = 4$

$$3 + x = 7$$
$$3 - 3 + \underbrace{x = 7}_{0} - 3$$
$$x = 4$$

2. $x = 36$

$$\frac{x}{3} = 12$$
$$\frac{3}{1} \cdot \frac{x}{3} = 12 \cdot 3$$
$$x = 36$$

3. $x = 8$

$$x - 8 = 0$$
$$x - \underbrace{8 + 8}_{0} = 0 + 8$$
$$x = 8$$

4. $x = 15$

$$5x = 75$$
$$\frac{5x}{5} = \frac{75}{5}$$
$$x = 15$$

Exercise 4: Translating English to Algebra
page 328

1. $\frac{x - y}{3}$ **4.** $2x - 7$

2. $x^2 + y^2$ **5.** $\frac{x^3}{4}$

3. $4(x + 10)$ **6.** $\frac{5x}{2x}$

Exercise 5: Translating Sentences to Equations
pages 329

1. $\frac{1}{4}x = 18$ or $\frac{x}{4} = 18$
2. $9 + \frac{1}{2}x = 13$ or $9 + \frac{x}{2} = 13$
3. $x - y = 8$
4. $2x - 3 = 5x + 9$
5. **(1)** $x - 5 = 19$
6. **(4)** $\frac{x}{7} = 5$
7. **(1)** $x + 6 = \frac{7}{6}x$

Exercise 6: Solving One-Step Algebra Word Problems
pages 329–330

1. $x = \$20$

$$\frac{1}{8}x = 2.50$$
$$\frac{8}{1} \cdot \frac{1}{8}x = 2.50 \cdot 8$$
$$x = \$20$$

2. $x = \$192$

$$72 = x - 120$$
$$72 + 120 = x - \underbrace{120 + 120}_{0}$$
$$\$192 = x$$

3. $x = 12$ ft

$$x - 5\tfrac{1}{2} = 6\tfrac{1}{2}$$
$$x - \underbrace{5\tfrac{1}{2} + 5\tfrac{1}{2}}_{0} = 6\tfrac{1}{2} + 5\tfrac{1}{2}$$
$$x = 12$$

4. $x = \$5793.75$

$$927 = .16x$$
$$\frac{927}{.16} = \frac{.16x}{.16}$$
$$927 \div .16 = x$$
$$\$5793.75 = x$$

Exercise 7: Combining Like Terms
page 330

1. $9x + 9y$ **4.** $12\,a^2 + 5a$
2. $7x^2 + 5x$ **5.** $9xy + 6x - 3y$
3. $x + y$

Exercise 8: Removing Grouping Symbols
page 331

1. $5(3x + 2) = \mathbf{15x + 10}$

2. $6x + 2(12x - 7) = 6x + 24x - 14$
$$= \mathbf{30x - 14}$$

3. $3(2x + 4 - 3y) = \mathbf{6x + 12 - 9y}$

4. $-6(5x - 12) = \mathbf{-30x + 72}$

5. $2(x - y) = \mathbf{2x - 2y}$

Exercise 9: Solving Multi-Step Equations
page 332

1. $x = 14$

$$2x - 26 = 2$$
$$2x - 26 + 26 = 2 + 26$$
$$2x = 28$$
$$x = 14$$

2. $x = 15$

$$\frac{x}{3} + 4 = 9$$
$$\frac{x}{3} + 4 - 4 = 9 - 4$$
$$\frac{x}{3} = 5$$
$$x = 15$$

3. $x = 21$

$$\frac{4x}{3} - 14 = 14$$
$$\frac{4x}{3} - 14 + 14 = 14 + 14$$
$$\frac{4x}{3} = 28$$
$$4x = 84$$
$$x = 21$$

4. $x = 1$

$$2(5x - 11) + 12x = 0$$
$$10x - 22 + 12x = 0$$
$$22x - 22 + 22 = 0 + 22$$
$$22x = 22$$
$$x = 1$$

Exercise 10: Setting Up and Solving Multi-Step Equations
pages 332–333
1. **(4)** $3(x + 32) = 123$
2. **(4)** $2x + 24 = 56$
3. **(4)** $(2x - 6) + x = 42$
4. **(5)** $4800 + 36x = 10{,}200$
5. **(5) not enough information is given**
   You do not know how many attendees were contest winners.

Exercise 11: Number Line
page 334
1. $1\frac{1}{2} > -1$ 2. $-4 < -2\frac{1}{2}$

Exercise 12: Signed Numbers
page 334
1. -3 yd   5. $-\frac{1}{4} > -\frac{1}{2}$
2. $+4\frac{1}{2}$ pt   6. $2\frac{1}{3}$
3. $-9 < -4$ 7. 3
4. $-3 < 1$

Exercise 13: Combining Signed Numbers
page 335
1. -17 3. -33 5. -19
2. -2 4. -3 6. -7.7

Exercise 14: Eliminating Double Signs
page 336
1. **1** $-6 + (-2) - (-9) =$
   $-6 - 2 + 9 = 1$
2. **total gain of 22 yd**
   $+23$ -4
   $+8$ -6
   $\underline{+3}$ $\underline{-2}$
   34 -12
   $+34 - 12 = +22$
3. **19°** $12 - (-7) = 12 + 7 = 19$
4. **$158**
   $+140$ -14
   $+\ 56$ -32
   $\underline{+\ 26}$ $\underline{-18}$
   $+222$ -64
   $+222 + (-64) = +158$

Exercise 15: Multiplying and Dividing Signed Numbers
page 337
1. 40 3. -84 5. 3
2. -144 4. -5 6. -4
7. **$-$22,284**
   $(-\$2476)\,(9) = -\$22{,}284$

Exercise 16: One-Step Inequalities
page 338
1. $x > -2$ $x - 3 > -5$
   $x - 3 + 3 > -5 + 3$
   $x > -2$
2. $x < -7$ $-3 + x < -10$
   $-3 + 3 + x < -10 + 3$
   $x < -7$
3. $x < -36$ $\frac{x}{-3} < 12$
   $-3 \cdot \frac{x}{-3} > 12 \cdot (-3)$
   $x > -36$
   Note change in direction.
4. $x \geq 4$ $x - 5 \geq -1$
   $x - 5 + 5 \geq -1 + 5$
   $x \geq 4$
5. $x < 4$ $-4x > -16$
   $\frac{-4x}{-4} < \frac{-16}{-4}$
   $x < 4$
   Note change in direction.

Exercise 17: Multiplying Algebraic Expressions
page 339
1. $24x^3$ $8x \cdot 3x^2 =$
   $8 \cdot 3 \cdot x \cdot x^2 = 24x^3$
2. $-28x^2y$ $7xy(-4x) =$
   $7 \cdot (-4) \cdot x \cdot x \cdot y = -28x^2y$
3. $-18a^3b^2$ $(-6ab^2)(3a^2) =$
   $-6 \cdot 3 \cdot a \cdot a^2 \cdot b^2 =$
   $-18a^3b^2$
4. $6y^3 - 12y^2 - 21y$
   $3y(2y^2 - 4y - 7) =$
   $3y(2y^2) + 3y(-4y) + 3y\,(-7) =$
   $6y^3 - 12y^2 - 21y$

Exercise 18: The Greatest Common Factor
page 339
1. $7x^2(3x - 2)$
   $21x^3 - 14x^2 =$
   $7x^2(3x) + 7x^2(-2) =$
   $7x^2(3x - 2)$
2. $11p^4(11p - 3)$
   $121p^5 - 33p^4 =$
   $11p^4(11p) + 11p^4(-3) =$
   $11p^4(11p - 3)$
3. $9x^2y^2(x + 4y)$
   $9x^3y^2 + 36x^2y^3 =$
   $9x^2y^2(x) + 9x^2y^2(4y) =$
   $9x^2y^2(x + 4y)$
4. $5x^2(x^2 + 5x - 4)$
   $5x^4 + 25x^3 - 20x^2 =$
   $5x^2(x^2) + 5x^2(5x) + 5x^2(-4) =$
   $5x^2(x^2 + 5x - 4)$

Exercise 19: Factoring by Grouping
page 340

1. $(x + 4)(x + 3)$
$$x^2 + 4x + 3x + 12$$
$$x(x + 4) + 3(x + 4)$$
$$(x + 4)(x + 3)$$

2. $(4y + 3z)(2y + 3z)$
$$8y^2 + 6yz + 12yz + 9z^2$$
$$2y(4y + 3z) + 3z(4y + 3z)$$
$$(4y + 3z)(2y + 3z)$$

Exercise 20: Ordered Pairs
page 341

1. $A\ (2,2)$ 4. $G\ (0,-2)$
2. $C\ (-3,1)$ 5. $H\ (1,-1)$
3. $F\ (-1,-4)$

Exercise 21: Distance by Counting
page 342

1. 9   2. 9   3. 6

Exercise 22: Distance Between Two Points
page 342

1. 5 $(x_1,y_1) = (0,-2)$
$$(x_2,y_2) = (4,-5)$$
$$d = \sqrt{(4 - 0)^2 + (-5 - (-2))^2}$$
$$= \sqrt{4^2 + (-3)^2}$$
$$= \sqrt{16 + 9}$$
$$= \sqrt{25} = 5$$

2. 6 E and F are on the same vertical line. Count the units from $(1,4)$ to $(1,-2)$; $d = 6$

3. $5\sqrt{2}$ $(x_1,y_1) = (-2,3)$
$$(x_2,y_2) = (-1, -4)$$
$$d = \sqrt{(-1 - (-2))^2 + (-4 - 3)^2}$$
$$= \sqrt{(-1 + 2)^2 + (-7)^2}$$
$$= \sqrt{1^2 + (-7)^2}$$
$$= \sqrt{1 + 49}$$
$$= \sqrt{50} = \sqrt{25 \cdot 2} = 5\sqrt{2}$$

Exercise 23: The Slope of a Line
page 344

1. $\frac{4}{3}$ $\frac{4 - 0}{3 - 0} = \frac{4}{3}$
2. $\frac{1}{11}$ $\frac{0-(-1)}{6-(-5)} = \frac{1}{11} = \frac{1}{11}$
3. 1 $\frac{2 - 3}{-1 - 0} = \frac{-1}{-1} = 1$
4. 0   The line is parallel to the x-axis; the slope is 0.

ANSWER KEY
POST-TEST 1: WRITING SKILLS
Part 1: Conventions of English

1. **(2)** This sentence needs a verb (*is*) to make it complete.

2. **(1)** The original sentences have a time order relationship. Starting the new sentence with *After* best expresses this relationship.

3. **(3)** The three parts of the sentence that are separated by commas should all be in the same form, so the second one needs to have a verb added: *Relax, place . . . , and put . . .*

4. **(2)** The original sentence contains two independent thoughts run together. A semicolon separates them.

5. **(5)** The antecedent is *worries,* so the pronoun should be plural: *them.*

6. **(2)** To agree with the rest of the paragraph, the verb form should be in the present tense: *get.*

7. **(2)** The correct past tense form of this irregular verb is *threw.*

8. **(4)** This sentence is complex, with two subject-verb combinations: *Times are* and *it's* (*it is*). The two parts should be separated with the conjunction *and* and a comma.

9. **(5)** The pronoun refers to *people,* so it should be plural: *they.*

10. **(3)** Never separate the main parts of a sentence, the subject and predicate, with a comma.

11. **(2)** The original sentences have a cause-and-effect relationship. This is best expressed by *because.*

12. **(4)** To agree with the rest of the paragraph, the verb form should be in the present tense: *skip.*

13. **(2)** The three parts of the sentence that are separated by commas should all be in the same single-item form: *Pasta, rice, and grains.* In the original sentence, the third item is in the form of an infinitive phrase (*to eat other grains*).

14. **(3)** The original sentence contains two complete thoughts run together. Choice (3) correctly divides the two complete thoughts into separate sentences.

15. **(3)** The subject is singular (*person*), so the verb must be singular to agree with it: *misses.*

16. **(2)** You may need to memorize the spelling of this tricky word.

17. **(3)** Always use the relative pronoun *who* to refer to a person. *Which* is the correct relative pronoun for a thing.

18. **(4)** The main part of the sentence is an exception to the fact stated in the introductory clause. The conjunction *but* expresses this relationship. The new sentence would read, "A cold virus can't penetrate skin, but it can penetrate mucous membranes in your mouth, nose, and eyes."

19. **(5)** This sentence is correct as written.

20. **(2)** To agree with the rest of the paragraph, the pronoun should be in the second person: *you,* not *one.* *You* takes a plural verb, so change the verb from *is* to *are.*

21. **(3)** The possessive pronoun *their* has nothing to modify in this sentence. The correct word is the adverb *there.*

22. **(1)** This sentence is correct as written.

23. **(2)** You may need to memorize the spelling of this word.

24. **(4)** "To the *New York Times*" is a prepositional phrase. Prepositional phrases should not be set off by commas.

25. **(4)** The term *health foods* is a common noun, not a proper noun, so it should not be capitalized.

26. **(4)** The subject of the sentence must agree with the subject of the introductory clause, *they.* The plural form also makes this sentence agree with the rest of the passage.

27. **(4)** *Contents* is a plural noun, so the verb should be *vary* to agree in number with the subject.

Use the answer key on page 445 to check your answers to the Post-Test. Then find the item number of each question you missed and circle it on the chart below to determine the writing content areas in which you need more practice. The page numbers for the content areas are listed below on the chart. For those questions that you missed, review the pages indicated on the chart.

POST-TEST 1: WRITING SKILLS EVALUATION CHART

Content Area	Item Number	Review Pages
Nouns, Pronouns	20, 21	46–48, 56–60
Verbs	1, 7	48–53
Subject-Verb Agreement	15, 27	54–55
Pronoun Reference	5, 9, 17, 26	57–59
Sentence Fragments	4, 8, 14	45
Sentence Combining	2, 11, 18	61–67
Sequence of Tenses	6, 12	49–51
Parallel Structure	13	69–70
Capitalization	25	71–72
Punctuation	3, 10, 24	72–74
Spelling	16, 23	74
No Error	19, 22	

Part 2: The Essay

If possible, give your essay to an instructor to evaluate. That person's opinion of your writing will be useful in deciding what further work you need to write a good essay.

If, however, you are unable to show your work to someone else, you can try to evaluate your own essay. If you can answer *yes* to the five questions in the Essay Evaluation Checklist, your essay would probably earn an upper-half score (4, 5, or 6) on Part 2 of the Writing Skills Test. If you receive any *no* answers on your evaluation checklist, you should read your essay carefully to see how it could be improved and review Chapter 4 of the Writing Skills section.

Essay Evaluation Checklist

YES   NO

_____ _____ **1.** Does the essay answer the question asked?

_____ _____ **2.** Does the main point of the essay stand out clearly?

_____ _____ **3.** Does each paragraph contain specific examples and details that help prove the main point?

_____ _____ **4.** Are the ideas arranged and linked sensibly in sentences and paragraphs?

_____ _____ **5.** Is the control of grammar and usage effective enough so that you were able to read the essay easily and smoothly?

ANSWER KEY
POST-TEST 2: SOCIAL STUDIES

1. (1) The chart for income shows that 30 percent comes from social security and other personal taxes, 35 percent comes from income tax, and 7 percent comes from other taxes that apply to individuals.

2. (2) The amount taken in for social security, etc., was 30 percent, but the amount expended was 32 percent. None of the other choices is supported by the figures shown.

3. (1) Choice (2) is a definition of cultural learning. Choices (3) and (4) are examples of cultural learning by humans. Choice (5) is a fact about the other animals. They are all supporting statements that lead to the conclusion that only humans use cultural learning.

4. (2) The Federalists assumed that the Federal government had no power over what had already been decided by the states. Choice (1) refers to the Anti-Federalist position.

5. (3) The Founding Fathers were split into two groups over the Bill of Rights. The split was based on their ideas about the rights and powers of a central government.

6. (4) Replanting of trees whose roots would hold the soil would be a practical solution. Sheep (1) would be even more destructive than cattle. The natural process (2), further watering (3), or clearing (5) would result in further soil erosion.

7. (4) The group described began as an expressive crowd, sharing an entertaining experience. But emotions got out of hand and turned the crowd into an acting group.

8. (1) According to the passage, riddling, a form of verbal play, helps children develop language and logic skills in addition to being an amusement, so choice (5) is wrong. Psychologists are right to see social play as important, so choice (4) is incorrect. There is no evidence for choices (2) or (3).

9. (1) The secretary of commerce would oversee an agency that helped promote new businesses.

10. (3) Because national parks are public lands, this agency would be governed by the secretary of the interior.

11. (3) With more houses on the market, the seller would realize that a buyer could choose another house and so would likely accept a lower offer. Choices (1) and (2) apply to a situation in which there are more buyers than sellers. With many homes on the market, homeowners would be discouraged from putting their houses up for sale. Choice (5) indicates a buyer who knows little about the housing market.

12. (5) Chinese food is popular, as shown by the number of Chinese restaurants. Choices (1) and (2) are not examples of acculturation. Chinese lanterns are an occasional occurrence, not a cultural adaptation. Bicycles are not a uniquely Chinese form of transportation.

13. (1) The highest point of population for both developed countries and developing countries occurs at or before 1990. After that period, both figures are projected to decline.

14. (3) The graph shows that the population of developing nations increased sharply between 1950 and 1990. Improved health care and nutrition would mean that more babies would be carried to term, more children would live to be adults, and more adults would live to bear children, thus increasing the population. Improved birth control would be more likely to influence a decrease rather than an increase in population. The same is true of migration from developing to developed regions. The pregnancy rate in developed regions would not affect developing regions.

15. (2) Improved delivery would mean better communication. The other choices would not influence a decision about mail delivery.

16. (5) The transatlantic cable linked two distant places through improved technology. None of the other changes improved communication or involved a major technological advance.

17. (2) By forcing the withdrawal of the bill, Republicans showed their disapproval of it, which is the opposite of choice (3). Choice (1) might be true, but there is no evidence of how long Democrats could talk if they wanted to. There is no evidence that choices (4) or (5) are true.

18. (1) The artist compares mapmaking to war by using the setting of a "situation room," a term for a place used for planning military strategies.

19. (4) Protection of the environment is in the public interest.

20. (5) This group is concerned with a single law.

21. (1) Vegetable soup is made up of a variety of ingredients that retain their own characteristics and are not blended together into a single taste, choice (2), or at odds with each other, choice (3).

22. (4) The line for the effect of health control costs dips down to 0 by the year 2003. The other lines both show a continued federal deficit.

23. (1) The passage states that acid rain spreads miles from its source, so it is not a local problem. People cannot control the natural water cycle, so acid rain is difficult to contain to specific areas.

24. (2) The owners are limited by the number of licenses available. Until they can get one, they cannot compete with other businesses that serve alcohol.

25. (4) The other two video stores are already serving the market and would limit the number of customers available to the couple.

26. (2) Baird had broken a law. As a candidate for the highest legal position in the land, she would set a poor example for the American people. Another woman was appointed, so (1) is incorrect. The other choices have no support.

27. (2) The traffic accident is the only horrifying event that the person actually experienced. The other events are reports or observations.

28. (4) According to the passage, relationships are top on the list of makings of happiness. Faith comes in third. The others are not included as causes of happiness.

29. (3) The first paragraph gives several definitions of happiness but ends with the statement that happiness "all depends." The information does not support the other conclusions.

30. (2) The symbol in the map legend specifies the targets of air strikes.

31. (5) By focusing on the destruction of military centers, the Allies could expect that Iraq's defense would be weakened to the point of surrender.

32. (3) Immigrants who crossed the oceans to America came in search of better jobs and a better life for their families; these are the same goals as those of migrant Mexicans. Columbus crossed the water for economic reasons. Enslaved Africans came to America involuntarily. The other two choices refer to military events.

Use the answer key on pages 447–448 to check your answers to the Post-Test. Then find the item number of each question you missed and circle it on the chart below to determine the reading skill and content areas in which you need more practice. The reading skills are covered on pages 31–41. The page numbers for the content areas are listed below on the chart. Knowledge of reading skill and content area-based questions is absolutely essential for success on the GED Social Studies Test. The numbers in **bold-face** are questions based on graphics.

POST-TEST 2: SOCIAL STUDIES EVALUATION CHART

Skill Area/ Content Area)	Comprehension	Application	Analysis	Evaluation
Behavioral Sciences (pages 93–100)	3	7, 12	27, 28	8, 29
U.S. History (pages 101–113)	**30**	16, 21	4, **31**	5, 15
Political Science (pages 114–125)	17	9, 10	19, 20	26
Economics (pages 126–132)	**2**	24, 25	11, **22**	1
Geography (pages 133–138)	**13**	6, 32	**14, 18**	23

ANSWER KEY
POST-TEST 3: SCIENCE

1. **(4)** Although all five choices are facts, only choice (4), that helium-filled balloons rise, involves a relationship between the relative weights of helium gas and air.

2. **(2)** A base neutralizes an acid. Choice (1) would increase acidity. Choice (3) is incorrect because a neutral substance such as water would have no effect. Neither choice (4) nor (5) can be inferred from the action of the scientists.

3. **(4)** Besides sunlight, both carbon dioxide and water must be present for photosynthesis to take place. Only water is given as one of the choices. Glucose, choice (1), is a product of photosynthesis; oxygen, choice (2), is a by-product of the process; and nitrogen gas, choice (3), does not exist in a free state.

4. **(3)** Dust is the only choice that is not a form of water.

5. **(3)** The epidermis is a layer of cells, each of which is organized to perform the same activity, leading to its classification as a tissue.

6. **(4)** Because the pancreas is a structural unit containing several types of tissues, it is best classified as an organ.

7. **(4)** Choices A and D are facts, but neither shows that sunlight can be changed to heat energy.

8. **(3)** This statement is a hypothesis because it gives a reasonable but untested explanation of why celery helps lower blood pressure.

9. **(2)** Any experimental result or discovery is classified as a finding.

10. **(3)** A car with its windows rolled up is almost identical to a greenhouse. The glass lets light energy in but prevents heat energy from escaping.

11. **(5)** As Earth's temperature rises, the polar ice caps will likely melt. The water from the melting ice will cause a rise in ocean levels.

12. **(1)** Reducing our dependence on all types of fossil fuels would reduce the atmospheric greenhouse gases released.

13. **(3)** Choice A is incorrect because the percent of helium is not listed. Choice D is not correct because the table refers to pure dry air only.

14. **(3)** The amount of carbon dioxide gas will decrease as the temperature of the pop increases. The soda will then taste flat.

15. **(5)** The weight of water displaced by any floating object is equal to the weight of the whole object, regardless of how much of the object is floating above the water level.

16. **(3)** As the drawing shows, a convection current is air movement caused by temperature differences. Water convection currents occur in the ocean.

17. **(3)** The energy and water that are created by cellular respiration are used by the body. The CO_2 (carbon dioxide) is expelled by the lungs as a waste product.

18. **(2)** Since the switch and wall sockets are wired in series, if one goes out they all go out. Opening the switch breaks the circuit, and all sockets go out.

19. **(3)** Only choice (3) is true. Bulbs A and B are part of the same series circuit, and if one goes out, so will the other. Bulb C, though, will stay lit no matter what happens to bulbs A and B.

20. **(2)** Increasing efforts to educate citizens about AIDS can only help in the worldwide effort to conquer this dreaded disease.

21. **(5)** Cacti and other desert plants can survive in the desert only by conserving water. As a result, desert plants have evolved little or no leaf surface through which transpiration can take place.

22. **(2)** During summer months, the North Pole is tilted toward the Sun and receives sunlight twenty-four hours each day.

23. **(2)** As the passage states, the tilt of Earth's axis is responsible for differences in day and night hours and for seasonal differences.

24. (5) The left side of the face is controlled by the right side of the brain. The parietal lobe controls facial sensations.

25. (5) Choices A and B would seem to indicate that a larger brain implies greater intelligence. Choices C and D suggest that brain size is not a determining factor for differences in intelligence.

26. (4) An electrical discharge in a cloud causes both thunder and lightning. You see the lightning before you hear the thunder because light travels faster than sound.

27. (3) Marshmallows have a carbohydrate content of about 80 percent; the other choices contain less than 50 percent of carbohydrates.

28. (5) The two major substances in sea water are chlorine (Cl) and sodium (Na), the two elements that make up sodium chloride (NaCl), most often called salt.

29. (3) You can infer only that two shorter magnets are created. You can't tell from the drawing what the strength of these magnets is.

30. (3) When liquids don't freely mix, the one with the greatest density sinks to the bottom. The liquid with least density floats to the top.

31. (4) A rainbow forms because suspended rain drops act as tiny prisms and cause sunlight (natural white light) to separate into its color components.

32. (3) The correct way to show three carbon atoms and eight hydrogen atoms is with the formula C_3H_8.

33. (2) As the drawing shows, the inter-neuron receives the nerve impulse from the sensory neuron and transmits the impulse to the motor neuron.

Use the answer key on pages 450-451 to check your answers to the Science Post-Test. Then find the item number of each question you missed and circle it on the chart below to determine the reading skill and content areas in which you need more practice. Pay particular attention to areas where you missed half or more of the questions. The page numbers for the content areas are listed below on the chart. The numbers in **boldface** are questions based on graphics. For those questions that you missed, review the pages indicated.

POST-TEST 3: SCIENCE EVALUATION CHART

Skill Area/ Content Area	Comprehension	Application	Analysis	Evaluation
Biology (pages 141–155)	**24**, 27	5, 6, 8, 9	21, **33**	20, **25**
Earth Science (pages 156–171)	**16, 22**	4, 10	11, **23**	12
Chemistry (pages 172–185)	**13, 32**	2, 14	3, 17, **28**	1
Physics (pages 186–198)	**29, 30**	15, **18**	7, **19**	26, **31**

ANSWER KEY
POST-TEST 4: LITERATURE AND THE ARTS

1. **(3)** According to the quotation, neither wealth (4) nor beauty (5) were as admired as piety. From this statement of their values, you can infer that the people would not be impressed by fame (1) or power (2).

2. **(5)** Lines 4–6 state that Casey expects to become a first baseman for the Red Sox.

3. **(1)** Throughout the excerpt, the author gives examples of women's and girls' participation in baseball. She mentions female sportswriters, fans, and a bat girl.

4. **(4)** In lines 34–42, the author says, "At spring training batting practice . . . I look down at the crowd of kids. Half of them are girls. This is new." The final sentence gives a specific example of another new development—the traditionally male job of bat boy now being filled by a female.

5. **(1)** Throughout the except, the author is supportive of her daughter's and other females' interest in baseball.

6. **(4)** Details are arranged chronologically. At the beginning of the excerpt, it is 7:00 in the morning. The next major actions occur at 7:09, 8:01, and 8:30.

7. **(3)** Given the number of electronic voice messages that remind the family of important dates (a birthday, an anniversary, payments due), one can infer that the family valued being well organized.

8. **(1)** The excerpt is primarily about the interaction of people and technology of the future—more specifically, the absurdity of technology divorced from humanity.

9. **(1)** According to the first two sentences of the excerpt, "Life was very hard for the Whipples. It was hard to feed all the hungry mouths, it was hard to keep the children in flannels during the winter, short as it was. . . ."

10. **(5)** The middle of the first paragraph states that "Mrs. Whipple was all for taking what was sent and calling it good, anyhow when the neighbors were in earshot. . . . She couldn't stand to be pitied."

11. **(5)** According to details in the first paragraph, the story takes place in a location where the winters are short and it is possible to pick cotton for a living. These details point to a rural southern town.

12. **(2)** In the first two lines of the poem, the speaker says, "We come to hear the endings / of all the stories."

13. **(3)** This complex comparison rests on two analogies. The first similarity is between a stream that is drying up and an aging person whose life is "drying up." The second similarity is between rocks jutting out from a stream that is drying out and the increasing prominence of the facial bones of a person who is aging. Note that all the comparisons in the poem develop the idea of people changing and "turning into themselves" over the course of time.

14. **(5)** Typical of the poem's language is the vocabulary of the last three lines—"Look! We have all / turned into / ourselves." Note that the vocabulary in these lines is commonplace, easy to understand, and could be heard in an informal conversation between friends.

15. **(3)** Dolores's inner conflict is expressed in the first line of the excerpt—"I'll never be okay until I go home again."

16. **(5)** Javier shows a caring attitude toward his mother when he crosses the room to be closer to her, takes her hand in his, and tries to calm her by saying, "Oh Mom, don't do that."

17. **(1)** Javier displays confidence in his future when he says, "I think I can go far here" (lines 25–26).

18. **(3)** The last sentence states that the playwright was inspired to write the play because her father had fled Vienna to escape the Nazi takeover.

19. **(1)** In each incident—that which involved the White Rose and that which took place in Tiananmen Square—university students were executed for protesting against a government that they viewed as immoral.

20. **(4)** The sentence structure of the review tends to be sophisticated. Most of the sentences are complex, and even simple sentences contain many qualifying phrases.

21. **(1)** The anecdotes that Hunter-Gault chose to include—recollections of attending dinners at relatives' farms, shopping for prom dresses, and reading newspaper comic strips —exemplify a happy and normal childhood. Note that the reviewer characterizes Hunter-Gault's recollections as "amiable" (line 36).

22. **(4)** The excerpt is primarily informational, focusing on the content of the book rather than on criticism. Note that the reviewer never makes mention of the quality of the writing or of the strengths and weaknesses of the book.

23. **(1)** The second sentence of the excerpt says, "[Hunter-Gault's] memoir . . . is concerned less with that civil-rights triumph [the desegregation of the University of Georgia] than with what it was like to grow up as the daughter of a distinguished dynasty of preachers in a generally self-sufficient minority community."

Use the answer key on pages 452–153 to check your answers to the Literature and the Arts Post-Test. Then find the item number of each question you missed and circle it on the chart below to determine the reading skill and content areas in which you need more practice. The page numbers for the content areas are listed below on the chart. For those questions that you missed, review the pages indicated.

POST-TEST 4: LITERATURE AND THE ARTS EVALUATION CHART

Skill Area/ Content Area	Comprehension	Application	Analysis
Prose Fiction (pages 201–212)	7, 9, 10	8, 11	6
Poetry (pages 213–223)	12		13, 14
Drama (pages 224–232)	15, 17		16
Nonfiction Prose (pages 233–242)	2, 3	1, 5	4
Commentaries (pages 242–247)	18, 21, 22, 23	19	20

ANSWER KEY
POST-TEST 5: MATHEMATICS

1. (2) 8

$12 \div 1\frac{1}{2} =$

$\frac{12}{1} \div \frac{3}{2}$

$\frac{12}{1} \times \frac{2}{3} = \frac{24}{3} = 8$

2. (3) $\frac{1}{90}$

$\frac{\text{family members}}{\text{total tickets}} \quad \frac{4}{360} = \frac{1}{90}$

3. (3) 8

$3m + 6 = 30$

$\quad\; -6 \quad -6$

$\frac{3m}{3} = \frac{24}{3}$

$\quad m = 8$

4. (4) Dave's Duds

$\frac{x}{\$30} = \frac{10}{100}$

$100x = \$300 \qquad\qquad \$30$

$\quad x = \$3 \qquad\qquad \underline{-\ \$3}$

$\qquad\qquad\qquad\qquad\quad \$27$

5. (4) 408

$20^2 + 2^3 =$

$20 \times 20 + 2 \times 2 \times 2 =$

$400 + 8 = 408$

6. (3) 1:3

width:height $= 27:81 = 1:3$

7. (4) $\frac{7}{20}$

$35\% = \frac{35}{100} = \frac{7}{20}$

8. (3) B, D, C, A

$A = 0.9 = 0.900$

$B = 0.09 = 0.090$

$C = 0.895$

$D = 0.19 = 0.190$

9. (2) $\sqrt{3^2 + 3^2}$

$d = \sqrt{(x_2 - x_1)^2 + (y_2 - y_1)^2}$

$d = \sqrt{(5 - 2)^2 + (5 - 2)^2}$

$d = \sqrt{3^2 + 3^2}$

10. (3) 157

$C = \pi d$

$C = 3.14 \times 50$

$C = 157$

11. (4) 15

$\frac{\$12,000}{\$80,000} = \frac{3}{20}$

$\frac{3}{20} = \frac{x}{100}$

$20x = 300$

$x = 15\%$

12. (4) 300

$\frac{\text{parts}}{\text{hours}} \quad \frac{15}{2} = \frac{x}{40}$

$2x = 600$

$x = 300$

13. (3) 50

$c^2 = a^2 + b^2$

$c^2 = 40^2 + 30^2$

$c^2 = 1600 + 900$

$c = \sqrt{2500}$

$c = 50$

14. (3) $12 \times 8 \times 6$

$V = lwh$

$V = 12 \times 8 \times 6$

15. (1) 2

$12a - 5 = 4a + 11$

$-4a \qquad\; -4a$

$8a \quad -5 = 11$

$\quad\;\; +5 \quad +5$

$\frac{8a}{8} = \frac{16}{8}$

$\quad a = 2$

16. (1) $3(a - 4)$

Divide each term by 3:

$3a - 12 = 3(a - 4)$

17. (2) 35

$\quad 105° \qquad\qquad\quad 180°$

$\underline{+\ 40°} \qquad\qquad \underline{-\ 145°}$

$\quad 145° \qquad\qquad\quad\; 35°$

18. (4) 12

Point A is 5 units to the left of 0.

Point B is 7 units to the right of 0.

The points are $5 + 7 = 12$ units apart.

19. (2) 2.25

$(1.5)^2 = 1.5 \times 1.5 = 2.25$

20. (5) $\frac{1}{2} \times 13 \times 7$

$A = \frac{1}{2}bh$

$A = \frac{1}{2} \times 13 \times 7$

21. (4) $55 \times 3 + 40 \times 2$

22. (4) **75**

$\dfrac{MR}{MN} = \dfrac{QR}{PQ}$

$\dfrac{8}{5} = \dfrac{120}{x}$

$8x = 600$

$x = 75$

23. (1) **2**

$\dfrac{\text{change in } y}{\text{change in } x} \quad \dfrac{6}{3}$

24. (5) **42**

$2 + 1\frac{1}{2} = 3\frac{1}{2}$

$3\frac{1}{2} \times 12 =$

$\frac{7}{2} \times \frac{12}{1} =$

$\frac{84}{2} = 42$

25. (3) $2y - 20 = 58$

Maxine $= y$

Pilar $= y - 20$

sum $= y + y - 20 = 58$

$2y - 20 = 58$

26. (4) **20**

1990	42 gal
1975	$-\ 22$
	20 gal

27. (4) 9.8×10^{10}

28. (3) **$5.85**

$78 \text{ in} = 6\frac{1}{2} \text{ ft}$

$6\frac{1}{2} \times \$.90 =$

$\frac{13}{2} \times \$ \frac{.90}{1} = \$5.85$

Use the answer key on pages 455–456 to check your answers to the Post-Test. Then find the item number of each question you missed and circle it on the chart below to determine the mathematics content areas in which you need more practice. The page numbers for the context areas are listed below on the chart. The numbers in **bold type** are questions based on graphics. For those questions that you missed, review the pages indicated.

POST-TEST 5: MATHEMATICS EVALUATION CHART

Skill Area/ Content Area	Item Number	Review Pages
Decimals	19, 28	251–260
Fractions	1, **7**	261–274
Ratio & Proportion	**6**	275–278
Percent	4, 11	279–286
Measurement	**18**, 21, 24	287–296
Graphs, Statistics, & Probability	2, **26**	297–304
Numeration	**8**	305–310
Geometry	5, **10**, **13**, 14, **17**, **20**, 22	311–322
Algebra	3, 9, 12, 15, 16, 23, 25, 27	323–344

INDEX

A

Abolitionists, 105
Absolute monarchy, 114
Absolute time, 161
Absolute values, 334
Achieved status, 97
Acid, 182
Action and reaction, 186
Action verbs, 48
Acts, 226
Addition
  and decimals, 254–256
  and fractions, 268–270
  and measurements, 288
Adler, Alfred, 99
Adverbs, conjunctive, 64–65
Air masses, 171
Algebra, 323–344
  equations, 324–326
  expressions, 323–324
  in word problems, 326–333
Allegory, 37
Alliteration, 216
Alloys, 180
Amendments, 105
American Federation of
  Labor, 107
Amino acids, 149
Analysis, 34–39
Anaphase, 145
Ancestry, 115
Angles, 311. See also
  Triangles
  complementary, 311
  corresponding, 314
  right, 311
  supplementary, 311
  vertex, 313
  vertical, 312
Antecedents, 57
  agreement in number, 58
  compound, 58
  missing, 59
  and personal pronouns,
    59–60
  relative pronouns, 58
Anthropology, 93–95
Anti–Federalists, 103
Anxiety theory, 99
Apostrophe, 74
Application, 33
Approximation, of square
  roots, 306
Aqueous solution, 179
Area, 320–322
Aristotle, 186
Articles, nonfiction, 238
Articles of Confederation, 102
Art review, 245–246
Arts, evaluation charts,
  404, 454
Ascribed status, 97
Astronomy, 156
Atmosphere, 167, 202–203
Atom, 172–173
Atomic bomb, 111
Atomic theory, 172
Audience, 76
Autobiography, 236–237
Average. See Mean

B

Balanced budget, 132
Balanced equation, 178

Bandwagoning, 34
Base, chemical, 182
Base, mathematical, 305, 313
Base angles, 313
Behavioral sciences, 93–100
Beliefs, 38
Big bang theory, 156
Big business, 107
Biography, 233–234
Biology, 141–155
Black holes, 156
Bond, chemical, 180
Book review, 243–244
Brainstorming, 76–77
British Thermal Unit (BTU),
  190
*Brown v. Board of Education
  of Topeka*, 111
BTU. *See* British Thermal
  Unit
Budget surplus, 132
Bush, George, 113
Business cycle, 130

C

Calorie, 190
Capital, 126
Capitalism, 127
Capitalization, 71–72,
  215–216
Card-stacking, 34
Carter, Jimmy, 113
Catalyst, 184
Cause and effect, 36
Cells, 141
  and active transport, 143
  division of (meiosis),
    146–147
  division of (mitosis),
    144–145
  membrane of, 141
  structure of, 142
  types of, 141
Cellular respiration, 151
Characterization, 203, 227
Checks and balances, 119–120
Chemical bonding, 180–181
Chemical energy, 188
Chemical equation, 177–178
Chemical equilibrium, 184
Chemistry, 172–185
Chlorophyll, 151
Chloroplasts, 141, 150
Chromosomes, 142
Circle, 318
Circumference, 319
Cities. *See* Government, local
Civil rights movement,
  111, 112
Civil War, 105
Classes, social, 96
Classical conditioning, 97
Classification, 152–153
Clauses, 61–62
  commas with, 72
  dependent, 65
  independent, 61–62, 65
Climate, 136–137
Climax, in literature, 205, 227
Clinton, Bill, 113
Closed primary, 124
Clouds, 168, 171
Coefficient, 323
Cognitive perception, 98
Cold War, 111

Commas, 62–63, 72–73
Comma splice, 63
Commentary
  art, 245–246
  music, 244–245
  as nonfiction, 242
  on poetry, 223
  on prose, 211
  television, 246–247
Common denominator,
  266–267
Communism, 111, 127
Comparison (mathematical),
  265–268
Comparison and contrast,
  36, 83–84
Compensation theory, 99
Complementary angles, 311
Compounds (chemistry), 179
Comprehension, 31–33
Conditioning, 97
Conductors, 197
Confederate States of
  America, 105
Conflict (literature), 204–205
Congress, 116. *See also*
  Government, U.S.
Conjunction
  coordinating, 62
  subordinating, 65
Conjunctive adverbs, 64–65
Constants, 323
Constituency, 124
Constitution of the U.S.,
  102. *See also* Elastic
  clause; Government, U.S.
  federalism and, 115
  ratification of, 103
Continental drift theory, 159
Continuing tenses, 50
Contour lines, 137
Contractions, 56–57
Conversion, in measurement,
  287–288, 291–292
Coolidge, Calvin, 109
Coordinates, rectangular,
  340–344
Coordinating conjunctions, 62
Corresponding angles, 314
Corresponding sides, 314
Courts. *See* Judicial branch
Covalent bond, 181
Criteria, 38
Critical thinking. *See* Thinking
  skills
Criticism, 210, 242–244. *See
  also* Commentary
Crossing over, 146
Cross products, 276
Cuban missile crisis, 112
Cube, 322
Cubic units, 322
Cultural anthropologists, 93
Cultural relativity, 94
Cultural universals, 94
Culture, 93, 94
Cumulus clouds, 171
Current and constant dollars,
  131
Customs, 94
Cylinder, 322
Cytoplasm, 142

D

Dalton, John, 172

Dangling modifiers, 68
Darwin, Charles, 153
Data, 297
Decimal fractions, 251
Decimal point, 251
Decimals, 251–260
  adding and subtracting,
    254–256
  comparing, 252–253, 266
  fractions and, 263–264,
    267–268
  multiplying and dividing,
    255–259
  ordering, 252–253
  percents and, 279–283
  places, 251
  rounding, 253–254
  using, 251–254
  zeros in, 252
Declaration of Independence,
  102
Deductive reasoning, 35
Defense mechanisms, 99–100
Deficit spending, 132
Deflation, 130
Degrees, 311
Demand. *See* Supply, and
  demand
Democracy, 114
Denominator, 261
  common, 266–267
Dependent clause, 65
Depression. *See* Recession;
  Stock market crash
Descriptive writing, 80–81
Desegregation, 111. *See also*
  Civil rights movement
Détente, 112
Dialect, 208–209
Dialogue
  in drama, 224–225
  in prose fiction, 203
Diameter, 318
Dictatorship, 114
Diffraction, 194
Diffusion, 143
Diploid cell, 147
Discount rate, 131
Displacement, 99
Divine right, 115
Division
  and decimals, 255–259
  of fractions, 272
  and measurements, 289
  of signed numbers, 336–337
DNA, 142
Dollars, current and constant,
  131
Domains, 196
Drafting (writing), 78–79,
  85–86
Drama, 224
  elements of, 227
  interpreting, 224–232
  stage directions in, 226
  structure of, 226
Dred Scott decision, 105

E

Earth
  atmosphere of, 167–168
  changing, 163–164
  composition of, 162–163
  formation of, 159–160
  oceans of, 164

Reflection, 194
Refraction, 194
Regular verbs, 49
Relative humidity, 170
Representative democracy, 114
Repression, 99
Reserve ratio, 131
Resolution
  in drama, 227
  in prose fiction, 205
Respiration, cellular, 151
Reviewer, 210
Reviews. *See* Commentary
Revising, 79, 87
Revolution, 115
Revolutionary War, 102
Rhyme, 216
Rhythm, 216
Richter scale, 160
Right angle, 311
Rights, state vs. individual, 119
Right triangle, 314
Rising action, 227
RNA, 142
Roaring Twenties, 109
Rocks, 161, 163
Roosevelt, Franklin D., 109
Roots (mathematical), 306
Rough draft. *See* Drafting
Rounding, of decimals, 253–254
Run-on sentences, 62–63

S
Safety and security needs, 99
SALT treaties, 112, 113
Scalene triangle, 313
Scales, reading, 295
Scenes, 226
Science
  post-test evaluation chart, 451
  pre-test evaluation chart, 402
Scientific method, 34–35
Scientific notation, 309–310
Sea level, 136
Secession, 105
Secondary groups, 95
Sectionalism, 104
Sedimentary rocks, 161
Seismic waves, 160
Self-actualization theory, 99
Semicolons, 73
Senate, 115–116
Sentences. *See also*
    Punctuation
  combining, 61–62
  complete, 45
  inverted subject-verb order, 54
  run-on, 62–63
  structure of, 61
  supporting, 77
  topic, 77
Sequence, 36–37
Series, commas and, 73
Setting, 202
Shortage, 129
Short story, 201
Signed numbers, 333–337
  multiplying and dividing, 336–337
  operations with, 334–335
Similar triangles, 314
Simile, 210, 221
Simple tenses, 49–50

Simplification, of fraction problems, 273–274
Slavery, 105
Slope, 343–344
Snow. *See* Water cycle
Social class, 96
Social environment, 100
Social institutions, 95
Socialism, 127
Socialization, 96
Social mobility, 97
Social psychologists, 100
Social structure, 96–97
Social studies, 91
  post-test evaluation chart, 449
  pre-test evaluation chart, 400
Sociology, 95–97
Solar energy, 188
Solar system, 157–158
Solids, 190
Solute, 179
Solution (chemical), 179
Solution (math), 324, 325–326
Solvent, 179
Sound waves, 192
Soviet Union, 113
Space exploration, 111
Spanish-American War, 109
Species, 152
Speeches, 241–242
Spelling, 74
  of regular verb forms, 53
Spring tides, 166
Square, 318
Squared number, 305
Square roots, 306
Stage directions, 226
Standard English, 45
Standard measurement, 287
Stanza, 214
Stars, 156–157
State government, 121
Static electricity, 197
Stationary fronts, 171
Status, 97
Steam energy, 188
Stock market crash, 109
Stratification, 96
Stratosphere, 168
Stratus clouds, 171
Structure, parallel, 69–70
Style
  in essays, 239
  literary, 207, 208–210
Subject, 45, 46
Subject-verb agreement, 54–55
Subordinating conjunction, 65
Substitution (math), 308
Subtraction
  and decimals, 254–256
  with fractions, 268–270
  and measurements, 288
Summarizing, 32
Sun, 157–158. *See also* Solar energy
Superego, 99
Superiority theory, 99
Supplementary angles, 311
Supply
  and demand, 128
  and equilibrium, 129–130
  price and, 128, 129
Supporting reasons, 83
Supporting sentences, 77
Supreme Court, 118–119

Surplus, 129
Symbols
  algebraic, 330–331
  on maps, 133
Synthesis, 38
Syzygy, 167

T
Tariffs, 105
Television review, 246–247
Telophase, 145
Temperature, 190
Tenses, 49–51. *See also* Verbs
Theme, 206–207
Theory, 34
Thesis statement, 86
Thinking process, 97
Thinking skills, 31–39
Third-person narration, 205
Thirteenth Amendment, 105
Tides, 166
Time
  in fiction, 202
  geologic, 161
  measuring, 162
Time order, 36
Time problems, 293–294
Time zones, 135
Tincture, 179
Tone, literary, 207–208
Topics, 76
Topic sentence, 77
Topographical maps, 133
Topography, 136–137
Traits. *See* Genetics
Transferring, 34
Transverse wave, 192
Trial-and-error learning, 98
Triangles, 313–314
  similar, 314–316
  types of, 313–314
Troposphere, 167
Trough, 192
Truman, Harry, 111

U
Unions, 107
United States, government of. *See* Government, U.S.
United States history, 101–113
  Civil War, 105
  colonial period, 101
  early republic, 102–103
  expansion period (1701–1850), 103–104
  exploration and colonization, 101
  foreign affairs, 104
  industrialization, 107–108
  Jacksonian democracy, 104
  Mexican War, 104
  reconstruction, 105
  revolution and independence, 102
Unknowns (math), 308
Urbanization, 107

V
Values, 38, 94
Variables (math), 308, 323
Verbs, 48
  helping, 68
  irregular, 52
  spelling of regular, 52
  subject-verb agreement, 54–55
  tenses of, 49–51
Verse, 214
Vertex, 311, 313

Vertex angle, 313
Vertical angles, 312
Veto, 117, 119–120
Vietnam War, 112
Volume, 322–323
Voting
  electoral college and, 117
  electoral process and, 124–125
Voting Rights Act (1965), 112

W
Washington, George, 103
Water cycle, 169
Watergate scandal, 112
Wavelength, 192
Waves, 191–192
  light, 194
  sound, 192
Wave theory of light, 193
Weather, 171. *See also* Meteorology
Weather and climate maps, 133
Wind, 163
Word problems
  algebraic, 326–333
  percents and, 283–286
Work, in physics, 187
World War I, 109
World War II, 111
Writing activities. *See also* Essay writing
  from behavioral sciences, 93–100
  from social studies, 91
Writing process
  brainstorming, 76–77
  drafting, 78–79
  editing, 79
  organization, 78
  prewriting, 76
  structuring, 77
  topic sentence, 77
Writing sample
  essay, 84–88
  preparing for, 75–89
Writing skills
  post-test evaluation chart, 446
  pre-test evaluation chart, 397
Writing types
  descriptive, 80–81
  informative, 81–82
  narrative, 80
  persuasive, 82–84

X
X–axis, 340
X–coordinate, 340

Y
Y–axis, 340
Y–coordinate, 340

Z
Zeros, decimals and, 252